ANG-NGA
THE-HUNG
THE HUNG

THE WORLD AND ITS PEOPLES

Echo Bay, Ontario, Canada

CANADA

GREYSTONE PRESS/NEW YORK · TORONTO · LONDON

PHOTO CREDITS: S.E.F./Instituto Geografico de Agostini / Ashton-Potter Limited / Atlas / Les Baxter / Bell Telephone Company / British American Oil / Canadian Broadcasting Corporation / Canadian Government Travel Bureau / Canadian National Railways / Canadian Opera Company / Canadian Pacific Railway / Canadian Pulp and Paper Association / Carl Dean / Dept. of Northern Affairs, Natural and Historic Resources Branch / Dept. of Recreation and Conservation, B.C. / Dominion Bureau of Statistics / E.S.P. / Giacomelli / Hiram Walker and Sons, Ltd. / Hudson's Bay Company / Len Sirman Press / *Les Grands Ballets Canadiens* / Massey-Ferguson, Ltd. / Millerlist / The National Ballet Guild of Canada / National Film Board of Canada / National Harbours Board-Montreal / Ontario Dept. of Highways / The Public Archives of Canada / Royal Ontario Museum / *Théâtre du Nouveau-Monde* / Toronto Symphony Orchestra / Toronto Transit Commission / The Universal and International Exhibition of 1967, Montreal / Vancouver Fire Dept. / *the Chrysler Corporation for the end papers that keynote "The World and Its Peoples" theme.*

Library of Congress Catalog Number: 66-20876

Cover and Book Designed by Harold Franklin

MANUFACTURED IN THE UNITED STATES OF AMERICA
16069

Editorial Consultant for Canada

William Kilbourne, Ph.D.
Professor of Humanities
York University, Toronto

The World and Its Peoples—Editors and Contributors

Hugh W. Ashton
B.A. Sc., University of Toronto

John Joseph Baughman
Ph.D., University of Michigan
Associate Professor of History
De Pauw University

Judith Bonnycastle
B.A., University of Toronto

Pierluigi Bracco
Assistant Professor of History
of International Relations
University of Padua

Grace Bray
Writer-Research Assistant
South Porcupine Secondary School

Dr. M. W. Brown
Professor of Art
Brooklyn College

Limentani Ida Calabi
Associate Professor of
Greek and Roman Antiquities
University of Milan

Basilio Cialdea
Lecturer in History of
International Relations
University of Rome

John Crowther
Writer, Director,
Production Associate
Louis de Rochemont Associates

Dr. George D. Crothers
Producer and Broadcaster
Columbia Broadcasting System

Federico Curato
Professor of Modern History
University of Pavia

John S. Erwin
Composer, author and critic

John G. Garrard
M.A., Columbia University
Instructor of Russian
Carlton College

Dr. Richard Hayes
Instructor in Dramatic Arts
New York University

Ellen Hersey
B.A., Oberlin College

Robert Higgins
M.A., Cambridge University

John W. Hunter, Jr.
A.B., Yale University

Peter Hyun
Seoul National University, Korea
Author and Critic

George G. Jackson, Jr.
Ph.D., Columbia University
Assistant Professor of History
Hofstra University

Audrey R. King
Columbia University
Author and Critic

Dwight LeRoy Ling
Ph.D., University of Illinois
Associate Professor of History
De Pauw University

Nicholas Maestrellis
B.A., University of Wisconsin

George B. Manhart
Ph.D., University of Pennsylvania
Professor Emeritus of History
De Pauw University

Andre Michalopoulos
Professor of Classical Literature
Fairleigh Dickinson University

Gerald Needham
M.A., New York University
Lecturer in Art History
Brown University

William Nethercut
M.A., Columbia University
Instructor of Greek and
Latin, Columbia University

Joseph Newman
B.A., Williams College
Author; Editorial Board:
New York Herald Tribune

Riccardo Picchio
Professor of Polish
Literature and Language
University of Florence

Clark V. Poling, Jr.
A.B., Yale University

Marco Rosci
Associate Professor
University of Milan

Dr. Irving Settel
Assistant Professor of Marketing
Pace College

Ralph Shaw
Former China
Correspondent, Agence
France Press

Ashley Talbot
B.A., University of Michigan
Senior Editor
C. S. Hammond and Company

Joseph Than
Film producer, writer and critic

Leone Traverso
Professor
University of Urbino

Robert Van Nuffel
Professor of French Literature
University of Brussels

Katherine Vandegrift
Author, artist and critic

René Wellek
Ph.D., Charles University, Prague
Professor of Comparative Literature
Yale University

Karen Whiteley
Senior Editor
American Heritage Dictionary

H. W. Whittaker
Drama Critic
The Toronto Globe & Mail
Director, Designer,
and Adjudicator

Robert Worth
Ph.D., University of Chicago

United States Editorial Staff

Executive Editor: Joseph P. King, A.B., *Duke University*

Editors: Harvey Arden, *University of California;*
Howard Spivak, *University of California*

Editorial Production: Julian Hamer, *Pennsylvania State University;*
(Assistant) Judith Brandt, *Université de la Sorbonne*

The national flag of Canada

Table of Contents

CANADA

PAGE **THE LAND**

POSITION AND BOUNDARIES

Canada's area of 3,851,809 square miles makes it the second largest country in the world. In size it is surpassed by the Soviet Union, which has an area of over 8.5 million square miles. The United States is about 200,000 square miles smaller.

It is an autonomous state within the Commonwealth of Nations. Queen Elizabeth II is the nominal head of state and is represented by a resident governor-general, but Canada is, in fact, a completely self-governing federation of ten provinces and two territories.

Quebec, the largest province, is twice the size of the state of Texas. The provinces of Ontario and British Columbia are each four times as large as Great Britain.

Canada covers the entire northern part of the North American continent, except for Alaska, which the United States bought from Russia in 1867, and the small French-owned islands of St. Pierre and Miquelon in the Atlantic Ocean to the south of Newfoundland (all that remains to France of the "New France"). Yet the majority of Canadians live in latitudes more south-

The coast at the mouth of the Clyde River in southwestern Nova Scotia. Typical of the rugged Atlantic Coast of Canada, the shoreline of Nova Scotia is deeply indented with bays, coves and inlets. In the region of the Bay of Fundy occur tides (rising up to 70 ft.) that are among the highest in the world.

A view of Quebec reflecting the French heritage of the city. Founded in 1608 by Samuel de Champlain, Quebec is one of the oldest cities in Canada. French operations in North America were centered here, and to this day French remains the principal language of the region.

erly than those of many Europeans —Windsor, Ontario, is farther south than Rome, and Montreal and Venice are at about the same latitude.

The coastline is extremely irregular, particularly on the eastern seaboard and in the north, and has a total length of 14,820 miles. Lakes and rivers constitute a significant proportion of the total area of Canada. The most famous are the Great Lakes—Superior, Michigan, Huron, Ontario and Erie. Canada contains over one-third of all the world's fresh-water lakes.

The east coast of Canada is washed by the Atlantic Ocean, broken in the south by the Gulf of St. Lawrence, from the west of which extends the St. Lawrence River. From the Atlantic to the Pacific Coast there is a maximum distance of about 3500 miles. Canada is bordered on the south by the United States of America for a distance of almost 4000 miles. The northernmost tip of land is on Ellesmere Island, close to the north pole.

ORGANIZATION OF THE STATE

Administrative Divisions

CANADA IS A FEDERATION OF TEN provinces and contains, also, two territories not yet organized into provinces. The provinces are semi-autonomous regions (each with its own legislature) within the federation; the territories are administered partly by the federal government but retain certain independent powers. Canada has a federal Parliament at Ottawa and ten provincial legislatures. Each province has established a third form of government known as municipal or local government.

Federal Government

The basis of the Canadian constitution is provided by the British North America (B.N.A.) Act of 1867, which incorporated and modified earlier acts of 1774, 1791 and 1840. The Act of 1867 was further modified by the Statute of Westminster of 1931, which, although increasing Canada's actual independence of the British parliament, failed to provide proper methods for the amendment of the Canadian constitution by the Canadian parliament without reference to Britain. In practice, Canada is an independent nation, but legislative action to make this formally binding is not yet possible under the constitution.

The federal government as provided in the B.N.A. Act was to consist of the Queen, the Senate and the House of Commons, which together are known as the Parliament of Canada.

Queen Elizabeth II, the head of the British Commonwealth of Nations, is also the head of the federal government of Canada, since all legislation passed by the Canadian Parliament must receive the monarch's approval. This is granted through the governor-general and is never, in practice, refused. The governor-general is appointed by the monarch, but the royal nomination is now merely a formality.

THE GOVERNOR-GENERAL

The functions performed by the governor-general in relation to the Canadian Parliament are similar to those performed by the British sovereign in relation to the Parliament of Great Britain. The governor-general is responsible for decreeing the convening or dissolving of Parliament, for granting the royal assent to legislation, for representing the monarch at official and diplomatic functions, and for appointing officials in the monarch's name. After due consultation, the governor-general, by virtue of an act passed in 1947, may exercise the royal prerogative without first seeking the approval of the Crown in London.

THE PRIVY COUNCIL

The governor-general may call upon the Privy Council to assist him at any time during his term of office, which is normally of five years' duration. Once again, however, the powers of this body are purely formal. The Privy Council consists of about 90 members (there is no constitutional limit on the number), whose appointment for a life term is made by the governor-general after consultation with the prime minister. Membership of the Privy Council is normally limited to past or present members of the Canadian cabinet, though membership is also granted as a mark of honor to members of the royal family or to distinguished Canadians.

The Privy Council as a whole is never convened, but its functions in advising the governor-general are carried out under its name by members of the Canadian cabinet. These are automatically privy councillors and are presided over by the prime minister.

THE PRIME MINISTER AND CABINET

The executive branch of the Canadian government consists of a cabinet of ministers presided over by the prime minister. The prime minister is appointed by the governor-general and is normally the leader of the political party that has the support of the largest number of members elected to the House of Commons.

The prime minister is responsible for choosing the members of his cabinet from among the members of the House of Commons or, more rarely, the Senate. Although each cabinet minister is normally responsible for a separate government department, sometimes with the assistance of a minister without portfolio, all ministers are equally responsible for the actions of the executive, and a government may thus be forced to resign over an action committed by a single minister. The cabinet is responsible for submitting to Parliament at each session the government program of legislation.

HOUSES OF PARLIAMENT

The Parliament of Canada is bicameral, consisting of an upper house, called the Senate, and a lower house, called the House of Commons.

The Senate exists to provide a forum in which experienced politicians, many of them former cabinet ministers, may debate or examine in committee measures passed by the House of Commons and, if necessary, suggest alterations and amendments. All bills passed by the Commons must receive the Senate's assent before being passed to the governor-general for the royal approval. In practice the Senate has rarely refused to pass legislation approved by the Commons.

Senators, of whom there are 102, are nominated by the governor-general on the advice, in effect, of the prime minister. They serve until the age of 75. Each senator must be a native-born or naturalized Canadian citizen over the age of 30 and must possess property valued at more than $4000 in the province for which he is nominated.

Members of the House of Commons are elected for a term not exceeding five years by the universal suffrage of all Canadian citizens or British subjects of the age of 21 or over who have been resident in Canada 12 months prior to polling day, with certain exceptions, such as persons confined in penal institutions or mental hospitals, federally appointed judges and officers on electoral districts. General elections are usually held every five years, but provisions exist for the dissolution of Parliament in the event that the government in office is defeated or forced to resign.

Seats in the House of Commons are allocated to the various regions on a geographical basis, taking into account both size and population. The number of seats allocated to each province has been revised several times.

Both houses of the Canadian Parliament meet separately but at the same time, and Parliament must hold at least one session every 12 months. The federal government is entrusted with power to legislate with respect to the peace, order and good government generally, and in particular on such matters as national defense and coinage, Canadian citizenship, criminal law, postal service, trade and commerce, navigation and shipping, as well as having authority in all matters not specifically assigned to the provincial legislatures by the British North America Act or subsequent acts. Both houses have the right to initiate legislation, but only the House of Commons may initiate measures dealing with matters of taxation or national expenditure.

The golden Mace, which rests on the table in front of the Speaker when the House is in session, is the symbol of authority of the House of Commons, the primary legislative body of Canada. Part of the Speaker's chair, seen in the background, is made of wood taken from Admiral Nelson's flagship, the Victory.

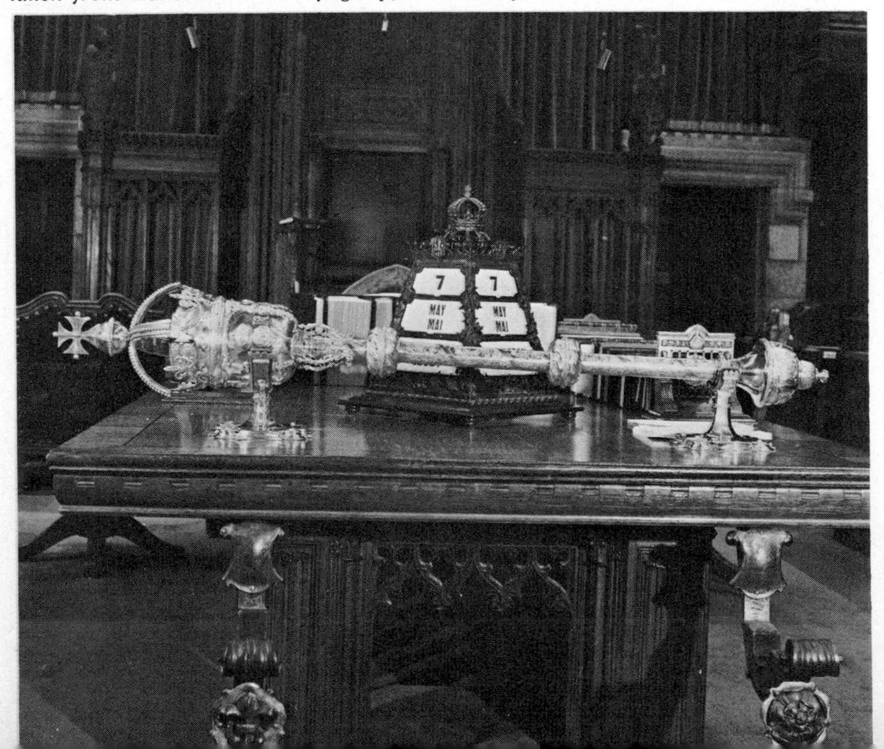

Provincial Government

Each province is nominally headed

by a lieutenant-governor, the representative of the Crown, who is appointed by the governor-general on the advice of the federal prime minister and fulfills the same functions on a provincial level as the governor-general on a federal level. The usual term of office of the lieutenant-governor is five years, and the provincial legislatures have no power to pass laws affecting his office.

EXECUTIVE AND LEGISLATURE

The lieutenant-governor appoints the members of the Executive Council (Cabinet) on the advice of the prime minister (premier), who is normally the leader of the political party having the support of the largest number of members elected to the Legislative Assembly. In every province except Quebec the legislature consists of a single house, the Legislative Assembly, which is elected for a five-year term by universal adult suffrage.

QUEBEC

Quebec differs from the other provinces in that, although the internal workings of its executive and legislature are similar, it has another, separate legislative body appointed by the executive. This is known as the Legislative Council and consists of 24 members, who are appointed by the lieutenant-governor and who hold office for life. It considers and must approve bills put before it, before such bills are submitted to the lieutenant-governor.

The provincial Parliament Buildings at Victoria, capital of the province of British Columbia. Canada is a federation of ten provinces—Alberta, British Columbia, Manitoba, New Brunswick, Newfoundland, Nova Scotia, Ontario, Prince Edward Island, Quebec and Saskatchewan—and two territories—the Northwest Territories and the Yukon. While the provinces are self-governing, the two northern territories have not yet progressed to full self-governing status.

Territorial Government

The two large territories of northern Canada are controlled from Ottawa by the federal government, though both have achieved some self-governing powers. They also have one elected representative each in the House of Commons.

The government of the Northwest Territories is vested in a full-time commissioner, who is appointed by the federal government and has his seat in Ottawa. He is assisted by a council of nine members, four of whom are elected for three-year terms by universal adult suffrage from among the residents of the Territories and the remaining five of whom are appointed by the federal government. The Council meets annually in the territories and at least once each year at Ottawa.

The government of the Yukon Territory differs somewhat from that of the Northwest Territories in that the commissioner, who also holds office from the federal government, resides within the Territory, at Whitehorse, and his Legislative Council is composed of seven members elected by universal adult suffrage for a period of three years from among the residents of the Territory.

The commissioner and council for each territory are empowered to legislate on most matters concerning the internal administration of the territory.

The Judiciary

The judiciary of Canada is independent of the executive and legislature and consists of both federal and provincial courts.

The highest court is the federal Supreme Court of Canada, which sits at Ottawa and has both criminal and civil jurisdiction over the whole country, acting as the final court of appeal in all cases.

Also situated in Ottawa is the Exchequer Court, incorporating the Admiralty Court, which deals with cases brought by or against the Crown and also with cases dealing with probate, divorce and admiralty matters. The only appeal from the Exchequer Court is to the Supreme Court.

Each province has a supreme or superior court, whose powers on a provincial level are similar to those wielded by the federal Supreme Court. Below these are county courts and divisional courts, whose power in dealing with offenders is limited. Below these again are the police courts and the justice of the peace courts, together with special courts to deal with offenses committed by juveniles.

The judges of all courts from the Supreme Court of Canada down to the provincial and divisional courts, with the exception of the judges of the courts of probate in New Brunswick and Nova Scotia, are appointed by the governor-general after consultation with the Privy Council—that is, in effect, by the Cabinet. Their salaries are paid by the federal authorities and they must retire at the age of 75. They cannot be removed from office except by Parliament itself, for misbehavior. Justices of the peace and magistrates who preside over police courts are appointed by provincial authority.

The justices of the Supreme Court of Canada, which sits in Ottawa. The federal Supreme Court of Canada is the highest court of the land, and has both criminal and civil jurisdiction over the nation. It acts as the final court of appeal in all cases.

Religion

There is no established church in Canada. Most of the major Christian denominations are represented, with the Roman Catholic Church accounting for about 45 per cent of the total Christian population.

In 1961 there were 8,342,826 Roman Catholics in Canada, over half of whom were resident in the predominantly French-Canadian province of Quebec. Roman Catholics were also in the majority in New Brunswick, Ontario, Prince Edward Island, Newfoundland, Nova Scotia and Northwest Territories. Elsewhere, Protestant sects are in the majority. In spite of bitterness and suspicion in the past, a spirit of mutual respect and toleration now generally prevails throughout the country.

The second largest religious body in Canada is the United Church of Canada, which was formed in 1925 by the union of the Congregational, Methodist and Presbyterian churches (although many Presbyterian congregations remained independent) and has since been joined by other nonconformist bodies. In 1961 the membership of the United Church of Canada was 3,644,008 (around 20 per cent of the population), with the largest congregations resident in Ontario, British Columbia and Alberta.

The Anglican Church of Canada, the third largest religious body in the country, had 2,409,068 adherents in 1961 (about 13 per cent of the population), nearly half of whom lived in Ontario.

The Presbyterian Church in Canada, composed of congregations remaining outside the United Church, had 818,558 members in 1961; the Evangelical Lutheran Church had 662,744 members and incorporated a number of Lutheran sects. The Baptist Church had 593,553 members.

In 1961 there were 254,368 persons of the Jewish faith in Canada. Their synagogues are in the main cities but not in rural districts. Moslems have a mosque in Edmonton, and there are some 10,000 Buddhists, the majority of whom are of Japanese extraction. There are 17 Buddhist temples in Canada, the largest of which is in Toronto.

Education

Under the provisions of the British North America Act each Canadian province may adopt and maintain its own school system. In recent years, however, the whole pattern of education has been undergoing a transformation, and a considerable degree of educational uniformity has been established, except for Quebec and Newfoundland, where education has been divided along denominational lines. In Quebec, for example, the system of education for Roman Catholic students has been strictly separated from that for Protestants. But even here, a royal commission has proposed a system much more secular in character, and other reforms were put into effect in 1964.

PRIMARY AND SECONDARY EDUCATION

Many elementary schools throughout the country are denominational, but most secondary education is on a non-sectarian basis.

In 1963-64 there were 24,700 primary and secondary schools, both public and private, in Canada, and a total of 4,787,098 pupils and 193,862 teachers. In almost all areas education is both free and compulsory up to the age of 16.

ADULT AND VOCATIONAL EDUCATION

Great advances have been made in recent years in the provision of facilities for adult education and vocational studies. In 1962-63 there were 125 teachers' training colleges, with 20,956 students and 1610 instructors.

There are many full-time institutions giving apprenticeship or pre-employment training in a number of trades, while more advanced technical training is provided by institutes of technology.

UNIVERSITY EDUCATION

In 1962-63 Canada had 365 educational institutions providing full-time education up to university degree standard, with a total of 141,388 students and 11,670 instructors. The largest faculties were those for arts and sciences (with a total enrolment of 74,665), engineering (15,200), commercial and business training (8200), medicine (4850), and law (3000), and there were over 20 other courses of instruction available.

As well as Canadian nationals, about 9500 students from foreign countries, nearly 80 per cent of them from the United States, are studying at Canadian universities.

Language

Canada has two official languages, English and French, which have equal status in federal institutions and in the province of Quebec.

By far the largest linguistic group is that of English-speaking citizens, who are in a majority in every province except Quebec. According to the 1961 census, some English was spoken by almost 80 per cent of the population, and it was the mother tongue of over half of all Canadians.

In 1961 French was spoken by almost one-third of the population and was the mother tongue of nearly the same number. Only in the province of Quebec, where French is spoken by 87 per cent of the population, are French-speaking Canadians in the majority; in all other provinces, except New Brunswick—where almost half of the people are French-speaking—the percentage of those speaking French runs from 1 to 10 per cent. Northern and Eastern Ontario and the old Red River district in Manitoba once led by Louis Riel contain the only other large French-speaking communities.

There are a large number of linguistic minorities in Canada, as might be expected of a population built up by large-scale immigration from many countries.

Currency

The basic unit of currency is the Canadian dollar, which is divided into 100 cents. Gold coins of 5, 10, and 20 dollars have been issued and are legal tender, as are American and British gold coins, but these are not in general circulation.

Coins of bronze, nickel, steel and silver are in circulation, with values of 1, 5, 10, 25 and 50 cents, and 1 dollar. Commemorative silver dollars have been issued on such occasions as the Silver Jubilee of King George V in 1935, the state visit of King George VI and Queen Elizabeth in 1939, and the entry of Newfoundland into Confederation in 1949. The Bank of Canada issues banknotes in denominations of 1, 2, 5, 10, 20, 50, 100, 500 and 1000 dollars.

The rate of exchange of the Canadian dollar has been found recently at about 1.07 Canadian dollars to the U.S. dollar and 3 Canadian dollars to the pound sterling.

Weights and Measures

The system of weights and measures in present use in Canada is a mixture of the British and American systems, although it is probable that the metric system will be introduced over the next few years, in line with the growing international trend.

Measurements of length are in imperial yards, feet and inches, and measurements of capacity in imperial gallons, quarts and pints, as in Great Britain; but the American hundredweight (100 pounds avoirdupois) and ton (2000 pounds avoirdupois), rather than the British, are commonly used.

PHYSICAL GEOGRAPHY

THE VAST COUNTRY OF CANADA extends for about 2800 miles from north to south and about 4000 miles from east to west. It is washed on the east by the Atlantic Ocean, on the west by the Pacific Ocean, and on the north by the Arctic Ocean. Its physical geography is extremely complex and consists of several physiographic, climatic and vegetational zones.

NATURAL DIVISIONS

The territory of Canada may be divided into five major areas. These are: the Appalachian region in the east, which includes the provinces of New Brunswick, Nova Scotia and Prince Edward Island, together with Newfoundland Island, the extreme southeast of Labrador, and the part of Quebec province lying to the south of the St. Lawrence low-

The Martyrs' Shrine Church near Midland, Ontario. In Canada there is no established state church, and freedom of worship prevails. While almost all the major religions are represented, most of the Canadian population belongs to Christian denominations, with the Roman Catholic Church, the United Church of Canada—made up of Congregational, Methodist and some Presbyterian churches—and the Anglican Church of Canada the three largest religious bodies.

CANADA

Physical Features

Albanel, lake F19
Albany, riv F16
Amadjuak, lake C19
Amunden, gulf . . . . B 8
Arctic, ocean k27
Aston, cape B20
Athabasca, lake E12
Athabasca, riv E11
Atlantic, ocean I20
Attawapiskat, riv F16
Baffin, bay . . . . n 35, B19
Baffin, isl . . . . n 34, B19
Banks, isl . . . . B 9
Barrow, strait . . . . n 31, B14
Beaufort, sea . . . . B 4
Belle Isle, strait F22
Black, lake E12
Bonavista, bay G23
Boothia, gulf B15
Boothia, pen B14
Breton, cape G21
Brodeur, pen B16
Bylot, isl . . . . n 35, B18
Chidley, cape D21
Churchill, riv E14
Clearwater, lake E18
Coast, mts . . . . E 7
Cree, lake E12
Cree, riv E12
Cumberland, sound C20
Davis, strait B21
Dease, strait C12
Devon, isl . . . . m 32, A15
Dolphin and Union, strait C10
Dubawnt, lake D13
Ellesmere, isl . . . . . . k 33, A16
Erie, lake H17
Fort George, riv F18
Fox, pen C18
Foxe, basin C17
Foxe, channel C17
Franklin, mts . . . . C 8
Fundy, bay H20
Garry, lake C13
Goodhope, mtn . . . . F 9
Great Bear, lake . . . . D 9
Great Slave, lake D11
Grizzly Bear, mtn . . . . C 9
Hamilton, inlet F22
Hay, riv E10
Hayes, riv E15
Hazen, strait m28, A11
Hecate, strait . . . . F 7
Henrietta Maria, cape . . . E17
Home, bay C20
Hopes Advance, cape D20
Horn, mts D10
Hudson, bay D15
Hudson, strait D19
Hunt, mtn . . . . D 8
Huron, lake G17
Island, lake F15
James, bay F17
James Ross, strait B14
Kaniapiskau, riv E20
Keele, peak . . . . D 7
Kellet, cape . . . . B 8
Lake of the Woods, lake . . G15
Lancaster, sound n33, B16
Larch, riv E19
Leaf, riv E19
Liard, riv . . . . E 8
Liverpool, bay . . . . B 7
Logan, mtn . . . . D 5
Mackenzie, bay . . . . C 6
Mackenzie, mts . . . . C 7
Mackenzie, riv . . . . C 8
Maclean, strait m29, A12
Manitoba, lake F14
Manitoulin, isl G17
McClintock, channel B13
Melville, isl m29, A10
Melville, lake F21
Mercy, cape C21
Michikamau, lake F21
Minto, lake E18
Mistassini, lake F18
Nass, riv . . . . E 8

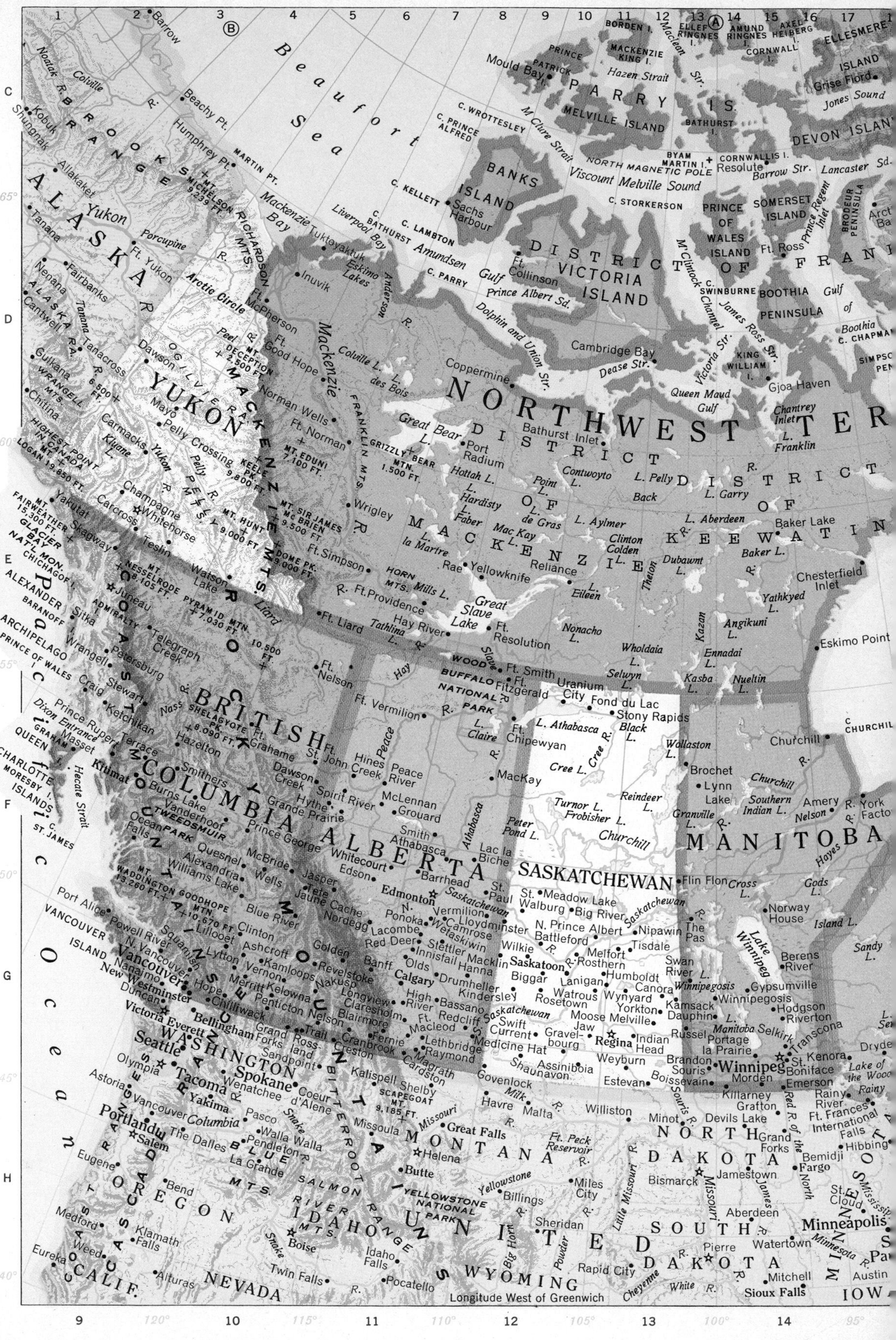

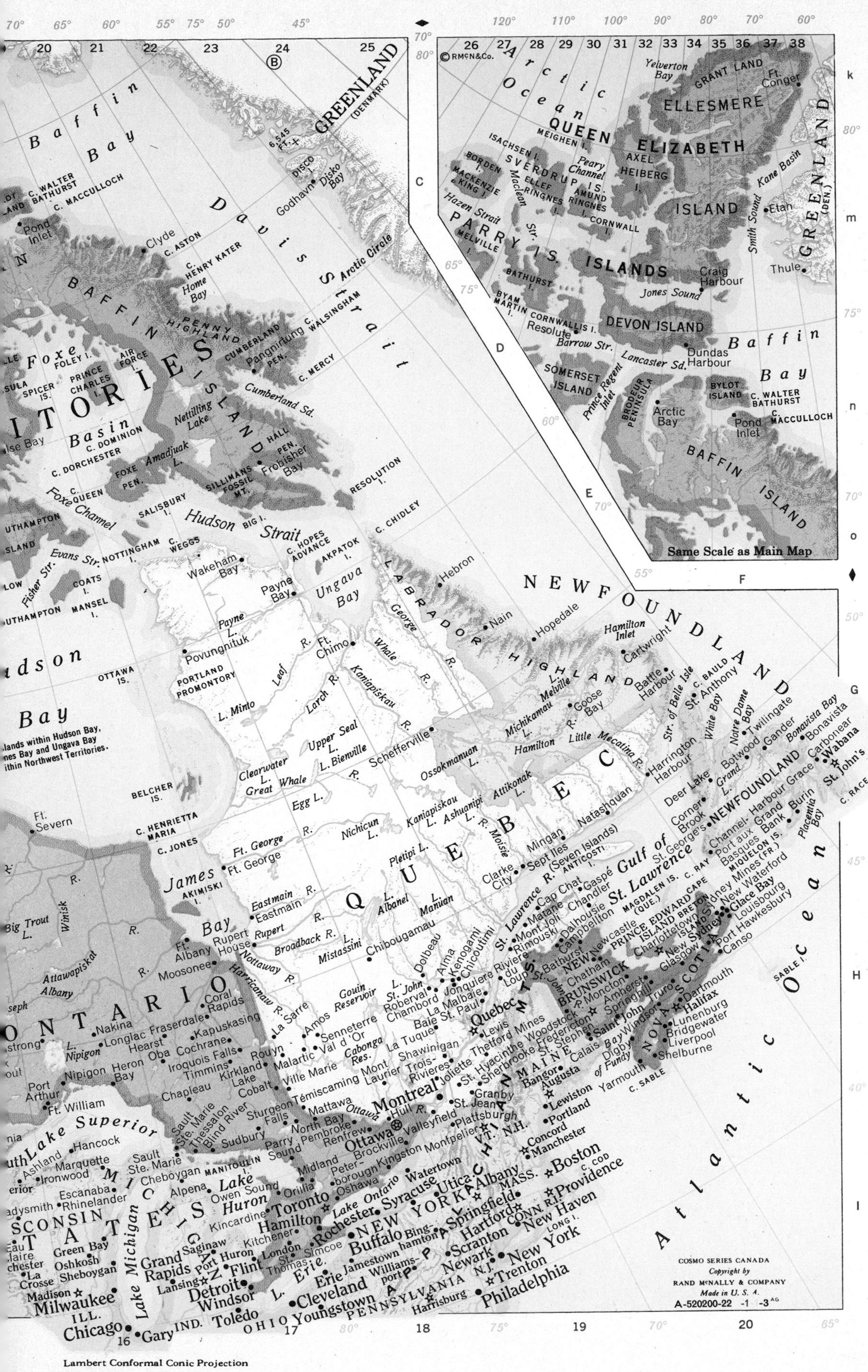

Lambert Conformal Conic Projection
SCALE 1 : 17,638,000 1 Inch = 277 Statute Miles

PROVINCIAL AND TERRITORIAL CAPITALS

Kicking Horse Canyon near famous Kicking Horse Pass, the highest point (5339 ft.) on the Canadian Pacific Railway's transcontinental route. Traveling east to west in Canada, one moves progressively through the Appalachian region of New Brunswick and Nova Scotia, the lowlands of the St. Lawrence, the Laurentian Plateau country, the plains of the interior and the great Rocky Mountain chain to the Pacific Coast, traversing a distance of about 3500 miles.

lands; the Laurentian Plateau, often called the Canadian Shield, which runs in a great arc of about 1,850,000 square miles embracing the greater part of Labrador, Quebec province and Ontario, northern Manitoba and northern Saskatchewan, and most of the mainland and the southern islands of the Northwest Territories; the plains and lowlands of the interior, including the great western prairies, the Mackenzie River lowlands in west Northwest Territories, the lowlands in the south of the Arctic Archipelago, and the plains of northern Ontario and the Great Lakes-St. Lawrence River region; the Cordilleran region, embracing the three great mountain chains of Yukon Territory, British Columbia and the southwest of Northwest Territories and Alberta; and the Innuitian region (so-called from the Eskimo *Innuit* meaning "the people"), comprising the northern islands of the Arctic Archipelago.

The Appalachian Region

The Appalachian region of Canada is situated at the northern end of the great ranges known as the Appalachian Mountains, which extend southwest for about 1700 miles from the Gulf of St. Lawrence to Alabama and the Gulf of Mexico. This system, formed in the late Paleozoic period, has been much eroded, and its highest peak, in North Carolina, is below 7000 feet. The main mountain ranges of the Canadian Appalachian area are situated in eastern Quebec province.

NEWFOUNDLAND ISLAND

Newfoundland Island, which together with Labrador on the mainland to the northwest and adjacent islands, makes up the province of Newfoundland, has an area of 43,359 square miles. It is situated in the Atlantic Ocean and is separated from eastern Labrador and Quebec by the 60-mile-long Strait of Belle Isle, which has a maximum width, at its southern end on the Gulf of St. Lawrence, of 15 miles. Newfoundland Island's Cape Spear is the most easterly point in North America, and its western shores are washed by the 100,000-square-mile Gulf of St. Lawrence.

Newfoundland Island is basically triangular in shape, with its apex at Cape Norman in the north and its base extending between Cape Ray in the extreme southwest and Cape Race on the Avalon Peninsula in the extreme southeast. Its coastline is very irregular, with many promontories, bays and inlets.

Many small islands lie off the rugged coastline, which is fringed by cliffs up to 400 feet in height along much of its length and up to 1000 feet around the Bay of Islands. Fogo Island, named after one of the Cape Verde Islands (Portuguese *fuego*: fire) and having an area of 100 square miles, is situated in Notre Dame Bay and is the largest of these offshore islands. Random Island (90 square miles) lies in Trinity Bay.

Most of the interior of Newfoundland Island is, like the coastline, rugged and rocky. Much of the southern half of the island consists of high, well-forested plateaus, the major elevations occurring in the northwest, where the Long Range Mountains extend northward along the coast for about 120 miles from Bonne Bay. The maximum elevation reached is 2651 feet in the peak of Gros Morne, at the southern end of the range.

The island is sufficiently watered but as a result of glacial disruption of old river systems, drainage lines are haphazard. There are many lakes, mainly in the west and south, the largest being the 205-square-mile Grand Lake, southeast of Corner Brook.

PRINCE EDWARD ISLAND

Prince Edward Island, the smallest of the Canadian provinces, has an area of 2184 square miles. It lies in the south of the Gulf of St. Lawrence, and its southern shore is washed by the 200-mile-long Northumberland Strait, separating the island from New Brunswick and Nova Scotia and varying in width between 10 and 25 miles. The coastline of Prince Edward Island is extremely irregular, like that of Newfoundland.

Apart from its coastline, Prince Edward Island is the least typical part of the Appalachian region. It is flat, the greatest altitude being approximately 450 feet above sea-level, and fertile and is watered by many small rivers.

NOVA SCOTIA

The province of Nova Scotia, which has an area of 21,425 square miles, consists of a large peninsula, about 380 miles long and between 50 and 100 miles wide, connected to New Brunswick on the northwest by the Isthmus of Chignecto. Cape Breton Island, to the northeast, also forms part of the province. The

Canso Causeway, opened in 1955, forms a road and rail link between the island and the mainland. Nova Scotia is bounded by the Atlantic Ocean along its eastern, lower side, and much of its western, upper side is washed by the Bay of Fundy, which extends for about 100 miles, dividing into two arms at the Isthmus of Chignecto. North of the Isthmus, the Northumberland Strait separates Nova Scotia from Prince Edward Island.

Cape Breton Island, 110 miles long and with a maximum width of 85 miles, lies two miles off the northeast coast of the peninsula, across the Strait of Canso, which joins the Gulf of St. Lawrence to the Atlantic Ocean. The island has an area of 3975 square miles, about one-third that of Vancouver Island, and a further 360 square miles are occupied by the salt-water Bras d'Or Lake, which lies in the center of the island and is connected to the Atlantic Ocean by channels in both the north and south. The coastline of Cape Breton Island is rugged and extremely irregular, with many bays and promontories, and the central and western parts of the islands are hilly, reaching a maximum elevation of 1747 feet in the highlands northwest of the city of Sydney.

The Nova Scotia peninsula is heavily forested and has a gently undulating surface. Elevations rise toward the coasts, which are rocky and fringed with low hills. The coastline is extremely irregular and is broken by many inlets, notably Chignecto Bay, which is the 50-mile-long northern arm of the Bay of Fundy and which terminates in Shepody Bay and the Cumberland Basin.

The Isthmus of Chignecto, which links the peninsula of Nova Scotia to eastern New Brunswick, is about 60 miles wide at its broadest point and about 17 miles wide along the New Brunswick border. The name is of Micmac origin, meaning "the great marsh district."

Nova Scotia is watered by a number of small non-navigable rivers. There are also a large number of lakes, notably Lake Rossignol, named after an early French trader, (16 miles long and 10 miles wide), in the south of the island.

NEW BRUNSWICK

The province of New Brunswick is roughly rectangular in shape and has an area of 28,354 square miles. It is bordered by the Isthmus of Chignecto on the southeast, by Quebec province to the north, and by the state of Maine to the west. Its shores are washed by the Bay of Fundy to the south, the Northumberland Strait and the Gulf of St. Lawrence to the east, and Chaleur Bay to the north. About 85 per cent of the land area of New Brunswick, which is generally flat except to the northwest, is covered by productive forest.

The rugged southern coast is broken by several bays and inlets of the Bay of Fundy, and it is there, almost in the center of the southern shore, that Saint John, the major city and port of the province, is situated. An interesting phenomenon are the rapids known as the Reversing Falls, where the St. John River meets the sea at the head of Saint John Harbor. At low tide the river water rushes through a 325-foot gorge with banks 95 feet high and makes a 17-foot descent to the sea. Then for a few minutes at slack tide the seething rapids become almost completely calm and ships may pass through. Later, as the tide rises, the ocean waters force themselves upstream tumultuously. This awe-inspiring event occurs twice every 24 hours.

West of Saint John, on the Maine border, Passamaquoddy Bay, containing several small islands, extends for 30 miles inland. In the extreme northeast of the Bay of Fundy the Chignecto Bay divides into two arms: Shepody Bay to the north and Cumberland Basin to the south. The east coast, along the Northumberland Strait and the Gulf of St. Lawrence, is level and marshy.

The northwest of the province is more rugged: spurs of the Appalachian system rise to over 2000 feet, reaching a maximum elevation of 2690 feet in Mt. Carleton, about 50 miles southwest of Dalhousie. The south of the province is well watered and dotted with many lakes, the largest being the 67-square-mile

Signal Hill, overlooking St. John's, Newfoundland. The island of Newfoundland is part of the Appalachian region of Canada, being an extension of the Appalachian Mountains (a formation almost 1700 miles long) which run southwest from the Gulf of St. Lawrence to the Gulf of Mexico coastal plain.

Grand Lake, north of the St. John River. The St. John flows into the Bay of Fundy.

SOUTHEAST QUEBEC PROVINCE

The southeastern part of Quebec province, bordered by the St. Lawrence River to the west and north, the Gulf of St. Lawrence to the northeast, New Brunswick and Maine to the east, and Vermont to the south, is a part of the Appalachian region. The southwest of this long, narrow strip is known as the Eastern Townships, of which Sherbrooke is the major center. In the northeast the Gaspé Peninsula extends into the Gulf of St. Lawrence.

Southeast Quebec contains the major elevations of the Canadian Appalachian system. The south and center of the area are traversed by the Notre Dame Mountains, a northeastern extension of the Green Mountains of Vermont, which rise to a maximum elevation of 3500 feet in the southwest of the Gaspé Peninsula. Near the head of the Gaspé Peninsula they merge into the Shickshock Mountains, which extend for about 100 miles on a west-east axis near the coast. This range reaches its maximum elevation of 4160 feet in Mt. Jacques Cartier.

The Laurentian Plateau (Canadian Shield)

The largest single physical division of Canada is the Laurentian Plateau, often called the Canadian Shield, which extends in a great arc across eastern and central Canada, covering a total area of about 1,850,000 square miles. The Laurentian Plateau extends from the Atlantic coast of Labrador through the whole of Quebec province, apart from the narrow southeastern strip of the Appalachian region, through southern and central Ontario, bending northwest through northern Manitoba and Saskatchewan, north over the Northwest Territories east of the Mackenzie River, and northeast to include most of the Melville Peninsula and Baffin Island.

The Laurentian Plateau is the oldest geological area of Canada and consists of rocky, undulating uplands, watered by many lakes and rivers but lacking good agricultural areas. It is, however, extremely rich in minerals. The northwestern mainland part of the area—that is, the area north of latitude 59°N. and contained between the Mackenzie valley on the west and Hudson Bay on the east—is usually known as the Barren Grounds, or Barren Lands. The appearance of the country is that of a vast rolling plain covered with short grass, sedge, saxifrages and other flowering plants, with the underlying Laurentian rock rising sometimes into rounded hills. Of special interest is the fact that the ground is permanently frozen to within a few inches of the surface and in warm weather is constantly wet.

The Gatineau River region is typical of the Laurentian Plateau country, of which almost the entire province of Quebec is a part. The Laurentian Plateau, also called the Canadian Shield, extends in a great arc across eastern and central Canada from the coast of Labrador to the Northwest Territories east of the Mackenzie River.

LABRADOR

Labrador, the mainland and larger part of Newfoundland province, has an area of approximately 110,000 square miles. Its rugged and irregular coastline is washed by the cold Labrador Current of the Atlantic Ocean, and the climate is severe.

Scoured by glaciation and eroded by water, Labrador is mainly an undulating plateau, lakestrewn in parts and with huge areas of swamp and muskeg. Bare rocky ridges rise above the generally featureless landscape; the valleys between vary from sand plains to lake clay patches. The northeast part is in sharp contrast. There, the Torngat Uplift, sometimes called Devil Mountains, extends from Hebron Fiord to Cape Chidley. The name is derived from the Eskimo *Tomgarsuak*—"the ruler of all sea animals." These are the highest mountains of the Pre-Cambrian Shield, reaching 5500 feet.

QUEBEC PROVINCE

Quebec province has an area of 594,860 square miles, and almost all of this territory, with the exception of the southern strip mentioned under the Appalachian and Lowland regions, falls within the Laurentian Plateau region. The northern part of the province is fairly rugged, with extensive forests and rich mineral deposits, but in the south the soil is more fertile.

HUDSON STRAIT

The northern shore of Quebec province is washed by the Hudson Strait, a 450-mile-long arm of the Atlantic Ocean, which separates Quebec from Baffin Island and has a maximum width of 150 miles. At the east end of the Strait, at the Atlantic confluence, are Resolution Island (30 miles in both length

The beautiful setting of Prince Albert National Park is situated in central Saskatchewan between the Saskatchewan and Churchill rivers. The park, which was established in 1927, covers an area of 1496 sq. mi., and is a wooded sanctuary for such wild life as moose, elk, deer, caribou and bear.

and width) and Killinek Island (20 miles long, and between two and nine miles wide), both being formed by Precambrian rocks just off the northern tip of Labrador. Toward the southeast, the Hudson Strait penetrates the Quebec mainland for about 200 miles in the 160-mile-wide Ungava Bay. In the center of the bay's mouth lies Akpatok Island (about 30 miles long and half as wide), with a precipitous coastline. The name comes from the Eskimo, "place of birds."

HUDSON BAY

Almost completely enclosed within the Laurentian Plateau, bordered by Quebec to the east, Ontario to the south, Manitoba to the southwest and by the Northwest Territories to the north and northwest, is a vast gulf or inland sea—Hudson Bay. Its vastness encompasses almost 500,000 square miles. An arm of either the Atlantic or Arctic Ocean, it connects with the former by Hudson Strait; with the latter, by Foxe Channel. Scotland, with its pastures for sheep and cattle, is in the same latitude as this vast, bleak, generally icebound inland sea of Canada.

Hudson Bay contains many islands. The largest of these is Southampton, with an area of almost 16,000 square miles, situated in the west of the bay's mouth.

THE LAURENTIAN MOUNTAINS

The interior of Quebec province north of the St. Lawrence lowlands is generally hilly. The southern edge of the Laurentian Plateau is marked by the Pre-Cambrian (and hence the world's oldest) mountains, the Laurentians, extending from the border with Ontario almost to Labrador, dividing the river systems emptying into Hudson Bay from those flowing into the St. Lawrence. The mountains reach a maximum elevation of 3905 feet a little to the northeast of the city of Quebec, while farther north, between Quebec City and the Lake St. John area, in the tourist center known as Laurentian Park, elevations of up to 3800 feet are reached. Toward the southwest, above Montreal, Mont Tremblant rises to 3150 feet.

CENTRAL ONTARIO

The Laurentian Plateau extends over most of central and southern Ontario. To the north, an extensive

A panoramic view of the vast plains of Canada. These flat prairie lands extend from the Winnipeg area in the south of Manitoba west across Saskatchewan to eastern and northern Alberta. It is the center of Canada's agricultural region.

lowland area fringes the western side of James Bay and the southern coast of Hudson Bay, while in the extreme southeast the lowlands of the St. Lawrence-Great Lakes area extend from Ottawa to Detroit. The plateau area of Ontario is heavily forested and there are few agricultural settlements, but it is one of the most important sources of mineral wealth in the world.

The wooded hills and valleys of the Ontarian Plateau are well watered and interspersed with many lakes. The Great Lakes, which mark the border with the U.S., will be dealt with under the section entitled Hydrography.

Grain fields in Alberta, near the foot of the Rocky Mountains, which may be glimpsed in the background. The greater part of Alberta consists of gently undulating, fertile prairie lands. Grain cultivation is widespread and is highly mechanized. Stock raising flourishes throughout the region.

CENTRAL MANITOBA

The province of Manitoba may be divided into three zones, of which the northern zone, around Hudson Bay, consists of forested plains, the central zone forms part of the Laurentian Plateau, and the southern zone is extensive prairie land. The major elevations of the province are situated not in the plateau area, which is generally undulating, forested and rich in minerals, but to the south and to the southwest.

The southern edge of the Laurentian Plateau in Manitoba is marked by Lake Winnipeg, which is the largest lake in the province and one of the largest in Canada, and an important fishing center and transportation route. The lake, about 240 miles long and 55 miles wide, extends along a northwest-southeast axis in the south-central part of the province, covering an area of 9398 square miles. The Saskatchewan River is the largest of its tributaries.

NORTHERN SASKATCHEWAN

The southern edge of the Laurentian Plateau covers the northern part of Saskatchewan province, which is an undulating, forested region, with rich deposits of copper, gold and, in the extreme northwest, pitchblende. The major elevations are found in the prairie area to the south and west.

The major features of the Saskatchewan Plateau are its large lakes, interconnected by rivers.

CENTRAL AND EASTERN NORTHWEST TERRITORIES

The Laurentian Plateau covers the greater part of the Northwest Territories, including the central and eastern part of Mackenzie District, all of Keewatin District, and the southeastern part of Franklin District (which includes the Hudson Bay islands, dealt with earlier). The plateau area proper is about 350 miles wide, extending from the foothills of the Rocky Mountains in the west to the lowlands that run along the shore of Hudson Bay in the east. The greater part of the area is infertile, although there are rich mineral deposits that are not yet fully exploited, and the nature of the terrain in general is adequately expressed by the name given to the southeastern part of the area—the Barren Grounds or Barren Lands.

The major elevations of the Northwest Territories are found in the west and will be dealt with under the Cordilleran Region.

CHAIN OF LAKES

The western edge of the Laurentian Plateau is marked by a chain of lakes connected with the Mackenzie River system. Great Slave Lake, the fifth largest lake on the continent, with an area over 11,000 square miles, lies in the southwest of the territory, near the border with Alberta, and is irregular in shape. It is roughly 300 miles long and between 30 and 140 miles wide, extending northwest in the 80-mile-long North Arm and northeast in the 80-mile-long McLeod Bay. It was named after the Slave Indians who formerly lived on its shores. The lacustrine chain is continued toward the northwest by Lac la Martre and Lakes Grandin, Tache and St. Therese, until eventually Great Bear Lake, the fourth largest on the continent, on the edge of the Arctic Circle, is reached. This lake, which has an area of around 12,000 square miles, is extremely irregular in shape.

There are a number of smaller lakes in the eastern sector of the Laurentian region in Northwest Territories.

FRANKLIN DISTRICT

A number of the islands of the Canadian Arctic Archipelago, which make up the District of Franklin in Northwest Territories, form part of the Laurentian Plateau region. The physical features of the Arctic islands will, however, be dealt with as a whole under the heading of the Innuitian Region.

Canadian Plains and Lowlands

The plains and lowlands of Canada form only a small part of the country's total area, but they are the focus of intensive agriculture, the site of the major industrial developments and the home of about 80 per cent of the population. Not only is the soil fertile and well watered, but also there are great deposits of oil and natural gas and coal, while the northern lowlands are rich in timber.

The Canadian lowlands may be divided into three major areas. These are: the prairies of southern Mani-

Beautiful Lake Waterton in Waterton Lakes National Park in the Rocky Mountains of Alberta. The park, as can be seen here, is quite mountainous, with heights rising to 9600 feet. This park is the Canadian part of Waterton-Glacier International Peace Park, located on the border of Alberta and Montana, which was created in 1932 by acts of the United States Congress and the Canadian Parliament.

toba and Saskatchewan and eastern and northern Alberta, together with the lowland areas of the Arctic Archipelago; the lowlands of northern Ontario and northeastern Manitoba, along the south shore of Hudson Bay, together with the Foxe Peninsula lowland in southwestern Baffin Island; and the St. Lawrence-Great Lakes lowland, the economic and industrial heart of Canada, in southern Ontario and Quebec.

THE WESTERN PRAIRIES

The vast, flat prairie lands of the west, interpersed by low mountain ranges and growing increasingly heavily wooded toward the northwest, extend west and north from the Winnipeg area in southern Manitoba across Saskatchewan, rising to high plain in eastern and northern Alberta and sinking to forested lowlands along the Mackenzie River in western Northwest Territories. Their eastern border is roughly marked by a line running from Lake of the Woods, through Lake Winnipeg, western Lake Athabaska, Great Slave Lake and Great Bear Lake to Amundsen Gulf, a large arm of the Beaufort Sea, and their western border is marked by the foothills of the Rocky Mountains.

SOUTHERN MANITOBA

The grain lands of southern Manitoba, centering on Winnipeg, slope gently toward the border with Saskatchewan. In the south of the province, the Pembina Mountains, which have a maximum elevation of about 2000 feet, extend for about 60 miles southeast from west of Winnipeg to the border with North Dakota. Farther west, near the border with Saskatchewan, the Riding Mountains extend through the 1148-square-mile Riding Mountain National Park, a lake-studded resort.

Two ranges mark the border between Manitoba and Saskatchewan. North of the town of Dauphin, the

Duck Mountain range extends for about 50 miles, reaching a maximum elevation of 2727 feet in Mt. Baldy, while the 60-mile-long Porcupine Mountain range a little to the north rises to 2700 feet in Hart Mountain.

SOUTHERN AND CENTRAL SASKATCHEWAN

Southern and central Saskatchewan form a part of the western lowlands, with the main wheat-growing areas in the south. Stock is raised in the higher country toward the border with Alberta, where the average elevation increases from around 1500 to over 4000 feet in the Cypress Hills. There are extensive tracts of forest in the central part of the province, where the Prince Albert National Park extends over an area of 1496 square miles, with a network of connecting streams suitable for canoe travel. At Lavalée Lake there is a nesting colony of jet black cormorants contrasting with a colony of white pelicans. Mining, mainly for coal, is concentrated along the southern border of the province.

A number of hill ranges run across the southern part of Saskatchewan. The highest elevations are found near the border with Alberta, where the Cypress Hills run for about 60 miles along the border with Montana, from Maple Creek to Medicine Hat rising to over 4500 feet.

Central Saskatchewan is well watered and contains many lakes. The largest of these are near the edge of the Laurentian Plateau.

ALBERTA

The greater part of the province of Alberta, except in the southwest where the Rocky Mountain system extends across the province and into Montana, consists of undulating prairie land, well watered and interspersed with tracts of forest in the north and central regions. Grain cultivation and stock raising are widely distributed, and there are large deposits of coal, oil and natural gas.

There are no significant elevations in Alberta outside of the Rocky Mountains, but the province is dotted with many lakes.

MACKENZIE DISTRICT

The lowlands of Mackenzie District in the Northwest Territories are less extensive and more heavily wooded than those of the prairie provinces. The main lowlands extend in a narrow strip along the Mackenzie River valley, bordered on the west by the Rocky Mountains and on the east by the Laurentian Plateau, the edge of the latter being roughly marked by the 300-mile-long chain of the Franklin Mountains, which lie between the Mackenzie valley and Great Bear Lake.

Coastal lowlands extend along the northern shore of Mackenzie District, washed by Amundsen Gulf. There are also extensive lowland areas in the islands of the southern Arctic Archipelago.

THE HUDSON BAY LOWLANDS

An extensive belt of lowlands, heavily forested and watered by many small lakes and rivers, extends along the southern shore of Hudson Bay. The lowlands extend inland for up to about 200 miles in an arc extending roughly from Cape Churchill in northern Manitoba to the Ontario-Quebec border on the southern shore of James Bay. North of Hudson Bay, the lowlands of Foxe

The valley of the Bow River and the town of Banff in Alberta, situated on the eastern slopes of the Canadian Rocky Mountains. This is part of the Cordilleran region of Canada, a great, rugged mountainous belt about 1000 miles long and nearly 500 miles wide, made up of the northern ranges of the Rocky Mountain system.

Peninsula may also be considered as part of this region.

THE GREAT LAKES - ST. LAWRENCE LOWLANDS

The lowlands around the Great Lakes and the St. Lawrence River, in southern Ontario and Quebec provinces, constitute the economic and industrial heart of Canada and are the home of about 60 per cent of the population. Intensive agriculture is practiced, but rapidly increasing industrial development has relegated the raising of crops and stock to a secondary position.

The southern Ontario lowland extends south of a line drawn roughly from Parry Sound on Lake Huron to Ottawa to Cornwall, near the St. Lawrence River and the Quebec border. It is bounded by Lake Huron on the west and by Lakes Erie and Ontario on the south and east. On the southeast, the Niagara River, containing the mighty Niagara Falls, one of the largest cataracts in the world, connects Lake Ontario to Lake Erie. The falls had their origin in the quaternary ice age when the Dundas Valley became blocked by ice and debris and a new outlet for Great Lakes drainage in the Niagara River caused the river to erode from the escarpment at Queenston Heights over an estimated period of some 25,000 years.

A narrow, densely populated lowland strip extends between the north bank of the St. Lawrence River and the southeast edge of the Laurentian Plateau, in south Quebec province. This strip, the site of the great cities of Montreal and Quebec, narrows toward the mouth of the St. Lawrence. In the Gulf of St. Lawrence lies Anticosti Island, an undulating, wooded island some 140 miles long and 30 miles wide, situated about 30 miles south of the mainland.

The Cordilleran Region

The Cordilleran region of Canada consists basically of a great mountainous belt about 1000 miles long and nearly 500 miles wide, made up of the ranges of the northern Rocky Mountains (or Rockies) system. The general form is like a mighty wall with mountain sides and elevated platform between. The Rockies, which rise on the Bering Strait in the Arctic Circle, sweep southeast through Alaska and into western Canada, covering the greater part of Yukon Territory, the southwestern strip of Northwest Territories, most of British Columbia and its off-shore islands, and southwestern Alberta. The system runs the length of the U.S. to New Mexico and has a total length of over 3000 miles.

The Canadian Rockies form an extremely complex system. They have a base of ancient crystalline rocks, but their formation dates mainly from the Upper Cretaceous and early Tertiary periods. The ranges are interspersed with internal plateaus, formed by erosion during the Pliocene period, and further orogenic and glacial action throughout the Pleistocene period made their reliefs even more complex.

For the sake of clarity and brevity, it is convenient to divide the Canadian Rockies into three groups, forming three separate, parallel systems. These are often referred to as the Foothills, the Mountains proper, and the Trench. It should be remembered, however, that this is a large simplification, since the system as a whole consists of many ranges lying on widely differing axes and is broken by the courses of the many rivers flowing either to the Pacific or Atlantic systems, for which it acts as a watershed. In the present context, however, it will be convenient to examine the Rockies under three headings: the western, the central and the eastern regions.

A herd of caribou in the snowy wastes of the Yukon Territory. While the Yukon is generally a plateau, it is crossed by the Mackenzie and Pelly mountains in the south and east. Mt. Logan (19,850 ft.), the highest peak in Canada, is located here.

THE WESTERN CORDILLERAN REGION

The western chain of the Canadian Rockies may be divided into two systems: the insular system and the Pacific, or coastal, system. The main peaks of the insular system are found in the ranges that dominate Vancouver Island—a long, narrow mass lying off the British Columbia mainland, from which it is separated by the Queen Charlotte and Johnstone straits, the Strait of Georgia, Haro Strait and the Strait of Juan de Fuca. Vancouver Island has an area of 13,049 square miles, and its southern tip descends below the 49th parallel, where the Juan de Fuca Strait forms the border with the U.S.

The mountains of Vancouver Island represent a westward extension of the Coast Mountains of British Columbia and the Olympic Mountains of Washington. They are interspersed by fertile, well watered valleys and are rich in minerals.

To the north of Vancouver Island, across the Queen Charlotte Sound, lies the archipelago of the Queen Charlotte Islands, which are separated from Alaska to the north by the 40-mile-wide Dixon Entrance. The forested Queen Charlotte Mountains, rising to over 4000 feet, extend from north to south over the three main islands of the group: Graham Island (2485 square miles), Moresby Island (1060 square miles), and Kunghit Island (83 square miles).

The main range of the Pacific system is the Coast Mountains, which represent a northward extension of the Cascade Range of the western U.S., the Fraser River marking the dividing line between the two ranges. The Coast Mountains run north for about 1000 miles to the Yukon border, where they are continued into Alaska by the higher St. Elias range. The Coast Mountains rise to a maximum height of 13,260 feet in Mt. Waddington.

The northern part of the western Cordilleran region is formed by the St. Elias Mountains, which, although they extend north on the mainland from the Coast Mountains, are structurally part of the insular system.

This range, interspersed by glacier-filled valleys, extends for about 200 miles in a northwesterly direction across southwest Yukon Territory and into Alaska. It contains the highest peak in Canada, the 19,850-foot Mt. Logan, at the head of the Seward Glacier about 180 miles west of Whitehorse. Although 9000 feet lower than the world's highest peak, Mt. Everest, its glacier ranks among the world's largest.

A Canadian ship forges through ice-jammed Norwegian Bay, Ellesmere Island. Ellesmere Island is one of the most northerly of the Canadian Arctic Archipelago. The severe climate, with short summers and long, frigid winters, greatly limits vegetation and human habitation on these islands, although there are a number of Eskimo settlements which subsist on hunting and fishing.

THE CENTRAL CORDILLERAN REGION

The central Cordilleran region of western Canada consists of a number of mountain chains extending from the border with the U.S. to the center of southern Yukon Territory, and lying roughly on a southeast-northwest axis. They are separated from the coastal systems by the valleys of the major rivers and from the Rockies proper by a series of plateaus and trenches. The area is well forested and is interspersed by many small lakes. It is generally divided into the Columbia system to the south, the central Cassiar system, and the Yukon system to the north.

In the south of the central Cordilleran system, the Monashee Mountains stretch north and west from the U.S. border for a distance of about 200 miles. The range, which has important mineral deposits, rises to a maximum elevation of 10,560 feet in Hallam Peak, while Cranberry Mountain rises to 9470 feet. East of the Monashee Mountains and roughly parallel with them, the Selkirk Mountains rise for a distance of about 200 miles from the boundary with Idaho and Montana.

Large areas of the Selkirk Mountains are contained within the specially preserved park areas in which British Columbia is rich.

To the west and north of the Selkirk Mountains, the Cariboo Mountains extend northwest for about 200 miles along the western edge of the Fraser valley. Large tracts of commercial forest and hunting areas are interspersed by many lakes, but the goldfields that attracted so many prospectors to the area in the later 19th century are now little worked. The range rises to over 9000 feet in the 9920-foot Mt. Spranger, but the unsurveyed Mt. Titan farther north is believed to rise to nearly 12,000 feet.

In central British Columbia, in the Cassiar system, the 100-mile-long range of the Babine Mountains reaches a maximum elevation of 7827 feet in Cronin Mountain, while the 250-mile-long Stikine Mountains, farther north, rise to 8200 feet.

Farther north again, the mountain ranges of central and east Yukon Territory have not, as yet, been fully surveyed, and there are many unnamed peaks and plateaus. The Pelly Mountains, extending about 200 miles northwest from the British Columbia border, reach a maximum elevation of about 9500 feet.

THE EASTERN CORDILLERAN REGION

The eastern Cordilleran region of Canada consists of the Rocky Mountains proper and their associated chains, extending from the Arctic Circle to the Montana border and separated from the systems to the west by the depression known as the Rocky Mountain Trench, the source of many major rivers.

The extreme northwest of the Rockies system is marked by the Brooks Range of Alaska and by the Richardson Mountains of northwest Yukon Territory. There are a number of other ranges and individual peaks in this area that have not yet been explored or named.

To the southeast of the Richardson Mountains, the Mackenzie Mountains extend for about 500 miles across the east of Yukon Territory and into southwestern Northwest Territories. They are extended to the west by the 150-mile-long Ogilvie Range, and farther east, across the Mackenzie River, the Franklin Mountains run roughly parallel to the Mackenzie range for about 300 miles.

The highest peak in the Yukon sector of the Mackenzie Mountains is Mt. Hunt, near the Northwest Territories border, which rises to 9000 feet. In the Northwest Territories sector is the 69,440-square-mile game reserve known as the Mackenzie Mountains Preserve. In the same area, the range reaches its maximum elevation of 9049 feet in Mt. Sir James McBrien.

The Rocky Mountains proper run along the border between British Columbia and Alberta, where they form the Continental Divide. They rise to their highest Canadian elevation, 12,972 feet, in Mt. Robson, which is situated in the Mt. Robson Provincial Park, B.C.

Jasper National Park (4200 square miles) in Alberta is an important tourist center and game preserve, east of Mt. Robson and Hamber Provincial parks, and contains peaks over 10,000 feet.

Banff National Park, to the south, has an area of 2564 square miles and also contains a number of important peaks.

A little to the south lies Mt. Assiniboine Park, which contains Mt. Assiniboine (11,870 feet), and to the northwest is Yoho National Park (507 square miles).

Farther south, near the border, is Mt. King George (11,226 feet), and south again is Waterton Lakes National Park (204 square miles); this is the northern part of the Waterton-Glacier International Peace Park.

The Innuitian Region

The Innuitian region is a term commonly applied to the more northerly islands of the Arctic Archipelago, but it is used here, for the sake of convenience, to denote all the islands off the north coast of Canada, some of which have already been mentioned as forming a part of other Canadian regions. The term is derived from *Innuit*, the name used by the Eskimos.

BANKS AND VICTORIA ISLANDS

In the southwest of the Arctic Archipelago is Banks Island, which is about 250 miles long and has a maximum width of 110 miles. The greater part of its 23,230-square-mile area is fairly level and dotted with lakes, but in the south hills rise to around 2000 feet. The 250-mile-long Amundsen Gulf separates the island from the mainland.

To the southeast of Banks Island, across the Prince of Wales Strait, which has a maximum width of 20 miles, is Victoria Island, which is 425 miles long and up to 350 miles wide, with an area of 81,930 square miles. Its irregular coastline is penetrated on the southwest by Prince Albert Sound and on the southeast by Cambridge Bay. The interior of the island rises to 3000 feet. Victoria Island is separated from the mainland by, from west to east, the 100-mile-long Dolphin and Union Strait, the 130-mile-long Coronation Gulf, the 130-mile-long Dease Strait and the 140-mile-long Queen Maud Gulf.

MELVILLE AND PRINCE PATRICK ISLANDS

To the north of Victoria Island, across the 100-mile-wide Viscount Melville Sound, lies Melville Island (16,503 square miles), the largest of the Parry Islands. Melville Island is about 200 miles long and varies between 30 and 130 miles in width; its hilly interior, broken by glacier-filled valleys, rises to around 1500 feet. Its coastline is deeply indented and is washed on the southwest by McClure Strait, a 170-mile-long channel connecting with the Beaufort Sea.

Eglinton Island (504 square miles) divides the western arm of McClure Strait, the 60-mile-long Fitzwilliam Strait, into the Crozier Channel and the Kellet Strait. About 30 miles west of Melville Island, across the Fitzwilliam Strait, is Prince Patrick Island (6081 square miles), a long, narrow mass rising to a maximum elevation of around 1500 feet in the central high plain. It is the fifth largest and the most westerly of the Queen Elizabeth Islands.

To the northeast of Prince Patrick Island, across the 80-mile-long Ballantyne Strait (which contains the 414-square-mile Brock Island to the north) is Borden Island.

THE SVERDRUP GROUP

About 60 miles east of the Borden Islands, across the 140-mile-long Prince Gustav Adolph Sea, is Ellef

Ringnes Island (4266 square miles), the most westerly of the Sverdrup group. The island, which is about 150 miles long and has a maximum width of 70 miles, rises to 2000 feet on the central high plain and is extended to the northwest by the 55-mile-long Isachsen Peninsula.

Amund Ringnes Island (1764 square miles), lying southeast across the Hassel Sound, is about 70 miles long and up to 45 miles wide. It has a maximum elevation of about 2200 feet. Meighen Island (360 square miles) is situated in the 70-mile-long Good Friday Gulf about 50 miles to the northeast, and to the east is Axel Heiberg Island (13,583 square miles), the largest of the Sverdrup group.

Axel Heiberg Island is about 220 miles long and irregularly shaped, varying in width between 20 and 100 miles. It is rugged and mountainous, reaching a maximum elevation of over 6000 feet in the northeast. It is divided from Ellesmere Island to the east by the 90-mile-

Near Kingston, Ontario is the picturesque district known as The Thousand Islands. There are over 1500 small islands in this stretch of the St. Lawrence River, and the area boasts many popular and beautiful summer resorts and wonderful recreational possibilities. Thousand Islands International Bridge, which links Canada and the United States at this point, is over 6½ miles long and was completed in 1938.

long Nansen Sound on the northeast and the 180-mile-long Eureka Sound farther south.

ELLESMERE ISLAND

Ellesmere Island, the largest and most easterly of the Queen Elizabeth Islands, about 30 miles east of Axel Heiberg Island, has an area of 77,392 square miles. It is situated only a few miles from the west coast of Greenland, from which it is separated, from northeast to east, by the 50-mile-long Robeson Channel, the 80-mile-long Kennedy Channel, the 110-mile-long Kane Basin and the 55-mile-long Smith Sound, which connect the Lincoln Sea in the north to the 700-mile-long Baffin Bay in the south. Baffin Bay has a maximum width of 400 miles; it is usually icebound, since it is traversed by the cold Labrador Current.

Ellesmere Island is extremely irregular in shape with an indented coastline, being about 500 miles long and varying in width from 25 to 300 miles. Its rugged and heavily glaciated surface is divided by long, narrow bays into four main areas: Grant Land to the north, where the 250-mile-long United States Range reaches a maximum elevation of over 11,000 feet; the central Grinnell Land; King Oscar Land to the southwest; and Ellesmere Land to the southeast. Cape Columbia, the northern extremity at latitude 83°7′ N., longitude 70°28′W., is the most northerly point of Canada.

DEVON AND PRINCE OF WALES ISLANDS

To the south of Ellesmere Island, across the 250-mile-long Jones Sound, is Devon Island (21,606 square miles), separated from the Sverdrup Islands to the northwest by the 70-mile-long Belcher Channel. Devon Island is about 320 miles long and has a maximum width of 100 miles; it reaches a maximum elevation of about 3000 feet in the heavily glaciated eastern region.

About 35 miles southwest of Devon Island, across the 120-mile-long Wellington Channel, is Cornwallis Island (2592 square miles), part of the Parry group. Farther west, across the McDougal Sound and the Crozier Strait, is Bathurst Island, in the same group, a rugged, irregularly shaped mass about 160 miles long and up to 100 miles wide, with an area of 7272 square miles.

South of Bathurst Island, across the island-dotted Barrow Strait, a 150-mile-long channel linking Viscount Melville Sound in the west to Lancaster Sound in the east, is Prince of Wales Island (13,736 square miles). This rugged and irregularly shaped island, about 190 miles long and between 40 and 130 miles wide, is separated from the Boothia Peninsula, on the mainland to the southeast, by the 110-mile-long Franklin Strait, which has a maximum width of 60 miles, and from Victoria Island, about 80 miles to the southwest, by the 170-mile-long McClintock Channel.

SOMERSET AND BAFFIN ISLANDS

About 30 miles east of Prince of Wales Island, across the 110-mile-long Peel Sound, which links Barrow Strait in the north to Franklin Strait in the south, is Somerset Island (9594 square miles), which is about 160 miles long and up to 105 miles wide, rising to a maximum elevation of around 2500 feet near the rugged east coast. It is separated from the mainland Boothia Peninsula, only

The International Bridge over the St. Marys River links Sault Ste. Marie, Ontario, with its counterpart in Michigan. A drive over the magnificent bridge gives a visitor a panoramic view of the famous Sault Ste. Marie Locks, the busiest inland waterway in the world, which handle around 100 million tons of shipping a year.

The Saint Lambert Lock on the St. Lawrence Seaway near Montreal. The importance of the St. Lawrence River as a major artery of shipping and trade was greatly increased with the opening of the Seaway in April 1959. For the first time the interior of the North American continent was made accessible to deep draft, ocean-going vessels. The development of the St. Lawrence Seaway in effect created a fourth seacoast for both Canada and the United States.

about six miles to the south, by the 30-mile-long Bellot Strait and from Cornwallis Island to the north and Devon Island to the northeast by Barrow Strait.

East of Somerset Island, across the 150-mile-long Prince Regent Inlet, which connects Barrow Strait to the Gulf of Boothia farther south, is the largest and the most easterly island of Canada—Baffin Island (183,810 square miles). This irregularly shaped mass, which is about 900 miles long and between 200 and 500 miles wide, is cut by several large bays into a number of peninsulas.

These are the Borden Peninsula in the north; the Brodeur Peninsula in the northwest; the Cumberland Peninsula in the east, where heavily glaciated mountains reach a maximum elevation of around 8000 feet; the Hall Peninsula to the southeast; and the flat and marshy Foxe Peninsula and Great Plain of the Koukdjuak to the southwest.

Baffin Island is separated from the mainland by the Hudson Strait, the 200-mile-long Foxe Channel and the 300-mile-long Foxe Basin, which runs into the 100-mile-long Fury and Hecla Strait. It is separated from Devon Island, 40 miles to the north, by the 200-mile-long Lancaster Sound and from Greenland on the east by Baffin Bay.

Hydrography

The hydrographic system of Canada is closely related to its relief. The Rocky Mountains system provides the watershed between the Pacific and Atlantic systems. Since the western rivers are near the coast, they tend to be fairly short. Rivers of great length flow east of the Rockies, but tend to empty into Hudson Bay or the Arctic Ocean rather than into the Atlantic Ocean.

Some of the rivers flowing west to the Pacific Ocean, however, have extremely long and complex courses, since they are forced into detours by the coastal ranges. The rivers flowing east to Hudson Bay form a complex network linked with many lakes, and their courses are often unstable because of a lack of definite reliefs and of a clear watershed. Often they form numerous branches, with the river basins separated by narrow strips of land known as portages, across which light craft may be carried from one river branch to another.

THE GREAT LAKES

The Great Lakes mark the Canada-U.S. border, extending for over 1000 miles between Ontario on the north and the states of Minnesota, Wisconsin, Michigan, Ohio, Pennsylvania and New York on the south. The lakes are, from west to east, Superior, Michigan, Huron, Erie and Ontario, and the international boundary runs roughly through the center of each, except for Lake Michigan, which is completely within the U.S.

The total area of the Great Lakes is about 95,000 square miles, just over a third of which is Canadian territory. They constitute the largest freshwater lacustrine system in the world, and their great importance as a communications and trade route, linked by a system of rivers and canals, was increased further by the opening of the St. Lawrence Seaway, which made the route between the Atlantic Ocean and the western shore of Lake Superior, a distance of well over 2000 miles, accessible to large, ocean-going craft.

The most westerly of the Great Lakes is Lake Superior, which is the largest body of fresh water in the world, with an area of 32,843 square miles, about 11,500 square miles of which are in Canada. It is 350 miles long and 160 miles wide, and its waters, which have a maximum depth of about 1290 feet, are fed by the Kaministikwia River, which flows 60 miles south and east from Dog Lake, and the Nipigon River, which flows 40 miles south from Lake Nipigon.

To the southeast, Lake Superior empties into Lake Huron through the St. Marys River, a rapids-obstructed channel flowing for 60 miles along the international border, through three small lakes, to Detour Passage. The commercial route between Lakes Superior and Huron is the Sault Sainte Marie (or Soo) Canals, two parallel channels, one on each side of the border, which bypass the St. Marys River rapids.

Lake Michigan, which lies south of Lake Superior and west of Lake Huron, has an area of 22,400 square miles and lies entirely within the U.S.

Some 15,353 square miles of the 23,860 square miles area of Lake Huron are in Canada. Lake Huron is 206 miles long and about 183 miles wide. It includes the large Georgian Bay to the northeast, which is 120 miles long and 65 miles wide and is separated from the main body of the lake by Saugeen Peninsula and the 1600-square-mile Manitoulin Island, the largest lacustrine island in the world and a popular holiday resort. Also in Georgian Bay are the 30 tiny islands which make up the Georgian Bay Islands National Park.

As well as receiving the waters of Lake Superior, Lake Huron receives the waters of Lake Michigan through the Straits of Mackinac. It discharges to the south, into Lake Erie, by way of the 40-mile-long St. Clair River, which flows into the 460-square-mile Lake St. Clair, which in turn discharges into the 31-mile-long Detroit River.

Lake Erie has an area of 9940 square miles, of which 4912 square miles are in Canada. It is about 241 miles long and between 30 and 57 miles wide. In the southwest of the lake lies Pelee Island (18 square miles), off the south coast of which is Middle Island, a small islet marking the southernmost point of Canada. It is by far the shallowest of the Great Lakes, having a maximum depth of only 210 feet. This makes it subject to rising to a dangerous level during storms, to pollution and to freezing in its shallower parts. Lake Erie empties into Lake Ontario, to the northeast, by way of the 34-mile-long Niagara River. About two-thirds of the way along its length are the famous Niagara Falls.

NIAGARA FALLS

The Niagara Falls, which lie between the cities of Niagara Falls, Ontario, and Niagara Falls, New York, form part of the international border. The Canadian Falls to the west, sometimes called the Horseshoe Falls because of their shape, are about 160 feet high and around 2500 feet wide.

Besides being an important source of hydroelectric power, the Niagara Falls are one of the world's major tourist centers, and both the Canadian and United States governments have preserved much of the area as parks.

The main commercial route between Lakes Erie and Ontario is the 27-mile-long Welland Ship Canal, opened in 1932. This channel, which rises 326 feet through a series of eight locks, carries traffic between Port Weller, at the northern end, and Port Colborne and Humberstone, at the southern end. It is also an important source of hydroelectric power.

Lake Ontario, the smallest and easternmost of the Great Lakes, has an area of 7313 square miles, of which 3849 square miles are in Canada. It is about 193 miles long and 53 miles wide, and conveys the waters of the Great Lakes system to the northeast, through the St. Lawrence River, into the Atlantic.

As well as the Welland Ship Canal, two other important canal systems lead off Lake Ontario. The

Niagara Falls in winter. The falls are fed by the Niagara River, which forms the link between Lake Erie and Lake Ontario. A spectacular attraction, the falls bring visitors from all over the world. Canadian Horseshoe Falls, seen here, is about 160 feet high and over 2500 feet wide. About 196,000 cubic feet of water flow over the falls per second.

The winding Kootenay River in British Columbia, with Lake Kootenay in the distance. The Kootenay River is one of the many tributaries of the great Columbia River system. Most of the western rivers of Canada, because they originate near the coast, tend to be relatively short.

Trent Canal flows about 220 miles from the Bay of Quinte, on the south, to Georgian Bay on Lake Huron. The greater part of the system consists of the 150-mile-long Trent River, which rises in Rice Lake and incorporates a number of other small lakes, rivers and artificial channels.

An important commercial route is the Rideau Canal, which flows north for about 126 miles from Kingston to Ottawa. The system was constructed in 1826-32 and incorporates the Rideau River, Rideau Lake and Cataraqui River.

THE ST. LAWRENCE RIVER AND SEAWAY

The importance of the St. Lawrence River as Canada's main route of shipping and trade, a position which it has held since pioneering days, was increased in recent years by the series of improvements that led up to the opening of the St. Lawrence Seaway, providing a route for large, ocean-going craft from the Atlantic Ocean to the heart of the American continent.

The length of the St. Lawrence River proper, from the northeast extremity of Lake Ontario to the Gulf of St. Lawrence above the Gaspé Peninsula, is 744 miles. The river, cutting through the southeastern edge of the Laurentian Plateau, has an extremely fertile valley and is the site of intensive agricultural and industrial development. There are hydroelectric plants on the major rapids, which are bypassed by canals for navigational purposes.

The St. Lawrence Valley is the main east-west axis of the Canadian transportation system. The St. Lawrence Deep Waterway (the Seaway) makes the St. Lawrence system the greatest inland oceanic route in the world.

The first part of the St. Lawrence River's course northeast from Lake Ontario—the 110 miles or so that mark the border between New York state and Ontario province—is dotted with many small islands. The main group, at the southern end, near Kingston, are known as the Thousand Islands, where the river is spanned by the Thousand Islands International Bridge, built in 1938. This group of about 1500 islets, on either side of the border, is a popular tourist center, and some islands in the Canadian sector form the St. Lawrence Islands National Park.

In south Quebec province, after flowing over the 50-mile-long International Rapids, the river widens to five miles to form the 30-mile-long Lake St. Francis, and then, after a further series of rapids, forms the 18-mile-long and seven-mile-wide Lake St. Louis. It is here, south of Montreal Island, that it receives its main tributary, the Ottawa River. After descending the three-mile-long Lachine Rapids, the river flows past Montreal, where it is spanned by the Jacques Cartier Harbour Bridge, built in 1930.

Near Trois Rivières, the St. Lawrence widens again to nine miles to form the 30-mile-long Lake St. Peter, where it receives its most important southern tributaries. Beyond Quebec the river is tidal, gradually widening toward the Gulf of St. Lawrence and reaching a maximum width of 90 miles at its mouth.

The main southern tributaries of the Saint Lawrence River, which enter the river on Lake St. Peter, are the 75-mile-long Richelieu River, which provides part of the communications link between the St. Lawrence and the Hudson River of New York state; the 150-mile-long St. Francis River; the 110-mile-long Yamaska River; and the 100-mile-long Nicolet River.

The main northern tributary of the St. Lawrence is the Ottawa River, which, for the greater part of its 696-mile course from its source on Grand Lake Victoria in southwest Quebec, marks the border between Ontario and Quebec provinces. The Ottawa River flows west, south and east in a wide arc, interrupted by many lakes and rapids, the latter providing the power for several important hydroelectric plants.

THE HUDSON BAY RIVERS

Very many rivers empty into Hudson Bay on the east, south and west, but the most important are those which make up the western system. These may be divided into three major groups: the rivers discharging into Lake Winnipeg; the rivers flowing from Lake Winnipeg to Hudson Bay; and the rivers flowing directly to Hudson Bay.

THE SASKATCHEWAN

The most important of the rivers that discharge into Lake Winnipeg is the Saskatchewan River, which is formed in central Saskatchewan province, east of the town of Prince Albert, by the junction of the North Saskatchewan and South Saskatchewan rivers. The North Saskatchewan River pursues an irregular easterly course of 760 miles from its source in the Rocky Mountains foothills in western Alberta, receiving the waters of the 175-mile-long Vermilion River and the 130-mile-long Clearwater River.

The South Saskatchewan River, which waters an important agricultural area, rises in the Rockies farther south, at the confluence of the 315-mile-long Bow River and the 250-mile-long Oldman River. It pursues a course of 550 miles east and north to its confluence with the North Saskatchewan River, receiving as it does so the waters of the Red Deer River (385 miles). The combined Saskatchewan rivers then flow eastward to Lake Winnipeg for a further 340 miles. The Saskatchewan River's total length, from the source of the Bow River to Lake Winnipeg, is 1205 miles.

THE RED AND ASSINIBOINE RIVERS

The second important river to discharge into Lake Winnipeg is the Red River of the North, which discharges into the southern end of the lake. Although the greater part of its 533-mile course from its source in North Dakota is through the U.S., its major tributary, the 600-mile-long Assiniboine River, waters the main grain-producing areas of southeastern Saskatchewan and southern Manitoba.

THE SOURIS AND NELSON RIVERS

The Souris River flows east, south and west in a 435-mile arc, through southeastern Saskatchewan, northern North Dakota and southern Manitoba, to discharge into the Assiniboine.

The Nelson River (400 miles long), which flows from the northeast of Lake Winnipeg to Port Nelson on Hudson Bay, is sometimes considered to constitute a single system with the Saskatchewan River, and the entire length of these two rivers is sometimes called the Nelson River.

The mighty Peace River rises in the Rocky Mountains of northern British Columbia and flows through Alberta for a distance of 1054 miles. In Northwestern Alberta, at the remote spot seen here, not far from the town of Peace River, the Smoky River joins the Peace. Flowing to the northeast it joins the Slave River north of Lake Athabaska. Most Canadian rivers that originate on the eastern slopes of the Rockies have their outlets either in the Arctic Ocean or Hudson Bay.

Over 500 species of wild birds have been recorded in Canada and its coastal waters. Pictured here, on their migration southward, Canadian geese take respite at the Jack Miner's Bird Sanctuary near Kingsville, Ontario.

THE CHURCHILL RIVER

North of the Nelson River, the Churchill River enters Hudson Bay at the settlement of the same name. The Churchill River pursues an irregular course of about 1000 miles through northern Saskatchewan and Manitoba, interrupted by many lakes, rapids and falls.

RIVERS OF BRITISH COLUMBIA

The most important river of British Columbia is the Fraser River (850 miles long), which drains the southern part of the province. It rises in the Rocky Mountains at Yellowhead Pass and flows northwest through the Rocky Mountains Trench for about 350 miles. North of the Cariboo Mountains it bends sharply back on itself, flowing south for about 400 miles almost to the border with Washington state. Between Lytton and Yale it runs in a deep canyon through scenery of unusual impact. Here is to be found Hell's Gate with important fish ladders. The last part of its course is a short stretch west to the Strait of Georgia, which it enters a few miles south of Vancouver.

The great Columbia River, the second largest system of North America, also rises in British Columbia. Only a part of its total course of 1200 miles is in Canada, however; this is between its source in the Rocky Mountains and northeastern Washington state.

THE MACKENZIE RIVER SYSTEM

The Mackenzie River, in the Northwest Territories, is named after Sir Alexander Mackenzie who, in 1789, explored this—one of the world's largest rivers—to its mouth. The name actually applies only to that part from Great Slave Lake to the north, but the drainage basin (about 700,000 square miles) includes a large area in the western provinces drained by such great

Lake Fortune in Quebec. This region of the province contains numerous such lakes, which were formed by glacial action during the Ice Age. The mixed-forest zone prevails here, and both conifers and broad-leaf trees are typical of the area.

Above: *Mt. Alberta in the Rocky Mountains overlooks a typical western Canadian landscape of streams and forests. In this region of vast forests, pine and fir trees, as well as other conifers, generally predominate.*

Below: *Banff National Park in western Alberta abounds in wild life. Here the buffalo, saved from extinction, may be seen grazing, and visitors can often catch sight of the Rocky Mountain goat feeding on the precipitous slopes of the mountains.*

rivers as the Peace, Athabasca and Slave. From the source of the most distant stream, the Finlay River in British Columbia, to the Arctic, the distance is 2635 miles.

The most southerly of the rivers that constitute the system is the 765-mile-long Athabasca River, which rises in the Rocky Mountains near the British Columbia-Alberta border and pursues an irregular course, mainly north and east, interrupted by many lakes and rapids, to empty into the southwest of Lake Athabasca.

Lake Athabaska empties into Great Slave Lake to the north by way of the Slave (or Great Slave) River, which has a northwesterly course of 258 miles. Near its source at Athabaska Lake it receives the waters of the Peace River, which is formed in northeast British Columbia by the confluence of the Finlay River with the 160-mile-long Parsnip River. From this confluence, the Peace River flows east and north through a rich agricultural area to its junction with the Slave River, having a total length (including the Finlay River) of 1054 miles.

THE YUKON RIVER

The Yukon River, the main river

A view of Quebec city showing the Château Frontenac, the lower town and the impressive St. Lawrence River. Quebec was one of the first permanent white settlements in the region of Canada, being founded in 1608 by the French. French culture and tradition remain paramount in both the city and the province of Quebec.

of northwestern North America, has a total length of about 2000 miles, about 714 miles of which are in Yukon Territory. The main headstreams of the Yukon River are the 330-mile-long Pelly River and the 338-mile-long Lewes River.

From the confluence of these two rivers, the Yukon River pursues a northwesterly course through Alaska to its delta on the Bering Sea. Its main tributaries in Yukon Territory are the 200-mile-long White River, which rises in Alaska; the 600-mile-long Tanana River and the 525-mile-long Porcupine River, which rise in the Yukon and flow into Alaska; and the 320-mile-long Stewart River and 100-mile-long Klondike River, both of which lie entirely within Yukon Territory.

Climate

The climate of Canada embraces extremes of highs and lows, as may be expected of a country so large and so diverse in reliefs. Climatic zones range from the temperate strip on the Pacific coast, west of the coastal mountain ranges, to the polar regions of the extreme north. The greater part of Canada, however, has long, severe winters and relatively brief summers, with moderate rainfall.

Five separate climatic zones may be distinguished. These are: the Arctic zone; the northern zone; the Prairie zone; the Cordilleran zone; and the Pacific zone.

THE ARCTIC ZONE

The Arctic climatic zone includes the greater part of Yukon and Northwest Territories and the islands of the Arctic Archipelago. Winters are long and very severe. The average annual temperature in Whitehorse, Yukon Territory, is 31.1°F. (ranging from an average January temperature of 5.2°F. to an average July temperature of 56.2°F). In Aklavik, Northwest Territories, it is as low as 15.8°F. (ranging from an average January temperature of —18.2°F. to an average July temperature of 56.4° F.). Winter temperatures below —60°F. have been recorded at both these centers. Precipitation is light, with an average of 10.67 inches annually at Whitehorse and 9.77 inches annually at Aklavik. Snow is light, but freezing temperatures persist for over 200 days in every year.

THE NORTHERN ZONE

The northern climatic zone extends roughly across northern Alberta, Saskatchewan and Manitoba, and over most of Ontario, Quebec and the Maritime Provinces, and is thus the largest climatic zone of the country. As may be expected, significant variations occur from place to place, with heavier precipitations and snowfalls to the east, lessening toward the northwest. Temperatures tend to rise toward the west and south. There is an average annual temperature of 38.9°F. at Gander, Newfoundland (ranging from an average January temperature of 18.6° F. to an average July temperature of 61.6°F.), and of 47°F. at Toronto (ranging from an average January temperature of 24.5°F. to an average July temperature of 70.8°F.). Average rainfall varies from about 39 to 53 inches annually in Newfoundland to about 14 to 44 inches in Quebec and about 24 to 38 inches in Ontario.

THE PRAIRIE ZONE

The Prairie climatic zone extends over the great grain-growing areas of Manitoba, Saskatchewan and Alberta. Temperatures are fairly uniform throughout this zone, with an average annual temperature of 36.6°F. in Winnipeg (ranging from an average January temperature of 0.6°F. to an average July temperature of 68.4°F.) and 36.8°F. in Edmonton (ranging from an average January temperature of 7.7°F. to an average July temperature of 62.9°F.). Temperatures, however, are subject to violent alterations over a short period. Rainfall is fairly low, with an annual average of 19.72 inches in Winnipeg and 17.63 inches in Edmonton. In southern Saskatchewan and southeastern Alberta, it is less than 14 inches annually.

THE CORDILLERAN ZONE

The Cordilleran climatic zone has a fairly complex nature, since climate depends more on altitude than on geographical position. In general, temperatures tend to decrease toward the east, where Fort Nelson, in British Columbia, has an annual average temperature of 30.2°F. (ranging from an average January temperature of —7.3°F. to an average July temperature of 61.7°F), while rainfall varies from 30 inches annually to less than 15 inches annually in the interior valleys.

THE PACIFIC ZONE

The Pacific climatic zone is extremely small, consisting only of British Columbia, west of the mountain chains, and the offshore islands. The climate is temperate, with Victoria, British Columbia, experiencing an average annual temperature of 50.2° F. (ranging from an average January temperature of 39.2°F. to an average July temperature of 60°F.), and the annual precipitation is the highest in Canada, with Victoria receiving an average of 26.19 inches annually and other coastal areas receiving greater amounts ranging as high as 100 inches annually on the west coast of Vancouver Island.

Flora

There are between 5000 and 6000 species and major varieties of flowering plants, ferns and fernlike plants in Canada, distributed among 148 families and about 750 genera. They grow according to their climatic and ecological preference. There are several easily recognizable floristic zones or forests, determined largely by temperatures, precipitation and length of the growing season.

In the Arctic regions, there is low or dwarf growth adapted to a short growing period and extremely low temperatures. The subarctic or Hudsonian zone extends from the southern coast of Labrador to the Mackenzie Delta, with its northern limit the tree line and its southern limit forming the northern limit of the agricultural crop zone. White and black spruce, jackpine and tamarack and other conifers are the chief trees of the forest but tend to be stunted because of bedrock and swamp. South of the subarctic zone is the mixed-forest zone, conifers along with poplar and birch.

The hardwood-forest zone to the south of the mixed zone is made up mainly of broad-leaved, deciduous trees such as maple, ash, oak, elm and yellow birch. There are many varieties of plants and the eastern part of the zone has been cleared for agriculture.

In the Carolinian zone, a small section of southern Ontario from Lake Erie north to the north shore of Lake Ontario and Lake St. Clair, the flora in some ways resembles that of the hardwood forest, but it also includes species found nowhere else in Canada such as black walnut, tulip-tree and the Kentucky coffee tree.

The prairie zone of vast grassland steppes has been developed for

An Eskimo summer campsite. The Eskimos, along with the Amerinds (a term used to cover the many North American Indian tribes), were the earliest inhabitants of this continent. It is estimated that well before 10,000 B.C. Eskimos began to migrate from eastern Asia across the Bering Strait to settle in North America.

A group of Canadian youngsters recite their lesson in a school in the north. In 1968 the population of Canada was estimated at over 20,000,000, and included people of every race from every part of the world. The largest ethnic groups in the population are those of British, French and German origin. About 7,000,000 Canadians are under 15 years of age.

agriculture and contains also some distinctive prairie wild flowers.

The mountain regions of the West have floristic zones determined chiefly by the topography of the country with varying precipitation and temperature. On the mainland of British Columbia and Vancouver Island the vegetation is almost subtropical, with plants not found in other parts of Canada. Trees in the Coast Ranges are huge—notably the Douglas fir, which can reach great heights and have diameters of up to 20 feet at the base. In the interior valleys (the Okanagan and Kamloops districts) there is sagebrush, but fruit trees also abound. Coniferous forests cover the slopes of the Selkirks, with alpine sections famous for brilliant flowers.

The southern parts of Canada have many plants common to the United States.

Fauna

The study of life of past geological periods has produced fossils indicating that, at one time animals of the type now found only in the Eastern Hemisphere were present, but today the animal life of Canada belongs distinctly to the Western Hemisphere. However, at one time there must have been land connections between the two hemispheres over which animals traveled. It is probable that the land connections were broken and reformed several times, resulting in complexities that make it difficult to chart accurately the course of evolution. The topography of the Bering Strait supports the conclusion that the land connection was in the far northwest. This would explain the similarities of fauna in the northern regions of Asia and America.

The ocean currents influenced the distribution of animal life. The cold Arctic currents chill the eastern shores while the final sweep of the Japan Current warms the west coast. The bleak Labrador shores are in almost the same latitude as southern British Columbia, but the animal life of the two regions is vastly different. Altitude has an influence too. At their peaks, the mountains present Arctic conditions, and typically northern animals reside where otherwise only southern animals might have taken shelter. There are three zones of fauna—the Arctic, the Hudsonian and the Canadian. The Arctic to the north is the home of the polar bear, caribou, musk-ox, Arctic fox, ermine, hare, lemming and ptarmigan. South of this, in the Hudsonian zone, from Alaska to the Gulf of St. Lawrence, are found the woodland caribou and distinctive species of birds. The Canadian zone contains mammals and birds recognized as distinctive to the country, such as the moose, lynx, beaver, blue jay and the Canada goose. In the temperate, more thickly settled parts of Canada, there are many varieties of water and shore birds, warblers, woodpeckers and thrushes, as well as many smaller animals such as the mink and raccoon.

Canada has eight species of frogs and six of tree frogs.

Reptiles in Canada include the lizard, snake and turtle. There are six species of small lizards, 35 varieties of snakes. There are 13 kinds of turtles, of which the marine species are the largest.

Canadian mammal fauna includes 105 genera with about 185 species. Among the mammals to be found are the antelope, badger, bat, bear, beaver, bison, caribou, chinchilla, chipmunk, cougar, coyote, deer, fox, gopher, hare, lynx, mink, mouse, muskrat, porcupine, seal, skunk, squirrel, weasel, wolf and wolverine.

Over 500 species of wild birds, representing 63 families and 18 orders, have been recorded in Canada and its coastal waters.

HUMAN GEOGRAPHY

The Primitive Population

THE POPULATION OF CANADA, BEFORE the beginning of European colonization, consisted of Amerinds (a wide term used to cover the many North American Indian tribes) and Eskimos. As far as Canada is concerned, settlement is all post-glacial. It is probable that primitive colonization of Canada by these peoples began some time before 10,000 B.C., when a land passage may have opened between the Continental and Rocky Mountain ice sheets. There is still some doubt as to whether the Canadian Indians migrated directly from Asia, as seems to be the case of the Eskimo, or came from regions in the south.

The indigenous population of Canada does not appear to have ever been very large; it is estimated that, at the time of the earliest European immigrations in the 16th century, there were about 200,000 Amerinds in Canada, out of a total North American population of around one million (excluding all areas south of Texas).

Since the Indians did not have wheat, they could not cultivate the Canadian prairies. However, the Amerinds of Canada were less dependent than those of the United States upon the buffalo. Consequently, they suffered less from the coming of the European settlers. Although there were instances of harsh treatment and minor massacres, the great extent of Canada and the relative smallness of its population meant that the Amerinds were able to avoid open conflict with the invaders of their domain, while the need of both French and British settlers for the support or at least non-opposition of the indigenous peoples during their colonial wars in the early 18th century led to a certain degree of toleration.

In 1966 there were approximately 225,000 Indians, and their number is increasing at the rate of three per cent each year.

Canada's Eskimos, who numbered 13,600 in 1961, are distributed in fairly small communities along the

The Chief of an Indian tribe in Banff, Alberta. About 225,000 Indians live in Canada at the present time, with an annual increase of over three per cent (the highest for any ethnic group). The Indian population is organized into 558 bands; which vary in size from fewer than ten members to more than 7000. The reservations and Indian settlements number about 2265, and occupy almost 6 million acres.

Arctic coastline. Hunting and fishing are their main occupations, with the musk-ox, reindeer, seal and walrus providing both the main dietary items and materials for clothing, dwellings and artifacts.

EARLY EUROPEAN SETTLEMENT

Permanent settlement of the territory that is now Canada did not take place until the early 17th century. Cartier, Roberval and Gilbert had attempted to establish settlements, but the early settlers could not withstand the severity of the winter climate. Samuel de Champlain (1567-1635) was the real founder of New France. His settlement at Quebec in 1608 was strategically located because the narrowness of the St. Lawrence River here assured control of traffic, which meant control of the fur trade. The British founded the Hudson's Bay Company in 1670 and its post at Moose Factory was the earliest European settlement in Ontario. They established settlements in Nova Scotia, New Brunswick and Prince Edward Island in the 18th century. Settlement in New France in the later 17th and the 18th centuries was hampered both by the hostility of powerful Indian tribes such as the Iroquois and by the unceasing rivalry, expressed in open warfare, between French and British forces, which did not end until 1763, when Canada was ceded to Britain. The number of French settlers who came to New France was very small compared to the numbers of English and other Europeans who came to the 13 British colonies to the south.

INCREASE IN IMMIGRATION

During and after the American War of Independence (1775-83), the number of British-born immigrants to Canadian territory increased greatly. United Empire Loyalists came from the United States in large numbers to the Maritime provinces, to the Eastern Townships of Quebec and to Upper Canada. Between 1791 and 1840 the main area of settlement in Canada was divided into two provinces: Lower Canada, in what is now Quebec province, where French colonists predominated; and Upper Canada, now Southern Ontario, where settlers of British stock were in the majority, though joined by sizable groups of the German-speaking "Pennsylvania Dutch." Toward the end of the 18th century the population of Canada was estimated at above 100,000.

At the beginning of the 19th century a period of intense immigration commenced. Immigrants from the U.S. were attracted by the fertile lands around the Lower Great Lakes. After 1820 the tide of immigration was swelled by a big influx of Brit-

POPULATION: CANADA

PROVINCES	AREA (Sq. miles)	POPULATION (1968) *
Ontario	412,582	**7,321,000**
Quebec	594,860	**5,930,000**
British Columbia	366,255	**2,010,000**
Alberta	255,285	**1,529,000**
Manitoba	251,000	**972,000**
Saskatchewan	251,700	**961,000**
Nova Scotia	21,425	**760,000**
New Brunswick	28,354	**625,000**
Newfoundland	156,185	**508,000**
Prince Edward Island	2,184	**110,000**
TERRITORIES		
Northwest Territories	1,304,903	**31,000**
Yukon Territory	207,076	**15,000**
TOTAL	**3,851,809**	**20,772,000**

*estimated

St. John's is the capital of Newfoundland. The city is situated on the east coast of the island and is the most easterly city of Canada. With its excellent sheltered harbor, the city early developed into a great fishing center; today it also engages in a variety of manufacturing and trade.

ish settlers consisting of soldiers discharged after the Napoleonic wars, agricultural workers whose livelihood had been affected by the aftermath of the industrial revolution, and Irish and Scots peasants deprived of their lands by grasping landowners and faced with famine at home.

THE LATE NINETEENTH CENTURY

By 1851 the total population of what is now Canada was about 2.5 million, almost entirely located in what are now Nova Scotia, New Brunswick, Ontario and Quebec. The tide of immigration slackened somewhat at this time, partly due to the attractions of the rapidly developing United States and the prosperity of Great Britain. But the natural growth in population was considerable, and by 1861 the total population had increased to nearly 3.25 million. It was during this period that some of the remote areas of the older colonies were opened up to settlement by the development of a railroad system. The later decades of the 19th century show a population increase of 14.2 per cent in 1861-71, 17.2 per cent in 1871-81, and 11.8 per cent in 1881-91.

A view of Fredericton, the capital of New Brunswick, on the St. John River. The site of Fredericton was first settled by Acadians in 1740, but the present city was laid out in 1785 by the United Empire Loyalists, who left the United States at the time of the American Revolution. Fredericton's main industry is lumbering and woodworking. It is also a hunting and fishing center.

The Early Twentieth Century

In 1901 the population of Canada, excluding Newfoundland, which remained an independent colony until 1949, had reached 5,371,315. The greatest increases in population since 1891 had occurred in British Columbia (an increase of 82 per cent) and in Manitoba (an increase of 67 percent). But the development of Saskatchewan and Alberta had hardly begun, while the aftermath of the gold fever of the 1890s actually saw a reduction in the population of parts of the Northwest Territories.

In the decade 1901-11, due chiefly to the western wheat boom, Canada experienced the largest increase in population ever recorded in the country, and the largest percentage increase of any country in the world at that time. The total population of 7,206,643 in 1911 was 34.2 per cent higher than that of 1901. During this decade, Manitoba's population almost doubled, while that of Saskatchewan and Alberta increased five-fold. The number of immigrants in this period totaled 1,760,000. Natural increase accounted for about another 1 million. On the other hand, the old established trend toward emigration to the United States continued, with nearly 900,000 people leaving the country, and this trend has remained a factor in the population figures up to the present day, though it has been balanced in periods of prosperity such as the 1900s and the mid-1950s and mid-1960s by considerable immigration from the United States.

Heavy immigration shortly before World War I was counteracted by war deaths, the influenza epidemic and continued emigration, all which held down the population increase to 21.9 per cent, in spite of total immigration figures of 1,612,000 for the decade 1911-21. Once again, the chief population increase occurred in the prairie provinces and in British Columbia. The Peace River country, in northern Alberta, was a new area being opened up.

BETWEEN THE WORLD WARS

Between 1921 and 1941, as immigration and the birth rate declined, the population increase slackened. There were about 1,200,000 immigrants in 1921-31, and only 150,000 in 1931-1941, mainly due to the economic depression. The total population of the country increased from 8,787,949 in 1921 to 11,506,655 in 1941, accounted for by an increase of 18.1 per cent in the period 1921-31 and 10.9 per cent in the period 1931-41.

SINCE WORLD WAR II

After World War II there was a period of considerable increase both in immigration and in the natural growth of population, resulting in a 21.8 per cent increase during the decade 1941-51 in the total population, to 14,009,429. All provinces except Saskatchewan showed an increase. The decade 1951-61, with a population increase of 30.2 per cent, showed an increase comparable to that of the early part of the century. At the 1961 census, the total population was 18,238,247. Total immigration in 1951-61 was 1,542,853, and the trend toward urbanization was stronger than ever.

Between mid-1961 and January 1965 a total of 323,664 immigrants entered the country. Immigrants from Britain and the Commonwealth countries accounted for about 40 per cent of this figure, while the largest single groups came from Britain, Italy, and the United States, in that order. Though the birth rate declined from its postwar high of 28 per thousand, it did not return in the early sixties to the low level of the depression. The total population reached 20 million during 1966.

Distribution of the Population

Some parts of Canada, particularly in the north, are virtually uninhabited. Settlement in the south is concentrated in the great trade and industrial centers around the Great Lakes and near the United States border. The highest density is found in the country's smallest province, Prince Edward Island, which has 47.9 inhabitants per square mile (1961 census).

Excluding the sparsely populated Yukon and Northwest Territories, the overall density of the Canadian population is 8.66 persons per square mile; this figure falls to a mere 5.12 persons per square mile when the northern territories are included. Apart from Prince Edward Island, mentioned above, densities are as follows: 36.1 inhabitants per square mile in Nova Scotia; 21.5 in New Brunswick; 18.1 in Ontario; 10 in Quebec; 5.3 in Alberta; 4.5 in British Columbia; 4.3 in Manitoba; 4.2 in Saskatchewan; 3.2 in Newfoundland; 0.07 in Yukon Territory; and 0.02 in Northwest Territories.

In recent years there has been a growing trend toward urban development, and in 1961 it was estimated that about 70 per cent of the population lived in cities, towns or villages of over 1000 inhabitants. In addition, some 53 per cent of the population were resident in regions classified as urban fringe areas, while the farm population amounted to only 12 per cent.

Halifax, the capital of Nova Scotia, showing the old fort (to the left) and some of the port facilities. With its natural anchorage, Halifax has served as a strategic naval base since the American War of Independence. A large shipbuilding industry is located there, and the city is also the leading commercial center of the Maritimes.

REGIONS AND CITIES

The Maritime Provinces

ALTHOUGH THE MARITIME PROVinces of the eastern seaboard—Newfoundland, Nova Scotia, New Brunswick and Prince Edward Island—are surpassed by the central provinces in size, population, industrial and commercial development, and lack the great resources of British Columbia, they may be considered along with the French-Canadian areas on the St. Lawrence River as the traditional home of early settlement, and they still maintain close ties with Europe and with New England.

NEWFOUNDLAND

The largest of the Maritime Provinces is Newfoundland, which has a total area of 156,185 square miles (43,359 square miles of which are accounted for by Newfoundland Island) and a population of 508,000 (1968 estimate). Newfoundland Island is the most easterly part of Canadian territory and is rugged and sparsely populated. Its climate is moderately severe, though not unpleasant, and its soil unsuited to intensive agriculture, though sheep are raised in some areas. The principal occupations are lumbering, which supplies the important paper and pulp industry, including the world's largest newsprint mill at Corner Brook; fishing off the famous Grand Banks and fish canning and processing; hunting, trapping and breeding fur-bearing animals; and mining, especially the important deposits of iron ore. Mainland Newfoundland known as Labrador has similar characteristics, and the main areas of settlement in both areas are along the coast. Huge iron ore deposits are situated inland, and the hydroelectric potential of the Churchill Falls, greater than that of Niagara, is only now being developed.

NEW BRUNSWICK

New Brunswick, which has an area of 28,354 square miles and a population of 625,000 (1968 estimate), is much less rugged, and about 85 per cent of the province is covered by productive forest. Rainfall is high, and heavy snow

The rugged, barren coast of Newfoundland, with its many inlets and coves, is dotted with numerous small fishing communities, such as Hibbs Cove, seen here. Since the soil of Newfoundland is unsuitable for intensive cultivation, the major occupations of the islanders are fishing, lumbering and mining.

occurs regularly during the harsh winters. As in Newfoundland, the lumbering and pulp and paper industries are of great importance, but the mining of copper and other minerals is the fastest growing of the province's industries, and the great mineral potential of northern New Brunswick had only begun to be exploited in the sixties. There is currently in progress a great program of hydroelectric power development. Agriculture—mainly the raising of cereals and fodder crops for large dairy herds—is concentrated in the central and southern regions watered by the St. John River.

NOVA SCOTIA

Nova Scotia is a peninsular province east of New Brunswick, extending into the Atlantic and dominated in its economy and culture, like Newfoundland, by the sea. It has an area of 21,425 square miles and a population of 760,000 (1968 estimate). It is heavily forested, and lumbering and fishing are the main occupations in the central and eastern areas. The mining and oil-refining industries are well developed, and there are large deposits of coal in the north, which attracted a large iron and steel industry early in the 20th century. Agriculture is predominant in the sheltered western areas, where cereals, fruits and vegetables, and feed crops for dairy herds are raised. The Annapolis Valley is famous as one of Canada's three great fruit orchard regions. The traditional industries of fishing, shipping and shipbuilding are still important.

PRINCE EDWARD ISLAND

Prince Edward Island, the smallest of the Canadian provinces, lies in the Gulf of St. Lawrence off the northern coast of New Brunswick and Nova Scotia, across Northumberland Strait. Its coastline is extremely irregular, like that of Newfoundland. It has an area of 2184 square miles and a population of 110,000 (1968 estimate). It is fairly level, and its fertile red soil and temperate climate are well suited to intensive agriculture: cereals, vegetables (notably potatoes) and fodder crops are raised, and cattle are bred for meat and dairy produce. Fishing is also of importance, with large canneries and noted oyster and lobster fisheries. Its Indian name *Abegweit* means "cradled in the waves," and there is no settlement in the island far from the sound of the sea. It ranks with Banff and Quebec City as one of Canada's three greatest summer tourist areas.

Cities of the Maritime Provinces

NEWFOUNDLAND

ST. JOHN'S *(pop. 79,884)*

St. John's, the capital of the province of Newfoundland and the educational and commercial center of the island, is situated on the Atlantic Ocean in the extreme east of Newfoundland Island. The approach to the harbor, known as The Narrows, is flanked on either side by 500-foot-high cliffs. The site was first visited in 1497 on June 24, the feast of Saint John the Baptist (hence its name), and was one of the first British settlements in Canada. It was at St. John's that Sir Humphrey Gilbert took posses-

The silhouettes of church spires at twilight dominate the skyline of Charlottetown, the capital of Prince Edward Island. Originally the French town of Port La Joie, the city was ceded to the British in 1763 and later renamed in honor of Queen Charlotte, the wife of King George. Charlottetown has been called the "Cradle of Confederation," for it was the site of the historic meeting in 1864, at which the first steps were taken toward confederation.

sion of Newfoundland in the name of Queen Elizabeth in 1583. The city developed as a fishing center, but little of its ancient character remains today, for its timber buildings were ravaged by disastrous fires in 1816, 1846 and 1892. As the nearest Canadian center to Europe, it was chosen by Marconi for his early experiments in radio communication and was the departure point for the first Atlantic crossing by airplane, made by Sir John Alcock and Sir Arthur Brown in 1919.

St. John's is the site of the provincial government of Newfoundland and of the Memorial University of Newfoundland, founded in 1924, as well as a number of other educational and cultural institutions. There are two cathedrals, Roman Catholic and Anglican, both of which are dedicated to Saint John the Baptist. The city lies on the Avalon Peninsula, to the west of its fine natural harbor in Freshwater Bay. Many transatlantic and North American sea-routes converge upon the harbor of St. John's, and there is an international airport a little to the north of the city.

The main industries of St. John's are based on the catch of the several Newfoundland fishing fleets. Shipbuilding yards and marine engineering plants supply the fishing fleets, while other manufactories produce beer, electrical goods, clothing, footwear, furniture, margarine, metalware, leather goods, soap, paint and tobacco products.

A view of the historic city of Quebec, showing the harbor, the old wall atop Cape Diamond, and, at the far left, the Plains of Abraham. Since the time of the first French settlement in 1608, Quebec has been an important trade and communication center. It is a seaport with extensive shipping facilities, grain elevators and refrigeration plants. Quebec possesses numerous buildings known for their historic and architectural interest, including Kent House (1636), the Talon Brewery (1668) and the Citadel, the summer residence of the governor-general of Canada.

CORNER BROOK (*pop. 25,185*)

Corner Brook, the second largest city of Newfoundland, is situated at the mouth of the Humber River on the west coast of Newfoundland Island and on the main railway line. It is a modern city, formed in 1956 by the amalgamation of four pulp- and paper-milling centers. Its site, in an area rich in timber, with a good harbor near the head of the Bay of Islands, has made it one of the most important centers of the paper industry. It has the largest single paper mill in the world. The mills, together with cement works, iron foundries and furniture workshops, are supplied with power from the Deer Lake hydroelectric works.

NEW BRUNSWICK

FREDERICTON (*pop. 22,440*)

Fredericton, the capital of the province of New Brunswick, is situated on both sides of the St. John River in the south center of the province. A small Acadian settlement on the site dates from 1740, and the city has been the capital of the province since just after the creation of New Brunswick in 1784. Parliament House is the seat of the provincial government, and the former Government House is now the New Brunswick headquarters of the Royal Canadian Mounted Police. Other important buildings include the 19th-century Anglican Cathedral and the University of New Brunswick, originally founded in 1785 by United Empire Loyalist immigrants from the United States. The city is a noted cultural center and possesses, in the recently established Lord Beaverbrook Gallery, one of the finest art collections in Canada. Fredericton has been designated by the Historic Sites and Monuments Boards of Canada as the "Poets' Corner of Canada," after the first important school of Canadian poets that grew up there.

Fredericton is a lumbering center, with timber mills and woodworking shops as well as factories for the manufacture of plastics, leather goods and footwear. It is an outfitting center for sportsmen wishing to hunt and fish in the Burpee Game Reserve.

MONCTON (*pop. 45,847*)

Moncton, in southeastern New Brunswick, is situated on the Petitcodiac River about 25 miles from the Bay of Fundy. It was founded by the French and still has a large French-speaking population. In 1755, when it was known as The Bend, it was captured by the British and named after the British commander—Robert Monckton.

Moncton serves as a trade center for an area noted for mink breeding, dairy farming, and the extraction of oil and natural gas. The city is a center of communications and has an international airport and large railroad workshops. Industries include textile milling, iron smelting and food processing, as well as the manufacture of biscuits, chemicals and paint, soft drinks and wooden furniture.

SAINT JOHN *(pop. 51,567)*

Saint John, the largest city of New Brunswick and a major port on the Bay of Fundy, is situated in the south of the province at the mouth of the St. John River. It was founded as a military post by the French in the 1630s, passed into British possession in 1758, and in 1783, after the Revolutionary War, was re-established as Parr Town by United Empire Loyalist settlers. It became Canada's first incorporated city in 1785, when it took its modern name, and thereafter developed as a center of shipbuilding. Much of the old, timber-built city was destroyed by fire in 1877.

Saint John is situated in pleasant surroundings, dominated by Fort Howe, on Portland Point, built by the British in 1778. Popular sightseeing spots include the Horticultural Gardens, the Lepreau Game Refuge, and the 325-foot-long gorge of the Reversing Falls Rapids, where the flow of the river is reversed at high tide.

The port, which is never icebound, can accommodate the largest vessels on the transatlantic or North American routes and has a modern dry dock that is among the largest in the world.

Saint John's industries include pulp and paper milling, textile milling, oil refining, brass founding and the refinement of other minerals, and the canning of locally caught salmon, as well as the manufacture of building materials, textiles, molasses and sugar.

NOVA SCOTIA

HALIFAX *(pop. 86,792)*

Halifax, the capital of Nova Scotia, is situated on Halifax Harbor, a natural anchorage on the southeast coast of the province. The British built a fort on the site, and the port has served as an important center of naval strategy in the American War of Independence, the Anglo-American War of 1812, and World War I and II. Over 17,500 ships sailed in convoys out of Halifax during World War II. It was the scene of disaster in 1917, when a great explosion of military stores in the harbor caused the loss of 1630 lives and damage amounting to $35 million, and again in 1945, when a lesser explosion caused $4 million worth of damage.

Halifax, like many others among the older Canadian settlements, is largely built of timber. It extends over a peninsula with an area of about 10 square miles between Halifax Harbor in the north and the bay known as North West Arm in the south. Older buildings include Saint Paul's Church (1750), the oldest Anglican foundation in Canada, the Citadel (1794-97), Government House (1800), and the Georgian Province Building (1818). The Halifax Memorial Library (1951) is a notable modern foundation. There are several institutes of higher education, notably Dalhousie University.

Halifax has been a center for the building of merchant vessels and warships since the late 18th century, and the modern harbor has large shipyards as well as docks for the largest vessels. The large outer harbor, to the south, is spanned by a mile-long steel suspension bridge with a clearance of 165 feet; it is lined with refrigeration plants and grain elevators, as is the smaller Bedford Basin to the north. The port is one of the chief outlets for Canadian exports in the winter months, when the St. Lawrence Seaway is icebound.

Halifax is the leading commercial center of the Maritimes, handling one-third of the retail trade and two-thirds of the wholesale trade for the province. The industries of Halifax include the processing and canning of local agricultural and fishing produce, sugar refining, oil refining, and the manufacture of clothing, confectionery, footwear, furniture and marine engines.

Dartmouth, on the north shore of Halifax Harbor, is joined to the city of Halifax by a mile-long suspension bridge erected over the harbor in the 1950s and by a ferry service first started in 1752.

SYDNEY *(pop. 32,767)*

Sydney, a city in northeast Nova Scotia province, is situated on Cape Breton Island, 10 miles from the open sea, about 210 miles northeast of Halifax. The harbor cuts athwart the Sydney coalfield, which extends on either side of the harbor mouth for a total distance of 32 miles. Sydney was founded by United Empire Loyalist settlers in 1783 and attracted many Scots immigrants in the early 19th century, when it was the capital of Cape Breton province. Its modern development dates from the construction of a railroad, and from the expansion of the iron, steel and coal-mining industries in the last decade of the 19th century. Sydney is an important seaport for the shipping of coal to other parts of Canada and for the export of metal products. There are extensive shipbuilding yards on Sydney Harbor, and the main anchorage is in the inlet known as South Arm.

Since 1901 Sydney has been a center of the iron and steel industries, importing metal ores from Newfoundland. The Dominion Steel and Coal Company (Dosco) normally employs between 4000 and 5000 men. Other industries include food processing and the production of bricks, chemicals and coke.

PRINCE EDWARD ISLAND

CHARLOTTETOWN *(pop. 18,427)*

Charlottetown, the capital of Prince Edward Island, is situated on a peninsula on the south-central coast, on a good harbor at the confluence of the Yorke and Hillsborough rivers. It is only a few miles from the Nova Scotia peninsula, to which it is connected by a train ferry and by steamer services. It had been a French fortified port before 1720, when a party of 300 colonists arrived and named it Port La Joie, presumably to express joy at their safe arrival. It was ceded to the British in 1763 and renamed in honor of Queen Charlotte, the wife of King George III, in 1768.

The remains of Fort Edward, dating from the 18th century, are situated in Victoria Park, overlooking the harbor and river confluence to the south; the park is also the site of Government House (1833), the residence of the lieutenant-governor of the province. In the center of Charlottetown is Queen's Square, the site of the provincial government building, a number of institutes of higher education and an experimental agricultural station. The city is the island's major port and trade center, dealing mainly in agricultural produce, principally potatoes, and has an airport. Most of the city's industries, notably meat canning, wool milling and the processing of lumbering and dairy farming products, rely on agriculture and forestry, and there are also shipbuilding yards.

Quebec Province

Quebec, in eastern Canada, is the

largest of the Canadian provinces, with an area of 594,860 square miles. Its population, estimated at 5,930,000 on July 1, 1968, is second only to that of Ontario. It is the heartland of French Canada, the French language being spoken by about 87 per cent of the population. The main region of settlement, and the economic center of the province, is the south, where the major towns are concentrated along the St. Lawrence River to the east and the Ottawa River to the west.

The north of Quebec province is occupied by a wide lowland, the Laurentian Plateau, an easterly part of the Canadian Shield region, which is extremely rich in minerals, notably iron, copper, lead, zinc and asbestos, and is well forested. The southeasterly part of the province contains the northern peaks of the Appalachian mountain system.

The lumbering and pulp and paper industries are the most important in the province. Intensive agriculture is concentrated in a large, rich, fertile area to the southeast of Montreal known as the Eastern Townships, where dairy and stock farming, the raising of feed and textile crops and cereals, and market gardening are all widely carried on and of primary importance. The province has great reserves of hydroelectric power, and its industrialization has proceeded rapidly.

The skyline of Montreal, Quebec. Montreal is the largest city in Canada, and the second largest French-speaking city in the world. The city is a commercial and financial center of Canada, produces a wide range of industrial products and is the leading port of the country. A major cultural center, Montreal has many fine museums, theaters, libraries and art galleries, notably the Montreal Museum of Fine Arts and the Château de Ramezay, built in the early 18th century.

An aerial view of the Montreal metropolitan area showing the pier called Cité du Havre, on the left, and the Île Sainte-Hélène and the Île Notre-Dame in the St. Lawrence River, the sites of the Canadian World Exhibition, Expo 67. Canada planned this immense and colorful world's fair in 1967 to celebrate the 100th anniversary of the formation of the Canadian Confederation, the birth of modern Canada.

Cities of Quebec

QUEBEC *(pop. 166,984)*

Quebec, the capital of the province of the same name, is situated on the north bank of the St. Lawrence River about 400 miles from the Gulf of St. Lawrence, at the confluence with the St. Charles River. A French settlement was established on Cape Diamond (a 300-foot bluff overlooking the St. Lawrence) in 1608, on the site of an Indian village reported by Cartier in 1535. During the 17th century, when it was the capital of the Royal Province of New France, and during the early 18th century, the city was the site of a number of conflicts between British and French forces, culminating in its capture by the British under General Wolfe in 1759. In the mid-19th century the city was for a few years the capital of Canada, and was the site of the Confederation Conference of 1864. About 90 per cent of the present population are of French extraction. The old town of Quebec still retains its 17th-century character, and it is noted for its steep, narrow streets and ancient buildings.

The older part of Quebec is the Upper Town, situated on Cape Diamond and the Plains of Abraham, overlooking the St. Lawrence. (The highest point is 333 feet above the river.) Remains of the old fortifications exist, and Battlefield Park to the southwest commemorates the battle of 1759 with a monument to General Wolfe. Among the city's historic buildings are Kent House (1636), the Talon Brewery (1668), the Hotel-Dieu du Précieux-Sang (1639), one of the oldest hospitals in North America, and the General Hospital (1692). A small area of the Upper Town is circled by walls with historic gates.

Quebec has long been a religious center and possesses many fine churches, both Roman Catholic and Protestant. The Ursuline Convent, the Quebec Seminary and the Chapel of Notre Dame des Victoires all date from the 17th century, and the Roman Catholic Basilica (founded in 1647) was extensively rebuilt in 1922 after a fire. The city is also an important cultural center, possessing several universities, notably Laval University (founded in 1852), and other institutes of higher education, together with museums, art galleries and theaters.

Quebec is an important trade and communications center, with a modern harbor capable of accommodating over 30 large ships at a time. Seven miles above the city is the great steel bridge that spans the St. Lawrence and is used by railroad and road traffic.

The industrial development of Quebec has increased considerably in recent years. The production of newsprint and other products is very extensive, and in addition there are breweries, metal refineries, tanneries, textile mills and brickworks, together with plants for food processing, tobacco processing and the production of footwear and other leather goods and fine furs.

HULL *(pop. 60,176)*

Hull, a city in southwestern Quebec province on the border with Ontario, is situated at the point where the Ottawa River is joined by the Gatineau River. Hull, on the north bank of the Ottawa River, faces the city of Ottawa on the south bank. It was founded in 1800, was completely rebuilt after a disastrous fire in 1900, and is now the judicial, social and economic center of southwestern Quebec.

Hull is one of the largest lumber and pulp and paper centers of North America and has fine-paper plants that are among the most modern in the world. There are also iron and steel works and heavy machinery plants. It is a center of the printing industry, and other manufactories include textile mills, meat canneries and plants for the production of cement, furniture, matches, mattresses and jute sacking. The population is 90 per cent French and is increasing rapidly.

MONTREAL *(pop. 2,436,817)*

Montreal, the largest Canadian city, and the second largest French-speaking city of the world, is situated on Montreal Island at the confluence of the St. Lawrence and Ottawa rivers in the south of Quebec province. The first European settlement on the site, called Place Royale, was established by Champlain at the beginning of the 17th century and was destroyed by hostile Indians. In 1642 the stockaded mission settlement of Ville Marie was established, and by 1725, when a stonebuilt defense system was constructed, it had become an important fur-trading post and a base for colonization of the province. From its earliest period, Montreal has been an important port, and its great period of expansion began in the 19th century when the population (estimated at about 2.25 million in 1964) increased from 9000 in 1800 to 328,172 in 1901.

The heart of Montreal centers on the Place d'Armes and Dominion Square, and the city spreads out around the 900-foot volcanic formation of Mount Royal, from which its modern name is taken. The city has now expanded beyond the confines of the island, and its suburbs, such as Verdun, have become cities in their own right.

Montreal is a cultural and educational center. As befits a city with the second largest French-speaking population in the world, its major educational institution, along with the English-speaking McGill University (founded in 1829), is the French Université de Montreal, which was founded in 1876 as a subsidiary of Laval University and became a separate institution in 1889. There are many other institutes of advanced education, as well as excellent museums, theaters, libraries and art galleries, notably the Montreal Museum of Fine Arts and the early-18th-century Chateau de Ramezay, originally the residence of the French governor, which houses a collection of Indian and early colonial objects. There is, also, the new Place des Arts, as well as a number of theaters and concerts halls built in connection with the development of Place Ville Marie and Expo 67.

There are many fine religious foundations, both Roman Catholic and Protestant, notably the seminary of Saint Sulpice, founded in 1710; the Grey Nunnery (1738); the church of Notre Dame de Bonsecours, founded in 1657 and, after destruction by fire in 1771, rebuilt in 1824 on the model of Notre Dame in Paris; the Protestant Christ Church Cathedral, a mid-19th-century Neo-Gothic building originally founded in 1789; the Roman Catholic Cathedral of Notre Dame (1870-94), a smaller imitation of the basilica of Saint Peter in Rome; and the Church of Saint Patrick (1841).

Montreal is a center of highway and railroads. Its international airport is a crossroads for the airlines of the world, and Montreal is, logically, headquarters for the International Civil Aviation Organization. The port of Montreal serves traffic on the St. Lawrence Seaway and from the Great Lakes, as well as from the seven seas. It is the world's foremost grain port. The modern harbor, which can serve the largest ocean-going vessels, can, with its more than 10 miles of docks, accommodate over 100 ships.

Montreal has access to three Canadian and three American television networks and is itself the main production center for the French-language broadcasting of Radio Canada's television and radio programs.

Montreal also has highly developed industries supplied with power from a number of hydroelectric stations. The city has steel mills, railroad workshops, meat packing plants, breweries, sugar refineries, tanneries, metal refineries, and paper, pulp, flour and textile mills. Other products include airplanes, cement, chemicals and pharmaceuticals, clothing, cigars and cigarettes, footwear, furniture, furs, electrical appliances, glass, heavy machinery, paint, plastics and rubber goods. Montreal is the head-office location of many international companies, and its beautiful and functional Place Ville Marie is connected with the modern Queen Elizabeth Hotel and the Canadian National railway station. Its new Place Victoria will be a vast international trade center.

SHERBROOKE *(pop. 76,284)*

Sherbrooke, a city in the south of Quebec province, in the Eastern Townships, is situated at the confluence of the St. Francis and Magog rivers, about 80 miles east of Montreal. The early settlement, known as Les Grandes Fourches, (Great Forks), a French trading post, was destroyed by Indians in 1759 and was re-established by Loyalist settlers in 1794. Sherbrooke is now a commercial and industrial center with a modern university and a number of important religious and educational foundations. It is the center of the Roman Catholic archdiocese of Sherbrooke, presided over by an archbishop. One of the oldest Anglican Churches in the Eastern Townships is St. Peter's, built in 1844. More than 80 per cent of the city's population is of French origin, but the city has long observed a custom of alternating between En-

The Parliament Buildings of Ottawa, the capital city of Canada. The city was chosen by Queen Victoria in 1858 to be the capital of Canada, and it remained the capital after the confederation in 1867. Ottawa, situated in beautiful surroundings, has many lovely parks and fine edifices, including the impressive buildings of the government.

glish-speaking and French-speaking mayors.

Sherbrooke is at the center of a railroad and highway network and is the distributive center of a region noted for forestry, stock-raising, and the mining of asbestos and copper. Its industries, which are supplied with power by a large city-owned hydroelectric plant, include lumber mills and plants for the processing of dairy products and the manufacture of stockings, gloves and other articles of clothing, footwear, furniture, mining equipment and rubber goods.

TROIS RIVIÈRES *(pop. 57,540)*

Trois Rivières, Quebec, is situated about 80 miles northeast of Montreal at the confluence of the St. Maurice River with the St. Lawrence. The city was an important fur-trading post when Champlain first established a fort there in 1634. It thereafter developed as a garrison town and a base for further colonization. Many of the city's religious and educational foundations date from the 17th century, but few old buildings survived the great fire of 1908.

The harbor of Trois Rivières is one of Canada's larger ports and is the outlet for the agricultural and mineral products of the surrounding region, notably grain and ferrous metals. The main industry of the city is its newsprint mills, which are among the most modern in the world and produce about 10 per cent of the world's requirements. In addition to timber-processing plants, there are textile mills and clothing factories, shoe factories and plants for processing dairy produce.

The Province of Ontario

The province of Ontario, in the south-central part of Canada, is the second largest of the Canadian provinces, with an area of 412,582 square miles. It has the largest population of all the provinces, estimated at 7,321,000 in July 1968, and seven of Canada's fifteen largest metropolitan areas are in Ontario. The north of the province, along the south shore of Hudson Bay and the west shore of James Bay, consists of a vast lowland area with great forests and many lakes and rivers, and of the Canadian Shield area north of the Great Lakes from the Ottawa River to the Manitoba border. The main center of settlement, agriculture and industrial development lies in the extreme south, between the Quebec border and the state of Michigan.

Lumbering is of importance throughout the northern part of the province, but the main wealth of northern Ontario is in its extensive deposits of minerals. The minerals worked include gold, silver, cobalt, copper and a large portion of the total world supply of nickel and uranium. Besides the valuable tobacco crops of southwestern Ontario, and the cherries, peaches and grapes of the Niagara Peninsula, Ontario has the largest mixed farming region in Canada. Southern Ontario is one of the most concentrated and varied industrial regions in North America, with ready access to hydroelectric and thermal power, raw materials and the richest markets of the United States and Canada.

Hamilton, Ontario, is one of Canada's leading inland ports, and is a major industrial center with over 600 plants. Several excellent educational institutions are located in Hamilton, including McMaster University, shown here.

Cities of Ontario

OTTAWA *(pop. 296,248)*

Ottawa, the capital city of Canada, is situated in the eastern part of the province, about 100 miles west of Montreal, at the confluence of the Rideau and the Ottawa rivers. The city was founded in 1826, when it was established as the northern headquarters for the construction of the Rideau Canal to Kingston on Lake Ontario. The work was supervised by Colonel By, and the city was originally called Bytown, only taking its present name in 1854. It became the capital of the United Province of Canada in 1858, and remained the capital after the creation of the Dominion of Canada in 1867. It developed as an administrative and lumbering center in the latter half of the 19th century.

On a high bluff above the river and dominating the city are the large Parliament Buildings, the center of federal government, originally built in 1859-65 and reconstructed again in the Gothic-revival style, after a fire in 1916. Among Ottawa's notable new buildings are those of Carleton University, the airport and the city hall. Besides the vast complexes of the various federal department's buildings, the city contains such a variety of institutions as the Royal Mint, the Dominion Observatory, the National Art Gallery and Ottawa University. The major churches are the Roman Catholic cathedral of St. Joseph and the basilica of Notre Dame, and the Anglican Christ Church Cathedral. The neoclassical Rideau Hall, the official residence of the governor-general, is situated in a pleasant park.

The main industries of Ottawa, paper milling, woodworking and

Queen's University, Kingston, founded in 1841. Kingston, Ontario, originally called Cataraqui, was a fortified French trading post until destroyed by the British in 1758. The site was occupied by United Empire Loyalists, who gave the settlement its present name. The city has a fine harbor on Lake Ontario, and its industries include the manufacture of aluminum, locomotives and engines, ceramics, textiles and mining equipment.

printing and publishing, are based on forestry production, and there are also iron and steel works, food processing plants, breweries and plants for the production of chemicals, clothing and watches. The factories are supplied with hydro-electric power from the large plant on the Chaudière Falls.

TORONTO *(pop. 697,422)*

Toronto, the capital of Ontario and the second largest Canadian city, is situated at the mouth of the Humber River on Lake Ontario.

In the early 18th century it was the site of a fort and trading post, and in 1793 Loyalist settlers established the village of York. The city was the capital of Upper Canada from 1796 to 1840 and again from 1849 until 1867, when it became the capital of Ontario. It was badly damaged in the Anglo-American War of 1812, when it was captured on two occasions by U.S. troops, who burned the government buildings as the English forces did in Washington, D.C.

Toronto extends for about ten miles along the foot of a bluff on the northwest shore of Lake Ontario. It is the principal partner in the federation of 13 municipalities established in 1953 under the name of Metropolitan Toronto (pop. 2,158,496). The new City Hall, begun in 1958, occupies the central position in a well-planned modern quarter, and there are many broad streets and open spaces, notably Riverdale Park, the 400-acre High Park, containing the Howard Museum, and the 350-acre Exhibition Park with a lake frontage of a mile and a half, to the west of the city. The last-named has been, since 1912, the site of the annual Canadian National Exhibition, said to be the largest annual fair in the world, which is visited by about 3 million people each year.

Toronto is a sprawling, thriving center of trade with a modern transit system including a north-south electric subway under and along its main thoroughfare, Yonge Street, and a ten-mile east-west subway. Toronto has many educational, cultural and scientific institutions, such as the University of Toronto with its many faculties and colleges and the allied Royal Ontario Museum; York University, being built as a large complex on a suburban 487-acre site, its modern hospitals including the famous Sick Children's Hospital; the Banting and Best institutes for medical research; the Pontifical Institute of Mediaeval Studies; Ryerson Institute of Technology; and the Royal Conservatory of Music, the Toronto Symphony orchestra with its subscription concerts at Massey Hall, the Royal Alexandra Theater, the Ontario College of Art and the Art Gallery of Toronto. Two of the city's most attractive buildings are adjacent to each other: Osgoode Hall, begun by John Ritchie in 1829-32 and altered and extended by Frederick Cumberland, the architect of St. James Cathedral; and the modern City Hall, designed by Finnish architect Viljo Revell, with its curving twin towers and 11-acre civic square.

The city of Winnipeg on the winding Red River is the capital of Manitoba province. The eighth largest city of Canada, it is the main commercial and distributing center for the prairie provinces, and is one of the great grain centers of the world.

Toronto has an excellent natural harbor with modern installations on Lake Ontario and is served by an airport on Toronto Island and the International Airport in the suburb of Malton. It is a railroad and highway junction and is the financial center of a large mining industry. The city's industries, which receive hydroelectric power from Niagara Falls, include food processing, meat packing, metal refining, printing and publishing, railroad workshops and shipbuilding yards, as well as the manufacture of automobiles, agricultural machinery and mining equipment.

BRANTFORD *(pop. 59,854)*

Brantford, about 60 miles southwest of Toronto, the county seat of Brant County, is situated on the Grand River in southern Ontario. It was established as an Indian settlement in the late 18th century, and was first named Brant's Ford after Joseph Brant, chief of the Mohawk Indians and leader of the Iroquois nations. European settlement began around 1805, and the city developed as an industrial center after the construction of a canal to Lake Erie in the 1840s and the coming of the railroad a little later.

Brantford has many monuments to its Indian origin, notably Her Majesty's Chapel of the Mohawks, established on the orders of King George III in 1785; the Brant Historical Society Museum, with Indian and early colonial remains; and the bronze statue of Joseph Brant in Victoria Park. It is still a center for the administration of Indian affairs. The city is an important railroad and highway junction, with an airport, in an area rich in agriculture and forest resources. It is widely known as the Telephone City, for near here, in the summer of 1874, Alexander Graham Bell invented the telephone.

Modern Brantford is one of Canada's more important industrial centers, with more than 150 manufacturing industries.

HAMILTON *(pop. 293,397)*

Hamilton, the third largest city in Ontario in population, is situated about 36 miles southwest of Toronto on the south side of Hamilton Bay at the western extremity of Lake Ontario, not far from Niagara Falls and the border of New York state. The area was first settled in 1778 and the present city was planned in 1813, the year in which it was the site of the battle of Stony Creek, which is now commemorated by a memorial park.

Hamilton has many fine buildings and open spaces, such as Dundurn Park, which contains the Wentworth Historical Society Museum in Dundurn Castle (founded in 1889), the central Gore Park and the 1800-acre Royal Botanical Gardens (laid out in 1941). There are Roman Catholic and Anglican cathedrals, and one large institution of higher education, McMaster University.

Hamilton Harbor, once called Brulington Bay, is an excellent natural anchorage about five miles long. It ranks third among Canadian ports in terms of tonnage handled. Its mouth, on Lake Ontario, is closed by Hamilton Beach, a four-mile sandbar pierced by the Burlington Canal, constructed 1823-32. The harbor can accommodate large steamers and is a center for the importation of coal and iron ore for local industry. Hamilton is a railroad junction for Canadian and American systems and possesses extensive railroad workshops.

Its position near the American border and on the main Great Lakes shipping routes has made Hamilton an important commercial center, but it is also one of Canada's main industrial centers, with more than 600 industrial plants. The iron and steel industries are the most important—over half Canada's basic steel is produced here. There are also cotton and woolen mills, automobile factories, canneries and heavy machinery plants, as well as plants for the manufacture of agricultural machinery, ceramics, chemicals, clothing, electrical appliances, felt, glass, household utensils, railway cars, rubber goods, soap, tobacco products, typewriters and wire.

KINGSTON *(pop. 54,685)*

Kingston, in southeast Ontario, is situated at the mouth of the St. Lawrence River and of the Cataraqui River in northeast Lake Ontario, about 150 miles northeast of Toronto. It was established as a French fort in the second half of the 17th century and was twice destroyed by the British, in 1689 and 1758. In 1784 a Loyalist settlement was established, and the city developed as a trading and shipbuilding center and, later, as a popular holiday resort.

Kingston was an important naval base during the War of 1812, and remains of its fortifications include Fort Henry (established in 1812 and rebuilt in 1840-46) and four Martello towers dating from 1846, one of which is now a museum. Queen's University was founded in 1841, and other institutes of higher education include the Royal Military College on Point Frederick, founded in 1876. Other notable buildings include Roman Catholic and Anglican cathedrals (built in the late 19th century), and the former Government House of Upper Canada, built in the classical style in 1841-44.

Kingston has a good natural harbor and is linked to Ottawa by the Rideau navigation canal. In the early 19th century, before the development of land communications, it was an important grain-shipping center, and it still has flourishing shipbuilding yards and marine workshops. The city's industries include lumber milling and food processing and the manufacture of aluminum (much the most important), automobile batteries, biscuits, ceramics, chemicals, leather goods, locomotives, mining machinery, textiles and artificial fibers.

LONDON *(pop. 200,455)*

London, a city on the Thames River in southern Ontario, is situated about 100 miles southwest of Toronto. The site of the city was chosen as the location of the new capital of Upper Canada in 1792 and was named after the capital of England, but the project was abandoned and

Regina, the capital of Saskatchewan, was founded in 1882 on the Canadian Pacific Railway's newly completed rail route, and a year later the city was made the capital of the Northwest Territories. It was in 1905 that Regina became the capital of the newly created province of Saskatchewan. It also serves as the western headquarters of the Royal Canadian Mounted Police.

settlement did not begin until 1826. It is the site of the University of Western Ontario, founded in 1878.

Modern London is the trade center for an important agricultural area, producing cereals, fruit and vegetables and dairy produce. It is also a communications hub served by railroad, highway and air traffic. It is a major manufacturing center with over 300 industries, including textile mills, breweries, tanneries, airplane assembly plants, iron and steel mills, metal refineries, food processing plants and printing works, as well as factories for the production of automobiles and diesel engines, biscuits, electrical goods, cardboard, cereal foods, cigars, domestic utensils, footwear and leather goods.

ST. CATHARINES *(pop. 97,101)*

St. Catharines, a city of southern Ontario about 35 miles south of Toronto, is situated on the southwest shore of Lake Ontario, a little to the northwest of Niagara Falls and the United States border. It was established as an Anglican mission settlement in 1792 and is now an important agricultural and industrial center, a popular holiday resort with mineral springs, and the site of an annual regatta and horse show.

St. Catharines is situated on the 28-mile-long Welland Ship Canal (constructed in 1932 to replace an earlier canal of 1833), which links Lake Ontario with Lake Erie to the south. It is the trade center for a rich agricultural region noted for fruit growing, and has railroad and highway communications and an airport. It is a manufacturing center with more than 100 industries, including paper, textile (silk and woolen) mills, fruit and vegetable canneries and food processing plants, automobile workshops, and factories for the production of agricultural machinery, carpets, clothing, electrical goods, metal products, marmalade and jams, fruit-juice and wine.

WINDSOR *(pop. 192,544)*

Windsor, a city of southern Ontario about 230 miles southwest of Toronto, is situated on the Detroit River on the U.S. border, opposite the city of Detroit, Michigan.

Windsor is an important port on the Great Lakes shipping routes and is the largest entry-point to Canada for visitors from the U.S., about 6 million of whom pass through the city every year. It is a junction of railroad and highway communications, with a large airport, and is linked to Detroit by the Ambassador Suspension Bridge and by road- and rail-tunnels and ferries. It is a major industrial center with more than 500 industries, the most important being the manufacture of automobiles. Other industries include steel mills, salt refineries, heavy machinery plants and food processing works, as well as plants for the manufacture of chemicals, pharmaceuticals and liquor.

The Prairie Provinces

The prairie provinces of western Canada—Manitoba, Saskatchewan, and Alberta—are the main centers of cereal production and also have important mineral and oil deposits. Agriculture is still of primary importance, but industrialization and mining here increased rapidly in recent years. The main agricultural regions lie in the lowlands of Alberta, southern Saskatchewan and southern Manitoba; the main mineral deposits are found in the Canadian Shield region of northern Saskatchewan and Manitoba, with the chief oil deposits in Alberta.

MANITOBA

Manitoba is the farthest east and the smallest of the prairie provinces, with an area of 251,000 square miles and a population estimated at 972,000 on July 1, 1968. The north of the province is rich in timber and minerals, while agriculture, notably the cultivation of wheat and fodder crops for large dairy herds, is concentrated in the prairie lands of the center and south. The main urban developments are in the south of the province, in and around metropolitan Winnipeg.

SASKATCHEWAN

Saskatchewan, the central prairie province, has an area of 251,700 square miles and a population estimated at 961,000 on July 1, 1968.

A view of Victoria, the capital of British Columbia, on Vancouver Island. Founded in 1843 by the Hudson's Bay Company, the city began as a fur-trading post named Fort Camosun, later changed to Fort Victoria. The area continues to be a busy trading center and port. The town itself was laid out in 1851-52, and its pleasant surroundings and moderate climate attract many visitors.

Its topography and climate are very similar to those of Manitoba, with extensive forests in the north and rolling prairie to the south, although minerals are more widely distributed; there are extensive oil deposits near the Alberta border. Stock raising and mixed farming are practiced in the south-central and southwest areas, but wheat is the most important single product, with 20 million acres devoted to it, making the province one of the great granaries of the world. Like Manitoba and Alberta, Saskatchewan is well supplied with hydroelectric resources from its many rivers and lakes.

ALBERTA

Alberta, the farthest west and the largest of the prairie provinces, has an area of 255,285 square miles and a population estimated at 1,529,000 on July 1, 1968. Its surface is flatter than that of its eastern neighbors, although the foothills of the Rocky Mountains system rise along its western border. The growing of grain and vegetables and stock raising are concentrated on the southern lowlands, while the well-forested northern area is rich in timber and game. Some of the most attractive scenery in Canada is found in such specially preserved areas as Banff and Jasper National Parks. Large deposits of coal, oil and natural gas have encouraged the development of heavy industry in recent years, and since the oil boom began in 1947 and oil and gas pipelines were constructed to the west coast and to eastern Canada, Alberta has rapidly become very rich.

Cities of Manitoba

WINNIPEG *(pop. 257,005)*

Winnipeg, the capital of Manitoba province and the major grain center of North America, is situated in the southeast of the province at the confluence of the Red and Assiniboine rivers, about 60 miles north of the U.S. border. A stockaded settlement established in 1738 and called Fort Rouge was re-established in the early 19th century, when it became a fur-trading center of the Hudson's Bay Company known as Fort Garry. Large-scale immigration into the area dates from the coming of the railroad in the 1880s; the population increased further from 42,340 in 1901 to 136,035 in 1911. Amost half of Manitoba's population is now concentrated in and around greater Winnipeg. A brief period of decline occurred during the post-World War I depression, when Winnipeg's importance as a trade center was lessened by the opening

Known as the "City Beautiful" and the "City of Bridges," Saskatoon, Saskatchewan, owes much of her present beauty and prosperity to the pioneers who selected her location on the South Saskatchewan River and laid out wide streets and parks in 1882. The city is an important hub of railroad, highway and air communications. It is also the distributing center for a large cattle-raising and farming region.

of the Panama Canal and the subsequent development of the port of Vancouver.

Winnipeg is noted for its cultural foundations, in particular the Manitoba Repertory Company, the Winnipeg Symphony Orchestra, the Royal Winnipeg Ballet, the Winnipeg Musical Festival and the University of Manitoba. Winnipeg is also a world center of Ukrainian culture and contains one of the highest Jewish populations per capita of any major North American city.

The situation of Winnipeg as the gateway to Western Canada has made it a major trade center, occupying a pre-eminent position in the North American grain trade. Huge stores and stockyards house the agricultural produce of the prairies, and the city is a major railroad junction, with large marshalling yards and railroad workshops. Its major industries, including meat packing, flour milling and the manufacture of agricultural equipment, are based on cultivation and these, like the plants for the production of automobiles, bricks, clothing and paper, are supplied with nearby hydroelectric power.

Edmonton on the North Saskatchewan River, the capital of the prairie province of Alberta, is the most northerly of the major cities of Canada. An important grain and agricultural center, Edmonton has also become a big oil center with the discovery and opening of oil fields in the vicinity of the city.

ST. BONIFACE *(pop. 43,214)*

St. Boniface, which is situated across the Red River from Winnipeg, has developed along similar lines to Winnipeg since its foundation in 1817. It is a major French-Canadian center, with a Roman Catholic cathedral and educational institutions. It is an important railroad junction, with stockyards even larger than those of Winnipeg. The industries of St. Boniface include meat packing, timber and flour milling, oil refining, brewing and the production of bricks, cereal foods, furniture, paint, sheet metal, tar and wire.

Cities of Saskatchewan

REGINA *(pop. 140,000)*

Regina, the capital of Saskatchewan, is situated on Wascana Creek in southern Saskatchewan, about 100 miles north of the U.S. border. It was founded in 1882 on the Canadian Pacific Railway's newly built main line and was the capital of the Northwest Territories until 1905, when the province of Saskatchewan was founded and Regina became its capital. Regina is the headquarters of the provincial legislature, which is housed in a neoclassical building overlooking an artificial lake.

Regina is the trade center and distributive point for the produce of an important agricultural area and has extensive grain storage facilities and stockyards. It is a center of railroad, highway and air communications. The city's industries include oil refining (oil being supplied by a pipeline from Alberta), meat packing, printing and publishing, and woodworking.

SASKATOON *(pop. 125,892)*

Saskatoon is situated about 150 miles northwest of Regina on the South Saskatchewan River. The city was founded in 1882-84 by settlers belonging to the Temperance Colonization Society, an anti-alcohol organization, and it developed as a center of trade and communications after the coming of the railroad in 1890.

Saskatoon is an important hub of railroad, highway and air communications and has extensive stockyards and grain-storage facilities. The city lies on both banks of the river, which is spanned by three highway and three railroad bridges. Industrial development has been rapid in recent years, and there are now more than 500 industries, notably brewing, meat packing, flour milling, iron founding and tanning, as well as the manufacture of agricultural machinery, cereal foods, chemicals, confectionery, powdered eggs and soap.

Cities of Alberta

EDMONTON *(pop. 376,925)*

Edmonton, the capital of the province of Alberta, is situated astride the North Saskatchewan River in central Alberta. The first settlement on the site was in 1819, when a fort was built to replace a post 25 miles to the south, which had fallen to Indian attacks. The population increased considerably in the 1890s, when it was reachable by railroad, and it served as a center for the 1898 gold rush to the Klondike. The city further increased in size by amalgamation with its sister city of Strathcona in 1912.

Edmonton has several impressive modern buildings and cultural foundations, including the University of Alberta. Older buildings include the McDougall Memorial Church and the Legislative Building (1912); the much restored Fort Edmonton, site of the city's foundation in 1819, is now a Mounted Police barracks.

Edmonton is the distributive center for an important grain- and stock-raising district. It is also the transportation center for the mining towns of the Yukon and Northwest Territories and a center of air, railroad and highway communications. Its modern airport is one of the largest air-freight centers in the world, and it is the southern terminus of the Alaska Highway.

In recent years, Edmonton has become a major center of oil production. Large modern refineries were connected by pipeline to Sarnia, on Lake Huron in Ontario, 1765 miles away, and to Vancouver, about 720 miles to the west. Large coal deposits are also worked in the area. Other industries include brewing, meat packing, flour milling, tanning and woolen mills, as well as the manufacture of butter and dairy products, cereal foods, chemicals, clothing, furniture, heavy machinery, paint, plastics, sheet metal and soap.

CALGARY *(pop. 330,575)*

Calgary, situated at the confluence of the Bow and Elbow rivers in southern Alberta, is just east of the foothills of the Rocky Mountains and about 138 miles north of the U.S. border. It was founded in 1875, as a Northwest Mounted Police post, and has developed as a center of agriculture and oil drilling since the early 20th century. It is a pleasant, modern city with a number of important educational and cultural foundations, and is famous for the annual Calgary Exhibition and Stampede, an evocation of the pioneering days that attracts many tourists to the city.

Calgary is the refining and distributive center for large oilfields to which it is connected by pipelines. Stock raising is also widely carried on, and there are large stockyards and meat packing plants. The city is a center of railroad, highway and air communications, and there is a military air base at Currie Field to the south.

In addition to oil refining and meat packing, Calgary's industries include flour and steel milling, iron founding, brewing, tanning and saw milling, as well as the manufacture of biscuits, cereal foods, chemicals, clothing and knitted goods, explosives, fertilizers, heavy machinery and paint.

British Columbia and the Northern Territories

BRITISH COLUMBIA

British Columbia, the westernmost province of Canada, has an area of 366,255 square miles and a population estimated at 2,010,000 in July 1968. Its potential resources are very great, both agriculturally (it possesses large regions ideally suited to the growing of cereals, fruit and vegetables and to stock raising) and industrially (it has large mineral deposits, great tracts of forest and ample hydroelectric resources). Most of the province is mountainous, lying between the Rocky Mountains on the east and the Coast Mountains on the west, but the terrain is broken by a number of sheltered, well-watered valleys. Along the coast there is heavy rainfall and the climate is temperate, particularly on Vancouver Island, which is the mildest region of Canada. There are a number of specially preserved areas among the wild and awe-inspiring mountains and valleys and giant rain forest. There are a number of islands off the west coast, the largest being Vancouver Island.

YUKON TERRITORY

Yukon Territory, to the north of British Columbia, has an area of 207,076 square miles and a population estimated at only 15,000 in July 1968. Its Arctic climate severely limits agriculture, but there are mineral deposits—notably of gold, silver, coal and lead—and the area has abundant game and fish. Most of the territory consists of high plateau broken by mountain peaks, with the Rocky Mountains system rising to the south and east.

NORTHWEST TERRITORIES

The Northwest Territories, which extend from latitude 60°N. to the north pole, including the islands of the Arctic archipelagic region, form the largest single region of Canada, with an area of 1,304,903 square miles. The population was estimated at only about 31,000 in 1968, of which around 60 per cent were Eskimos or Indians. The eastern and central mainland has many large lakes, and the Rocky Mountains system rises toward the west. Much of the land is unproductive, especially the plains known as the Barren Grounds to the south, but in the west there are rich deposits of oil and pitchblende, and there is gold at Yellowknife on Great Slave Lake. Fur-trapping is important, though game is strictly preserved over much of the territory. The climate is generally severe, with very heavy snowfalls in the north and west.

Cities of British Columbia

VICTORIA *(pop. 57,453)*

Victoria, the capital of the province of British Columbia, is situated on the Strait of Juan de Fuca in the southeast of Vancouver Island, about 55 miles southwest of Vancouver city. It was founded as a Hudson's Bay Company trading post in 1843 and was known first as Fort Camosun and later as Fort Victoria. It developed as a trading center and a base for gold prospectors, but its importance declined with the growth of Vancouver. Its pleasant scenery and moderate climate attract many tourists.

Victoria has an excellent natural harbor, comprising an outer anchorage for large vessels and an inner anchorage for smaller craft and for the large fishing fleet. Esquimault harbor, to the west, is the Pacific headquarters of the Royal Canadian Navy, and there are extensive military and civil dockyards. The main exports of the port are cement, fruit, fish and timber products. Victoria is connected to the mainland by car and train ferries and by air services from the air field at Patricia Bay.

The main industries of Victoria—fish canning, paper and saw milling, dairy processing and mining-machinery plants—are dependent upon local produce, and there are also large grain elevators and refrigeration facilities.

VANCOUVER *(pop. 410,375)*

Vancouver, in the southwest of British Columbia, is situated on the Strait of Georgia opposite Vancouver Island, a short distance from the border of Washington. Since 1931 it has been the third largest city in Canada. It was founded in 1875, when it was called Granville, and was renamed when reached by railroad in 1886. Its early development was as a center of fur trapping, gold prospecting and saw milling, but it rapidly increased in importance as a port after the opening of the Panama Canal in 1915, the population increasing from 13,709 in 1891 to 163,220 in 1921 and to 246,593 in 1931. The population of the greater Vancouver region will probably reach one million over the next few years.

A large part of Vancouver was destroyed by fire in 1886. It is now a well-planned modern city, with many important religious, cultural and educational foundations, notably the University of British Columbia, housed in a modern complex in the western suburb of Point Grey. Its spectacular setting amid sea inlets and mountains, its moderate climate and excellent bathing and winter-sports facilities attract many tourists.

Vancouver is Canada's second most important port and is served by many international lines. The excellent natural anchorage on the south of Burrard Inlet is accessible throughout the year and has modern dock installations and extensive grain and refrigeration storage facilities. The main exports are grain, fish, and mining and forestry products. The city is an important railroad terminus and is served by an international airport on Sea Island to the west. Burrard Inlet is spanned by Second Narrows Bridge and Lions Gate Bridge, and there are ferry services to the suburb of North Vancouver.

The main importance of Vancouver is as a center of commerce, and the major industries include fish canning and timber processing. There are modern steel mills and shipbuilding yards, as well as furniture factories. The Trans-Mountain Pipeline, completed in 1953, connects it with Edmonton and brings oil from Alberta to the Pacific Coast.

Settlements of the Northern Territories

The sparsely populated northern territories have no large cities or towns.

The largest settlement is Whitehorse (pop. 5031), in Yukon Territory. Situated at the head of navigation on the upper Yukon River, it was an important center of the oil industry during World War II and is still an important center for communication with the mining communities of the north. It is connected by railroad to Skagway, Alaska, 90 miles to the south, and by the Alaska Highway to Edmonton. There is a civil and military airport and an important meteorological station.

Other centers in the northern territories include, in the Yukon Territory: Dawson (pop. 881) and Watson Lake (pop. 500); and in Northwest Territory: Yellowknife

The boating area of Vancouver. Mountains, forest and sea provide a magnificent natural setting for Vancouver, British Columbia. Founded in 1875, Vancouver developed rapidly, benefited by a superb harbor and an abundance of natural resources. Today it is the major economic center and port on the Pacific Coast of Canada, and the third largest city in the country. The city's spectacular setting and moderate climate provide a wide range of recreational opportunities.

(pop. 3245), Inuvik-Aklavik (pop. 2119) and Fort Smith (pop. 1681).

ECONOMIC GEOGRAPHY

IN THE PRESENT CENTURY, ESPECIALLY since World War II, the economic expansion of Canada has been striking. The country is one of the world's largest exporters of wheat, and also occupies a leading world position with regard to minerals and metal products, particularly nickel and aluminum, and forestry products (it produces almost half the world's newsprint). The development of industry has been rapid, and industrial production has now replaced agriculture as the basis of the national economy.

General Situation

There have, however, been three major obstacles to economic development. The vastness of the country long imposed severe communications problems. These were met in the first place by the creation of great railroad systems and highway networks; and, more recently, by the development of air transport.

The harshness of the climate over a large part of the territory limited the amount of land available for agriculture to less than 10 per cent of the total land area. This problem has, however, been offset by the intense cultivation of suitable areas and by increasing mechanization.

The relatively small population has limited the amount of labor available. This problem has been approached by the continued encouragement of immigration and by the use of automated industrial processes.

On the other hand, the economic expansion of Canada has been aided both by the country's great natural resources and by overseas investments, notably from Britain and, to a greater extent in the last few decades, from the United States. Canada has great reserves of hydroelectric power, vast areas of commercial forest, rich mineral deposits and wide prairie lands ideally suited to grain cultivation; and both agriculture and industry are now capable of producing large surpluses for sale abroad.

Agriculture

Although agricultural production has now been surpassed by indus-

Above: *A view of an apple orchard in the fertile South Thompson Valley near Kamloops, British Columbia. Apples are the most important fruit crop of Canada. The nation as a whole produces more than 20 million bushels, with more than 5 million bushels coming from this Pacific Coast province.*

Below: *A herd of cattle in the Great Sand Hills region of Saskatchewan. Beef cattle production has grown significantly in Canada since World War II, with the number of cattle increasing from 8,400,000 head in 1951 to 12,817,000 in 1964. The wide open spaces and abundance of feed grains make the prairie provinces the center of the beef raising industry.*

trial production as the most important single factor in Canada's economy, it still occupies an important position. In 1964 it employed around 624,000 workers, or almost 10 per cent of the total labor force. Wheat is still one of the most valuable of Canada's exports, while other important sectors of agriculture include the raising of other grain and field crops, dairy and stock farming, mixed farming—including the cultivation of fruit and vegetables and such specialized crops as sugar beet and tobacco—poultry farming and the raising or trapping of fur-bearing animals. The production of eggs and cheese is one of the largest in the world. Over a million head of beef cattle are slaughtered annually.

OCCUPIED FARMLAND

In 1961 it was estimated that occupied farmland in Canada amounted to about 173 million acres, or about 7 per cent of the country's total area. The total number of farms was 481,000, but just under one-third of these holdings were extremely small and played no significant part in total production. In recent years a trend toward larger farms and the amalgamation of smaller units has developed.

WHEAT

The cultivation of grain crops centers on Manitoba, Saskatchewan and Alberta, where about 80,400,000 acres of land, nearly one-half of the country's total agricultural land, are under cultivation. The main crop is wheat, of which Canada is one of the world's leading producers. In 1964 the total area taken up by wheat cultivation was 29,685,000 acres; of this area more than half was in Saskatchewan. The total wheat yield in 1964-65 was 16,341,000 tons.

Above: *A tobacco farm in Ontario. The main areas for the growing of tobacco are Ontario and Quebec. In this region agriculture is diversified and many different types of crops are raised.*

Center: *Digging potatoes on Prince Edward Island. In the Atlantic provinces the agricultural land areas are relatively small. It is crops like cabbage, potatoes and other root crops that are generally cultivated.*

Below: *A poultry farm in Nova Scotia. Between 1951 and 1961 the output in Canada of fowl and chicken meat almost doubled, and egg production rose by almost 50 percent. Poultry raising is centered near the major cities, and in New Brunswick and Nova Scotia.*

SECONDARY GRAIN CROPS

Secondary grain crops are also concentrated in the prairie provinces and, to a lesser extent, in Ontario and Quebec. Production in 1964-65 amounted to 5,508,000 tons of oats, 3,632,000 tons of barley, 326,000 tons of rye, over 1,300,000 tons of mixed grains, and 1,345,000 tons of corn.

OILSEEDS AND ROOT CROPS

A rapidly expanding sector of agriculture in Canada is the cultivation of oilseeds. Rapeseed is grown in the north of the prairie provinces, while flaxseed, and to a lesser extend mustard seed and sunflower seed, are raised in the south. Canada is now the world's leading exporter of rapeseed.

Production in 1964 amounted to 18,855,000 bushels of flaxseed, 11,068,000 bushels of rapeseed, 39,750,000 pounds of sunflower seed, and 47,750,000 pounds of mustard seed.

The two major field root crops are potatoes (280,700 acres under cultivation in 1964) and sugar beet (101,312 acres under cultivation in 1964). Quebec, New Brunswick and Ontario are the major potato-producing areas, and total national production in 1964-65 amounted to 2,122,000 tons. Sugar beet is mainly grown in Ontario and Quebec; national production in 1964-65 amounted to 1,168,000 tons. In 1964 the area devoted to other root crops was 26,100 acres, yielding 294,000 tons of produce.

OTHER CROPS

Other important crops include soybeans, pulses, tame hay and tobacco. Soybeans are grown mainly in Ontario and had a total acreage of 231,000 acres in 1964 and a total production of 6,976,000 bushels. Peas and beans are widely grown in Quebec, Ontario and Manitoba: in 1964 total acreage amounted to 76,000 acres of beans and 70,500 acres of peas. Production in 1963 amounted to 1,456,000 bushels of beans and 1,064,000 bushels of peas.

The acreage devoted to tame hay in 1964 was 12,507,000 acres, mainly in Quebec, Ontario and the prairie provinces, and production amounted to 21,365,000 tons. The main areas for the cultivation of tobacco are Ontario and Quebec; there are recently established plantations in New Brunswick, Nova Scotia and Prince Edward Island. The total area under tobacco in 1963 was 113,893 acres; these gave a yield of 201,144,000 pounds in the same year.

FRUIT AND VEGETABLES

The production of fruit and vegetables is of increasing importance to the Canadian economy, and the processing and canning industries have developed rapidly over the last few years. Ontario and British Columbia are by far the largest fruit-producing areas, and extensive orchards are also found in the Atlantic provinces and in Quebec. The total cash value of the Canadian fruit crop in 1963 was estimated at $67,276,000. Most fruit is grown for home consumption, but considerable quantities of apples and blueberries are exported.

Apples are the most important fruit crop. There are large orchards in Nova Scotia and New Brunswick, as well as in southern Ontario, Quebec and central British Columbia. In 1964 an estimated 20,286,000 bushels of apples were harvested. Dessert grapes and grapes for the making of wine and soft drinks are grown chiefly in south-central British Columbia and in the Niagara district of Ontario. Other notable fruit crops include apricots, cherries, loganberries, peaches, pears, plums, raspberries and strawberries.

In 1964 about 244,000 acres were devoted to the raising of vegetables, and in 1963 the total cash value of the vegetable crop amounted to $64 million. Pulses have already been dealt with, and other crops of importance to the canning industry include tomatoes and corn. The production of vegetables is mainly carried on in fairly small market gardens near the larger towns.

STOCK RAISING

The raising of stock for meat and dairy produce, and poultry farming —which is largely acccomplished on extensive mixed farms or on the large ranches of Saskatchewan and Alberta—form a significant part of agricultural production, on which increasing economic emphasis is being placed in the prairie provinces. The raising of hogs is widespread in Quebec and Ontario. Although the demands of the home market are high, large quantities of meat and dairy produce are exported, mainly to the U.S.

In 1963 the number of head of livestock in Canada was estimated at 2,915,000 head of milk cows; 9,391,000 head of other cattle; 5,210,000 head of hogs; 1,340,000 head of sheep; 448,000 horses; and 73,788,000 head of poultry. In general, recent years have shown a gradual decline in sheep farming (which is mainly concentrated in Alberta and Ontario); and, too, the number of milk cows has also declined. However, the value of dairy produce has increased, due to the adoption of modern methods of breeding and processing.

In 1963, meat production figures included 1,408,784,000 pounds of beef; 978,252,000 pounds of pork; 127,901,000 pounds of veal; 31,209,000 pounds of mutton and lamb; 92,263,000 pounds of canned meats; and 98,500 pounds of offal.

Ontario and Quebec are the main centers of dairy farming. Production in 1964 included 18,490,639,000 pounds of milk.

POULTRY PRODUCTION FIGURES

Poultry farming, like dairy farming, shows a decline in the number of head of stock but a rise in production—the latter due to the introduction of modern methods of production and distribution. Large poultry farms are established near most of the major population centers, especially in Ontario (where turkey-breeding is of great importance), and in New Brunswick and Nova Scotia. In 1964 Canadian poultry farms—excluding Newfoundland, where poultry raising is of little importance—produced 437,906,000 dozen eggs, 483,349,000 pounds of fowl and chicken meat, 162,448,000 pounds of turkey meat, 4,922,000 pounds of duck meat, and 3,020,000 pounds of goose meat. Exports in

Harvesting wheat on a farm in the vast, flat prairie land of Canada. The prairie provinces of Manitoba, Saskatchewan and Alberta constitute the "breadbasket" of the country, where 80,400,000 acres, almost half of Canada's total agricultural land, are under cultivation. The rich soil and high degree of mechanization produce an enormous outflow of grains and oilseeds. As a result, Canada is one of the world's leading exporters of agricultural commodities.

1964 included 2,374,000 dozen eggs and 680,000 pounds of poultry meat.

FURS

Fur farming has developed considerably in recent years, with mink and chinchilla breeding occupying a predominant position. Trapping is also of considerable importance, particularly in the northern territories, but the value of ranch-raised pelts now considerably exceeds that of wild products. The total value of ranch-raised furs in 1963-64 was $22,179,953, of which mink accounted for around 98 per cent. Pelts of ranch-raised animals included 1,390,139 mink pelts; 12,308 chinchilla pelts; 3411 nutria pelts; and 837 fox pelts. The value of wild pelts in the same period amounted to $13,079,473, the most important animals trapped, in order of value, being beaver, mink, muskrat, lynx, white fox, marten, squirrel, ermine, other fox, rabbit and raccoon.

Forestry

Canada's extensive forest areas are one of the country's greatest sources of wealth, and their products account for around one-third of all Canadian exports. The total forested area is about 1,714,000 square miles —nearly half of the country's total area—of which about 1 million square miles consists of forest producing timber of commercial value.

The ownership of more than 80 per cent of the productive forests is divided among the provincial governments. Advice on the administration and conservation of the forests is provided by the federal department of forestry, established in 1960, whose powers were reinforced by the Agricultural Rehabilitation and Development Act of 1961, the enforcement of which became the department's responsibility in 1964.

The most important commercial forests in Canada consist of softwoods, which occupy an area of about 345,299,000 acres. The principal softwoods are balsam, cedar, Douglas fir, hemlock, maple, pine, poplar, spruce and yellow birch, which supply the bulk of Canada's lumber production. Balsam, fir, hemlock, jack pine, poplar and spruce are also widely used in the manufacture of pulp and paper. Hardwoods, such as birch, box, elm, maple and oak, are less widely distributed, occupying a total area of around 73,511,000 acres, mainly in southern regions. A further 114,384,000 acres are classified as mixed forest.

The province of British Columbia is the major lumber-producing area, accounting for about 68 per cent of the country's total production in 1962, followed by Quebec, 13.2 per cent; Ontario, 7.4 per cent; the Maritime Provinces, 6.4 per cent; and the Yukon, Northwest Territories and the prairie provinces, 5 per cent.

The major sawmills are located in western British Columbia, while Quebec and Ontario lead in the production of paper and allied products. Logging and the production of pulpwood are important throughout the country. The bulk of timber production in Prince Edward Island is for fuel.

In 1962 the total output of the logging industry was 3,431,802,000 cubic feet of timber, and the lumber industry produced around 9,277,244,000 feet of lumber in 1963. Of the greatest importance is the pulp and paper industry: Canada is the second largest producer and exporter of wood pulp in the world (about 74 per cent of the total output being processed within the country) and supplies about half of the world's newsprint. In 1962 newsprint production amounted to 6,648,170 tons, accounting for about 75 per cent of all manufactured paper products and 93 per cent of all such products exported.

A tug hauls booms of logs on the Gatineau River in Quebec. Canada is the second largest producer and exporter of woodpulp in the world, and supplies about half of all the world's newsprint. (*photo:* Malak)

Fishing

The total production of Canada's rich fresh-water and sea fisheries has increased considerably in recent years, especially since the entry of Newfoundland into the confederation. Canada is now one of the dozen or so countries in the world with a total catch exceeding 1 million tons annually and ranks with Japan and Norway as the leading country for fish exports. The industry is estimated to employ 60,000 sea fishermen, 20,000 lake fishermen, and 15,000 workers in processing plants.

The most important fisheries are those of the Atlantic coast, which produce about 60 per cent of the total value of the salt-water catch. The most important fish produced by these fisheries are cod, lobster, haddock, herrings and sardines. Of a catch valued at $76,608,000 in 1963, the value of the cod catch was $20,998,000, the lobster catch, $21,281,000, the haddock catch, $4,916,000, and the herring and sardine catch, $3,086,000. Other important fish were halibut, mackerel, redfish, salmon, swordfish, flounder, hake and pollock. There are large processing plants in the main coastal centers.

The fisheries of British Columbia, on the Pacific coast, produce about one-third of the total value of the salt-water catch. Salmon herring and halibut are the most important fish: of a catch valued at $40,466,000 in 1963, the value of the salmon catch was $22,790,000, the halibut catch, $8,249,000, and the herring catch, $6,477,000. Other important fish were tuna and shellfish, including clams, crabs, oysters and shrimps. There are large salmon and tuna canneries, as well as plants for the production of fishmeal and other products.

The main inland fisheries are situated on the Great Lakes, the lakes of Manitoba, and Great Slave Lake in the south of Northwest Territories. In 1963 the total value of the fresh-water catch was $13,302,000 the most important catches being those of whitefish and of yellow pickerel.

A view of the industrial area of Winnipeg, Manitoba, showing the big slaughterhouses and meat-packing plants. Canadian manufacturing, particularly those industries connected with the processing of agricultural and forestry products, has grown very rapidly since the beginning of World War II. In 1939 the value of factory shipments was only $3,474,784,000; by 1964 it had increased to over $31,000,000,000.

Natural Resources

Canada possesses rich mineral resources, and the development of the mining industry has been rapid, especially since World War II. The total value of the Canadian mining industry's output was $3,397,000,000 in 1964. In that year the leading products, in order of importance, were: crude petroleum, iron ore, nickel, copper, zinc, natural gas and asbestos. The major mineral-producing provinces were Ontario, accounting for 26.8 per cent of the total value of output, Alberta, 22 per cent, Quebec, 19.8 per cent, Saskatchewan, 8.2 per cent, British Columbia, 7.9 per cent, and Newfoundland, 5.6 per cent.

METALLIC MINERALS

In 1964 the most important metallic mineral produced was iron ore, with important mines in Ontario, Quebec and Labrador. Total production of iron in 1964 amounted to about 38,664,500 tons, valued at $402,892,490. Second was nickel, of which Canada is now the world's leading producer: 232,875 short tons valued at $381,996,719 were produced, notably from mines in Ontario and Manitoba. Third place was occupied by copper, mainly mined in Ontario and British Columbia, with a total production of 494,017 tons, valued at $328,233,604.

Zinc, found mainly in Quebec and New Brunswick, occupied fourth place, with a production of 682,000 tons, valued at $193,285,404. Next was gold, found mainly in Manitoba and British Columbia, with a total production of 3,810,738 ounces, valued at $143,855,362. Sixth place was occupied by uranium, dug mainly in Ontario and Saskatchewan, with a total production of 13,828,369 pounds, valued at $85,418,271.

Other important metallic minerals (together with production and value figures for 1964) are: lead (200,000 tons, valued at $53,863,546), silver (31,111,943 ounces, valued at $43,556,719), platinum (374,988 ounces, valued at $25,196,159), cadmium (2,800,761 pounds, valued at $8,950,213), cobalt (3,196,322 pounds, valued at $6,484,255), magnesium (18,041,900 pounds, valued at $5,592,989), columbium (2,250,000 pounds valued at $2,305,000), and selenium (448,750 pounds, valued at $2,213,182).

NON-METALLIC MINERALS

The most important non-metallic mineral produced in 1964 was asbestos, totaling 1,377,079 tons, valued at $148,370,312; about 80 per cent of this amount was produced in Quebec. Second was potash (mainly produced in Saskatchewan), with a total production of 862,440 tons, valued at $30,660,000.

An open cut cuprite mine at Mudochville on the Gaspé Peninsula, Quebec. Canada possesses varied and abundant mineral resources, and in 1964 the value of the mining industry's output was more than $3 billion. The leading products were crude petroleum, iron ore, nickel, copper, zinc, natural gas and asbestos.

Third place was occupied by salt, with a total production of 3,892,636 tons, valued at $23,075,518. In fourth place was titanium dioxide and allied substances, whose total production was valued at $20,981,935.

Other important non-metallic minerals (together with production and value figures for 1964) are: sulphur (1,611,181 tons of elemental sulphur and 434,776 tons of sulphur in smelter gas, valued at $15,409,943 and $4,493,182 respectively), gypsum (6,373,765 tons, valued at $12,397,828), peat moss (245,117 tons, valued at $7,177,608), sodium sulphate (330,178 tons, valued at $5,328,220), quartz (2,130,837 tons, valued at $4,602,864), and nepheline syenite (292,042 tons, valued at $3,397,106).

PETROLEUM

The most important fuel deposits in Canada are those of crude petroleum, which is found mainly in Alberta, Saskatchewan and British Columbia. The major refining center is at Sarnia, Ontario, which is joined by pipelines to the Edmonton oilfields and to Superior, in Wisconsin. This pipeline is the longest in the world, having a total length of 1793 miles. In all, there are around 11,000 miles of oil pipeline, together with about 40,000 miles of natural gas pipeline.

In 1964 Canadian oilfields produced 274,250,125 barrels of crude petroleum, with a total value of $674,478,151. This represented an increase of over 6 per cent of the 1963 figure, but there are still immense reserves; the oilfields around Edmonton are among the richest in the world. About one-third of the total production of crude petroleum and natural gas (of which 1,363,814,214,000 cubic feet was produced in 1964) is exported to the U.S. The total value of natural gas production in 1964 was $183,505,880, and natural gas by-products were valued at a further $75,096,676.

COAL

Canada is not a large producer of coal, and much coal is imported from the United States. The main coal deposits are not yet fully exploited, since they are situated in the mountain foothills of the west, in the north of the prairie provinces, and in Cape Breton Island, northern New Brunswick, and Nova Scotia—in other words, away from the main industrial areas. Nevertheless, total coal production in 1964—11,072,776 tons, valued at over $72,109,300—represented an increase of 5 per cent over that of 1963.

HYDROELECTRIC POWER

The relative paucity of coal supplies in Canada is offset by the richness of the country's hydroelectric reserves. The great quantity of electricity that can be produced at low cost has expedited industrial development and has made possible the electrification of many scattered rural communities. Many plants have been established in recent years under the supervision of the Central Electric Station, and an agreement made with the United States government in 1961 and ratified in 1964 provides for the joint development of the hydroelectric resources of the Columbia River basin over a period of 60 years.

In January 1965 the installed generating capacity, both hydroelectric and thermal, totaled 27,099,000 kw., of which 20,331,000 kw. were installed in hydroelectric plants. About 75 per cent of the total hydroelectric capacity is installed in the St. Lawrence River-Great Lakes region, where industrial needs are greatest; British Columbia also has large installations, notably on the Fraser and Columbia rivers. Of all the Canadian provinces, only Prince Edward Island has no hydroelectric installation.

Industry

Canadian industry, particularly those industries relying on the processing of agricultural and forestry products, has developed very rapidly since World War II. In spite of a lack of coal resources and, more important, of manpower, the introduction of modern methods and automated processes and the ample supply of electrical power enabled industrial production to reach a record figure in 1964, when the total selling value of all factory shipments was estimated at about $31,171,694,000 compared with approximately $2,820,811,000 in 1917, $3,474,784,000 in 1939, $12,479,593,000 in 1949, and $22,830,836,000 in 1959.

LABOR AND PRODUCTION

In 1962 Canadian manufacturing industries employed 1,391,426 workers (the 1964 estimate was 1,499,000). The major industrial province was Ontario, which accounted for about half of total production. Quebec came next, with 29.7 per cent of the total production, followed by British Columbia with 8.2 per cent and Alberta with around 4 per cent. In order of industrial importance, the remaining provinces were Manitoba, Nova Scotia, New Brunswick, Saskatchewan, Newfoundland and Prince Edward Island, with the northern territories playing only a very small part in total production.

In order of selling value of factory shipments, the leading industries in 1962, together with the number of employees, was as follows: food and beverage industries (210,156 employees, and a total selling value of factory shipments amounting to $5,375,339,000), primary metal industries (91,923 employees; $2,969,096,000), transportation equipment industries (104,850 employees; $2,343,690,000), paper and allied industries (100,710 employees; $2,333,578,000), metal-making industries, excluding machinery and transport equipment industries (109,472 employees; $1,722,554,000), chemical industries (63,905 employees; $1,543,593,000), electrical industries (96,595 employees; $1,389,382,000), coal and petroleum products industries (16,277 employees; $1,294,070,000), wood-working industries (83,468 employees; $1,154,377,000), and textile industries (67,810 employees; $982,129,000).

A fully automated pipeline terminal at Edmonton, Alberta, which can move to distant markets butane, propane and other liquefied petroleum gases. Canada has around 11,000 miles of oil pipeline and about 40,000 miles of natural gas pipeline. Around one-third of the total production of crude petroleum and natural gas is exported to the United States.

Above: *Because of its vast distances, Canada has concentrated on developing efficient transportation networks. The railroad system operates on 58,511 miles of track, and motor transport can use almost 500,000 miles of highway. Shown here is a completed section of the Toronto By-Pass, the first 12 lane highway in Canada.*

Below: *Toronto's busy International Airport is symbolic of the importance of air transportation to Canada, with its great distances and rugged northern terrain. Toronto's new airport, capable of handling the largest jets, was officially opened in 1964. The modern terminal, shown here, is efficient and unique. The center building is a seven-story parking garage which can accommodate 2400 cars, while the circular structure does away with the long passages generally found in most air terminals.*

Trade

Canada's exports and imports reached an all-time high in 1966 when the total value of foreign trade was $18,579,400,000 an increase of 37 per cent over 1963 and a figure which placed Canada sixth among the trading nations of the world. In 1966 exports totaled $9,501,760,000 in value, while imports were valued at $9,077,640,000 Canada achieved a favorable balance of trade in 1961 for the first time in ten years and maintained this position in the early sixties.

In 1964 Canada's principal exports, in order of value, were: wheat ($1,023,112,000), newsprint ($834,646,000), wood pulp ($460,854,0.00), lumber ($449,732,000), iron ore and concentrates ($356,007,000), aluminum and alloys ($317,937,000), petroleum and products ($262,023,000), aircraft and parts ($248,785,000), nickel and alloys ($197,145,000), and copper and alloys ($190,363,000).

The principal countries to which exports were shipped were, in order of value, the United States (which received about 53 per cent of all exports), Britain (which received about 15 per cent), Japan, the U.S.S.R., the Federal Republic of Germany, Australia, the Chinese People's Republic, the Netherlands, Belgium and Luxembourg, France, South Africa, Norway, Mexico, Venezuela, India, Poland, Italy, Cuba, Czechoslovakia and New Zealand.

Canada's principal imports in 1964, in order of value, were non-agricultural machinery and parts ($874,125,000), automobile parts, excluding engines ($555,456,000), electrical equipment ($335,229,000), petroleum ($320,637,000), tractors and parts ($220,342,000), engines, other than aircraft ($193,014,000), automobiles and trucks ($163,776,000), aircraft and parts ($154,648,000), and agricultural machinery, other than tractors, ($152,290,000).

CHIEF COUNTRIES OF ORIGIN

The principal countries from which goods were imported were, in order of value, the United States (which sent about 69 per cent of all imports), Britain (which sent about 8 per cent), Venezuela, Japan, the Federal Republic of Germany, France, Italy, Australia, Belgium and Luxembourg, Jamaica, the Netherlands, Brazil, Sweden, Switzerland,

India, Guyana (British Guiana), the Netherlands Antilles, Malaysia, Iran and South Africa.

Communications

Because of its great size, Canada depends heavily upon efficient transportation systems. Road development has been tremendous in this century. In late 1962 Canada had 478,362 miles of highway, 291,300 miles being of surfaced road, 145,800 miles of improved road, and the remainder of earth road.

Most highways are maintained by the provincial authorities, although the federal government contributed $145,286,574 of the total $777,432,336 spent on highway maintenance and construction in 1961-62.

In 1963 Canada was estimated to possess one motor vehicle for every 3.1 inhabitants, compared to a figure of one for every 2.3 persons in the U.S. Registered motor vehicles included 4,788,896 automobiles, 1,225,981 trucks and buses, and 37,186 motorcycles, out of a total of 6,074,655 registered vehicles.

In January 1964 Canada had a total railroad mileage of 58,511 miles, of which 43,623 miles were primary maintrack and 14,888 miles secondary maintrack, sidings or railroad yards. The operation of about 80 per cent of this track was accounted for by the federally owned Canadian National Railway System (22,937 miles of primary maintrack) or the joint stock corporation known as the Canadian Pacific Railway Company (16,278 miles of primary maintrack).

Railroads have been of the utmost importance to the commercial and social life of Canada, and development continues: a 430-mile line opening up the Northwest Territories was constructed between Peace River, Alberta, and Pine Point on Great Slave Lake in 1961-64. Modern automatic freight-sorting yards are being installed across Canada by both major railroads.

In 1963 Canadian railroads carried 20,600,000 passengers (19,500,000 accounted for by the two major companies). Freight was carried for a total of 75,796,000,000 ton-miles (65,864,000,000 by the two major companies).

Water transport is of great importance. There are excellent ports on the Pacific, Atlantic and Arctic coasts, and on the 2687-mile-long St Lawrence Seaway. In 1963, the coastal traffic amounted to 46,119,756 tons of cargo, about 90 per cent of which was carried in Canadian-registered vessels. About 20 major ports handle about 150 million tons of freight annually, and in 1963 international cargoes amounted to 114,586,111 tons, of which about 27 per cent was carried in Canadian-registered vessels. In 1963, the total number of Canadian-registered vessels, including canal and river craft, was 22,796, with a total of 2,858,746 gross tonnage.

Civil aviation in Canada is supervised by a federal government department. The largest airline is Air Canada, and there are many smaller passenger and freight lines; Canada's major airports are served by international flights of the world's major airlines. In 1963 there was a total of 360 seaplane bases and 302 airfields registered with the Department of Tranport

In 1963 Canadian airlines carried 5,427,344 passengers and a total of 125,529 tons of freight. In the same year, Air Canada's traffic included 3,966,547 passengers carried for a 2,887,239,000 revenue passenger-miles, and totals of 32,023,000 ton-miles of freight and 12,859,000 ton-miles of mail.

A Russian ship being loaded with Canadian grain at Montreal harbor. Canada possesses excellent harbors on its three coasts and the 2687-mile-long St. Lawrence Seaway. Twenty-one Canadian ports each handle more than 2 million tons of freight every year. Montreal, in the east, with about 20 million tons, and Vancouver, in the west, with nearly 18 million, are the two busiest ports.

PAGE	THE PEOPLE

Lake Louise in its spectacular Rocky Mountain setting at Banff National Park, in Alberta. A world-famous resort, Lake Louise boasts several large hotels with extensive entertainment and sports facilities. Here, visitors to the park are entertained by Scottish pipers and drummers.

POPULATION PATTERNS

ALTHOUGH CANADA IS THE LARGEST country in the western hemisphere and the second largest in the world, it has a population of only 20 million. More than half of the population is concentrated in the two provinces of Ontario and Quebec. Throughout the rest of Canada the distribution of the population is uneven. Whereas, for example, the great tracts of the Northwest Territories, which extend into Arctic regions, contain only a few Eskimos and a handful of white specialist workers, the smallest of the provinces, Prince Edward Island, with less than 1 per cent of the total Canadian population, is the most densely populated, with almost 48 people per square mile. The largest province, Quebec, has 8 per square mile.

NATIVE PEOPLES

The aboriginal peoples, the Indians and Eskimos, who were in possession of the land before the arrival of Europeans in Canada, today number about 225,000. The Indians are most numerous in the Prairie provinces, Ontario and British Columbia. Most of them still live on reserves, although many are being integrated into the general population.

Canada's Eskimos live mainly around the Arctic coast. Only one small group is found inland, in the region near Hudson Bay known as the Barren Grounds.

THE BRITISH AND FRENCH

The largest single population group in Canada, forming some 44 per cent of the total population, can trace its origin to the British Isles. The most numerous are of English stock, but Scots and Irish are also well represented in Canada. People of British stock are scattered throughout the provinces, but Cape Breton, Nova Scotia, is an enclave of Scottish culture where Gaelic is still spoken.

The French, who were the first Europeans to settle in Canada, constitute some 30 per cent of the population. The majority are concentrated in Quebec province, although a considerable number form minorities in the other provinces. In New Brunswick, in particular, there is an increasing French population, which will soon comprise half the total. In the most populous province, Ontario, over one-tenth of the population is of French extraction, concentrated chiefly in the north and near the Quebec border.

OTHER EUROPEAN GROUPS

Immigrants to Canada have come from almost every European country, and while many have been assimilated into the life of the country in a general sense, others tend to congregate in sections of large cities, maintaining their own culture and observing their own festivals and religious customs. Classes in English and French, opportunities for upgrading or adaptation of skills and welfare assistance are provided to newcomers from other lands.

People of German extraction constitute slightly more than 6 per cent of the population; many are descended from German immigrants who entered Canada several generations ago. These are now, with the exception of those belonging to certain religious sects (such as the Dunkards, Hutterites, Amish and Mennonites), indistinguishable from people of British origin, even the names in many cases having been Anglicized.

Ukrainians form another significant ethnic group. Although some Ukrainians are fully assimilated, others still prefer to live in exclusive communities in which they can preserve their own language and traditions. Many such communities are found in the prairies, where there are also communities of Icelanders.

In British Columbia and Saskatchewan there are colonies of Doukhobors, members of a religious sect which had its origins in Russia. Despite passionate rebellion by dissident elements (such as the "Sons of Freedom" group in British Columbia) most Doukhobors are being assimilated into the Canadian way of life.

ASIATICS AND NEGROES

Non-European immigrant elements in Canada are very small. Asiatics—mainly Chinese and Japanese—are most numerous in Vancouver on the west coast, but there are sizable numbers of Chinese and Japanese Canadians in Toronto and certain other cities.

Negroes, for the most part the descendants of runaway slaves, form a very small minority group. A number of Canada's Negroes are concentrated in the maritime provinces, particularly in a district of the city of Halifax, Nova Scotia, which has acquired the name "Africville." There is a small percentage of West Indians, and recent changes in immigration laws will open the doors of Canada for more of these citizens of the Commonwealth.

An Indian trapper from the Yellowknife district of the Northwest Territories proudly displays a white wolf skin. Furs remain an important source of income for the Indians in this area, but the tribes of the Northwest Territories are generally poor, and those bands not yet settled on reservations are facing extinction.

FEATURES OF CANADIAN SOCIETY

IN CANADA, AS OPPOSED TO THE U.S., there is a tendency for some European ethnic groups to maintain their racial identity rather than to fuse their national traits with those of other Canadian citizens. There is a basic dualism in Canadian society, which rests on the official status of Canada's two official languages, English and French, the languages of the country's two founding peoples.

Cultural Differences

French Canada is racially more homogeneous, since almost all French-speaking Canadians are of French descent. Anglo-Saxons, as the English-speaking members of the community are sometimes (rather inaccurately) called, include not only people of British stock, but also all those non-British immigrants who have adopted the way of life of the English-speaking Canadians. This way of life is in many ways distinct from that of the French Canadians, who are determined to preserve their own culture. This is no simple matter for them, living as they do among 20 million English-speaking North Americans, whose language is necessary for economic survival and advancement, sometimes even in the heart of French Canada.

MINORITY GROUPS

A tendency toward separate identity is not confined to the French Canadians. The Ukrainians are still partly unassimilated into the English-speaking culture in Canada, particularly some members of the pacifist Doukhobor sect who refuse to recognize any public authority.

The German Mennonites (particularly the Old Order Amish), and other divisions of so called "Plain

Folk" who emigrated from Germany and Russia, also are pacifists and prefer to live in exclusive communities in which only German is spoken. These are found mostly in Ontario and Manitoba.

On the whole, however, members of the present generation, many of whom were born in Canada, are increasingly breaking away from their ethnic origins and cultural backgrounds and assimilating into the life of either English or, more infrequently, French Canada.

American Influence

The most obvious feature of English-Canadian society today is its similarity to that of the United States, Canada's immediate neighbor. It is sometimes asserted that Canadians take as much interest in public affairs in the United States as they do in events in their own country; it is certainly true that more American than Canadian magazines are read in Canada.

Although in general, Canadian habits in the more superficial aspects of life, such as housing, eating and dress, all testify to a strong American influence, a very different history, a distinctively northern geography and climate and the presence of French Canada have helped the country to retain a definite identity of its own.

THE INDIANS

NUMERICALLY SMALL BUT OF GREAT interest as the first human inhabitants of Canada are the Indians. It is generally believed that they crossed the Bering Strait into America from northeastern Asia some 20,000 years ago.

Indians Today

Once widespread throughout Canada, the Indians began losing control of their land some 300 years ago. The Europeans, who took it from them, introduced a new way of life, and the Indians became dependent on them for food and clothing as their own natural food supplies dwindled with cultivation of the land. Thousands fell victim to diseases such as tuberculosis and smallpox brought by the white men. Eventually reserves were set aside for Indians, and steps are now being taken to integrate reserve schools into the public school systems.

A member of the Blood tribe of Alberta. The Indians of the Prairie provinces are the most numerous in Canada, numbering about 70,000. Though the tribes do not play a significant role in the national economy, many Indians have left the reservations to take their place in Canadian society alongside other citizens.

DISTRIBUTION OF THE TRIBES

The Algonquian-speaking tribes of eastern Canada are today greatly reduced, and the Indian population of the Maritime Provinces is very small. Remnants of the once-powerful Iroquois nation are still found in Quebec province and Ontario. Notable among these are the Indians of Caugnawaga near Montreal, whose immunity to vertigo and sureness of foot have enabled them to became invaluable employees in skyscraper construction work throughout Canada and the United States.

The Indians of the Prairie provinces number about 70,000. Remnants of fierce Plains' tribes such as the Blackfoot and Stony Indians, they play little part in the general economy of the country. The Indians of British Columbia, on the other hand, where the most advanced of Indian cultures flourished before the coming of the Europeans, are somewhat more active in the economic life of the province, some of them owning successful salmon-fishing enterprises.

The poverty-stricken tribes of the Northwest Territories and Yukon, who have not been settled on reserves, are facing extinction.

INDIAN STATUS

Divided into almost 600 separate communities known as bands, the Canadian Indians occupy or have access to more than 2200 reserves, varying in size from a few acres to more than 500 square miles. Although they have given up their rights to the traditional tribal hunting grounds, they have the right to hunt on Crown lands. Government cooperation in introducing new techniques has increased productivity in fishing and contributed to the conservation of fur-bearing animals. Registered Indians live under special Indian legislation which gives them a peculiar status in Canadian society. They are, for instance, exempted from paying taxes and cannot be sued for debt. They are provided with government medical care. But if they live on the reservations they may not vote. Many Indians have chosen to leave the reservations and acquire the same status as other Canadian citizens. Some of these have achieved prominence in many walks of Canadian life.

The Indian Economy

The traditional way of life of the various Indian tribes depended on the environment and the resources at hand. For most groups this meant a hunting economy, which entailed a nomadic existence. Only the Iroquois tribes of southern Ontario and Quebec and the coastal people of southern British Columbia were partly sedentary at the time of the arrival of the Europeans.

THE HUNTERS

The tribes of the northeastern woodlands hunted the moose, caribou and bear. In the northwest the economy was almost wholly dependent on the caribou, whose seasonal movements dictated the migrations

Women of the Stony Indian tribe don colorful, traditional outfits to celebrate the opening ceremonies of the Banff Indian Days festival. The picturesque clothing formerly worn by Canada's Indians is generally seen today only on such occasions and is preserved mainly as a tourist attraction.

of the hunters. The caribou provided meat for food, and hides for clothing and shelter. The Indians of the Plains were similarly dependent on the buffalo.

Skill in hunting was learned by the Indian male from earliest boyhood. He learned to track his prey by means of almost imperceptible signs left by its passage. He could dress in the hide of a beast and imitate its call, thus enabling himself to approach close enough to kill his prey.

At the season of migration large-scale hunts were organized in which the whole tribe participated. A herd of moose, buffalo or caribou might be simply surrounded and as many of the animals killed as possible, but more sophisticated hunters used the method of impounding. A whole herd could thus be guided into a corral and trapped.

SEA HUNTING AND FISHING

The tribes of British Columbia were mainly dependent for their livelihood on the products of rivers and sea. The Nootka of Vancouver Island, for instance, were intrepid hunters of the whale, which they attacked with harpoons from insubstantial dugout canoes.

Fishing was an important activity among all but the Indians of the Plains, where rivers and lakes are few. One of the most effective methods of large-scale fishing was the communally constructed weir. Fish caught in such weirs provided certain British Columbian tribes with a great part of their annual food supply.

TRAPPING

Although trapping is generally associated with the early European pioneers in Canada, the activity had long been practiced by Indians. Many Indians of the north were induced to abandon their old methods of large-scale hunting in order to concentrate on trapping the small animals whose fur was desired by European traders.

The breakdown in the old hunting economy and the Indians' increasing dependence on the whims of the white trader were primary factors in the decline of Indian culture in the north.

IROQUOIS AGRICULTURE

The Iroquois of Ontario and the St. Lawrence valley had some knowledge of agriculture before the arrival of the Europeans. With rudimentary stone tools they broke the surface of the soil to grow corn, beans, squash and sunflowers, the last-mentioned providing a useful oil. The products of the fields were stored underground for use during the winter.

Iroquois methods of cultivation were so primitive that the soil was quickly exhausted. The life of a settlement was thus limited to the time during which the soil would continue to bear a crop.

ECONOMIC LIFE TODAY

With increased educational facilities some Indians have been able to take up positions in the professions. The majority, however, are employed in the timber and fishing industries or in agriculture, and a considerable number still work as trappers. The Indian Act (revised in 1951) established an Indian Trust Fund made up of moneys derived from Indian assets. The fund is owned by separate bands, and expenditures are permitted for purposes in the interests of the band or its individual members. When an Indian gives up his rights under the Indian Act he is paid a proportional share of the fund of the band to which he belongs.

Dwellings

The wigwam and tepee, impermanent tent-like structures, were the dwellings of the nomadic hunters of North America. Both types of tent were made from skins stretched over a conical framework. The wigwam, which was the home of the Indians of eastern Canada, often was set over a partly excavated floor to increase warmth. The tepee, used by the Plains' Indians, differed from the wigwam in having two cowls for smoke holes projecting from the tent, like ears.

LONG HOUSES

The rectangular houses of the agricultural Iroquois communities were constructed on the same principle as the conical tents of the hunters; they were based on a framework of poles covered with skins. As many as 25 families often lived in one of these large houses.

The wooden houses of the coastal Indians of British Columbia were the most substantial built by Canadian Indians. Examples are still preserved in this region, although the Indians no longer build them. Made of cedar-wood planks, these houses consisted of an inner and outer section, the latter being detachable.

Some of them measured several hundred feet in length and 50 to 60 feet in width. Each family of the extended household was allotted a prescribed amount of space along one side of the building. Its hearth was shared with the family living in the corresponding space opposite.

GABLED HOUSES

Some Pacific coast tribes built houses of a quite spectacular nature. In these the frame was square instead of rectangular, and the roof was gabled. Their most striking features were the fantastic carving of the pillars supporting the roof beams, the painting of the façade, and the presence of a carved totem pole before the entrance.

INDIAN VILLAGES TODAY

Indian houses today are not always immediately distinguishable from those of non-Indian families living at a similar economic level. Most are built either from logs or weatherboard, and the commonest type is rectangular with a gabled roof. Overcrowding is common in these houses, which are generally very small, consisting of a single room with a kitchen annex. Such facilities as electricity, running water and adequate plumbing are often lacking.

Dress

The picturesque costumes formerly worn by Canada's Indians are seen today only on ceremonial occasions and are preserved mainly as a tourist attraction. Indians now wear the same type of clothes as their fellow Canadians, although in some more isolated regions moccasins and jackets made of skins still form part of everyday dress.

In most parts of Canada the outfit of the male Indian consisted of a thigh-length shirt, a breechcloth, leggings and moccasins. A common type of headgear was a cap decorated with an animal's brush. For most occasions a voluminous robe formed the top garment.

On the tidal marshes of the James Bay area, snow geese and blue geese often pause on their southern migratory flights. Expert Indian guides and their families set up living quarters close to fly-in camps to assist well-to-do hunters who visit the region every fall. As seen here, Indian women and children dress each day's kill.

The Plains' Indians often wore a lighter version of this costume, consisting of a sleeveless shirt with breech-cloth and moccasins.

Women's costume did not include the breech-cloth, but otherwise was generally similar to that of their menfolk, except that the shirt was long enough to cover the knees and the leggings were shorter.

The women of the Iroquois often wore a blouse and skirt instead of the usual long shirt.

Decoration of women's dress, as also of men's, consisted mainly of fringes and tassels on the hem of the shirt and on the leggings. Decorative effects were also produced by porcupine-quill embroidery and painted leather.

PACIFIC COAST DRESS

The Indians of the southern coast of British Columbia wore a lighter costume, better suited to the unusually equable climate of the region.

The basic garment worn by both men and women was a rectangular covering made from skins or cedar bark cloth, draped under the left arm and over the right shoulder, and belted at the waist. A short cape was sometimes worn as a top garment.

CEREMONIAL DRESS AND ORNAMENTS

The robes worn on ceremonial occasions were elaborately painted with tribal emblems or with scenes of warfare. The magnificent feathered headdresses—the most celebrated item of Indian costume—were reserved for ceremonial occasions. The ceremonial headdress of some of the Pacific coast Indians was made from bears' claws.

Most of the personal ornaments worn by the Indians were hunting trophies. They included bracelets of antelope teeth and necklaces made from pieces of antler and sometimes headdresses decorated with porcupine quills, animal claws or white ermine skins.

TATTOOING AND BODY PAINTING

The practice of tattooing the face and body, now almost obsolete, was confined to the tribes of the north and the Pacific coast. Tattooing, which was extremely painful, was accomplished by puncturing the skin and passing a thread, coated with pigment, through the hole. It was more widely practiced by men than women; the latter generally limited themselves to a few lines on the face, whereas men sometimes covered their bodies with tattooed designs.

All Indian tribes practiced face and body painting. They were acquainted with many pigments that provided them with a wide spectrum of colors. Among the Indians of the Plains and the eastern regions certain painted designs were associated with success in battle or with particular religious beliefs.

Political and Social Organization

Forms of political and social organization among the Indian tribes of Canada varied from the simple to the extremely complex.

LOOSE BANDS OF THE NORTH AND EAST

The primitive hunters of northern and eastern Canada had no clearly defined political organization. The tribe was composed of a number of bands, each led by the man who displayed greatest prowess in hunting. There was no tribal chief or other central tribal authority.

The survival of the band was largely dependent on a spirit of mutual co-operation. Each family unquestioningly helped less fortunate neighbors, for misfortune occurred indiscriminately and help might be required at any time. The custom of mutual aid, inherent in all Indian society, may still be observed in Indian settlements today.

THE BANDS OF THE PLAINS

The buffalo hunters of the Plains had a less amorphous political system. They, too, were divided into bands, but the affairs of each of these were managed by an informal council composed of its leading men, one of whom acted as chief. In summer the whole tribe would amalgamate for the great buffalo hunts under the leadership of an elected chief.

The social system of the Plains' Indians was given added complexity by the subdivision of the tribe into fraternities, membership in which did not coincide with band membership.

With the introduction of the horse and firearms the society of the Plains' Indians acquired a semi-military character. No longer was prowess in hunting the sole criterion for success, for skill in

A cluster of tepees at the Blood Indian Reserve at Cardston, Alberta. The wigwam and tepee were the dwellings of the nomadic hunters of North America. Both types of tent traditionally were made from skins stretched over a conical wood framework though modern fabrics are now employed. The rectangular houses of the agricultural Iroquois were constructed of wood frameworks covered with skins. As many as 25 families would live in one of these large houses. In British Columbia the Northwest Coast Indians built substantial houses made of solid cedar planks.

raiding was now felt to be of equal importance. Much of the Indians' energy was concentrated on horse-stealing raids and intertribal warfare.

This Mohawk Indian is made up for the Indian Pageant at Brantford, Ontario. Indian tribes traditionally practiced face and body painting with a wide range of color pigments. Among the tribes of the Plains and eastern regions, specific painted designs were associated with success in battle or with particular religious beliefs.

THE IROQUOIS LEAGUE

The energetic Iroquois had a relatively advanced political system. By the 17th century they had formed a confederacy of five tribes known as the Iroquois League. Although each tribe regulated its domestic affairs, external matters were the responsibility of a central council representing all five tribes. The League council, which was all-male, consisted of about 50 *sachems,* or clan chiefs. The functions of the council were to settle intertribal disputes, to receive embassies from outside tribes, and to decide on matters of war and peace. Although civil authority rested in the hands of the *sachems,* they were often opposed by rival leaders who had proved themselves in war. About 1720 the Tuscarora were admitted and the League became known as the Six Nations.

CLANS AND FAMILIES

The Iroquois social system was also complex. Each tribe consisted of a number of clans, members of which were scattered throughout the villages of the tribe. The clans themselves formed two groups, or *phratries,* which came into their own on ceremonial occasions, although they played little part in everyday life.

Each clan was divided into a number of "maternal families," for descent was through the female line. The family was headed by the oldest female member and consisted of her children, the children of her daughter and the children of any other direct female descendants. These matriarchs had considerable political power, since it was they who nominated the *sachems* for the League council.

PACIFIC COAST SOCIETY

Among the coastal tribes of British Columbia society was graded into nobles, commoners and slaves, the last being generally prisoners-of-war. In Pacific coast society there were no noble families but only noble individuals within each family. The noble members of a family where those belonging to the main line of inheritance, whereas the commoners belonged to subsidiary lines. The whole household, nobles, commoners and slaves, occupied a single large house. The union of two or more such households formed a clan.

It was in this part of Canada that the institution of the "potlatch" flourished. A potlatch was a feast given by one clan or clan-chief for another to demonstrate wealth and generosity. However lavish the gifts given at such a feast, the recipient aspired to surpass them at the return potlatch which social convention obliged him to give. To refuse an invitation to a potlatch, or to fail to honor the debt incurred by acceptance, meant a loss of prestige and status.

Childhood, Marriage and Death

Until very recent times the Indian child was not weaned for two or more years, and was seldom separated from its mother, who carried it on her back in a portable cradle. Although allowed considerable freedom, children absorbed much training in the various tasks they would have to perform in later life. They also learned tribal history and tradition through stories and legends.

The Indian child of today still enjoys considerable freedom from

The wood carvings of the Northwest Coast Indians are famous the world over. The brilliantly painted carved columns in Stanley Park, Vancouver, are powerful examples of this art. Generally made of cedar, these fascinating poles range from 10 to 70 feet in height and from 1 to 3 feet in diameter.

discipline, but the old forms of education are being increasingly replaced by formal education in school. The younger generation is thus losing contact with the tribal tradition and way of life.

ADOLESCENCE

Among all Indian tribes adolescence was the great testing time, for it was at this stage of life that the Indian made contact with his personal guardian spirit. Seclusion and fasting were two aspects of the discipline which the young Indian had to undergo, and boys and girls were kept strictly apart.

None of the mystery associated with adolescence remains among Indians today. It is, in fact, the young people of this age-group who show the most determination to forget the tribal past.

MARRIAGE

Until recent times Indian marriages were arranged by the parents, betrothals often taking place in infancy or even before birth. The usual age for marriage was 18 or 19 for the man and slightly younger for the girl.

A young man of the Plains' Indians simply purchased his bride, whereas in northern and eastern Canada it was the custom for the bridegroom to serve his wife's parents for a year. In coastal British Columbia the husband claimed his wife in a series of potlatches.

Young Indians today generally choose their own marriage partners, as do most Canadians, and the old customs connected with marriage negotiation and ceremonials are practically extinct. Only in mid-coastal British Columbia is the occasional potlatch still held to celebrate a marriage, but the custom has lost most of its social significance. Marriage is generally based on the Christian sacrament and follows the pattern common among Canadians of European ancestry.

ATTITUDE TO DEATH

The Indian attitude to death was one of stoical acceptance. Among the nomadic Indians the old and sick were sometimes deliberately killed when their condition made them unfit for the hard life of the wandering hunters.

The Indians believed in an afterlife and in a heaven, which they conceived of as a "happy hunting ground." The journey there, however, was long and dangerous, and in order to aid the departed soul on this journey food and other offerings were placed in the grave.

DISPOSAL OF THE DEAD

Today most Indians are buried in Christian cemeteries, but in the past methods of disposing of the dead differed widely from tribe to tribe. The forest Indians left their dead on raised platforms or in trees. In some cases, as among the Iroquois, the bones were later collected for burial in the ground. In treeless areas the dead were often buried under stone cairns. Cremation, a much rarer rite, occurred among some tribes of south central Canada.

Pastimes

Frequent periods of enforced idleness, inevitable in the Indian way of life, which was dependent on seasonal events, led to inventiveness in the matter of leisure-time activities.

GAMES AND GAMBLING

Although the Indians enjoyed such energetic activities as running, wrestling, lacrosse (invented by the Indians of eastern North America) and a type of football, their favorite pastimes were games of chance. One gambling game widely played in eastern Canada was a form of dice involving the throwing of a number of counters with surfaces of different colors. Another, played by the Carrier Indians of the west, involved the guessing of markings on a number of small sticks.

FESTIVALS

Festivals, which played an important part in the social life of the tribes, were held at the seasonal gatherings. Iroquois festivals, of which there were six important ones, included the Maple Festival, held in spring when the syrup flows in the maple trees. The main festival of the Plains' Indians was the Dance of the Sun, a religious festival that is sometimes revived today. The Dance of the Sun lasted about four days, and participants frequently reached a pitch of ecstasy at which they voluntarily inflicted mutilations upon themselves.

Among such British Columbian coastal tribes as the Bellacoola and the Kwakiutl, festivals were the major winter activity. The festivals, promoted by the great secret societies that dominated the social life of these tribes, included feasts, masked dances and ritual dramas.

Religion

Like all primitive peoples, the Canadian Indians sought to interpret the universe, as they saw it, through myths. North American Indian myths do not, however, form a single system, for each tribe recounted and interpreted the common myths in its own way.

THE GREAT SPIRIT

All Indian tribes believed in a Great Spirit, generally conceived of as a sky-god. Among the Algonquin tribes of the east he was Gitchi Manitou, the father of all life. The Bellacoola Indians of British Columbia called him Alkuntam.

Although recognized as the supreme spirit, the sky-god was generally considered to be too remote to intervene in human affairs and thus seldom was the object of elaborate rituals of worship.

SUN AND MOON

The sun and moon were worshiped as anthropomorphic deities who had their domain above the clouds. The Algonquin Indians conceived of them as brother and sister. According to one of their myths the Sun went out to hunt one day, staying away so long that his sister, the Moon, became afraid for him. She searched for 20 days

"The Mother Bear," a carving of the Haida Indians, one of the tribes of the Northwest Coast. Noted for its technical precision, Haida art placed less emphasis on color than was usual in Northwest Coast art.

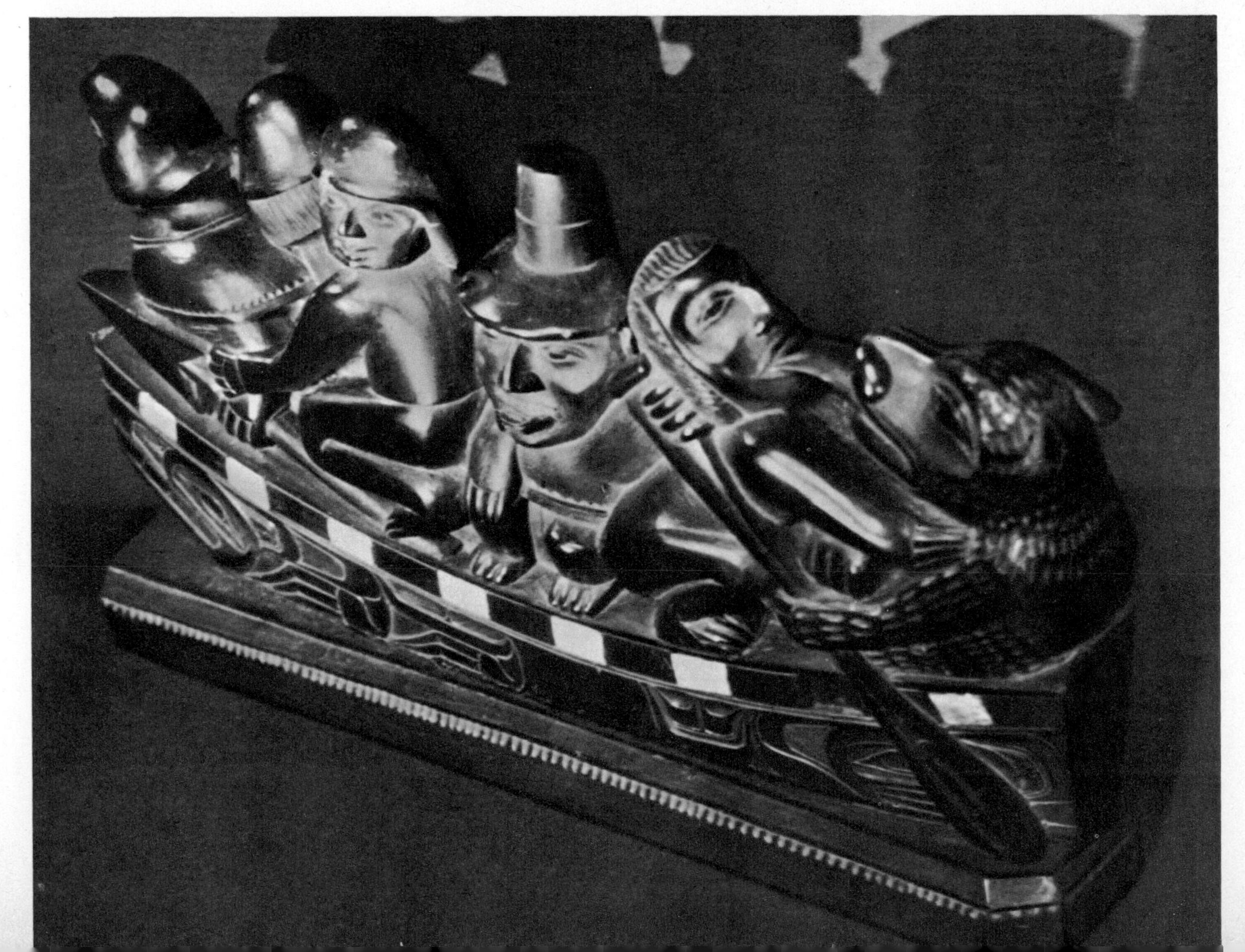

before finding him; since then the Moon has regularly made 20-day journeys across the sky.

THE THUNDER-BIRD

Another important deity, common to all Indian tribes, was the spirit of thunder, conceived of as a great bird. The thunder-bird was always accompanied by a flock of smaller birds, the flapping of their many wings causing the rumbling sound heard as thunder. It was believed this deity sent water to the earth, and was thus a fertility god.

MOTHER EARTH

As in many other mythologies, in Indian mythology the earth was conceived of as a great mother. Among the Algonquin Indians she was called Nokomis, the Grandmother, who fed all life at her breast.

The Iroquois possessed a legend not dissimilar to the Greek myth of Demeter and Persephone. Onatha, the daughter of Mother Earth, was carried off by the Spirit of Evil, who imprisoned her under the earth, where she remained until she was rescued by the Sun. Since Onatha is the spirit of Wheat, this myth apparently seeks to explain the mystery of growth.

THE BIRTH OF GOOD AND EVIL

None of the Indian tribes has a true creation myth, since these people were unable to conceive of a state of chaos preceding the emergence of the universe. There are, however, numerous myths describing the creation and peopling of the present world.

According to the Iroquois myth the earth is the shell of a gigantic turtle which rose out of the primeval lake. The first being on earth was Ataensic, who was cast out of heaven by her jealous husband. She gave birth to a daughter whose twin sons, Ioskeha and Tawiscara, were the spirits of good and evil. Ioskeha learned the secrets of agriculture, hunting and medicine, and it was he who created the first man. Tawiscara tried to imitate his brother, but succeeded only in creating evil things.

PAGAN BELIEFS

North American Indian religion was based on a belief in mysterious forces, or spirits, inherent in all phenomena. All religious strivings were aimed at acquiring the best possible life on earth, and the Indian sought to enlist the aid of these forces in his struggle with life.

The major purpose behind religious practice was to ward off the influence of evil spirits and to gain the cooperation of friendly ones. Propitiatory offerings and sacrifices were made before important undertakings, and also to appease a spirit which appeared to be angry. Another common practice was to leave offerings at such places of supernatural danger as waterfalls, rapids, mountain passes or lone rocks.

Common to all North American Indians was the belief that, by prayer, fasting and ceremonial purification, a person could acquire the personal protection of a spirit.

Of great importance in the religious life of the Indians were the many taboos affecting the social behavior of the individual and the tribe. Some taboos were in force only during particular phases of a person's life, such as puberty or

Carved posts of a Haida village on Queen Charlotte Island. It is erroneous to refer to such columns as "totem poles," as the Indians of the Northwest Coast did not practice totemism—a belief that certain animals are related by blood to specific groups or clans. The most important function of carved posts was to provide a heraldic emblem for the family or tribe. The sculptured creatures served as symbols of family or tribal lineage and were sometimes used to tell the story of individuals or groups.

Young men of the Blood tribe in costume for the Sun Dance. Though Indian rites are now generally shown as tourist attractions, the Dance of the Sun was once a major religious festival of the Plains Indians. The Dance of the Sun lasted about four days, and the celebrants frequently reached such a pitch of ecstasy that they inflicted mutilations upon themselves.

mourning, others were enforced at particular seasons of the year. Other taboos were permanent, since they concerned the food supply of the tribe. Eastern Indians, for instance, were forbidden to throw beaver bones to the dogs, since this would outrage the Beaver Spirit and cause him to withhold supplies of beaver.

'SHAMANS'

Although every Indian was sure to have a vision from the supernatural world once in his life, a few individuals claimed to possess superior powers in this field and to be able to commune with the unseen universe at will. These were the *shamans,* or medicine men, who acted as mediators between the tribe and the spirit world.

In general the position of the *shaman* was much more influential in the loosely organized tribes of the north and east, where the strength of the individual personality was the only criterion for influence. Elsewhere the regulation of religious affairs was in the hands of tribal leaders.

CHRISTIANITY

The devastating effect of the European invasion on Indian economic life was alone enough to shake the foundations of the traditional religion. It soon became clear that the necessities of life were now in the control of the white man rather than of the supernatural powers which had hitherto been held responsible for good and ill fortune.

The Indians were eventually converted to Christianity—almost all Canadian Indians describe themselves as Roman Catholics or Anglicans or, to a lesser extent, as members of Protestant Churches. The Christian God was naturally identified with the sky-god, who was already worshiped as the supreme deity but who was invested with none of the ethical qualities of the Christian God.

THE ESKIMOS

In the far north of Canada, where snow and ice cover the ground for much of the year, live the country's 13,000 Eskimos, whose culture is uniquely adapted to the harsh conditions of the Arctic. Most of the Eskimos are scattered around the coast of the Northwest Territories and the Arctic islands, although a few, perhaps 2000, live around the southern part of Hudson Bay.

Origins and Characteristics

It is generally accepted that the Eskimos, who are found in all Arctic regions, originated in northeastern Asia. The Canadian Eskimos probably migrated to the New World by way of the Bering Strait, as did the ancestors of the North American Indians.

A probable chronological gap of 14,000 years between the arrival of the Indians in America and that of the Eskimos, along with their northern environment, serves to account for cultural disparities between the two groups.

Although present-day Eskimo culture, in all parts of the Arctic, is primarily coastal, it is thought by anthropologists that the Eskimos were originally an inland people. If this is true, then it would seem that the so-called Caribou Eskimos of

At all times the basic rule of the hard Eskimo life has been mutual assistance. Carrying this spirit of cooperation and sharing into modern life, a major development in the Eskimo economy has been the introduction of cooperatives. Here, at Port Burwell, an Eskimo hunter brings a polar bear skin to the Eskimo manager of a cooperative store to trade for other provisions.

the Barren Grounds, inland from Hudson Bay, approximate most closely the way of life of their ancestors of northeastern Asia.

White travelers who have lived among the Eskimos have frequently remarked upon the superior character traits commonly encountered among these people. Such qualities as tolerance, hospitality, willingness to share all possessions, and equability of temper are all regarded not merely as preferable, but as essential if a group is to survive in the inhospitable regions of the north.

The Search for Food

Until the last decade the Eskimos of Canada were the least privileged and most neglected section of the Canadian people.

Today, while they are not legally wards of the Canadian government, the Department of Northern Affairs has assumed a responsibility for the Eskimos and helps them to abandon the nomadic life in favor of a settled existence. Eskimos are being taught to adapt their traditional economy to modern methods, and thus to ensure themselves a year-round supply of food. More and more are responding to the government's training programs, and it seems likely that all groups will eventually choose a life of security over the challenging but hazardous life of their forefathers.

HUNTING THE SEAL

The economy of the coastal Eskimo is largely dependent on the seal, although other creatures such as the whale and the bear are also hunted. The flesh and internal organs of the seal provide food, its blubber (fat) serves as fuel, and its skin is used to make tents and clothing.

In summer, when the sea is not frozen, the seal can be hunted with the harpoon from a kayak, the Eskimos' one-man skin boat. When the sea is frozen, however, the hunter of the seal requires enormous patience if he is to be successful. He waits, sometimes for hours, beside a blowhole, a small hole in the ice which the seal periodically visits in order to breathe. When the snout of the seal appears at the hole the hunter strikes through the ice, killing the creature with a blow on the head.

THE CARIBOU ESKIMOS

Coastal Eskimos supplement their diet of seal and other sea animals with the meat of the caribou when it is available, but the Eskimos of the Barren Grounds are unique in relying solely on the caribou for all necessities of life. Unfortunately, indiscriminate killing of the caribou, by both Eskimos and other Canadians, led to serious depletion of the herds and a breakdown in the regular pattern of migration. The Caribou Eskimos were themselves in danger of extinction, until in recent years their plight came to the notice of the authorities.

COOPERATION

At all times the basic rule of Eskimo life has been mutual assistance. The proceeds of a good hunt are shared among all members of the community, and, in bad times, a family will share what little food it has with another, even poorer family.

The spirit of cooperation and sharing has been carried over into modern life. The most important innovation in the Eskimo economy has been the introduction of cooperatives. In these, by learning new skills and using modern equipment, the Eskimos have enabled themselves to find a reliable source of support from what they produce.

PRODUCTS OF THE NORTH

The first cooperative was formed on the George River, near Ungava Bay, in 1959, and specializes in the catching and freezing of fish, much of which is sent to southern Canada. Other cooperatives—of which there were 19 in 1963—specialize in production of carvings, timber, sealskins, furs and other such products of the north. Handicrafts have been recognized as a valuable commodity, and the Eskimos—especially the women—are being encouraged to produce traditional articles for sale in the south. The Ookpiks, the Arctic owl, has become the symbol of the Department of Trade and Commerce at foreign fairs and exhibitions, and the sale of sealskin model Ookpiks has brought revenue to the Eskimos.

MODERN ESKIMOS

In 1963 there were some 3000 Eskimo children receiving a regular education which will fit them to enter the life of modern Canada. New programs of education and instructional materials adaptable to their northern life and culture have been introduced. Many younger Eskimos have shown great aptitude for dealing with machinery; it is hoped that they will soon be able to take over both the technical and administrative management of the cooperatives without the assistance of their non-Eskimo advisers. Territorial grants have been made to stimulate the learning of trades and to encourage study at universities, technical institutions and teachers' colleges.

Dwellings and Transport

The traditional dwellings of the Eskimos were all of a temporary nature, although some Eskimos, who have abandoned the nomadic life, are now settled in permanent wooden houses.

TENTS

In the spring and summer, when the ground is free of snow, the Eskimo traditionally lived in cone-shaped tents, consisting of a frame of wood covered with skins, rather like the Indian wigwam.

Furnishings were extremely simple. A sleeping platform, lined with twigs and moss and covered with skins, took up much of the space around the sides of the tent, and a few other skins and some utensils completed the furnishings.

Tents are still used today, but the hand-stitched skin covering has largely been replaced by canvas, sewn on the family sewing-machine. The meager fire of twigs and blubber oil has been superseded by an oil-drum stove, but the sleeping platform, with its mattress of skins, still lines the walls of the tent.

IGLOOS

The most celebrated type of Eskimo dwelling is the temporary dome-shaped winter house, the igloo. The igloo is generally used for one night only, and can be built by one man in a single hour. Wedge-shaped blocks of snow are cut out with a special, long-bladed knife and are laid on top of one another in ever-narrowing rings: the first circle usually contains 15 blocks and the last five. The top is closed with a single block, in which a hole is bored to allow warm air to escape. Entrance is by way of a low tunnel which is constructed last.

Like the Eskimo tent, the igloo is furnished with a sleeping bench and little else. The only heating is provided by a blubber lamp and the body warmth of the occupants.

CANOES

The Eskimos use two types of canoe: the kayak and the umiak. The kayak, on which is modeled the one-man canoe used by sportsmen all over the world, is made from layers of sealskin stretched tight over a frame of wood or whalebone. It is used in both sea and river hunting.

The larger boat, the umiak, is less common in Canada than in other parts of the Eskimo world. It is also a skin-covered boat, not closed in like the kayak, and large enough to hold a whole family.

SLEDS

The Eskimos' traditional mode of land transport in winter is the dog-sled. These are quite large, reaching 18 feet in length although the width rarely exceeds two-and-a-half feet. The sled and its runners are both made of wood; the latter are given the necessary smoothness by the application of softened mud which, when frozen hard, is coated with water to make a thin layer of ice.

The ideal dog-team consists of ten or twelve animals, which are hitched to the sled in a double row.

MODERN MODES OF TRANSPORT

Modern technology has introduced new forms of motorized transport into the Arctic. Motorized sleds or "skimobiles" are constructed with skis on the front end and tractor treads on the back, and are driven by gasoline motors. The dog-sled is still, however, a common form of transport in the Arctic.

DRESS

The appearance of the traditional Eskimo costume—fur parka, trousers

Eskimo hunters at Pond Inlet in the north of Baffin Island haul up a freshly killed seal. The economy of the coastal Eskimos is largely dependent on seal, though bear and whale are also hunted. In the summer the seal can be hunted from a kayak with a harpoon, but in winter a hunter must sometimes wait for hours beside a break in the ice, hoping that a seal will come up to take a breath of air.

A team of huskies pulls a sled across the barren, frozen wastes of the Keewatin district. The dog sled, sometimes reaching 18 feet in length, is the traditional winter transport of the Eskimos. The husky, with his thick coat of fur and his stamina, is ideally suited to the harsh conditions of the north.

and boots—is well known. What is less well known is the fine tailoring that goes into the making of such a suit of clothes. The Eskimo women, to whom is entrusted the whole task of preparing the skins and making the clothes, are highly skilled needlewomen, and the clothing that they produce is remarkably efficient in protecting the wearer from the bitter conditions of an Arctic winter.

A DOUBLE SUIT

To withstand the coldest winds the Eskimos wear two complete suits of skin clothes, each made in a similar way. The inner suit is worn with the fur against the body, and the outer one with the fur outside.

The parka is a kind of hooded shirt reaching to the knees. Fur trousers, fur gloves and high boots, called *kamiks*, complete the winter costume. Soft harehide slippers are worn as inner footwear. All garments are loose to allow for ventilation as a precaution against chills.

WOMEN'S WEAR

The women's clothing is almost identical to that of the men, except that the parka is provided with an extra hood, the *amaut*, at the back, in which a mother carries her unweaned child. Women's boots are longer than those of the men and their trousers correspondingly shorter.

The summer costume is essentially the same as that worn in winter, except that the top layer of garments is discarded.

FINE WORKMANSHIP

Until quite recently Eskimo women still used needles made from bone, and thread made from animal sinews; with these they sewed seams of incredible fineness.

To increase the aesthetic appeal of their work the women sometimes insert sections of variously colored skin and fur into the main body of the garment, thus forming a graceful pattern. Other decorations include bead edgings and embroidery.

DRESS TODAY

Contact with the rest of Canadian society is having its effect on dress as on other aspects of Eskimo life. Women in the sedentary communities of the cooperatives now wear cotton dresses, and often their favorite headgear is a floral headscarf. Many men have replaced the fur parka with one of cloth, usually in a brilliant color. Sealskin boots, however, are still appreciated as the most adequate Arctic footwear.

Food

The natural diet of the Eskimos is almost exclusively one of flesh. The high content of fat and protein in meat has been proved to be essential to their health.

The delicacies that are dearest to them would be acceptable to few non-Eskimo people, since many of them are based on raw meat well supplemented with fat. One of the favorite delicacies is the outer skin of the whale with much of the blubber still attached. It is either served fresh or preserved in skin bags packed with blubber.

Fresh seal meat is boiled, but whole seals are often put aside for preservation. Meat does not rot in the Arctic, but ferments; particularly good, to the Eskimo taste, is the fermented liver of the seal.

In recent years plans have been put into effect to assure the Eskimos of a constant food supply by canning some of their favorite foods. The Arctic char has proved delicious to fish lovers in the south as well as to native Eskimos.

Eskimo Society

THE FAMILY

The basic and essential unit of society among the Eskimos has always been the married couple. A clear division of labor makes each of the two dependent upon the other. The husband, as hunter, is the provider of food; he also builds the houses. The woman's most important task is the preparation of skins and the making of clothes. She also tends the tent or house and prepares the food.

Any unmarried person without a family is in the unfortunate position of having to rely on the charity of neighbors in order to survive. Celibacy is therefore rare; it is generally thought, except among more cosmopolitan Eskimos, that it denotes a serious inadequacy.

Sterility is regarded as a misfortune, and the Eskimos treat their children with great affection and indulgence.

THE BAND

The only political unit of the nomadic Eskimos is the band, a number of related households which meet together at the seasons of the big seal and caribou hunts, but which hunt individually at other times of the year. There is no official chief, the accepted leader being the man most skilled in hunting.

Even in the new, settled communities of Eskimos, the groups remain confined to a few families that live in close proximity to one another and look on one particular head of a family as their leader.

The basic rule of Eskimo life has always been common labor and a share of the proceeds for all. The greatest sin against society is to break this rule, and anyone who does so—through laziness or greed—cannot escape the retribution of the community he or she has wronged.

The commonest form of punishment for such an offense is merciless ridicule. Great account is taken of public opinion, and only the most hardened sinner could long stand the shame of public ridicule. A more severe punishment is ostracism, for no man can survive alone in the Arctic.

Customs

BIRTH AND CHILDHOOD

Although childbirth is generally regarded by Eskimo women as little more than a temporary inconvenience—a woman often requires no more than a few hours' rest after giving birth—the event has been surrounded by a number of taboos, which are disappearing with exposure to modern civilization.

The soul is thought to be the principle of life, and its protection is thus regarded as essential to the well-being of the individual. For this reason a baby's soul is sometimes exorcised by an *angakok* (*shaman*) immediately after birth; in a magical rite the *angakok* hides the soul under the mother's lamp, where it is believed that it will be safe wherever the owner may wander.

Certain events during childhood call for ceremonial celebration. When a child wears out its first pair of boots the parents hold a great feast, and the boots are kept thereafter as talismans. A boy's first successful seal-hunt is similarly celebrated with a feast.

COURTSHIP AND MARRIAGE

Boys and girls are not kept apart during adolescence, and are allowed considerable freedom in their relations with one another. A strict code of etiquette must nevertheless be observed by a young man contemplating marriage with a particular girl. He may not propose directly to the girl, but must first pay a series of visits to her parents. During these visits he takes little notice of the girl herself, but may, after a while, bring her presents. Her acceptance or rejection of these indicates whether he may entertain any hope. If the girl appears favorably inclined the suitor then asks, generally in a casual way, for her parents' consent to the marriage.

In former times there was no marriage ceremony, the bridegroom merely taking his bride to his tent.

A cheerful Eskimo family seated on the sleeping platform of their igloo, a dome-shaped winter dwelling. Constructed of blocks of snow, a small igloo can be built by one man in an hour. In the spring and summer, with the ground free of snow, the Eskimo generally lives in a tent of wood frame covered with animal skins.

The bride herself, however delighted she might be at the marriage, was expected to put up a great show of unwillingness and resistance. Today most Eskimos are married according to the Christian sacrament.

DEATH

The Eskimos accept death without fear, for their hard life has always made it a constant companion. Suicide was, at one time, a frequent form of death. When an old person felt unequal to the hardships of the nomadic life, he or she might voluntarily remain behind when the rest of the family moved on; the cold brought a quick and relatively painless death.

Traditional burial customs are simple. The body is usually entombed in a cave or under a cairn of stones. Anything that has touched the corpse is regarded as unclean and must be abandoned. The tracks leading to the burial place must be erased to prevent the spirit of the deceased—now a thing to be feared—from following the living.

VISITING

Because of their frequent enforced solitude the Eskimos are, by nature, a sociable folk, and their favorite leisure time activity is visiting. Anyone who has had a particularly successful hunting expedition is expected to invite all his neighbors to a party.

The etiquette of these occasions must be strictly followed. The successful hunter disparages his prowess as a hunter and his wife's skill as a cook and hostess; he suggests that it would be too presumptuous of him to hope that his neighbors would deign to accept his poor hospitality. The guests respond by praising the hunter and the size of his catch. The host then tries a little of the meat, which he throws away in disgust, saying it is uneatable. This is regarded as an invitation to begin the feast, and all the guests immediately do so.

Eskimos at Pelly Bay, Northwest Territories, gather in a large igloo to watch a dancer perform. The Eskimos are by nature a sociable people, and their favorite leisure activity is visiting. Evenings are often enlivened with the gaiety of music and games as the Eskimos entertain one another with songs and dances of their own composition.

SONGS AND GAMES

A social evening is often enlivened with music and games. At a song-feast the Eskimos entertain one another with songs and dances of their own composition. The accompaniment is played on the *ayayut*, a large skin-covered drum that is held by a handle and beaten—not on the skin but on the frame—with a short stick. One performer plays the drum while another sings and dances. When one pair of performers is exhausted their place is taken by another, and the feast may continue for 20 hours at a stretch.

Like the Indians, the Eskimos are extremely fond of gambling games. Cat's cradle is another popular pastime, and many Eskimos are very skilled at the game; whole stories are woven into the complicated, constantly changing pattern of the string between their hands.

Mythology and Religion

Despite their conversion to Christianity many Eskimos still live in constant fear of spirits, which they believe share their hard world and control the various elements.

Although many of the spirits are both nameless and formless, the most powerful and dangerous are known by name and have the character of deities. To some Eskimos the greatest spirit is Torngasoak, the Good Spirit, a remote and nebulous being. To the Caribou Eskimos, however, the principal spirit is Kaila, a weather and sky god. Like the great sky-god of the Indians, Kaila stands aloof from men, requiring no ritual of worship.

SEDNA

The divinity held in most dread by the coastal Eskimos is Sedna, who controls the creatures of the sea. Hostile to men, Sedna is imagined as a one-eyed giantess lying at the bottom of the ocean.

Sedna, so the legend tells, was originally an Eskimo girl. According to one version of the legend she was an orphan abandoned by heartless neighbors. As she clung desperately to the side of one of the departing kayaks, its occupant chopped off her fingers. The severed members became the sea-mammals—seals, walruses and whales—and Sedna herself became their presiding deity.

OTHER SPIRITS

Among the friendly divinities of the Eskimos are Agoolik and Nootaiok, who give aid to the sea hunter; Koodjânut, a bird spirit who has power to heal; and Tekkeitserktok, god of the earth and of deer. Ataksak, who lives in the Eskimos' heaven, is a personification of joy.

Hostile spirits include Aipaloovik, a sea spirit who threatens the safety of boatmen; Keelut, an earth spirit; and Noesarnak, a female spirit. The evil spirit most dreaded by the Caribou Eskimos is Paija; nobody can see Paija and live to report the experience, for anyone to whom she appears dies with the sight of her frozen in his mind.

EARTH, SUN AND MOON

Like the North American Indians, the Eskimos believe that before the creation of the earth there existed a great primeval lake. Earth was created by a hail of rocks and stones from the sky, and in this world there was utter confusion until the creation of life, when each species recognized its own kind and its place in creation.

Sun and Moon are said to be a sister and brother who were originally mortals on earth. The Moon, full of incestuous passion for his sister, the Sun, pursues her across the sky but is never able to catch her. The feebler light of the Moon is due to the inadequately lighted taper which he snatched up before setting out in pursuit of his better provided sister.

Besides the rearing of children, one of the most important tasks of the Eskimo woman is the preparation of skins and the making of clothes. Here an Eskimo mother kneads a seal skin with her teeth to make it more pliable. The parka of an Eskimo mother is provided with an extra hood called the amaut, *in which she can conveniently carry her unweaned child.*

THE ANGAKOK

The traditional Eskimo religion has not yet fully succumbed to the influence of modern civilization. It has no organization and no formal priesthood, the nearest to a priest being the *angakok*, or *shaman*, who claims to have contact with the spirit world, which he can enter at will in a state of trance.

A youth who senses in himself the power to become an *angakok* puts himself into the hands of an older *angakok*, who teaches him the lore of spirits and demons, the traditional magic spells preserved in an ancient language and the art of inducing trances. Having learned all this, the novice is expected to seek out his *tornrak*, or guiding spirit. After a long period of fasting and seclusion the *tornrak* appears to him; only after he has struggled with it and gained mastery over it does the *tornrak* become his familiar spirit.

HEALING THE SOUL

One of the main functions of the *angakok* is healing. Illness is believed to be caused by sin or by the workings of an evil spirit; it has its roots in the soul. Physical suffering is thus seen as only a reflection of the sickness of the soul, and the *angakok's* healing efforts are directed at the soul rather than the body.

THE FRENCH CANADIANS

Canadians of French origin constitute about 30 per cent of the total population. The "French fact," as it has been termed, is an intrinsically valuable force in Canadian life, and no small part of the uniqueness of Canada depends upon it. By some English Canadians, particularly in the west where little French is spoken, it has also been considered the chief obstacle to Canadian unity.

Preservation of the Culture

Most other ethnic groups tend to merge into the English- rather than the French-Canadian way of life. The French Canadians, surrounded by 200 million English-speaking North Americans, have an understandable fear of losing their distinctive culture and identity. More than three-quarters of all French Canadians live in the Province of Quebec, where they constitute well over three-quarters of the population.

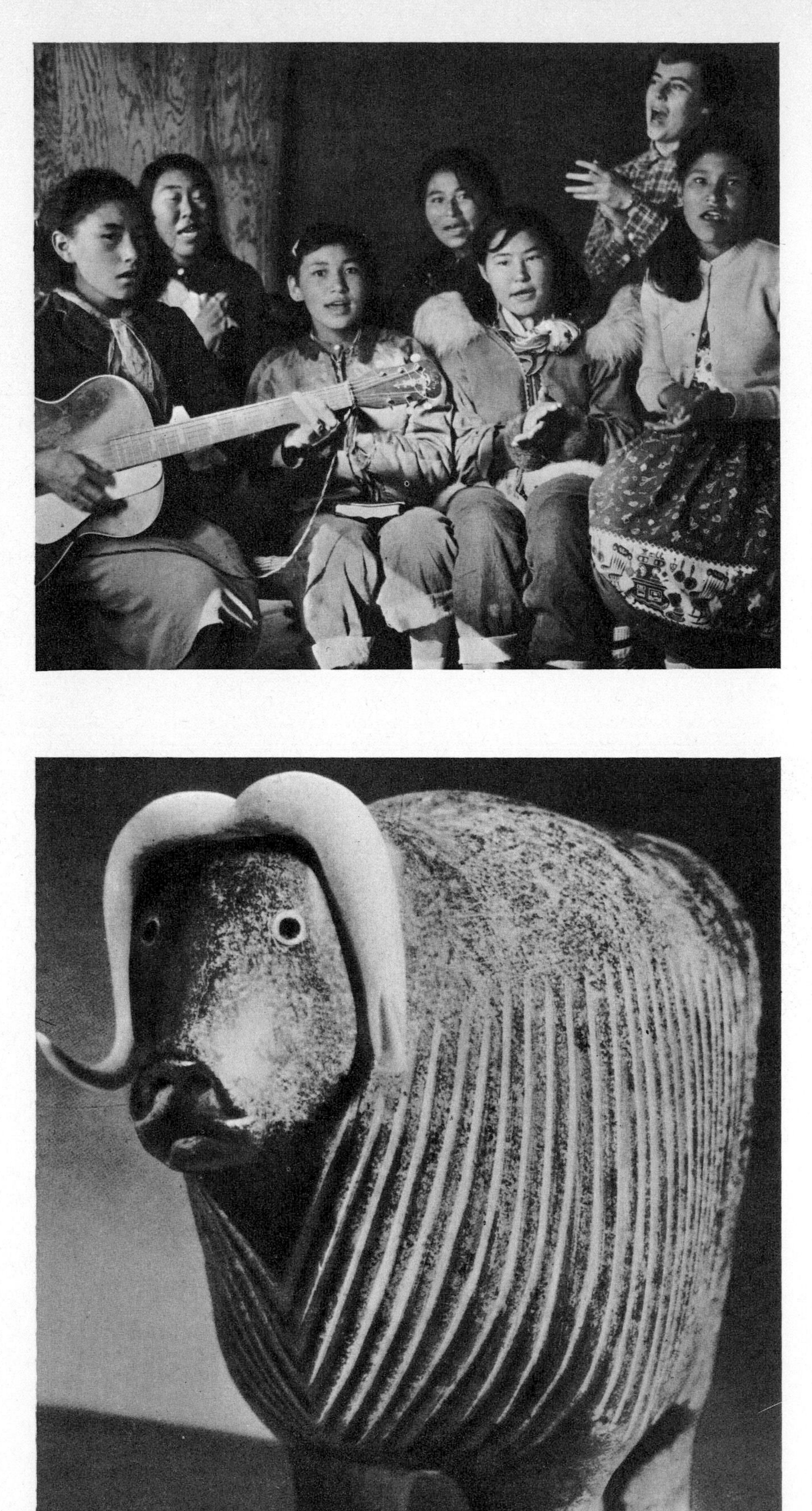

Eskimo girls learn a hymn at the government-run village school. The living habits of the Eskimos are undergoing steady change as contact with the rest of Canadian society increases. Learning about Western ideas through the schools and cooperatives, Eskimos have already adopted Christianity, and growing numbers are coming to accept Western dress and to live in settled communities.

The "quiet revolution" in Quebec, begun with the victory of the Liberal party in the 1960 provincial elections, and continuing under a reformed Union Nationale government in 1966, has aimed to give French Canadians the equality of political, economic and social status within Canada that they have never quite possessed. Even in Quebec the English-speaking element has tended to run big business and hold most of the economic power. Many English Canadians, particularly in Ontario and in Quebec itself, have welcomed the French-Canadian determination to be "masters in their own house," even though they do not wish to see the assertion of a special status for Quebec, as the political focus of French Canada, lead to a weakening of the federal power.

Contrary to general belief, Quebec's birth rate is now only slightly higher than the national rate of 27.2 and is surpassed by that of New Brunswick and Newfoundland. In New Brunswick there is a prospect of the French Canadians becoming a majority in the foreseeable future. Here nearly half of the population is of French origin. The ratio is about 1:6 in Prince Edward Island; 1:7 in Nova Scotia; 1:9 in Ontario; 1:13 in Manitoba; 1:17 in Saskatchewan; 1:18 in Alberta; 1:25 in the Northwest Territories and the Yukon; 1:40 in Newfoundland. In the decade 1941-51 the French-Canadian population of British Columbia doubled, but its ratio is still only about 1:29. Most of the French population of Canada are descendants of some 70,000 French in New France and Acadia at the time of the British conquest (1760).

Carved at Akiaktashuk, this musk ox is typical of Dorset Eskimo sculpture. Many Eskimos still believe in magic and spirits. Carvings, such as this one, of animals which had disappeared from Eskimo hunting grounds were believed to be endowed with magical qualities which would bring the animals back.

THE ACADIANS

The Acadians of the Maritime Provinces, on the Atlantic coast of Canada, are distinct by origin and temperament from the French of Quebec. The Acadians are, in fact, the descendants of the first French settlers in Canada, who came from Poitou in western France. They colonized Nova Scotia, southern New Brunswick and Prince Edward Island. Although they were expelled in 1755, many Acadians returned to settle discreetly in the more isolated regions of the Maritime Provinces, where they are still to be found today, following their old-established rural mode of existence.

The Acadians hold no bitterness for past wrongs and remain on friendly terms with their English-speaking neighbors. It is probably in this part of Canada that the traditions of the old rural France are preserved in the purest form, for the Acadians have not followed the trend toward urbanization to the same degree that other French-speaking Canadians have.

French-Canadian Characteristics

The French Canadians have retained, to an amazing extent, the characteristics of the European French; the physical appearance and mannerisms of the people of a French-Canadian town would not strike the eye as alien to the streets of any French town.

French Canadians possess an attractive animation and show genuine response to emotions. They tend to be affected by group reaction more than the individualistic English Canadian. They enjoy celebrations, parades and political rallies. The family is a large part of their lives, and anniversaries of all kinds bring as many members of the family together as possible.

Certain characteristics of the French Canadians have been passed down through generations of peasants. Most attractive among these are a natural courtesy and hospitality, the latter no doubt fostered, in the pioneering past, by the need for people to be ready to give and accept aid in a hostile environment.

FRENCH-CANADIAN CONSERVATISM

Another typical characteristic, still commonly encountered among French Canadians, is an innate conservatism. A distrust of innovations and an affection for the old institutions—particularly in the fields of education—have been partly responsible for keeping the French Canadian in an economically inferior position to his English-speaking compatriots.

This conservatism has bred its opposite in the radicalism prevalent among French-Canadians intellectuals, who have played an important political role in leading French Canadians toward a new status of equality, particularly since 1960. A few radicals have indeed during the 1960s even resorted to violence as a means of attracting attention and support to the cause of a separate and independent state for Quebec. But in spite of considerable popular sympathy for their aims, their methods are abhorrent to the vast majority of their compatriots.

FAMILY FEELING

Although the importance of the French-Canadian family as a social unit is now less than at an earlier time, there is no doubt that the family feeling of the French Canadian is still very strong. Much social life is confined to the family circle.

A French Canadian's feeling of family loyalty extends beyond those members of his family immediately known to him. Before an important anniversary of some event concerning a particular family, such as the original landing in Canada of their pioneering ancestor, an advertisement appears in the newspapers, inviting all holders of the family name to a renunion. Such family reunions are often attended by more than a thousand people. A recent allegation against a French-Canadian federal politician brought expressions of fear that an insult was being leveled against the family, rather than the typically English reaction that it only reflected upon the individual involved.

Rural Life

The earliest French pioneers in Canada were the *coureurs de bois*, who gained a livelihood from the land by exploiting the fur trade.

An ivory mace of the Territorial Council of the Northwest Territories, carved from a walrus tooth and adorned with whalebone, wood and musk ox horn. The Eskimos consider it a symbol of peace and concord and place it among them during discussions.

RESTAURANT
DAY & NIGHT
ON FERRY
JOS. E. LEMIEUX

Quebec still has 40,000 lakes and 30,000 square miles of forest, but furs are no longer of great economic importance. The modern *coureurs de bois* are apt to be weekend sportsmen, who fish and hunt game purely for pleasure.

FARMING METHODS

Farming is still important in the St. Lawrence valley. Here there are some of the old-style family farms, which are worked by the owner and his family. The typical conservatism of the French Canadian is expressed in his slowness to adopt modern farming machinery and his preference for traditional farming methods. Thus the sight of a patient horse harnessed to a plow is still not uncommon in the fields of the Quebec countryside. The Acadian farmers of the Maritime Provinces have traditionally taken great pride in their teams of oxen, resplendent in yokes of finely worked and studded leather.

LOGGING

In winter, when farming activities are reduced to a minimum, the traditional occupation of some French Canadians is wood-cutting. They leave their farms to move into the forests, where they spend the winter in lumber camps. These camps are filled with an atmosphere of conviviality, although the work is hard. It is probably true that many of the most popular of French-Canadian folk songs originated in the lumber camps: they include *Voyez Passer les Raftsmen* (See the Raftsmen Pass) and *C'est l'Aviron Qui Nous Mène* (It Is the Oar Which Takes Us).

In spring, when the thaw swells the rivers, the logs are floated down to the sawmills and paper factories. The sure-footed lumbermen leap from log to log in mid-stream as they drive the timber down the river, breaking the obstructing ice as they meet it.

VILLAGES AND HOUSES

The French-Canadian village is built around the church and the house of the parish priest. The typical village consists of little more than one main street flanked by two rows of houses, with some adjacent scattered cottages. There are, generally, a few stores, an inn, a post office and, still in a few cases, a blacksmith's forge. The modern world has long since reached rural French Canada, however, in the form of gasoline stations and hot-dog stands, juke boxes and television sets.

The traditional style of French-Canadian domestic architecture is extant in some old houses, but it has not been used for more than 100 years. These old houses, built of stone, are long and low with gabled roofs containing two rows of dormer windows. Their most characteristic feature is the presence of two chimneys, one at each end of the roof.

Modern houses are often built of wood, a material found in abundance in Quebec. These so-called *maisons de pièce* are square in plan and almost flat-roofed. The façades are often somewhat ornate, and it is customary to paint the doorways and window frames in bright colors. The most important room in a French-Canadian village house is the kitchen, which is sometimes entered directly from the front door. The article of furniture which immediately strikes the eye is an enameled kitchen dresser, usually ornamented with numerous mirrors. Each bedroom often has sacred symbols on the walls and a crucifix over the bed.

Town Life

Most of the population of Quebec now live in the town and cities of the province. Industry is today of much greater economic importance than agriculture, and Quebec is possibly the most urban and industrial of all the Canadian provinces.

QUEBEC CITY

Quebec City still retains much of its old European character despite encroaching industrial influences and its large modern suburbs. Still one of the two religious and cultural centers of French Canada, Quebec

The Château Frontenac, perched above a street at the foot of Cape Diamond in the French-Canadian city of Quebec. French Canadians have retained to a great degree the characteristics of the European French.

Old Saint-Pierre Street is now the center of Quebec City's financial district. La Maison Fargues (1781) is an outstanding example of the fine and solid houses built by the middle class in the 18th century.

is strongly influenced by the Roman Catholic Church. The historic center of Quebec City is clearly divided into the Lower and Upper Towns. The Lower Town has narrow, winding streets and old Norman-style stone houses. The Upper Town of Quebec, with its fine stone houses, its citadel, its seminary and its Ursuline Convent, still retains much of its 17th-century character.

MONTREAL

Montreal, Canada's largest metropolis, epitomizes the conflict between French-Canadian and English-Canadian society, for here the two cultures exist side by side or, some say, collide head-on. Originally a French-Canadian religious, military and fur-trading center, Montreal became the major commercial and industrial center of the dominant English-speaking Canadians after the conquest of 1760.

The division into two cultures is most clearly to be seen in the residential areas of the city. The eastern residential area houses the French-speaking part of the population, who have a lower economic status than the English Canadians. Until recently it was the general rule in Quebec province that top managerial posts were filled by English Canadians, while French Canadians performed the manual and clerical work.

In the French part of Montreal, east of St. Lawrence Main, many people live in a characteristic type of French-Canadian apartment house divided into two or three apartments. The desire of the French Canadian for personal and family privacy underlies the custom of having a curving iron outside staircase to give individual access to each apartment.

The night-life of Montreal is equaled by that of no other Canadian city. Nightclubs and restaurants of the American type abound, but the most characteristic Montreal clubs, which have something of the lightheartedness of Parisian night-life, are the *clubs de diseurs et de chansonniers,* with their special entertainment compounded of song and satire.

French-Canadian Society

The traditional French-Canadian social pattern is based on two main elements: the family and the parish. Although this type of society was essentially rural, and the majority of *habitants* (settlers-farmers) have moved to the towns, there is a close relationship between secular and religious life, and the family bonds are still strong.

THE PATRIARCHAL FAMILY

Since the earliest days of settlement in Canada, the most important social unit of the French Canadians has been the family. Unlike the old French type of household, which comprised a number of married brothers and sons with their families, the French-Canadian household consisted of a single family line, headed by a patriarch whose word was law among his children.

Each family formed an autonomous unit, although wider kinship links with neighboring households were of social importance.

According to the general rule of inheritance the farm passed to one son, usually the eldest, whose duty it was to provide for his parents in their old age and for his younger brothers and sisters. The other brothers and sisters eventually left the farm to seek their fortunes elsewhere. Girls either married or entered a religious order, whereas boys had a choice of careers, ranging from the Church and the professions to manual labor.

The rule of inheritance by a single son was by no means a right, however. Cases of division of the land among all the children of a family were frequent, and inheritance by a man's wife was not unknown. Legally, however, the status of a wife was restricted by the provisions of old French civil law, in which revisions in keeping with the modern rights of women have only recently been made.

French-Canadian families are generally large, and it has been usual for children to remain with their parents until marriage, although urbanization has made changes in this custom. It is in the family circle that French-Canadian culture—particularly the language, lore and religion—is preserved.

THE PARISH

The parish, traditionally the most important of all public institutions in French Canada, is still of importance even in the towns. The French Canadian has felt his first loyalty toward the Church and, in particular, toward his parish, rather than toward any secular institution. Great pride is taken in the parish church and the presbytery; many of the older churches were actually built by the work of the parishioners' own hands. It is a matter of pride among the parishioners to have a better church than that of the neighboring parish.

The parish priest is one of the most important persons in the community. His advice on all matters is respected, for he is almost inevitably a man of the people, who understands their problems.

Festivals

The French Canadians take great pleasure in all celebrations, public or private. Baptisms and weddings are marked by large parties, and funerals sometimes assume the pomp of public ceremonies.

The main feasts of the Church, however, are still kept as religious festivals and not merely as holidays for enjoyment.

EASTER

Good Friday and Easter Saturday are public holidays. The former day is spent quietly, as a time of mourning for the crucified Christ, but on Easter Saturday the holiday spirit prevails and people go out to do their Easter shopping. The shops themselves have a festive air, and hams, the traditional food with which the Lenten fast is broken, are gaily decorated with paper rosettes and ribbons.

The high spot of the Easter festival is the High Mass on Easter Sunday, for which the parishioners wear their newest and finest clothes.

CHRISTMAS AND THE NEW YEAR

The central event of the Christmas celebration is the Midnight Mass. The service is immediately followed by the Christmas wake, which begins with a banquet of meat pies (*tortières*), rissoles, chickens, tarts and other delicacies. After the banquet come dancing and games, which last until dawn. It is customary to prolong the Christmas season until Little Christmas (Twelfth Night), and many French Canadians observe the religious celebrations on December 25, but defer the giving of gifts until the January festival.

On New Year's Day it is the custom to visit relatives and friends and to ask for the blessing of the head of the house. Many people make a special effort to visit their parental home to receive the formal blessing of their father.

Another New Year's custom is the *guignolée*: on New Year's Eve children and young people don colorful and imaginative costumes, in which they go about the streets singing and begging alms on behalf of the poor.

'FÊTE-DIEU'

A major public religious festival in French Canada is *Fête-Dieu* (Corpus Christi Day), when the buildings and streets are hung with flags and religious banners. In some parishes people line the streets as the Host is carried in procession to a public altar; all kneel as the Host passes by in the midst of the procession of soldiers, clergy and little girls in white dresses. After a public service the Host is carried back to the church to the joyful pealing of bells.

SAINT JEAN-BAPTISTE

The patron saint of French Canadians is St. Jean-Baptiste (John the Baptist), whose day is June 24, which is celebrated both as a religious and patriotic festival. This is primarily an urban festival and is less marked in the countryside.

The celebrations of this feast are particularly spectacular in Montreal, where a grand procession is held. The procession includes bands of musicians and floats depicting scenes from the history of the French-Canadian people.

The fire of St. John is lit and blessed on the evening of June 23, and, as it burns, the people rejoice and dance in the streets.

THE SUGARING PARTY

One of the gayest times of the year in rural French Canada is "sugaring time," in spring, when the sap is tapped from the maple trees to be condensed into syrup or maple sugar. At this season a sugaring party is held every Sunday.

The focus of such a party is the delicious maple sugar candy made from the maple sap, but no opportunity is lost for other enjoyment. The guests are first served a substantial meal, which includes such items as salt pork with baked beans and eggs cooked in maple syrup. The meal is followed by lively dancing and songs.

In winter, when farming activities are at a minimum, some French Canadians traditionally switch to the occupation of lumbering. Winter is spent in the logging camps, and during the spring these skilled lumbermen help float the logs down to the sawmills and paper factories. Here, river drivers pole logs down the Ste. Anne River in Laurentides Provincial Park, Quebec.

WINTER FESTIVALS

Many towns of Quebec province break the monotony of the long winter by holding special winter festivals. The town of Sainte Agathe des Monts, for instance, the popular Laurentian ski resort, is famous for its Winter Festival, but the most famous is in Quebec City itself. The events include processions with allegorical and historical floats, folk-song sessions, and exhibitions of ice and snow sculpture.

THE GENERAL CANADIAN SCENE

THE TERM ENGLISH CANADIAN includes all those people who, whatever their country of origin, have adopted the English language and the way of life evolved by the British in Canada. Ordinarily they are simply called "Canadians."

The Canadian Character

Generalizations about the English-speaking Canadians are likely to be valid only for certain sections of the population, since the vastness of the territory and the varying histories and conditions of the provinces make for variety in the characteristics of different communities. There are nevertheless distinctively Canadian types, traits and characters—perhaps best expressed and discovered in literature, such as the writings of Stephen Leacock, E.J. Pratt, Hugh MacLennan, Morley Callaghan, and in Northrop Frye's conclusion to the *Literary History of Canada.*

The Canadian character is conservative and quiet. Canadians dislike noise and show for their own sakes. This characteristic is reflected in their style of dress, which, in the towns at least, is sober and unadventurous.

The pace of life generally in Canada is slower than in the U.S. The desire to keep abreast of innovations exists among Canadians, but leisure is not sacrificed for the sake of progress. The characteristic Canadian caution is also linked with the leisurely tempo of life in Canada.

The Canadian has, to some extent, inherited the British characteristic of reticence, so that a newcomer to Canada might at first feel a lack of friendliness in the people.

THE PATRIOTIC FEELING

The English Canadian is traditionally a supporter of the Commonwealth, of which Canada is a mem-

The parish priest strolls through the village of Île aux Coudres. The parish, a traditional institution in French Canada, is still of importance even in the towns. French-Canadian villages were often built around the church and the house of the parish priest.

"Sugaring time" in the spring, when the sap is tapped from the maple trees, is one of the gayest times of the year in rural French Canada. At this season a sugaring party is held every Sunday. Many tasty foods are served, but the main treat at such parties is the delicious maple-sugar candy made from the maple sap.

ber, and is a loyal subject of the British Crown. His first loyalty and affection are, however, toward Canada. The Canadians' pride in their country and in their achievements as a nation is one of their deepest passions.

Life in the Atlantic Provinces

A regional survey of life in Canada can begin in no better region than the Atlantic provinces, which saw the first European attempts to settle the American continent north of Florida. The Atlantic provinces comprise Nova Scotia, New Brunswick and Prince Edward Island—often known as "the Maritimes"—and Newfoundland, which became the tenth province of Canada in 1949.

In many ways this region is economically the most backward in Canada, but the people, with their varying ways of life, are resourceful and interesting.

NOVIA SCOTIAN COMMUNITIES

In Nova Scotia the mosaic of immigration to Canada is still very apparent in the varying types of speech and customs found in the different counties of the province. The Acadians, mentioned above in

A fisherman repairs the rigs on one of the many craft that jam the harbor of Lunenberg in Nova Scotia. In Nova Scotia the pattern of immigration to Canada is very apparent. The Acadians still retain their French language and customs, and the Scots of Cape Breton Island have preserved their Gaelic speech. Lunenberg County is the domain of the Germans, whose customs, cookery and folklore have been transplanted almost intact.

the section on French Canadians, retain their French language and customs, and the Scots of Cape Breton Island still preserve the Gaelic language. Dutch and German communities are also distinguishable by their accents and customs. The domain of the Germans is Lunenburg county, where old German customs, cookery and folklore have been transplanted intact.

A SCOTTISH COLONY

Cape Breton Island, to the north of Nova Scotia, has been described as a Scottish colony, and it is certainly in this region that the name "Nova Scotia" (New Scotland) has greatest validity.

The Cape Bretoners' love of Scotland and all Scottish customs sometimes exceeds that of born Scotsmen. At St. Anne's, situated amid picturesque "Highland" scenery with glens and inlets, there is a Gaelic College; and at Antigonish an annual *mod* (festival), with piping and Highland dancing and games, is held to preserve the Highland traditions. This preservation of the Scottish way of life is not, however, artificially achieved, for the Gaelic language has been continuously used in the home and the church, and Scottish crafts, such as blanket-making, are still practiced by the people of Cape Breton Island.

FRUITGROWERS OF THE ANNAPOLIS VALLEY

The Annapolis valley is famed, far beyond the borders of Canada, for its apples and other fruit. If Cape Breton Island appears to have been lifted out of Scotland, this valley is comparable to parts of rural England.

Most of the people of this region are descended from United Empire Loyalists who emigrated from the 13 colonies after the American War of Independence in order to seek a new life in the north. It was they who introduced the characteristic frame houses with their white shingles, and the barns with their high gables.

In spring, when the apple trees are in blossom, the valley is the scene of an Apple Blossom Festival that attracts many visitors. Each of the orchard towns chooses its "princess," and from these a "queen" is selected to be crowned on Apple Blossom Sunday, the climax of the festival.

HALIFAX

The principal city of Nova Scotia, in fact of all the Atlantic provinces, is one of the world's busiest ports, Halifax. The people of Halifax are very pro-British; they are proud of their geographical link with Britain and of the part played by Halifax in the two world wars. Even the atmosphere of the older streets, often sunk in the damp gloom of a climate in itself reminiscent of Britain, recalls that of English towns.

NEW BRUNSWICK

If the atmosphere of Nova Scotia is predominantly British, New Brunswick is becoming increasingly French. Even in communities that were formerly English-speaking, French is often now the principal language. The province's affinities are with Quebec, and with Maine, the bordering state of the United States. Both New Brunswick and Nova Scotia have old ties with New England, or "the Boston states," as Maritimers often call it.

Much of the territory of New Brunswick is covered with forest, and timber is the province's major source of revenue. Farmers, who find that agriculture is scarcely sufficient to keep a family, turn to logging as an additional source of income. As in Quebec province, the great log rafts are driven down the rivers in spring to the pulping mills. The forests of New Brunswick are also the domain of trappers and guides, whose presence recalls early pioneering days in Canada.

THE RIVERS

Rivers—until recently the main highways of the province—are central to the life of New Brunswick. The greatest river is the St. John, which flows the whole length of the western part of the province. Its banks are studded with small farms, some of them now sadly boarded up and abandoned, and quiet villages with wooden houses and churches.

The river crossings provide some of the most characteristic features of the New Brunswick scene. Narrow stretches are crossed by covered bridges, which, with their ridged roofs, look rather like long, narrow barns. Elsewhere ferries—some of them operated by the passenger himself—are the usual means of crossing the rivers.

SOME SUPERSTITIONS

In the past the New Brunswick people had a tradition of being superstitious by nature, possibly because of the proximity of the forest, always pregnant with mystery. It is said that sometimes, near a river, a green light arises out of the ground, and that anyone who is unfortunate enough to see it is doomed to die.

In the New Brunswick folklore there are tales of strange beasts in the forests and of buried treasure, as well as Indian tales of the god Glooscap, who is said to have caused most of the natural phenomena to be seen in the province.

CRADLED-ON-THE-WAVES

Prince Edward Island, the smallest of Canada's provinces, is something of a rural paradise. The Indians' name for the island is *Abegweit,* which is translated as "cradled-on-the-waves," a suitably poetic description for this peaceful region.

The people of Prince Edward Island are overwhelmingly dependent on the land for their livelihood, and this alone makes the island distinct from the other Atlantic provinces. The white-painted, high-gabled farmhouses sit in a landscape of luxuriant green meadows and rich red soil. The people themselves are generally hardworking and thrifty. They take great pride in their idyllic way of life.

A HORSE-BREEDING CENTER

Prince Edward Island has long been a center for the breeding of horses. The horse, as a working animal, has now been superseded by machinery, and more emphasis has been laid on the breeding of horses for harness-racing. Visits to fairs and local races are popular pastimes of the Islanders. The best known of the fairs is during Old Home Week held at Charlottetown, the provincial capital. Charlottetown is proud of its historical role in the creation of the Canadian nation and in 1964 held a Centennial Celebration to commemorate the meeting of the first Confederation conference.

The picturesque fishing village of Harbourville nestles snugly in a forested curve along the Bay of Fundy. The neat little community is on the shore route of the Annapolis Valley, famed for its apples and other fruit. Most of the people of this region are descended from the United Empire Loyalists who emigrated from the United States after the American War of Independence.

THE NEWFOUNDLANDERS

The people of Newfoundland, Canada's first-discovered but most recently acquired province, are mainly of English or Irish stock. Their accent is closest to that of the Irish, although it is as unmistakably unique as the character of their language, their place-names and their folk songs.

FISHING COMMUNITIES

For nearly 500 years the main source of livelihood for the people of Newfoundland was provided by the vast supplies of cod teeming in the seas around their island. Although they are now feeling the effects of modern transport and communication, the fishing communities' way of life has not been greatly changed.

The fishermen live in so-called outports. These are villages, each of which is situated on its own bay or cove. Until the introduction of modern forms of communication, the only means of contact between the villages was the sea.

The outport consists of a few houses scattered on the steep, rugged shore. A twisting path leads down to the shore with its "stations," in which the cod are stored and dried, and its moored boats.

Poor and lonely though the Newfoundland outports may seem, some of their names—Heart's Content, Thankful Hearts and Happy Adventure—suggest how welcome a sight they were to the fishermen returning from their conflict with the elements. The life of the cod-fishermen is still hard, and Newfoundland is still the poorest of the Canadian provinces.

Life in Ontario

Ontario is Canada's most prosperous province. Not only does it contain the largest proportion of the country's industries, it is also foremost in agriculture and in the production of valuable minerals, such as gold, uranium, nickel and copper.

This province has a strong American character. Its original settlers—who set a pattern in social behavior, architecture and a whole style of living—came not from the Old World, but from the 13 Colonies

This well-kept homestead is typical of the dwellings on Prince Edward Island. In addition to the rich lobster and oyster beds on its ocean shore, the fertile soil and emerald-green fields of Prince Edward Island have earned for the province the title "Million Acre Farm." The industrious population is about equally divided between Scottish, English, Irish and Acadian descendants.

to the south. They were United Empire Loyalists who left the Colonies after the American War of Independence, bringing to the largely unopened regions of the north generations of experience of life in the New World.

These first settlers quickly discovered the fertile lands of Ontario and the communication highways provided by the many rivers. More Americans soon moved north, and they were followed, in the 1820s, by the first large waves of immigrants from Britain. Not long thereafter came the many Irish who left Ireland as a result of the great potato famine of the 1840s.

Most of the immigrants from other European countries have come to Ontario during the 20th century, although an important community of Germans—Pennsylvania Dutch, as they are known—settled in one of the most fertile regions early in the province's history. Since World War II immigrants have arrived in large numbers from Germany, Poland, Holland, Italy, Hungary and other European countries.

RURAL ONTARIO

More than 70 per cent of the present-day population of Ontario is urban-dwelling, but there is still a large farm population.

Farming in Ontario is highly mechanized, except in several isolated Mennonite and Amish communities, notably in Waterloo County. Ontario farmers are generally prosperous, and the carefully tended fields and orchards reflect their well-ordered industry.

As in other fruit-growing areas of Canada, blossom-time in May is celebrated as a festival in the Niagara region. At this season thousands of sightseers flock from the towns to enjoy the spectacle of the trees in full blossom.

In the 19th century the farmers of Ontario were among the wealthiest and most influential people of the province. From this period date the large wooden farmhouses and the red-brick farmhouse-mansions still to be seen in the Ontario countryside.

THE CANADIAN CAPITAL

Situated in Ontario but scarcely typical of the province is Ottawa, the capital city of Canada. Ottawa has been described as a city of civil servants, and although it still retains a little of its flavor as a frontier lumber town, a great part of its population is employed in government offices.

On the east coast of Nova Scotia are many rocky reefs and headlands. Numerous small fishing villages have sprung up to fish the teeming Atlantic waters of the Maritime Provinces. The life of the fishermen is still hard, and the lonely outports in which they live usually consist of a few houses scattered on the steep, rugged shore.

TORONTO

Toronto, with a population of nearly two million, is the metropolitan center of Ontario, and increasingly it is becoming the center of all English Canada.

Toronto has been traditionally a city of Empire Loyalists, Protestant in religion and Conservative in politics.

However, with the large influx of European immigrants the picture has changed completely, and Toronto is almost half Roman Catholic, has a large Jewish population and is no longer predominantly British in its ethnic origins.

One of the nicknames given to this city is "Toronto the Good," derived from its strict Victorian observance of the Sabbath and its restrictive liquor and entertainment laws prevalent until recent years.

Toronto now, however, is one of the great jazz and popular music entertainment centers of North America and has a wide variety of entertainment bars and coffee houses. Toronto is also the center of English-language publishing and network television and radio production in Canada, and the metropolis for Canadian artists and the arts. Its superb new city hall is a symbol of its vitality and of a civic

Above: *Dressed in traditional costume, a couple zestfully performs a Ukrainian dance during a folk festival. One of the many peoples who settled the Prairies, the Ukrainians brought with them a love of the land and a willingness to work hard for a new life. Some Ukrainians still preserve their own language and customs.*

Below: *Determination and strong character come through in this portrait of a Prairie farmer. Although early immigration to Canada had been mainly from France, first, and then the British Isles, the opening of the Prairie wheatlands attracted immigrants from many other European areas—the Ukraine, Austro-Hungary, Germany, Scandinavia and Iceland. The wheat farmers of the Plains are thus of very mixed origin and many different cultural backgrounds.*

consciousness that makes it an attractive place to live.

Life in the Prairie Provinces

The three so-called Prairie Provinces—Manitoba, Saskatchewan and Alberta—are known chiefly as wheat-growing lands, and it was indeed the fertility of their rich soil that was responsible for the unparalleled swift development of the region at the beginning of the 20th century.

It should be remembered, however, that large areas of the Prairie Provinces are not, in fact, prairie. In the west of Alberta is the mountain country of the Rockies, and northern Manitoba and Saskatchewan have vast tracts of forest and tundra.

Today the economy of the Prairies is no longer so dependent on wheat. Alberta has always been an important cattle region, and in the last two decades a new source of revenue has been found in oil. As a result of the growth of commerce and industry that has accompanied the discovery of oil, the Prairie Provinces also have experienced the drift to the towns that is occurring in all parts of Canada.

PRAIRIE PEOPLE

The people of the Prairie Provinces—particularly the farmers and ranchers—have their own individual character, born of the environment and the difficulties encountered by their pioneering grandfathers. Their most endearing characteristic is a spontaneous hospitality and eagerness to assist their neighbors and visitors to their country. These were the qualities that enabled the pioneers to endure the hardships of the first Prairie settlement, when loneliness, made more intense by the vast empty spaces, could be a threat to sanity. They also helped farmers to survive the dreadful period of the drought in the 1930s, which crippled the Prairies.

Another characteristic of the Prairie people is their love for their own land. Many who leave the Prairies to live in other provinces of Canada are never completely happy away from the open spaces and the atmosphere of freedom in which they grew up.

THE WHEAT FARMERS

The first discovery of the Prairie wheatlands in the late 19th century attracted multitudes of settlers, not only from the British Isles but from the Ukraine, Austro-Hungary, Germany, Scandinavia and Iceland. The wheat farmers are thus of very mixed origin.

The average Prairie wheat farm consists of a square mile of land and is today highly mechanized. An increasing number of farmers now work on their property only during the times of seeding and harvest, spending the rest of the year in the towns.

THE HUTTERITES

Since the first settlement of the Prairies, groups of immigrants from various parts of Europe have chosen to form exclusive communities there. They include Ukrainians and Icelanders, who still preserve their own languages and customs. Perhaps most interesting of such communities are those of the Hutterites, a branch of the Mennonite sect, which has a fairly large following in Canada.

THE COMMUNAL LIFE

The Hutterites, who originated in Tyrol and Moravia in the 16th century, first came to Canada in 1918. They believe in a communal life, in which all property is shared, meals are taken in common and children are cared for in a communal kindergarten. In a *Bruderhof* (a Hutterite communal farm) the affairs of the community are controlled by the *Wirt* (household head), who is elected by the members. The work is carefully organized, each department being put in charge of one person, who must then distribute the various tasks and ensure that they are carried out.

Hutterite farming is efficient. The farmers have no prejudice against machinery and make use of up-to-date equipment. Each community is virtually self-supporting, only such goods as salt, leather and machinery having to be acquired outside.

ALBERTA. CATTLE RANCHERS

Among the most prosperous people of the Prairie Provinces are the cattle ranchers of Alberta, whose domain is in the foothills of the Rockies. Today, life on a cattle ranch bears a closer relationship to the traditional life of the plains than does the life of the wheat farmers. Spending much of their time in the saddle, the ranchers resemble the Indians of former times, who hunted the buffalo (now practically extinct in the Prairies) on horseback.

Space is of paramount importance in ranching, and some of the ranches are as large as 50,000 acres. The rancher is thus relatively isolated. Since the distance from the nearest market is inevitably great, it is often necessary to store enough supplies to last a month or more at a time.

In the hilly country of the cattle ranches the horse is still the most practical form of transport and is an indispensable item of equipment. Manpower, too, is of importance, for no machine has yet been devised to round up the cattle.

Toronto citizens board one of the city's modern subway trains. Toronto in the past was a city of United Empire Loyalists, Protestant in religion and Conservative in politics. However, steady immigration has so changed the composition of this thriving metropolis that now the city is about half Roman Catholic, with a large Jewish population. As a result of this ethnic diversity and its dynamic tempo, the metropolitan center attracts more immigrants yearly than any other community.

THE CALGARY STAMPEDE

The town of Calgary, in which a yearly festival is held, epitomizes the cattle country of Alberta. Visitors to the annual Stampede, which has been called "the Greatest Outdoor Show on Earth," come not merely from all parts of Canada, but also from the United States and Mexico.

During Stampede Week the symbol of the show, the white Stetson hat, is seen everywhere, and full cowboy dress is common. The Indians of the reserves dress in the glory of their traditional costumes to perform their tribal dances and take part in the displays of horsemanship.

RODEO AND CARNIVAL

The Stampede combines the excitement of a rodeo with the gaiety and pageantry of a carnival. It opens with a grand parade through the streets of Calgary. Indians on horseback, cowboys and their girls in wagons, "Mounties" (members of the Royal Canadian Mounted Police) in red jackets, wide-brimmed hats and knee boots, all bring back the color of the old days in the West.

Rodeo events include feats of horsemanship, wagon races, in which wagons are loaded as they were in the days of the Prairie pioneers, and tests of cowboy skills.

WINNIPEG

Like all the important cities of Canada, Winnipeg, the capital of Manitoba and home of almost half the population of the province, has its own atmosphere and character.

Today Winnipeg is a city of many ethnic groups, but its Scottish foundation is unmistakable. It has the highest Jewish population per capita in North America, and it is a world center of Ukrainian culture. The informality of the early settler days survives in social exchanges, and the people have the same friendly attitude toward strangers as have the farmers of the more remote regions. It is also, however, a cultural center, enthusiastically promoting the theater, ballet and literature.

The thundering chuckwagon race, one of the events of the Calgary Stampede. The annual Calgary Exhibition and Stampede, a combination rodeo and carnival, reflects the cattle and cowboy background of Calgary, Alberta. In the hilly country of the province, the horse is still the most practical form of transport. Ranchers, as they did in the old West, spend much of their time in the saddle far from the markets and towns.

CALGARY STAMPEDE
P
N

Life in British Columbia

British Columbians like to think that they are different from other Canadians, and certainly the mountain barrier to the east virtually isolates this province from the rest of the country. British Columbia tends to look toward Asia and the west coast of the United States rather than toward the lands of the Canadian east.

The majority of British Columbians are Canadian-born and of British descent. At one time the province was a favorite place for retired British army personnel, but this era is now past; few native Britons now settle in this part of Canada, although many Canadians, particularly from the prairies, retire here. Minority groups in British Columbia include the native Indians (more numerous per capita here than in any other province), the Doukhobors, who are members of a Ukrainian sect, and the Asians. There are also many Portuguese, Scandinavians, Germans and Dutch.

THE DOUKHOBORS

British Columbia's most famous minority group are the Doukhobors, who number about 12,000. A small segment of these, the so-called Sons of Freedom, who refuse to accept any form of secular authority, constitute a social problem.

The Doukhobors, who separated from the Russian Orthodox Church 300 years ago, first came to Canada in 1897, settling in Saskatchewan. Since then many, including the most dissident elements, have moved into British Columbia.

Originally the Doukhobors were pacifists; rejecting all violence and all material values, they believed in a communal life. They were led by outstanding individuals who were regarded by their followers as semi-divine.

THE SONS OF FREEDOM

Today the majority of Doukhobors, while retaining their language, culture and religion, have adjusted, as far as possible, to the Canadian way of life.

Only the Sons of Freedom cling to the old principles, resisting authority in such matters as the compulsory education of their children and the registration of births, marriages and deaths. One of their most famous forms of protest is that of stripping themselves naked, a unique type of passive resistance. Less passive is their occasional practice of setting fire to public and private property.

A swarming cargo of herring is taken on board a packer ship. Although commercial fishing is generally the business of the Indians in this area, other fishermen are quite active in the waters off British Columbia and Vancouver Island. In a region rich in many resources—the earliest settlements prospered in the fur trade—the people have traditionally engaged in lumbering, mining, farming and cattle raising.

LUMBERJACKS IN THE PAST

One of the archetypal figures of Canada is the lumberjack, who is particularly associated with British Columbia. For half the year, during the winter, he lived in the forest in a primitive lumber camp, deprived of the company of women and feeding on a monotonous diet of salt pork and baked beans. After such a period of deprivation it was small wonder that the lumberjack lived riotously on his return from the forest in the spring.

Methods of working were primitive and dangerous. Two men would attack the trunk of a huge tree, several hundred years old, with axes and saws. Mounted on "springboards," 12 feet above the ground, they would patiently chop at either side of the trunk until the tree was ready to fall. The accident rate was high, and diseases such as typhoid and smallpox bred easily in the unsanitary lumber camps.

MODERN LUMBERJACKS

In former times the loggers, after felling one section of forest, simply moved on to another. Today these destructive methods have been replaced by scientific "tree farming," by which complete denudation of forest areas is counteracted by careful planting of new trees.

Mechanized equipment has revolutionized felling methods, and the revolution has also spread to the sorting and movement of logs in the river at the spring thaw. Once a task carried out by nimble-footed "drivers," it is now performed with the aid of "boom-scooters," small boats which push and pull the logs in the required direction.

LIFE ON THE LAND

British Columbia is famous for its fish-packed rivers and seacoast, and commercial fishing is particularly the business of the Indians.

Farming, on the other hand, is the province of the settlers. Like the Prairie Provinces on the other side of the Rockies, British Columbia possesses both wheatlands and cattle country.

British Columbian cattle ranches are often even larger than those of Alberta, especially in the wild northern Cariboo country.

The orchard region of the Okanagan valley is unique to British Columbia. Most of its people are of

A dairy farm of Courtenay, British Columbia. The rugged mountainous terrain of the province tended in the past to give the people a feeling of isolation from the events and activities of the rest of Canada. Because of this, it was not unusual for the citizens of British Columbia to feel a greater connection to the West Coast of the United States than to the other provinces of Canada.

British descent, but other settlers came from Germany, Belgium and, more recently, Portugal.

VANCOUVER AND VICTORIA

If Vancouver has many of the characteristics of a big prosperous North American city, Victoria, the provincial capital, is a tourist's "English" city. Until recently Victoria was indeed the refuge of retired British people, who found in the surrounding landscape and the gentle climate a reminder of their own Devon and Cornwall.

The elderly Englishwoman, dressed in tweeds and serving afternoon tea, and her husband, who grew roses and wrote letters to the London *Times*, have almost vanished from Victoria, but their legend lives on. The Englishness of Victoria survives as a tourist attraction and a lure for Canadians who wish to retire to a mild climate and the most English city in Canada.

LEISURE IN CANADA

In Canada it is always possible, even for city-dwellers, to escape easily into virtually untouched sections of countryside. The presence of these empty spaces has, to a large extent, molded the leisure activities of the Canadians, and new immigrants quickly acquire the Canadian passion for the outdoor life.

Back to Nature

Every summer weekend it is a custom in Canada for many families to pack supplies into their automobile and set off for a cottage on one of Canada's thousands of lakes. It is still possible, in so extensive and sparsely populated a country, to buy land for a very small sum, and many people do this so that they may build a house away from the clamor of the city.

LOG CABINS AND MODERN COTTAGES

Those weekenders in whom the pioneering spirit is strongest sometimes emulate their forefathers and build a log cabin in the traditional manner. The less ambitious follow "do-it-yourself" plans and build themselves a cottage in the modern style.

Some cottagers still pride themselves on living a relatively primitive mode of life while they are there. Cooking is often carried out over wood fires, and washing in cold water is a rule for many. The daily activities are traditionally Canadian —canoeing, fishing, hunting and exploring. But more recently motorboating has become very popular and most cottages now have electricity and many of the conveniences of city living.

HOLIDAY LODGES

A common way of spending a summer holiday in Canada is to stay at a summer resort hotel or in a holiday lodge, some of which are situated in the country's vast national parks. At these lodges each family has its own cabin. Cooking facilities are sometimes provided, but many lodges have a communal dining-room for guests. The atmosphere is informal and friendly, and the peace and beauty of the surroundings are ideal for relaxation. Trailer parks are popular, as is camping in the provincial parks.

SPORT

Most Canadians are sports enthusiasts. Since 1948 three "halls of fame" have been established to honor the deeds of great Canadian

Canadians have always been sports enthusiasts, and Canada's climate offers a rich variety of sports during every season of the year. Although lacrosse, which was learned from the Indians, is the official game of Canada, ice hockey probably ranks as the national sport. Popular recreational activities include golf, cricket, curling (shown here), basketball, football, skiing, camping and all types of water sports.

athletes. The Canadian Amateur Athletic Hall of Fame is controlled by a committee of the Amateur Athletic Union of Canada, and the first names, enrolled in 1949, were Canadian gold medalists of the Olympic games. Canada's Sports Hall of Fame was founded at the Canadian National Exhibition, Toronto, in 1955. A national selection committee, composed of sports writers and broadcasters, including one member from each province, chooses names representative of professional as well as amateur achievement. In 1957 the Canadian National Exhibition devoted a room to hockey, separate from the Sports Hall of Fame.

ICE HOCKEY

Although lacrosse, learned from the Indian, is officially Canada's national game, ice hockey is really the national sport, played by both French Canadians and English Canadians, by professional teams and by thousands of lads aspiring to belong to either the famed Montreal Canadiens or Toronto Maple Leafs or another of the National Hockey League teams (now all in American cities). Amateur leagues exist right up to the Arctic. Canada, which formed its Amateur Hockey Association in 1887, was the first country to organize the sport on any scale. Today millions watch the games of the National Hockey League on television, and tickets to the games are always at a premium. Members of the professional teams are national heroes and have the admiration of Canadians of all ages.

OTHER SPORTS

Golf is gaining great popularity in Canada, and municipally operated courses have made it possible for more and more people to spend summer days on the golf course for a nominal fee. A few Canadians have gained top places on the professional circuit. Baseball is popular, although not as passionately so as with the Americans to the south. Football rivals hockey for fans' enthusiasm, and the climax of the organized football season is Grey Cup Day, when the top teams of East and West meet. The day is noted for the festivities of the thousands of fans, and the celebrations include the Grey Cup Parade through the main streets of the chosen city.

Other popular sports in Canada include curling, lawn and alley bowling, badminton, tennis, basketball, water skiing, sailing, horse racing, fishing (both in summer and in the winter, through the ice), sports car racing, and skating (both ice and roller). It is a rare Canadian who does not both enjoy watching organized sport and also have a favorite sport in which he himself indulges frequently.

That most English of institutions, cricket, is played across Canada but particularly in Vancouver and Victoria, and the European immigrants to central Canada have made soccer a popular game in the large cities.

FOOD AND DRINK

THE DEVELOPMENT OF A CANADIAN cuisine is a little like that of the Canadian identity. There is the distinctly French cuisine with its delicious recipes, the more conservative English dishes and those combining methods and recipes from several inheritances. The American influence shows in the ubiquity of such items as Southern fried chicken, hot dogs and hamburgers. Sophistication in food and drink has developed as the nation has grown from a pioneer wilderness to a predominantly urban community. Home cooking is still the most accepted fare in most small communities, although one successful Toronto restaurant now advertises: "If you like home cooking, stay at home."

In the 19th century, the hardworking man of the land ate a standard breakfast of meat, fried potatoes, sometimes porridge, and bread, and he drank tea or milk. Hunts yielded game for rarer foods such as stuffed beaver and lynx or squirrel stew. The lumbermen ate pork and beans and flapjacks smothered with black molasses.

In Confederation years, the main meal, dinner, was eaten at noon, and the evening meal was supper. As the century progressed, the English custom of afternoon tea became fashionable, and many ate a light meal at lunch. By this time bacon and various cold meats were introduced, along with coffee, and cocktails made with whisky, bitters, sugar and water.

It was, and in many instances still is, the fact that the menu depended on the natural conditions of the area. Fresh fruit was plentiful in the south but fresh fish was not, and the opposite was true in the north.

The French have always made better use of spices, herbs and wines in their cooking than have the English. It has been said that cheap spirits in the pioneer days deterred the English from using wines. At the time of Confederation, as much rye whisky as one could consume could be had for five cents, and some stores even had an open barrel with a dipper hanging beside it as an accommodation for their customers. The early Canadians were hard drinkers, and the Temperance Movement and restrictive liquor laws that followed were a reaction to such customs.

It is interesting to note that dining trains began in Canada. The Great Western Railway converted a car into a "hotel" or "palace" car in 1867, the forerunner of the modern dining car.

Canadian foods and dishes for which the country is famous are the maple syrup of Quebec and Ontario; the blueberries and apples of the Maritimes; the fiddleheads of New Brunswick (curled ferns cooked as a vegetable); the summer sausage, liverwurst, *schmier kase*, doughnuts, apple cider and other Mennonite and Pennsylvania Dutch foods of Waterloo County, Ontario; the Arctic char; the Winnipeg goldeye; the Brome Lake duckling; Ingersoll and Black Diamond cheddar cheeses; and French Canadian pea soup.

A French Canadian woman of Île aux Coudres prepares a repast on the family's decorative wood-burning stove. The development of Canadian cuisine parallels that of Canadian history in general. It ranges from distinctly French food with its use of herbs, spices and wines, to the more conservative dishes of the English, and to methods borrowed from each as well as from other ethnic groups. The American influence shows up in such items as Southern fried chicken, hamburgers and hot dogs.

THE HISTORY

Presented to the people of Iceland by the U.S. Congress in 1932, this bold statue in Reykjavik commemorates the great Viking Leif Ericsson, who may have landed in America when his ship was blown off course on a voyage from Norway to Greenland in 1000 A.D.

THE DISCOVERY OF CANADA

The Norsemen

SOME TIME AFTER THE END OF THE ice age, Asian peoples began to cross the Bering Straits from the eastern tip of Siberia. Over the next 20,000 years, they spread through North and South America. Among these were the nomadic tribes who were the first inhabitants of the vast country that is Canada.

The Norse Vikings were the first Europeans to discover Canada. Although their reputation for being merely barbaric pirates still persists, the Vikings were, in fact, a civilized people who were building a commercial empire stretching from the Baltic to the Black Sea, and from the Baltic westward to the Scottish Hebrides and Iceland. They discovered Canada by accident.

ERIC THE RED

In 982 Eric the Red discovered Greenland, and there he created a small settlement. Although he was considered a violent and restless man, even for those times, he settled there happily and brought up his sons, including Leif, later known as Leif the Lucky. According to the Icelandic "Saga of Eric the Red," it was Leif Ericsson who discovered Canada about A.D. 1000, while returning from a visit to Norway. After losing his bearings below Iceland, Leif sailed on blindly until he came to the shores of a land where grapes and wheat were growing wild.

THORFINN AND HIS CHILD

On his return to Greenland, an expedition was mounted under the leadership of Thorfinn Karlsefni, whose reputation for being an excellent navigator made him the obvious choice for heading the expedition. On the voyage one ship gave up and returned home, but Thorfinn pressed on until they came to shores that resembled the country Leif had described. By many scholars it is believed to be on or near the Gulf of St. Lawrence.

Thorfinn and his companions settled there, raising livestock and cultivating crops. Unfortunately for the colony, they were constantly harried by hostile natives, who made uneasy co-sharers of the new land the Norsemen had discovered. In 1006 Thorfinn was finally forced to abandon the settlement. The Vikings returned to Greenland, taking with them Thorfinn's one-year-old son, Snorri, the first European child to be born in North America.

Although they were the first European discoverers of Canada, the Norsemen played no part in the development of the country, for they never settled there again; but it is likely they visited it to load their ships with timber.

Columbus and Cabot

Although European sailors looking for new fisheries may have reached Newfoundland earlier, the age of European awareness of the New World began in 1492 when Christopher Columbus left the port of Palos, Spain, to seek out a westerly route to the Indies. Two months later, his three ships sighted land and Columbus set foot on one of the offshore islands of North America, in what is now the West Indies.

Five years later, in 1497, the Venetian mariner and navigator John Cabot explored the northeastern point of Cape Breton Island. He returned in the following year on behalf of English (Bristol) merchants, who had underwritten the cost of the expedition in the hope that he would discover new lands where they could trade. He was also armed with a charter from the English king, Henry VII, which authorized him to occupy, annex and govern the new lands for the Crown. But the trip was not regarded as a success, since Cabot was looking for a passage to the lands of the Great Khan and the trade of the Far East.

In the early 16th century the fishing fleets of Europe were frequenting the banks off Newfoundland, the favorite breeding places of the cod, for which there was a regular market. Unlike meat, which deteriorated rapidly, cod could be salted, dried and stored away. Portuguese and French vessels in particular came in great numbers every summer.

Jacques Cartier

Important as the early voyages were, they do not compare with the three voyages made between 1534 and 1541 by Jacques Cartier, the first European to sail up the St. Lawrence and explore the interior of Canada.

The French monarch Francis I had already sent the Italian navigator, Giovanni da Verazzano, to explore the North American coast in 1524, and this resulted in Verazzano's ascertaining that the New World was not a series of islands but a vast continent. Ten years later, in 1534, Francis sponsored another voyage led by the sea captain from Brittany, Jacques Cartier, to look for a northwest passage through North America to the East. Sailing from St. Malo, Cartier's first voyage took him through the Strait of Belle Ile and into the Gulf, along the west coast of Newfoundland. Cartier's first impressions of the country were unfavorable. The vista of stones and rugged rocks and the lack of soil led him to call it the land that God gave to Cain. The hostile and savage natives also dismayed him. He de-

Jacques Cartier (1495-1557), a French navigator, discovered the St. Lawrence River and was the first to sail into the interior of the continent. Between 1534 and 1541 he made three trips to the New World seeking a northwest passage to the Orient. These voyages and explorations by Cartier firmly established France's claim to the region of the St. Lawrence.

scribes them in his diary as having their hair tied up on top of their heads like a handful of twisted hay, "with a nail or something of the sort passed through the middle." He also noted that they clothed themselves with the furs of animals.

These unfavorable impressions were mitigated when he sailed around the southern and western parts of the Gulf of St. Lawrence; there he found trees, meadows and fields with self-sown oats, gooseberry bushes and strawberry vines. Seeking a passage to China, he gradually headed north until he came to the great bay that now separates New Brunswick from Quebec. Because of the summer heat he encountered, he named it Chaleur Bay. He spent several days on the Gaspé Peninsula, where he raised a large wooden cross bearing the words "Long Live The King of France." He met Indians from up river whose tales convinced him that the St. Lawrence was the northwest passage he sought. He took two of them back to France with him in the fall, determined to return the following year and explore the passage to the west.

On his second voyage, in 1535, Cartier explored the St. Lawrence River as far as the Indian village of Hochelaga, now Montreal, and went up Mount Royal. He wintered at Stadacona (now Quebec). On his return to France in 1536, he found the French king at war and uninterested in pursuing another voyage immediately.

When he set off for the third time in 1541, it was with the goal of colonizing. He was associated with a nobleman, Sieur de Roberval, who had been appointed commander-in-chief and also viceroy of New France. This was to be not just a voyage to seek out the reported mineral wealth of Canada, but to found a French settlement in the New World.

Cartier left before Roberval. The small settlement that he established above Quebec was not a success, any more than was the one established in 1542 by Roberval. Cold, scurvy and famine killed off many of the colonists, and the remainder finally abandoned the settlement.

Internal struggles and European wars kept France preoccupied for the rest of the century. But a claim to Canada was now established that would be taken up later.

FRENCH CANADA

FOR THE NEXT 60 YEARS THERE WAS no serious attempt to colonize the St. Lawrence valley. On the other hand, Frenchmen had begun to turn their eyes in the direction of the fur trade. The new felting process in the manufacture of hats now provided a steady market, and the fur traders began to concentrate on the beaver, which was to become the major reason for the growth of the trade.

Samuel de Champlain

With civil peace restored, France again gave serious thought to colonizing the country, and in 1603 a Royal Monopoly passed to a company that included Samuel de Champlain (c. 1567-1635), who was to become known as the Father of New France. The company was to have a monopoly of the fur trade in return for establishing a settlement.

Champlain was the ideal man to be involved in a project of this nature. He had been a sailor and a professional soldier; he was determined to find his destiny in the new world. He set sail on March 9, 1603, on an exploratory trip to seek out a suitable site for the colony. Further explorations during the following year, when Champlain was joined by the Sieur de Monts (c. 1560-1630), who had become the holder of the Royal Monopoly, led him to make the first settlement on the Bay of Fundy. It was a severe winter and a hard period for the settlers. They were short of drinking water and forced to drink snow water and feed only on salt meat. This diet caused a violent outbreak of scurvy, and many of the settlers died.

In the spring of 1605 the settlement was moved to Port Royal, which was to be, through many

For some 60 years after Cartier's last trip there was no serious attempt on the part of the French to colonize the St. Lawrence Valley. However, the vast virgin forests and the many rivers and streams sheltered countless fur-bearing animals. In Europe there was demand for these furs, and a new felting process in the manufacture of hats provided additional markets. It was this growth in the fur trade that began to attract Frenchmen to the New World.

vicissitudes, the early center of French history and interest in Acadia.

FOUNDING OF QUEBEC

In 1608 Champlain established a trading post on the site where formerly had stood the Indian village of Stadacona, the settlement known to Cartier, which had been destroyed in the meantime by inter-tribal wars. From this site grew the city of Quebec, named from the Indian word *Kebec*, "a narrowing of the waters."

EXPLORING WESTWARD

In the spring of 1609, Champlain received bad news from France when he learned that his backers' interest for the project was waning. But, reluctantly, they agreed to continue it for another year. Champlain now decided to explore the land westward and learn more about its potentialities, while making friends and allies of the Indians, which would ensure a steady flow of furs and make his investors happy. Leaving Quebec, he started out on the first of a series of remarkable journeys of exploration that took him as far west as the great freshwater sea of Georgian Bay and Lake Huron.

YEARS OF TRIUMPH AND DISASTER

For the next 20 years, Samuel de Champlain devoted all his energies to establishing a colony of France in the New World and to the conversion of the Indians to Christianity. On his death-bed in 1635, at the age of 65, he could look back on years of triumph and disaster.

He had made friends of the Algonquins and the Hurons and had given them official French support in their struggle with the Iroquois. He had explored vast areas of the country and recorded on paper a tremendous amount of information that has made it possible for historians to obtain a clear picture of this particular phase of Canadian history. He had seen the arrival of the Récollet priests and the Jesuits. On the reverse side of the coin, he had seen his country at war with England and the surrender of his beloved Quebec to the British. Fortunately, he had also lived to see it returned to France.

Champlain has been criticized for involving official French support in the tribal battles against the Iroquois. This inspired in them a deep-seated hatred of the French, with the result that they gave active support to the British in the wars that were to follow. But he deserves nothing but credit for his unswerving devotion to the cause of creating a French colony on the American continent and bringing to the New World the civilization of France, often in the face of violent opposition from traders and merchants, who were concerned only with making profits out of the country. He was truly the father of New France and the first great man in Canadian history.

The Company of One Hundred Associates

At first it seemed as if Champlain's visionary concept of a great French colony in France was to have the full support of those at home. This certainly was the intention of Cardinal Richelieu (1585-1642) when he, as chief minister of France, formed, in 1627, an organization known as the Company of One Hundred Associates. The company included people from all walks of life, including the clergy.

For the sum of 3000 *livres*, each member was to have the distinction of belonging to a company that had exclusive rights for 15 years to the entire trade of the colony, with the exception of the coastal fisheries. No duty was to be charged on the goods they imported to France; in return the Associates were committed to send 300 settlers to Canada each year. They were to support the settlers for three years and provide each community with three priests.

War with England

Unhappily for the settlers who were already there, King Charles I of England declared war on France just as the first French ships were making their first journey to Canada under the provisions laid down by Richelieu. They were attacked in Gaspé Bay and surrendered immediately. Quebec also surrendered.

This brief war ended in 1629, and Canada was officially handed back to France by the Treaty of St. Ger-

The stockade of Port Royal, Nova Scotia. In 1604, with the Sieur de Monts, who had received a Royal Monopoly for trade, Champlain established a colony on the Bay of Fundy at the mouth of the St. Croix River. After a disastrous winter the settlement was transferred across the bay to Port Royal. The colony was the center of French activity over the next few years.

Jesuit missionaries were the pioneers of a Church that played a powerful role in forming the culture of French Canada. The first missionaries worked mostly in the wilderness, living with the Indians. In Metropolitan France itself, the Jesuits were instrumental in keeping alive a considerable interest in the colony, which led to the sending of much-needed supplies and gifts. One of the most important achievements of the Church was the establishment of an educational system, including the 17th-century Jesuit school in Quebec (shown here).

main-en-Laye, signed in 1632. By then, the Company of One Hundred Associates was on the verge of bankrupty. Although it managed to struggle on, it became even more clear as time went by that the project was a failure. This was principally because of the greed of its members, who had failed to carry out the provisions laid down by Richelieu.

The First Iroquois Wars

Champlain's work of colonizing the settlement had been seriously hampered by the warring Indian tribes. In 1624 he had concluded a treaty with the Iroquois, by which it was agreed to maintain peace between France and her Indian allies on the one hand, and the Iroquois on the other. Hostilities between the tribes, however, repeatedly flared up, and inter-tribal affrays continued until Dutch merchants began trading with them around 1639. When the Dutch started issuing firearms to the Iroquois in exchange for beaver pelts, economic rivalries were added to the age-old hatreds between the tribes.

Inter-tribal battles and attacks on Europeans made it clear that a very serious situation was brewing for the colony. By 1649 the Iroquois had defeated the Hurons and wiped out the Jesuit missions in Huronia and were also astride the Ottawa River as well as the Richelieu and the St. Lawrence. The saintly Jesuits Jean de Brébeuf and Gabriel Lalemant had been cruelly murdered.

To counteract the Iroquois threat, the French had made Montreal one of their major defensive positions. Nevertheless, by 1660 it seemed that the situation would soon be out of control.

Intervention of Le Roi Soleil

By this time the government at home had awakened to its responsibilities towards New France. Louis XIV, Le Roi Soleil (The Sun King, 1638-1715), gained strong control over the French state, with Jean Baptiste Colbert (1619-83) as his chief minister. Between them they brought about a new era in the affairs of the colony.

Its government was reorganized as a department of France, with three officials, the governor, the intendant and the bishop; the first two derived their authority from the government in Paris, and each was responsible to that government. The work of the great Intendant Jean Talon is discussed below, but first the role of the Church will be examined.

The Roman Catholic Church in French Canada

The historical nature of New France, and indeed French Canada as it exists today, cannot be understood without awareness of the part the Roman Catholic Church played in its formation. The first four Récollet missionaries came to New France at the request of Champlain in 1615. Ten years later, in 1625, three Jesuits reached the new mission field. These missionaries were the pioneers of a Church which played the most powerful part in forming the culture of French Canada, giving it a character that exists to the present.

The first missionaries worked mostly in the wilderness, living like the Indians under conditions of extreme hardship. In 1648 the missions they had established in Huronia were attacked by their converts' enemies, the Iroquois; the mission stations were destroyed and the missionaries tortured and put to death.

In Metropolitan France the Jesuit missionaries kept alive a widespread interest in the colony. This inspired the sending of vital relief and gifts, as well as more missionaries, and induced many people from all trades and backgrounds to seek their fortunes in Canada. Much was done through the publication of the *Relations*, the Jesuits' reports to their superiors in France. The Jesuits were able to begin formal education of Indian boys as early as 1635 in Quebec, as were the Ursuline nuns for girls under Marie de l'Incarnation after her arrival in 1639.

The establishment of an education-

The monument to the Father of New France, Samuel de Champlain (1567-1635), on Nepean Point, Ottawa. In 1603 Champlain made his first journey to New France as a member of a fur-trading expedition. Two years later he established a colony at Port Royal, Nova Scotia; in 1608 he moved inland and founded the settlement of Quebec. Champlain's explorations carried him as far west as Georgian Bay. His later years were devoted entirely to the welfare of the colonists.

al system was perhaps the most important task, apart from the pastoral functions of the Church. And the foundations of this system were laid by the Jesuits, who, besides being priests, were trained teachers. The Jesuit school in Quebec was to develop into a college which taught the classical languages, philosophy, theology and mathematics. Standards were high, and, despite the difficulties of communications, schools spread throughout New France and during the 18th century rose to nearly 50 in number. An ever-increasing proportion of the French clergy began to be occupied in missionary work in Canada. But soon a native French-Canadian clergy had been created, and by the end of the 17th century stone churches and other substantial religious buildings were already springing up.

THE FIRST BISHOP

Francois de Laval had been appointed vicar apostolic to New France in 1659 and in 1674 became the first bishop. He was determined that the Church should be as independent of the secular order in New France and of the Gallican influence of the French Church at home as he could make it. He resolutely opposed traders who wished to get rich by providing cheap liquor for the Indians, and in this opposition he often clashed with the government. He built strongly, and the religious and cultural influence of the Church he built continues to the present day to give formation to French Canada. Its influence is felt far beyond the frontiers of its own nation.

JEAN TALON: THE GREAT INTENDANT

In spite of his jealousy for his Church's independence, Laval's dreams for a well-ordered Catholic society in the colony were closely related to the plans of Louis XIV's great minister, Jean Baptiste Colbert. He intended the colony to operate on the scale of a royal province. To do this, he appointed Jean Talon, previously an intendant of a French province, as the first intendant of New France. Together, he and Talon ushered New France out of its role as a missionary and fur-trading outpost.

Upon arrival in 1665, Talon, seeing it necessary to increase settlement, arranged for the emigration of shiploads of hardy French peasants and enticed retiring soldiers of the Carignan-Salières Regiment to settle with grants of land. King Louis dispatched shiploads of his protegées called *filles du roi* as prospectives mothers for New France. Talon, heartily endorsing marriages, gave presents of household provisions to all brides in the colony. Fines were imposed on parents with daughters unwed at 16 and upon bachelors over 20 years old.

Talon intended that New France look toward becoming self-sufficient, at least with respect to food and clothing. Production of the latter he encouraged by compelling farmers to grow hemp, withdrawing yarn from the market and leaving the women no alternative but to weave rough homespun cloth on the looms which he supplied.

He established a brewery to utilize surplus grain. Shipbuilding was started at Quebec, and lumbering was a winter employment for the colonists. Talon also had aspirations to a trade with the West Indies and France.

Under the zeal of its first intendant, New France achieved considerable prosperity and doubled its population to over 7500 during his 7 years in office. His achievements were significant for their social permanence rather than the economic diversity they brought, however. The fur trade remained the economic staple of the colony.

Talon and Colbert had tried to civilize the colony, including its Indians, and reproduce in the New World the pattern of French provincial life. To ensure public involvement with their aims they prohibited fur-trading without a license. However, the vast unexplored interior of the continent was much too tempting for young Frenchmen who wished to seek adventure and a fortune.

The great Canadian religious leader, Marie de l'Incarnation, once said that a Frenchman becomes an Indian more readily than an Indian becomes a Frenchman. The young man, Pierre Radisson, verified her statement.

The Hudson's Bay Company

On May 2, 1670, one of the most far-ranging and powerful business ventures the world has ever known came into being with the charter of "The Governor and The Company of Adventurers of England Trading into Hudson's Bay." Thus the Hudson's Bay Company was founded. Prince Rupert (1619-82), a cousin of the English king, Charles II (1630-85), was made first governor of the company.

GROSEILLIERS AND RADISSON

To understand how the Company came into being, it is necessary to go back to the time of the *coureurs de bois* (woods rangers), the early French fur traders. These traders were generally financed by the merchants of Montreal to travel up country to collect pelts under license. But a number of *coureurs de bois* were unlicensed traders.

Médard des Groseilliers and Pierre Radisson (the latter had been captured by Indians as a young man and spent two years living as one of them) were two particularly daring members of this group. In the spring of 1659 they pushed their way westward from Quebec to the unknown shores of Lake Superior. From there they headed northward and wintered with the Sioux, from whom they learned something of the character and extent of Hudson Bay, which had been discovered by the English navigator, Henry Hudson.

When they returned to Montreal after a year's absence, they were accompanied by 300 Indians and 60 canoes laden with furs. After he had sold his own share of the furs, Groseilliers announced his intention of making the journey on his own. Accompanied by six *coureurs de bois,* he set off once more. The voyage was successful; apart from the profit that Groseilliers made out of it, he was able to bring back with him this time definite information about a convenient route to Hudson Bay of way of Lake Superior.

In May 1662 Groseilliers set out once more for the west, this time accompanied by 10 men. Again he was away for a year; again he returned with an enormous number of furs. He was, of course, infringing on the rights of the general monopoly that had been granted by the French king under the charter of the Company of One Hundred Associates, but like the other private traders, he relied on the laxity of the authorities. Unhappily for him, a fresh patent for a new company was issued shortly afterward, and a new governor arrived on the scene, determined to take more rigorous measures against private traders. For people like Groseilliers the situation had now become difficult.

The new governor promulgated a law that no French subject could devote himself to the fur trade without a permit. Groseilliers immediately sought out Radisson, who was as indignant as he over the new official policy. They decided to enlist aid from outside New France to set up a Hudson Bay company. Armed with introductions, Groseilliers made his way to Boston, only to learn that there was no help forthcoming from that quarter. Although his scheme to set up a trading post on the Hudson Bay was welcomed by many leading citizens of the town, there was a scarcity of money available for projects of this nature, since much money had already been invested in building up their colony.

Groseilliers' visit to Boston, however, was not wasted; he met Zachary Guillaume, the captain and part-owner of a small vessel named the *Nonsuch,* which plied a trade between the colony and the mother country. Guillaume was eager to assist in any way he could, providing that sufficient funds could be found to subsidize any trips that he might make. Although Groseilliers was unable to find the needed

In 1670 the newly formed Hudson's Bay Company began to establish fur-trading forts around Hudson Bay. The settlers in New France challenged and opposed this English entry into the fur trade, and the struggle lasted for 90 years. With the English in possession of Forts Albany and York Factory, the French in 1697 sent a fleet of five ships to try to capture them. In the ensuing naval battle (seen herein a painting by Norman Wilkinson) the French emerged victorious, and Fort York Factory surrendered.

money at that particular time, his meeting with Guillaume was to prove of the utmost importance.

TO FRANCE AND ENGLAND

This meeting was followed by a series of further setbacks. Radisson, who was just as enthusiastic about the project as Groseilliers, eventually joined him in Boston. The two traveled on from there to France, hoping that they might get support from the French court. Again, their representations met with no success. Eventually, however, they were given a letter of introduction to Prince Rupert of England. Leaving Radisson in Paris, Groseilliers made his way to the English capital.

As a result of Groseilliers' first interview in 1667, Prince Rupert promised to support the scheme. Radisson then arrived in England, and there was a further meeting at Windsor Castle. Although Prince Rupert was able to enlist the support of King Charles II, there was considerable delay before further steps were taken. In the meantime, the two adventurers were given an allowance and were lodged in Windsor.

TWO SHIPS FOR THE WEST

In 1668 Radisson and Groseilliers set off for the west in two ships. One was the *Eaglet,* which had been supplied by the British, and the other was the *Nonsuch,* commanded by Groseilliers' Boston friend, Captain Zachary Guillaume. Unfortunately for Radisson, he was on the *Eaglet,* which was disabled early on by a storm and forced back to England. The *Nonsuch,* with Groseilliers on board, sighted Resolution Isle in August. Moving on to the Hudson Straits, they made their way through narrow channels and mountains of ice, until at last they came to the site of Vincent's Bay.

When the *Nonsuch* returned to England a year later, it brought a cargo valued at some $60,000, which was more than enough to convince all concerned that there was a fortune to be made in the bay. As a result, the charter for the Hudson's Bay Company was introduced and signed.

A SMALL REWARD

Radisson's and Groseilliers' reward was small and given in reluctant doles. The English looked on them as renegades, and as such, hardly suited to belong to a company that included so many distinguished names. As it was, the two adventurers remained in London throughout the winters of 1673 and 1674, while they tried to get some satisfactory terms for their services. The best they could get was a promised payment of $300 per annum as a joint fee, which might be increased if the conditions of the company prospered still further.

Disgusted with the situation, Radisson and Groseilliers went back to France and visited Jean Colbert, who promptly suggested that they come back to the service of France, with a salary three times as large as the one the Hudson's Bay Company had offered them. Although their hearts were set on going back to the fur trade, they agreed to Colbert's request that they join the French navy, and for the time being they disappeared from the scene. But they were the unrecognized pioneers of the Hudson's Bay Company.

THE COMPANY OF THE NORTH

Several years passed before the French-Canadian people realized that the time had come to contest the growing strength of the Hudson's Bay Company.

In the year 1680, a conference was held that was attended by the most important figures of the

When the French undertook the exploration of Canada in the 1600s they came into contact with the Algonquin Indian tribes, who were the first Indians to have their way of life changed by the coming of the white man. The French chose to support the Algonquins, who were enemies of the Iroquois; the English allied themselves with the latter. This choice became a significant factor in determining who would eventually control North America. This painting by Paul Kane depicts an encampment of the Ojibwa tribe of Algonquin Indians among the islands of Lake Huron. (Royal Ontario Museum, Toronto)

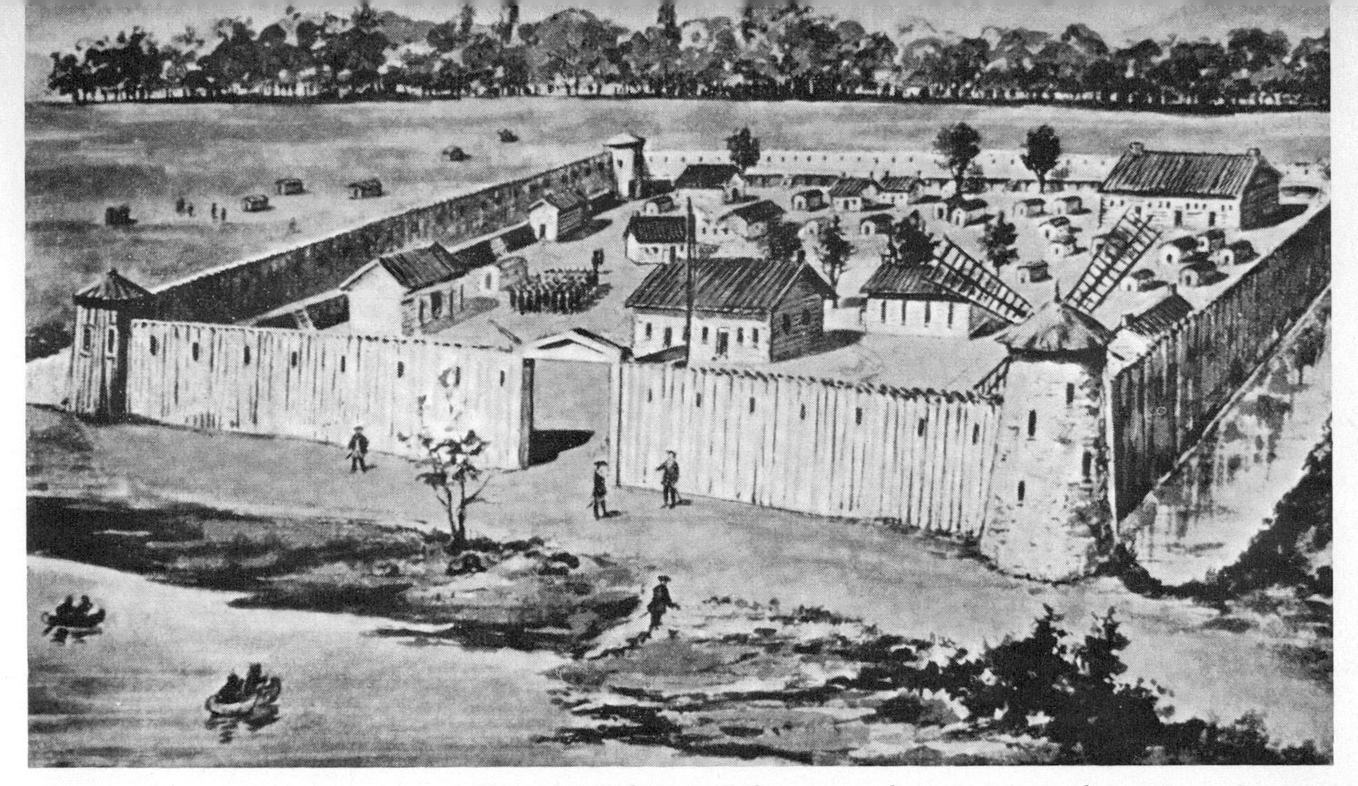

The fort at Lachine was built to protect the western approaches to Montreal and was a key outpost of the French in their wars against the Iroquois. In 1689, in retaliation for a French attack on the Senecas, the Iroquois overran Lachine and massacred about 60 of the inhabitants.

colony, including Radisson and Groseilliers. Out of this meeting was formed the Company of the North.

The new company was sorely needed in New France, if the colony was to maintain its financial interest in the fur trade. Up to this point, they had tried to centralize the trading by making the Indians bring their furs to market, rather than going out and seeking the furs for themselves, as the *coureurs de bois* had done.

WARS AND THE FUR TRADE

The system had not taken into account the fact that the continual inter-tribal wars were likely to interrupt the regular flow of trade traffic. To make matters worse, that adventurer of the forest, the *coureur de bois,* had been declared a criminal and was liable to be sent to the galleys for life for a second offense. As the French fur trade was now in a state perilously near decay, immediate action was necessary. A fur trader from Quebec, named Aubert de la Chesnaye, obtained the promise of Radisson and Groseilliers to take command of two ships for the company, which would venture into the north in a search for pelts.

Eventually, the two veteran traders set off in the *St. Pierre* and the *St. Anne*. It was an adventure that seemed destined for failure from the start, as the crews were inexperienced and the ships unseaworthy, but they returned with a large and valuable cargo. The enthusiasm with which they were greeted was quickly damped when it was learned that they had attacked the English posts in the Hudson Bay, and worse still, they had brought two prisoners back with them. Heavy fines against the two and diplomatic apologies followed.

END OF A GREAT ADVENTURER

In disgrace, the two friends parted. It is not known what happened to Groseilliers, but it is assumed that he went to Three Rivers and there lived out the balance of his life with his wife and children.

Radisson, deciding he could no longer trust himself to the mercy of the new French government, turned up again in London in 1684 and offered his services for the second time to the Hudson's Bay Company, which accepted him. Their faith in him was not misplaced. He went to the Hudson Bay almost immediately, in a ship named *The Happy Return*, and brought back 20,000 pelts. He continued to make profitable trips on behalf of the company to the Canadian North, and he died in London, at the age of 76, in 1702.

The Struggle for Supremacy

Although the vested interests of the French and English in Canada had already brought them into collision, an uneasy peace had existed between them from the time of the Treaty at St. Germain-en-Laye until 1685, when the ever-growing success of the English at Hudson Bay made some decisive action on the part of the French inevitable. New France was also still menaced by the Iroquois, who were still free to attack its exposed settlements and its fur trading posts in the wilderness.

At this vital stage in the history of New France, the Marquis de Denonville was chosen to be the new governor. As Denonville saw it, he had two immediate tasks to perform. First, he had to check the Iroquois' and their English allies' invasions into the country of the French missions and trading posts and to cement France's alliance with the western Indian tribes. Second, he had to introduce honest and efficient administration into New France (unlike that of his corrupt predecessors) to fortify Montreal and Trois Rivières and consolidate the defense of the colony.

In Denonville's opinion he could only regain the respect of the Indians by a show of force. In 1686 he decided, therefore, to send a militia force to seize all the forts and posts at James Bay in the Hudson Bay. The attack was successful, and after it was over Fort Hayes, Fort

Rupert and Fort Albany were in the hands of the French.

When the news of the raid reached London, there was such a clamor that King James II was forced to taken action. Demands were made for restitution and recompense for the losses sustained. As a result, a neutrality pact was signed at Whitehall.

Denonville's attacks on the Iroquois were to have long-term effects on their relations with France. Choosing the mighty Senecas, the most powerful of the Iroquois tribes, he attacked and put them to rout, but apart from the slaughter of the Senecas, all that he had achieved was to foster anew the hatred of the Iroquois for the French.

Denonville soon realized that the victories he had achieved were hollow. Famine now raged through the colony, and, as no furs had been delivered for two years, revenues were at a low ebb. It was also now obvious that the Iroquois were waiting for a suitable moment to exact their revenge.

HURON CHICANERY

The situation was worsened by a Huron chief named Krondiaronk (the Rat), who, with a war party, attacked three Iroquois deputies who had come to discuss the possibility of patching up the broken peace. Killing one of the chiefs and taking the others prisoner, he lied to the Iroquois by saying that he had been acting on Denonville's instructions. His prisoners, who were eventually released, returned to their tribes, more convinced than ever that any sort of peace with the white man was an impossibility.

Soon after, the Iroquois redoubled their raids on the settlements and harried the fur trade routes to the west. At daybreak on Aug. 5, 1689, some 1500 of them attacked the little village of Lachine, close to Montreal, where they massacred about three score of its inhabitants. It was the worst disaster in the history of the colony.

FRONTENAC

Denonville was recalled to France and succeeded as governor by the Comte de Frontenac, who had served a previous term as governor of New France from 1672 until 1682.

Frontenac was 70 years old, and grave problems awaited him in New France. The English revolution in 1688 had dislodged James II from the throne, and he had been replaced by William of Orange (1672-1702).

With the arrival of Frontenac in New France, Louis XIV decided on a bold and decisive course of action. A naval expedition, supported by an overland attack from Canada, was to be sent to capture New York. At the same time, Frontenac was to attempt the impossible task of imposing peace on the Iroquois. The scheme was bold; it also was impracticable. Denonville had not yet returned to France, and news of the Lachine massacre had not reached the mother country. Neither the king nor Frontenac, therefore, had any idea just how hostile the Iroquois were. As for the planned naval and military coup, the king had no idea of the inadequate manpower available to carry out such an operation. As events turned out, the two warships sent to attack New York from the sea did not do so.

THREE RAIDS

Deterred by this, and by the fact that he had found the colony in a sorry plight, Frontenac decided to carry out an offensive campaign as best he could with the means at his disposal. He organized three raiding forces and sent them into English territory. The attacks on Schenectady, N.Y., Maine and the frontier villages on the border of New Hampshire were in a sense successful and raised the prestige of the French with the Indians. But they also goaded the English into reprisals. In the following autumn a land force marched from New York to Connecticut, joined with a band of Iroquois and moved up to Lake Champlain with the purpose of attacking Montreal. A sudden outbreak of smallpox among the Indians prevented the attack from taking place.

In the meantime the English

Because the French court felt that the future growth of the colony depended on expansion through the St. Lawrence River and the Great Lakes, the Comte de Frontenac, one of the outstanding governors of New France, built Fort Frontenac in 1673 at Kingston, Ontario, then known by the Iroquois name of Cataraqui. Fort Henry (seen here) was built in 1836 on higher ground to protect Canada against attack by the United States. Among the stonemasons who helped construct the fort was Alexander Mackenzie, later to be a prime minister of Canada.

colonies had equipped a fleet under the command of Sir William Phips, who was convinced that the taking of Quebec would be easy. His attack was a dismal failure. The original plan was to bombard the town while land forces attacked. When it came to putting the plan into operation, the land forces were bogged down in the mud and underbrush and Phips was unable to give them adequate support with his guns, as his supplies of ammunition ran out quickly. The ground forces retreated and the fleet, as it withdrew, was badly hit by the batteries of Quebec.

Although their defeat at Quebec was a blow to British prestige, it did not relieve the situation in Canada for the French. Frontenac assumed that Phips would return with a larger force to make another attack, and he immediately set about strengthening the Quebec fortifications, but the attack that he had anticipated did not materialize.

FRONTENAC'S LAST CAMPAIGN

Five years later, in 1695, now in his 76th year, Frontenac decided to lead another expedition against the Iroquois. On July 4 of the following year he set off with 100 French militia and 500 Indians. His campaigns were partially successful and the Iroquois sustained heavy losses. He did not, however, succeed in crushing the Iroquois' insatiable desire to fight the French to the last man. They remained, as always, arrogant, defiant and prepared to support the English although the latter gave them nothing in return.

On his return to Quebec from the Iroquois country, Frontenac received a series of new instructions from the French court. He had tried to line his own pockets and stimulate the fur trade by issuing licenses freely. He was told that he was to issue no more licenses. He was told to make peace with the Iroquois, even though it might undermine the good relations he had with the Indian tribes that had supported France thus far. Convinced that he saw the interest of New France more clearly than did the court, Frontenac ignored the orders.

MARCH ON ACADIA

The new instructions had been given because the French court had decided that its best policy was to center its interests in the east. In 1696, together with their Indian allies, the French destroyed Pemaquid, on the New England coast, and launched a successful attack against the English colony at Newfoundland. Following this, Fronte-

The French and Indian War (1756-63) was the final struggle between France and England for the control of Canada. The English in America were almost 2 million strong, but French settlements were small, and the French had to depend on the help of the Algonquins and other tribes to the west. The English, however, received the powerful support of the Iroquois, who had a burning hatred of the French. This painting by Paul Kane is of Kee-A-Kee-Ka-Sa-Coo-Way (man that gives the war whoop), chief of the Crees. (Royal Ontario Museum, Toronto)

nac was ordered to prepare an army of at least 1000 men, who were to march overland to Acadia, which had already changed hands several times.

It was also part of the French plan to attack Boston, Salem, Portsmouth and other places, and to destroy them. The French fleet was then to go on and take New York, while another small fleet under Pierre le Moyne, Sieur D'Iberville (1661-1706), would go to the Hudson Bay to take Fort Nelson, leaving the French with no further competition in this area.

In May 1697 a fleet left France, but it never reached its destination. Delays and the shortage of supplies forced it to sail back to France without having fired a gun. As the fleet was a vital part of a complex plan, Frontenac was forced to call off his expedition to Acadia. The one successful operation was carried out on Hudson Bay by Pierre le Moyne. He was already a hero to the people of New France because of the conspicuous part he had taken in an earlier raid made on the Hudson Bay forts. After defeating three English ships, he took Fort Nelson and $60,000 worth of furs.

In the same year the war in New France ended abruptly with the Treaty of Ryswick, which also ended the war which Louis XIV had waged in Europe from 1689. Under the terms of the treaty, Acadia was handed back to the French.

Left: *Around Port Royal, as it was originally known, centered the long struggle between the French and the British for control of Acadia. During 100 years of conflict before the final French capitulation to a New England force under Colonel Francis Nicholson in 1710, the settlement changed hands a number of times. It was Nicholson who changed the name from Port Royal to Annapolis Royal, in honor of the reigning sovereign of England, Queen Anne. The present Fort Anne is an outgrowth of French fortifications built on this site and later additions made by the English.*

NEW FRANCE AT THE PEAK

By 1702 New France was at the peak of her power. The Iroquois had seemingly made a permanent peace. The attempted reprisals of the New Englanders and New Yorkers had failed. New France was straddled across the mouth of the Mississippi, and she also controlled the entrance of the St. Lawrence and, except for Fort Albany, the Hudson Bay. It was true that many of her troops were struggling to maintain France's position in Europe, in the War of the Spanish Succession, but the same situation applied to the English, which meant that France had more than a fair chance of preserving her colonial empire in America.

ECONOMIC CRISIS

It was at this stage, however, that New France found herself faced with an economic crisis brought about by the collapse of the fur trade. The ever-present competition from the English in Hudson Bay and the stopping of licenses to the *coureurs de bois*, by royal order in 1696, had badly disrupted the regular flow of furs. In a desperate attempt to remedy this situation, an amnesty was granted in 1704 to the *coureurs de bois*, together with a promise of the renewal of their licenses.

This attempt to bring the fur flotillas down once more to Montreal was only partially successful. In the years between the cancellation and the renewal of the licenses, many *coureurs de bois* had becomes restless and lawless. Many of them had formed ties of one sort or another in the up country, and they had no desire to settle again on the banks of the St. Lawrence. Many were now little more than adventurers, living from day to day in the wilderness on what-

The Death of General Wolfe *by Benjamin West. In 1759, with war raging between Britain and France, General Wolfe led an attack against the key French position of Quebec. For three months French troops under General Montcalm held off the English forces; finally, in a battle on the Plains of Abraham, they were defeated and Quebec was captured. Both Wolfe and Montcalm were killed. The fall of Quebec sealed the fate of New France, and when the war was officially ended, in 1763, Canada belonged to England.* (The National Gallery of Canada, Ottawa)

ever they could find by hunting or trapping.

From the commercial point of view, the English fur trade had had little to fear from the French since the inception of the Hudson's Bay Company, a monopoly which the French could not challenge with appreciable effect.

The sources for fur of the Hudson's Bay Company were too far away to be plundered by the *coureurs de bois*, and as the company had cheaper goods to offer the Indians, it could afford to wait in its trading posts and let the Indians come to them. The company also had the advantage of having a direct sea route to England. The French, on the other hand, had to go inland and then bring the furs back to Montreal and Quebec, before they could even start shipping them back to France.

IMPORTANCE OF NEWFOUNDLAND

If the English felt themselves seriously threatened at all, it was in Newfoundland, which had begun as an English colony in 1610. The harbors along the eastern coast had now become permanent fishing ports, and the whole territory was a training school for seamen, with an important naval base at St. John's that guarded the North Atlantic approaches to the American continent. Newfoundland was therefore doubly important to the English, since it provided trade for the sailors and a reserve of ships and men in case of war, as well as a vital overseas fishing station, providing dried fish for most of the southern European countries.

The Treaty of Utrecht

The general conflict ended with the Treaty of Utrecht in 1713. With it, the English drove a hard bargain. The captured posts at the Hudson Bay were to be restored to the Hudson's Bay Company; Newfoundland was to be officially recognized as a possession of England; all of Acadia (Nova Scotia) was to be ceded to the English, as well as the island of St. Kitts. The Treaty of Utrecht, in fact, marked the beginning of the end of New France. Even so, it brought a period of relative peace to North America, and during this period New France prospered and its population increased.

In the interval before the next series of wars, the French concentrated on the fortification of Louisbourg on Cape Breton, Nova Scotia, which eventually became the site of a new stronghold. When it was completed and garrisoned, the French were reasonably satisfied with their position in the east. In addition to Louisbourg, there was Quebec, occupying a highly advantageous position if the time ever came to defend it again. The French had also erected Fort Frédéric at the lower end of Lake Champlain, and this, with the earlier French forts at Fort Niagara and Detroit, enabled them to retain control of the outlets of the St. Lawrence river system.

With the outbreak of the War of the Austrian Succession in 1740, which broadened soon to include the colonial rivalry of France and England, New France found herself embroiled in a war that lasted until the close of 1748. Again it consisted of a series of skirmishes, which were a preparation for the final duel of the Seven Years' War in 1756.

THE TREATY OF AIX-LA-CHAPELLE

To appreciate why the peace treaty of Aix-la-Chapelle in 1748 provided nothing more than a breathing space for the two antagonists, it is necessary to understand the reasons for the continuation of the struggle in America. It had been the intention of France during the War of the Austrian Succession to win a large military preponderance in Europe, which would enable her to make diplomatic gains in America.

This emphasis on manpower had meant the sacrifice of seapower. As a result, the French navy had steadily declined. By 1748 it was in such a weak position that France's colonies were exposed to capture by the English ships, which could attack knowing that there would be no effective counterresistance from the French fleet. In the fight for the balance of power in Europe, France had therefore left herself dangerously vulnerable overseas.

In the circumstances, it was only natural that England should be tempted to pluck what seemed to be a ripe plum that could be had merely for the picking. Apart from the vested interests of the two countries concerned in Canada, there was also the actual nature of the antagonists.

France was over-confident, even though she knew that England was superior to her in naval power. England already saw Canada as a potentially valuable part of the British Empire in America. Unlike the French, the English colonies had opened their doors to large-scale colonization, so that when the final struggle came with France, the English had about 2,000,000 colonists in America.

The French and Indian War

Britain declared war on France on May 18, 1756, though the fighting was already well under way in America the previous year. A British force under the young Virginian George Washington and a second one under General Braddock had tried to drive the French out of the Ohio Valley, but both had been defeated. Of the four British attacks on French strongpoints, only the one on Fort Beauséjour had succeeded.

THE FRENCH COMMANDER

The French general in Quebec was Louis Joseph de Montcalm, a professional soldier who had entered the French army at the age of 12. A battle-hardened veteran and a humane aristocrat, he had more than 30 years of campaigning behind him by 1756. But his resistance to the English was hampered because he commanded only the French regular forces, the colonial troops being controlled by the Marquis Pierre François de Vandreuil (1698-1765), the governor-general.

Montcalm quickly saw that he would have to keep the British off balance so that they would be unable to gather their superior forces for a crushing blow against his lightly held defenses. His forces also were in constant need of supplies. With a few battalions of regular Indians and forest-wise Canadians, he quickly attacked the British posts of Fort Oswego and Fort William Henry and captured both. By 1758, however, the British had begun to organize themselves. Even so, Montcalm was still able to throw back a British advance up Lake George.

THE ENGLISH COMMANDER

The British general, James Wolfe, though only 32, was, like Montcalm, a war-tested officer. At 14 he had become a marine officer and by the age of 20 he was a brigade major.

The fall of Louisbourg in 1758 had opened the way into the capital of Canada, and in 1759 the British fleet sailed up the St. Lawrence and placed Wolfe's army below Quebec, which was being defended by Montcalm.

The stubborn resistance of the garrison entrenched in the upper town held up the British forces for three months until September 13, when, very early in the morning, Wolfe mounted an assault by way of a path that led up a steep cliff. The heights of the cliff were lightly guarded, and by dawn the British had struggled up to the Plains of Abraham, the weakly defended landward side of Quebec. Immediately Montcalm counterattacked to drive the British from the heights before they could bring up their

The influence of the French heritage in Canada is reflected in the architecture of this hotel in Alberta. Built in 1913, it imitates the style of 17th-century French châteaux.

main force. The counterattack failed, and the surrender of Quebec followed. Neither Montcalm nor Wolfe lived to see it, for both of them had been fatally wounded during the battle.

THE FALL OF NEW FRANCE

The fighting was not yet quite at an end, but the fate of New France was sealed. At Montreal the remaining French force rallied, then descended on Quebec to besiege in turn the British garrison there. The arrival of British ships in the spring, when the ice broke on the St. Lawrence, forced the French to retire to Montreal. They finally surrendered to a large force in September 1760.

Although New France had fallen with the surrender at Montreal, the war did not officially end until 1763, when a new age began in Canada's history, the age of British North America. Only two little islands were allowed to continue flying the French flag, the islands of St. Pierre and Miquelon. But the culture the French had brought to Canada endured and the 65,000 colonists of New France were to increase many times over.

THE CANADIANS UNDER BRITISH RULE

Initial Differences

INITIALLY NEW FRANCE CHANGED little with the coming of British rule. The French officials and merchants and members of the Society of Jesus were withdrawn from the colony and returned to Metropolitan France. But 65,000 French Canadians remained. With enduring tenacity they held to the language, the religion and the laws which they had derived from France. They were Canadians, too, however, and had a way of life which drew in part from the new country which they had pioneered.

It was natural that with the arrival of the English there should be friction between the two cultural groups. A small number of merchants came, settling mainly in Montreal and Quebec, where they began to take over the fur trade and to control the economic life of the colony. The French Canadians confined themselves largely to agriculture or to the professions and the Church.

EARLY BRITISH RULE

Although the British governor, James Murray, had been instructed to arrange for an elected assembly that would bar Catholics from political rights, and although he had fought against them in the siege of Quebec, he was very much on the side of the French-Canadian inhabitants.

His attitude was based on an aristocratic dislike for the political aspirations that were beginning to exist in the minds of the British merchants. His sympathies were more with the feudal *ancien régime.*

Deliberately temporizing, he moved slowly toward establishing a system of English law, while he steadily postponed calling an assembly. In 1765 he was recalled and his successor, Sir Guy Carleton (1724-1808), another soldier, took over. He, too, found himself on the side of the old French-Canadian society, whose aristocratic system he considered a bulwark against the bourgeois temper and attitude of the British merchants.

In 1766 Samuel Hearne joined the Hudson's Bay Company, and in 1770 he led a land expedition to the mouth of the Coppermine River. The trip opened up unknown territory and proved that there was no short northwest passage. To facilitate trade on the Saskatchewan, Hearne began the building of Cumberland House (shown here) in 1774. It was the first inland trading post of the Hudson's Bay Company.

The Quebec Act

As a soldier who had helped to defeat French Canada, Carleton was convinced that there was a strong possibility of further trouble from the French unless they were happily reconciled to British rule in Canada. In his opinion this could only be achieved by giving Quebec her own laws and institutions. Although he received violent opposition to this from the British merchants, who were still pressing for the promised assembly, the Quebec Act was passed eventually in 1774. This more than fulfilled Carleton's hopes. The government was to be by governor and an appointed council, which included both English and French members. English criminal law was to remain, but French civil law was to continue as it had done under the old regime. The Roman Catholic Church in Quebec was to be recognized, with the result that its legal right to tithes continued to be backed by the authority of the law. The Quebec Act was prompted by the desire to conciliate the French and turn them into potential allies against the enemies of Britain. It was, in a sense, an attempt at fairness in the recognition of the civil rights of the French Canadians.

RESENTMENT IN NEW ENGLAND

But instead of consolidating British rule in Canada, the Quebec Act complicated an already difficult situation. By putting the province of Quebec on a special basis, Britain found herself in the position of having antagonized her American colonists, who were already moving toward increasing independence. In addition to the establishment of a government without assembly in Quebec, a further cause for the discontent of the American colonies was the fact that the Quebec Act had annexed the western lands between the Ohio and upper Mississippi rivers to Quebec. This extension of the boundaries of Quebec was a blow to the Americans, who saw territories they considered their being given to the defeated French and placed under autocratic rule. They had already shown their resentment over the way that Britain was claiming the right to tax them and to enforce British trade laws. Now they were being asked to accept another action that would weaken still further their position. The Quebec Act contributed to the outbreak of the American Revolution, and within several months, Canada was again menaced with invasion.

THE ATTACK ON MONTREAL

The invasion was launched at the end of August 1775, after an appeal had been made to the Canadians to join the 13 colonies in revolt. The appeal met with little response. Those who did respond made up two small regiments. The American invaders attacked Montreal, which fell quickly.

Carleton escaped to organize forces gathering before Quebec. There, with about 1800 men, he found himself under a siege that lasted until the following May, when British ships came up river to his aid.

On July 4, 1776, the leaders of 13 former British colonies in America signed their Declaration of Independence and, although they had to continue their struggle for several more years, British rule over them was ended.

The United Empire Loyalists

With peace made in 1783 by the Treaty of Versailles, the British lost the 13 American colonies. America was an independent nation, free to develop in its own way. But in their brief struggle against the Americans the British had been supported by sympathizers within the colonies. These loyalists of the American Revolution, who became known as the United Empire Loyalists, had wanted to maintain the connection with the Crown of the United Kingdom.

Sir Alexander Mackenzie (c.1755-1820) and his band gaze at the Pacific Ocean. A member of the North West Company, Mackenzie set out on the first of his explorations in 1789 and followed the river that now bears his name to the Arctic Ocean. In 1793 he led an expedition across the Rocky Mountains to the Pacific Ocean, thereby accomplishing the first overland crossing of North America north of Mexico.

Territorial possessions in 1801.

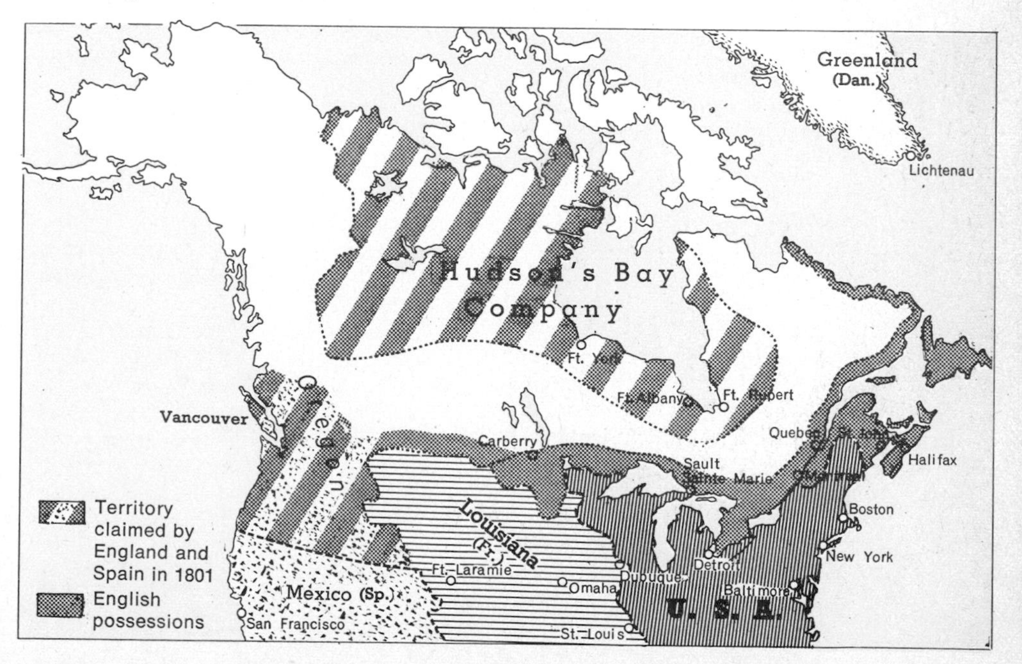

A rival to the Hudson's Bay Company emerged after the French and Indian War. Centered in Montreal, the North West Company became a serious threat to the older organization, and for 50 years the resourcefulness and enterprise of the "Nor' Westers" cut into the revenues of the Hudson's Bay Company. In 1821 the damaging and often bloody rivalry was resolved by an amalgamation of the two firms, in which the name of the older company was retained. This painting shows a Hudson's Bay Company canoe brigade at Lachine, near Montreal, in the 1820s.

Within the terms of the peace treaty Britain tried to ease the position of those who remained, but thousands of Loyalists began to leave the new independent America. About 30,000 settled in Nova Scotia and in New Brunswick (separated from Nova Scotia in 1784), and a smaller number came to what is now southern Ontario.

THE CONSTITUTIONAL ACT

It was the Loyalists who eventually created a Canada that was as much English-speaking as French. In 1791 the British parliament passed the Constitutional Act, to meet the changed conditions that had come about with the settling of the Loyalists in the Old Province of Quebec. Their language, religion and general outlook on life were different from those of the French-speaking population. The Quebec Act was not a workable proposition for a colony with an English as well as a French population, and the British authorities sought a solution that would assimilate both groups into a framework that could be controlled by representative government. It was assumed that this could be achieved only by creating two provinces.

The Constitutional Act, therefore, replaced the Old Province of Quebec with the provinces of Upper and Lower Canada, which to all intent and purpose were divided by the Ottawa River. Upper Canada was to be English-speaking, with English laws and institutions, and the lower province predominantly French, retaining the French civil law granted to it by the Quebec Act.

MENACE FROM FRANCE

Almost as soon as the new provinces had been formed, the British authorities found themselves faced by a fresh menace. The news of the French Revolution had brought to the French-speaking colonies a new concept of French glory, and French emissaries moved in from the United States and attempted to stir up public opinion, which had already been excited by the distribution of a pamphlet *Les Français Libres à leurs frères les Canadiens*, which promised that the new French government would free Canada. Riots broke out, but they were quickly suppressed, and gradually the response to the work of the agitators from France died away. The Roman Catholic Church was particularly concerned to side with the British authorities in resisting the atheistic and republican doctrines of the French Revolution.

The outbursts of unrest, however, had given the British officials new cause to distrust the French Canadians. Even the Roman Catholic Church was suspect until a number of emigré priests arrived in Lower Canada, full of stories of the terror stalking the streets of France under the new regime. Their strong support of the British attitude to the Revolution was noted with approval by the British authorities.

The War of 1812

To the long-standing friction between Americans and the British over the western fur trade, the Napoleonic Wars added the further American grievances of a British blockade, interference with American shipping and the impressment of sailors on American ships into service in the British navy.

The United States wished to assert herself as a nation, and the best place to do so was in Canada. If she could take Canada from the British, she would also be able to satisfy her need for continental expansion. All that was needed was an excuse for war.

It came soon. And the British provided it. The western Indians were in retreat before the advancing American settlements. Under the influence of the British, the Indians formed a league and attempted a last stand before it was too late. In 1811 they were defeated at the battle of Tippecanoe. Their resistance, although futile, was taken as proof by the Americans that the Indians were being supported by the British, and in June 1812 the United States declared war on Britain.

The war was waged on land and sea. Although the Americans did well in a number of small encounters at sea, they were unable to challenge Britain's general naval supremacy. In any case maritime New England had no desire to support a war that could only injure her overseas trade.

BROCK'S VICTORIES

With a population of over 7,000,000, the United States had the superiority on land, but its military leaders made a number of tactical errors. In 1813 and 1814 they mounted two attacks on Montreal, which failed because they were badly led and stoutly resisted by French-Canadian volunteers. Major General Isaac Brock struck a heavy blow against the Americans in the West early in the war, by capturing the western post of Michilimackinac.

This daring and spectacular feat, which had been carried out with only a few hundred Canadians and Indians, so impressed the western tribes that they were won wholeheartedly to the side of the British. Brock followed this by an attack on Detroit, which brought about the surrender of a large force that was ready to attack.

These two major actions were carried out in 1812 and contributed a great deal to the final outcome of the war. Brock was killed the same year, driving off an American invasion at Queenston Heights.

RAIDING AND BURNING

The two years that followed saw the raiding and burning of York by the Americans. Instead of following the obvious strategy of attempting to capture Montreal and cutting Canada in two, they dissipated their energies in a series of minor skirmishes that could have no possible effect on the final outcome. Their situation worsened when Napoleon was sent to Elba, leaving large numbers of British troops free to be sent to Canada as reinforcements. The British did no better, failing in their attempts to capture New Orleans (after the war had officially ended) and Lake Champlain, though they did succeed in burning the capital at Washington. The war petered out in 1814, in what was almost a stalemate.

AFTERMATH OF WAR

As the Americans seemed willing to continue the war if they were asked to yield a territory, the British did not press the point of boundary adjustments. The Treaty of Ghent (1814) restored the prewar boundaries. By the Rush-Bagot agreement of 1817, both the United States and Britain agreed to the disarmament of the Great Lakes. By the Convention of 1818, the frontier was defined from Lake of the Woods, beyond the Great Lakes, to the Rocky Mountains, along the 49th parallel.

The end of the war brought a much closer relationship between the French and British Canadians, who had fought together to defend their country.

The Expansion of the Provinces

Since the fall of New France, immigrants to British North America had come mostly from the 13 colonies. Now, with the war in Europe over at last, they began to flow in from Britain. With the postwar depression and unemployment in Britain and the dislocation of industrial change, many British people turned hopefully to the idea of a more attractive life in the colonies. Starting in 1815, and especially after 1820, there was a steady stream of British settlers pouring into British North America. Despite the problems that were to beset the colonies later on, this stream continued until the middle of the Victorian age of prosperity, and indeed has never since entirely abated except for the interruptions of war.

THE BACKBONE OF THE NEW SOCIETY

A small percentage of the wealthy and the aristocratic classes took part in this emigration, hoping to make their fortunes as gentlemen farmers or merchants. However, it

Immigrants at Montreal *by William Raphael. For 50 years after the fall of New France, most of the immigrants to Canada came from the 13 colonies. After the defeat of Napoleon in Europe, however, settlers began to arrive directly from England. This movement was given impetus by a postwar depression that resulted in widespread unemployment in Britain. From 1815 on, and especially after 1820, there was a steady stream of immigrants from the British Isles.*(The National Gallery of Canada, Ottawa)

was the great numbers of laborers from factories and farms, and of members of the urban and rural middle classes, who came over with little or no capital but their own skills and willingness to work, who were to provide the backbone of the new society. "Empty hands made Canada," as the saying goes.

Although Upper and Lower Canada attracted many emigrants, large numbers also went to Nova Scotia, which had had a checkered history since it had been founded by Champlain in the early 17th century as Acadia. Granted to Sir William Alexander in 1621, under the Scottish Crown by James VI (James I of England), under the name of Nova Scotia, it had changed hands a number of times before it was finally returned to the English with the Treaty of Utrecht, in 1713.

Nearly 40,000 emigrants settled in Nova Scotia between 1815 and 1838. A very large percentage of them were Scots, who were following in the footsteps of New Englanders and Loyalists. This was one of the few colonies that pursued the cause of reform without the complications of racial and religious side issues. The oligarchy was a major force here, as it was elsewhere. Its paternal rule was challenged by Joseph Howe, the editor of the *Nova Scotian*, a paper which supported the Nova Scotia Reformers. His constant attacks on the government led to an attempt on the part of the oligarchy to muffle his voice with a court action for libel. Conducting his own defense, he won the suit, and went on to join the asssembly in 1836. Howe's influence was important in the achievement of responsible government in 1848.

The Fur Trade

While the process of settlement was going on, an old commercial war was being waged afresh in the fur trade. The Canadian fur trade run by the North West Company out of Montreal was now a serious threat to the Hudson's Bay Company. Although the Hudson's Bay Company had the advantage of its geographical position, the North West Company had shown more enterprise. The situation between them was resolved in 1821 by an incident that reflects little credit on the "Nor' Westers."

RED RIVER SETTLEMENTS

Lord Selkirk (1771-1820), a philanthropic Scottish aristocrat who had joined the board of the Hudson's Bay Company, had conceived the idea of creating a settlement of Highland and Irish settlers on the Red River, in Manitoba. He did so on the grant of land that had been given to him in exchange for the controlling stock that he had bought from the company.

MASSACRE AT SEVEN OAKS

The Red River colony which Lord Selkirk had settled lay across the main trading routes of the "Nor' Westers." The "Nor' Westers" saw the little settlement as a Hudson's Bay scheme to threaten their whole organization. They therefore aroused the *métis* (half-breeds) who traded with them in pemmican. Something akin to a civil war began to develop on the Red River. The *métis'* assaults on them brought violent

William Lyon Mackenzie (1795-1861) came to Canada from Scotland in 1820. Through his journal, the Colonial Advocate, *he charged that the ruling oligarchy of Upper Canada was blocking needed economic progress and reform. A popular political leader, he was elected to Parliament in 1828 as a member of the Reformers. In the election of 1836, however, the Tory Party won a complete victory, defeating almost all the prominent Reformers, including Mackenzie. Embittered, Mackenzie joined with Papineau and other leaders in plans for rebellion, and in 1837 he led a mob in an attempt to seize Toronto. The rising failed, and Mackenzie was compelled to flee to the United States. He returned to Canada under the Amnesty Act of 1849.*

Louis Joseph Papineau (1786-1871), an aristocrat with great ability as an orator, took up the cause of French-Canadian grievances against the British rulers of Lower Canada. From 1815, when he became speaker of the Assembly, he was recognized as the leader of the French-Canadian Party. When the British rejected his appeal for governmental and financial reforms, Papineau joined other French-Canadian leaders in stirring up rebellion. He was forced to take refuge in the United States, returning to Canada only after the passage of the Amnesty Act of 1849.

reprisals from the settlers, and the climax was reached when Robert Semple, governor of the territories of the Hudson's Bay Company, attacked and destroyed the fort of the "Nor' Westers." They struck back in 1816 with the massacre of 22 settlers at Seven Oaks. Selkirk attempted to solve the problem by enlisting Swiss and Canadian veterans, and in his capacity of magistrate he took Fort William on Lake Superior, the chief fort of the "Nor' Westers." The "Nor' Westers" immediately brought legal action against him, and he was arrested and tried. He was fined £2000, and, with his health shattered, he went off to recuperate in the south of France, where he died.

UNION OF THE TWO COMPANIES

The two rival companies realized that the time had come for union, and in 1821 the "Nor' Westers" were absorbed by the Hudson's Bay Company. At that time a Scotsman named Sir George Simpson (1792-1860) became administrator of the Hudson Bay territory. Simpson was a remarkable man; controlling a vast area, and working often with violent and intractable employees, he could look back after the 35 years of his rule of the company and boast that there had been only 19 capital crimes during his period of office.

COLONIAL SELF-GOVERNMENT

The Need for Reform

BRITAIN'S RAPID RISE TO THE industrial leadership of the world, following the cessation of hostilities in Europe, caused her to lose interest in imperial matters. Little or no attempt was made to think out and pursue dynamic development policies that would meet the growing desire of the ever-expanding colonies of British North America to control their own affairs.

The imperial government did little more than maintain an outdated colonial system while grievances mounted.

Each of the provinces, with the exception of Newfoundland, was ruled by a British governor, with the assistance of an appointed council supported by an assembly, which was responsible for taxation and the sanctioning of new legislation. Effective power, however, usually lay in the hands of the executive council, who were men of wealth and social position. Known as the Family Compact in Upper Canada, and as the *Château Clique* in Lower Canada, they were an oligarchy, who had little in common with the ordinary people. They were suspected by them, sometimes with good cause, of corruption and nepotism, which took such forms as granting Crown lands to their relatives. In all fairness it has to be said that a large number of the oligarchy were men of the highest integrity, who sincerely believed that their upbringing and position in society best fitted them to rule. But it was obvious that the needs of the people could not be satisfied until the oligarchies had been removed from their positions of power or forced to share it more broadly.

The age of reform had already come to Europe; the social forces that were to culminate in the great 20th-century revolutions were fermenting throughout Europe. But it was to take an actual rebellion to jar the British government out of its complacency.

Rebellions in Upper and Lower Canada

The Family Compact was strong in Upper Canada, where its monopoly on government positions entrenched privilege and prevented the country from being developed rapidly with adequate roads, schools, banks and other instruments necessary for economic progress. William Lyon Mackenzie (1795-1861), an energetic Scottish immigrant, founded a journal, the *Colonial Advocate,* to support the cause of reform.

His violent attacks aroused the Compact. Some of its wilder members marched on the offices of the *Colonial Advocate,* wrecked them and threw the type into Toronto Bay. The action was ill-timed and helped make Mackenzie a popular political leader.

A struggle for power between the Reformers and the Tories began. Faced with a Tory assembly elected in response to a personal appeal for loyalty by the governor, in 1837 Mackenzie stimulated an armed revolt. The rebellion failed after Mackenzie had tried to organize an ill-equipped force to march against York. It was dispersed by the militia, and Mackenzie took refuge in the United States.

FRENCH AND ENGLISH

In the autumn of 1837, rebellion also broke out in Lower Canada. Here the situation had been further complicated by the basic divisions between two cultures. The French-speaking majority were already resentful because they felt the English-speaking population had the governor and his oligarchy on their side. They made uneasy partners, for the English-speaking minority had to contend with a French majority in the Assembly.

The French had a strong leader in Louis Joseph Papineau (1786-1871), who was both an aristocrat and a political radical. Papineau had great gifts as an orator; in 1815, at the age of 29, he became speaker of the Assembly, and he held that post almost continually until 1837.

The general discontent in Lower Canada came to a head in 1834, when the Lower Canadian Assembly, prompted by Papineau, presented a list of grievances, The Ninety-two Resolutions. These reflected goals and aims similar to those of the rebellious American colonies of 1776. Moderate elements broke with Papineau, as did the Catholic Church, which had finally wearied of his inveterate anti-clericalism and the violence of his public statements.

THE CRUSHED REBELLION

The situation worsened in 1837, when the British parliament stated, in Ten Resolutions, that it was not prepared to give Canada self-government. In response Papineau preached violence as the only solution to the problems of Lower Canada.

His supporters assembled themselves into a revolutionary party they named the Sons of Liberty. Fighting began near Montreal, and the British authorities issued warrants for the arrest of Papineau and his associates. After one rebel victory against a detachment of British troops, the rebellion was crushed within a few weeks. Papineau and his closest followers had crossed the border into the United States.

The Durham Report

The rebellions had made one thing clear. The Canadian people could not be contained much longer within the framework of the existing colonial system. Even then it seemed that the British government had not learned its lesson. Supression was the immediate answer. In Lower Canada, the prisons held many rebels under arrest, with the threat of the gallows hanging over their heads. Others were in hiding.

In Upper Canada Mackenzie was still defying the militia on Navy Island in the Niagara River, where he received supplies from the U.S. To make matters worse, other Reformers had fled to the U.S., where they were given a warm welcome. There was talk of another attack from over the border. Various raids across the border during 1838, though not officially condoned by the American authorities, led to a number of small battles and appeared at one point to be about to contribute to the outbreak of war between Britain and the U.S.

THE EARL OF DURHAM

The 1830s were an age of reform in Britain. England had already taken the first steps into electoral reform with the extension of the franchise in 1832. She had abolished slavery and passed the Factory Act, which curbed child labor. At last she turned her attention to reforming her colonial empire.

Realizing that the existing situatian could not be allowed to continue in Canada, Lord Melbourne, the British prime minister, appointed the Earl of Durham (1792-1840) as governor-in-chief of British North America. His task was to calm the provinces, report on their grievances and recommend a new form of government for the Canadas.

In response to the rebellion that shook Canada in 1837, the prime minister of England, Lord Melbourne, in 1838 appointed the Earl of Durham (1792-1840) governor-in-chief of British North America. It was to be Durham's task to calm the provinces, report on their grievances and propose a new form of government for the Canadas. Quartered in Quebec (a view of the Château Frontenac, which dominates the city, is seen here), he worked with intense energy for the five months that he held the post. His report, issued in England, recommended that Upper and Lower Canada be united, that self-government be instituted for local matters, but that steps be taken to suppress the French language and culture so that eventually Quebec province might be made English. French Canadians reacted with great hostility to the Durham report.

Durham was a proud, quick-tempered man who had played an important part in the passage of the Reform Bill of 1832, and although an aristocrat, he was an avowed liberal who was the hope of the British radicals.

Durham reached Quebec in 1838, escorted by warships. Two days later he rode through the city on a white horse, accompanied by an impressive retinue and cheered by an admiring population. This passion for display did not interfere with his work. Although he was already dying of consumption, he worked with feverish energy for the five months he was in Canada, dealing with the enormous task on his hands. He had to govern, hear grievances and at the same time make a plan for the future that would be more satisfactory than anything Canada had known in the past.

One of his first acts there was to lead to his eventual undoing. He restored a more settled atmosphere to the country by dropping the charges against all those who had been accused of rebellion, except for Papineau and Mackenzie, and he exiled nine self-confessed rebels. Durham had no legal authority either to condemn or to exile. The political forces in England who were looking for an opportunity to discredit him seized on this action as an instrument to attack him. Rebuked by Melbourne, he resigned.

THE DURHAM REPORT

Within two months of his return to England he produced his report. It had one grave defect. It ignored the nationalism of the French, with what seems a strange disregard for their hopes for national unity. He stated in the report that there should never again be an assembly at Quebec with the French in a majority. The French province must be made English, with English language and laws. There should be English teachers in the French schools, and the English and French children should be allowed to play together. He hoped that English culture would eventually prevail. Upper and Lower Canada should be united under one legislature, with English as the official language. The intention was quite clear—to stifle completely French-Canadian nationalism.

To understand Durham's attitude, one must realize that he had spent most of his five months in Canada in Quebec, where he was very much under the influence of the English population, many of whom considered all Frenchmen potential traitors. He saw them, too, as a backward farming community, who were opposed to progress. In his view, responsible government had to be granted in a way that would

assimilate the French, who would then be in no position to stop the march of progress.

Although anxious to stifle French-Canadian nationalism, he wished the French to have self-government by means of responsible government, a simple but effective formula he and his staff derived from the Canadian Robert Baldwin. The executive council should be replaced by a cabinet made up of members of the legislature and responsible to the elected house rather than to the governor. Local affairs, therefore, would be left to colonial self-government, and imperial affairs would be reserved for British control—such matters as modifications to the constitution of the colonies, foreign affairs and commerce, and the disposal of public lands.

Quite understandably, the French Canadians reacted angrily to Durham's report. In effect it would have destroyed their way of life.

THE COMING OF RESPONSIBLE GOVERNMENT

The Melbourne government decided not to grant responsible government. They did, however, decide to unite the Canadas, and a bill was introduced in 1839, only to be with drawn, in order that the new governor-in-chief might first win the consent of Upper and Lower Canada. The man who had taken over the post was Charles Poulett Thomson, later Lord Sydenham, who had gone to Canada in 1839. Confident in his own abilities, he began his rule with a council of his own choice, as in fact Durham had done.

An experienced diplomat, Thomson soon established good working relations with a central group of Canadian polititians. He then wrote to Lord Russell (1792-1878), the British colonial secretary, that all was now well in Canada.

He held the view that responsible government by the colonists was not practicable for Canada. On the other hand, he realized that public opinion could not be ignored. He therefore set himself the task of persuading the people to accept something less. If he could provide a popular and efficient government, all might be well.

A brilliant administrator, Sydenham had a strategy that meant, in effect, destroying the political patterns keyed to the old colonial constitutions; he proposed to supplant these with modern, efficient governmental departments. With an election in the offing, following the passing of The Act of Union by the British parliament in July 1840, he set out to undermine the power both of the entrenched forces of the Family Compact and the radical elements in Canada. He achieved this to a large degree by a careful manipulation of elections, and by the obviously high caliber of his administration. As a result, in the first legislature of the Union, only a handful of Compact Tories and Reformers were represented. Among the defeated was the French leader, Louis Hippolyte Lafontaine (1807-64).

Robert Baldwin (1804-58), Canadian statesman. In the early 1840s Baldwin, with Francis Hincks, arranged a coalition with the farsighted leader of the French Reformers, Louis Lafontaine. It was hoped that such a partnership would block those forces attempting the political suppression of the French Canadians and strengthen English Reformers in their appeal for greater self-government for Canada. However, the governor, Sir Charles Bagot, and his successor, Sir Charles Metcalfe, implemented the policy of the British government to block the Reformers and prevented the achievement of responsible self-government.

A FRENCH-CANADIAN STATESMAN

Lafontaine, who was to become an important figure in French politics for the next decade, had succeeded Papineau as chief of the French Reformers. Unlike his predecessor, he was a moderate and practical man, governed by the belief that the French way of life must be defended at all costs, but also that the two peoples of Canada must develop a system of government, a society, in which they could live side by side in reasonable harmony. Although opposed to the union, he had decided to accept it in the hope that it might lead to responsible government. In the meantime, participation in the union would at least give the French an opportunity to have some say in their affairs. He made a vital decision that was to affect the whole course of Canadian politics.

BALDWIN AND HINCKS

Robert Baldwin (1804-58) and Francis Hincks (1807-85), the two leaders of the English Reformers, had already suggested to Lafontaine that the coalition of the French and

English Reformers would be a beneficial move for both parties. By means of such a union, the French would destroy the forces that could lead to their political suppression. In turn, the English would gain by their support for responsible government. Lafontaine, a farsighted leader, was naturally in sympathy with the suggestion. It would, he believed, work in the best way for all Canadians. He agreed to join Baldwin.

At almost the same time, Baldwin quarreled with Sydenham. He had requested that Sydenham remodel the council by replacing three Tory members with Reformers, or at least, more moderate Conservatives. Sydenham refused and Baldwin resigned.

After Sydenham's death in 1841, the next governor of the United Province was Sir Charles Bagot (1781-1843). He realized that if he were to carry on government at all, he must have the support of Lafontaine and his bloc, which had become a major political force.

He proposed to Lafontaine that he and two other members of the French Reformers should join the executive council. Lafontaine, who was demanding a cabinet government on English lines, refused. Bagot was now caught between the need to avoid disapproval of the British Tories, who had come to power at the time of Sydenham's death, and the practical political necessities of the time in Canada. Lafontaine was asked to join the ministry along with Baldwin and accepted.

Subject to fierce criticism for his decision, ill health through overwork and mental distress, Bagot resigned in the autumn of 1842. He died in the following year, the third governor literally to give his life to Canada.

After its amalgamation with the North West Company in 1821, the Hudson's Bay Company added to its immense domain the territory west of the Rockies and north of the Spanish possessions. Anticipating the Oregon boundary settlement with the United States, the Company founded Fort Victoria in 1843 and moved its western headquarters there from its previous location near Vancouver, Washington. This painting by A. Sherriff-Scott, depicts the Hudson's Bay Company steamer Beaver *off Fort Victoria in 1846.*

METCALFE'S POLICY

The new governor was Sir Charles Metcalfe (1785-1846), an experienced administrator who had spent 37 years serving the British government in India and Jamaica. Inclined to be liberal, Metcalfe nevertheless quickly showed that the British government intended him to restrain the Reformers from expanding and strengthening their position and to prevent the achievement of responsible government. The British government felt that its imperial grip on Canada was threatened by the ever-growing popularity of the Reformers.

A crisis was quickly precipitated by the ministry's demand that it should control all appointments to office. This Metcalfe would not accept and the ministry resigned.

Metcalfe's intervention in the ensuing elections gained him a slightly more amenable assembly to deal with, but he had really only succeeded in achieving a short postponement of an inevitable crisis.

The new British colonial secretary, Earl Grey (1802-84), was convinced that responsible citizens in office were the best judge of their own well-being; he was therefore anxious to see responsible government established in Canada. While a stop-gap governor was concerning himself with his routine duties, Grey sought the right man to carry out his policy. He found him in the Earl of Elgin (1811-63), who arrived in Montreal in January 1847, when the struggle for responsible government was nearing its climax.

With Grey prepared to grant responsible government, Elgin's task was easier than that of his predecessors. The elections of 1848 opened a way to apply a wiser policy. The Reformers' majority gave them control of the legislature, and Elgin called in their leaders, Baldwin and Lafontaine, to choose the members of the government. Lafontaine became prime minister and Baldwin, attorney-general. Responsible government had also been granted in Nova Scotia in January 1848. All of what was to be the British Commonwealth was eventually to follow the same pattern.

REFUGEES FROM STARVATION

At the same time, Elgin found himself confronted by complicated and tragic problems. In 1847 the

A Fort York Factory boat brigade arrives at Norway House, the Hudson's Bay Company establishment at the northern end of Lake Winnipeg in Manitoba, in the 1860s. The history of the Hudson's Bay Company as a great political empire ended in 1869 when the new Dominion of Canada acquired the Company's territory for £300,000 and thus ended its monopoly. Thereafter the Company became a gigantic corporation of diverse business interests.

great potato famine in Ireland had led to a fresh surge of emigration to North America. Many of these refugees from starvation had come in ships fit only for carrying cargo and with no facilities for accommodating a large number of passengers. Typhus and cholera were rampant on these death ships, and the emigrants carried the diseases into North America. There were too many of these hapless and long-suffering survivors of the famine to be sustained by Canada's weak, still relatively undeveloped economic structure. Unemployment was widespread, for, with the advent of free trade in 1846, Canada had lost her preference in the British market. The milling trade had disintegrated, and Canada's ships were idle.

As if this were not enough, Elgin and his ministers had to face the English-French problem anew, though in a different form. During the rebellions, when property in Upper Canada was destroyed, the owners had claimed compensation from the state. A measure had been passed, and they had been paid. French claims of a similar nature in Lower Canada had been the subject of a preliminary investigation by Metcalfe, but the matter had been put aside. A Rebellion Losses Bill, to compensate owners including rebel sympathizers in Lower Canada, passed the assembly and was formally approved by Elgin.

It was the immediate signal for a wildly hostile display by English and Irish Tory elements. That evening, while the members were in session, a hate-crazed mob attacked the Parliament building in Montreal. Smashing its windows with stones, they went on to invade it. Members were driven out and the building was ransacked, set afire and left a smoldering ruin.

Elgin was pursued through the streets of Montreal by an angry mob, who smashed the panels of his carriage as well as injuring him with a stone. The Tory press gave Elgin a week to leave the country. Through all this, Elgin maintained a calm front.

It had seemed to the Tory merchants of Montreal that Britain was casting them aside. And they would be commercial orphans. Now that they had been thrust into the ruthless competitive world markets of free trade, the imperial connection seemed meaningless. Without the old British trading system, they believed Canada's unsteady economic foundations would collapse.

Equally convinced, in their panic and despair, that the only hope for the future was to become part of the United States, they signed the Annexation Manifesto of 1849, which asked that Canada be absorbed into the United States. The Manifesto came to nothing, but it did discredit the old Tory merchant oligarchy.

RECIPROCITY WITH THE UNITED STATES

In 1851 Lafontaine was succeeded as prime minister by Francis Hincks, who took as his colleague the French-Canadian Reformer A. N. Morin. Both of them were anxious to solve the problem of increasing Canada's trade, which had recovered only slightly since its collapse following free trade. The best and most reasonable commercial outlet for Canada was the United States. But this great market could be exploited only by reciprocity: the trade traffic must be two-way. Commercial barriers between the two countries must be destroyed by removing customs duties on most goods. Elgin himself favored an agreement of this kind, and in 1854 he went to England to obtain permission to negotiate for the British colonies in North America. Given the approval of the British government, he went to Washington the same year, and left with a signed treaty.

The Railway Age

One thing now became clear. If Canada was to develop her enormous resources into profitable trade, she must build railroads to compete with the carrying trade of the American West. Railroad lines had been laid down in British North America earlier, but they were very short. By 1850 Canada still only had 66 miles of operating railroad lines.

There was, of course, the problem of finance, but this was solved by the likelihood of handsome profits to British shareholders. Work proceeded rapidly on a number of lines, including the Grand Trunk Railway, which was to become, for a while, the longest railroad in the world.

The railroad-building era produced a new prosperity. It brought into being new commercial and industrial patterns. New towns were rising, even in the remote regions of the Canadian forests where there had only been rugged pioneer settlements. Iron foundries and rolling mills sprang up beside the long iron tracks. Canada began to participate in the industrial revolution that was transforming the whole Western world.

'CLEAR GRITS'

The Hincks-Morin ministry fell in 1854 and in Hincks's place came Sir Allan MacNab, who was prime minister for two years, being succeeded by John A. Macdonald (1815-91), a moderate Conservative, who was to contribute most to the creation of a nation. He immediately found himself opposed by the "Clear Grits" ("all sand and no dirt, clear grit all the way through"), a new radical and liberal party. They were joined by George Brown, editor of the powerful Toronto *Globe*, who had entered politics in 1851. Brown, while fervently Canadian, strongly supported ties with Britain and admired the British constitution. Under his influence the "Grits" turned from their previous tendencies toward the United States. Holding fast to the tenets of free trade and parliamentary government, he was a British Liberal of the Victorian era.

The Future of the Northwest

The British lands in the northwest were still the domain of the Hudson's Bay Company. Even after the Oregon boundary dispute of 1846 was settled, the Northwest Territories remained the potential focus of an international crisis. The American frontier was moving west across the prairies. When gold was found on the Fraser River in British Columbia in 1856, American miners swarmed into the new colony. In the same year, Minnesota, close to the Red River colony, became a state. But the Hudson's Bay Company had not fulfilled its obligation to ensure that its vast regions were settled.

THE GRADUAL ENCROACHMENT

To the concern over American encroachment in the west was added a further source of British-American rivalry in 1861 when the Civil War broke out in the United States. The situation deteriorated rapidly. On Oct. 8, 1861, the British mail steamer *Trent* was stopped on the high seas near Cuba by an American warship. From the British ship the Americans removed envoys from the rebellious South to England and France, and carried them away as prisoners. This seizure of civilians on a neutral

The provincial parliament building in Toronto, Ontario. In 1841, following the recommendation of the Durham Report, Upper and Lower Canada were united, and Upper Canada became known as Canada West. With the creation of the Dominion of Canada in 1867, Canada West became the province of Ontario, with Toronto its capital.

British ship stirred up a great deal of ill-feeling in England, and for a little while it seemed as if there would be war. The danger passed, but there was still the feeling that the Northwest might fall into the hands of the United States, and that the miliary defense of eastern central Canada was inadequate.

The Toronto *Globe*, the most important paper in Canada, had under George Brown earlier begun a campaign for taking over the West, and the "Clear Grits" made this a main point in their political program. The British government initiated a parliamentary inquiry into the conditions in the territory and the role there of the Hudson's Bay Company. The inquiry's judgment was to the effect that the Hudson's Bay Charter of 1670 retained its legal validity. But it also decided that the monopoly held by the company in the area beyond Rupert's Land should end.

Final Steps Toward Confederation

In 1858, Brown defeated Macdonald's cabinet, only to be himself defeated in the House after a mere four days in office. From then on, successive cabinets carried on as best they could in a situation on the verge of deadlock. But in June 1864 the picture changed when Brown make the statesman-like gesture of proposing and offering full cooperation in a coalition of Liberals and Conservatives, which would seek general federation. Party differences were forgotten in the common cause, and a delegation of French- and English-Canadian leaders moved into the Maritime Provinces and undertook, at a conference in Charlottetown in September 1864, the difficult task of convincing the leaders of Nova Scotia, New Brunswick, Newfoundland and Prince Edward Island that they should enter into a federal union with the two parts of Canada to form a new British North American nation. In October 1864 the Quebec Conference met to work out the details of the proposed federation.

The conference passed 72 resolutions that formed the basis of the British North America Act of 1867, the written part of the Canadian constitution. A large majority of the Canadian parliament accepted these resolutions in 1865, but it took a long and difficult political struggle by Tupper and Tilley, the leaders in Nova Scotia and New Brunswick, to bring their provinces into confederation with Canada in 1867. The two island colonies rejected the proposal, only joining Canada at later dates(Prince Edward Island in 1873 and Newfoundland in 1949).

BRITAIN AGREES

Since cooperation with British ministers was necessary, members of the Canadian cabinet went to London in the spring of 1865. They found the British government in agreement with the decisions made by the Quebec Conference, and the active support of British governors and the colonial office was thrown into the balance in favor of Confederation during the next two critical years. In the spring of 1867 the British parliament passed the British North America Act. On July 1 the Dominion of Canada came into being. A few months later, in the fall of 1867, the Dominion's first parliament assembled in Ottawa.

THE DOMINION OF CANADA

Building a Nation from Sea to Sea

THE CANADIAN PRIME MINISTER, SIR John A. Macdonald, who had been

The Fathers of Confederation. In September 1864, delegates (shown here) from the legislatures of Canada, New Brunswick, Nova Scotia and Prince Edward Island met at Charlottetown, the "Cradle of Confederation." On this historic occasion the first steps were taken toward the eventual union of the colonies of British North America. In 1867, with the passage of the British North America Act, the modern Canadian federal state was established, uniting the provinces of Canada, New Brunswick and Nova Scotia into one country divided into four provinces: Ontario, Quebec, New Brunswick and Nova Scotia.

knighted for the great part he played in Confederation, was now faced with an enormous task. He was 52, a young man by later political standards, though an old veteran by the standards of his day, and one whose skill had been developed in political combat.

The problems that confronted him would have tested the greatest politician, demanding the utmost political skill and wisdom. In Nova Scotia a fervently anti-Confederate movement was still powerful, and public opinion was not reconciled to being "sold up the river" and into the Canadian Confederation by Tupper's small group of Nova Scotian Tories who supported the idea. But the only hope of the anti-Confederates lay in an appeal to the British government, which was strongly committed to their opponents. Macdonald managed to placate them for the time being by offering Nova Scotia larger federal subsidies, and by bringing the leader of the anti-Confederate cause, Joseph Howe, into his cabinet.

THE PROBLEMS OF THE WEST

The aftermath of the American Civil War made Canada's relations with the United States uneasy. Some American politicians still had hopes of absorbing at least part of British North America. And the Hudson's Bay Company still held the immense Northwest Territories. Beyond these, on the west coast, was the newest and most precarious of the North American colonies, British Columbia. Both of them would have to be acquired if Canada were to become a transcontinental nation. Left as they were, the pressure for their settlement by Americans and annexation by the United States might soon become irresistible.

To begin with, the problem of the Hudson's Bay Company seemed to present no major difficulty. In 1869 it was agreed that Canada should pay the company £300,000 for its rights as owner, leaving the company free to trade, but without monopoly. The great rule of the company was over at last.

Unfortunately, the matter was not to end there. The Red River settlement had grown used to the Hudson's Bay Company's authority and became alarmed by the sudden turn of events. By far the largest group in the settlement were the *métis,* half-breeds of French-Indian extraction. Politically conscious and well organized, they feared, with good cause, that the inrush of new Canadian settlers that was bound to follow would mean the end of their carefree life, which depended partly on hunting the buffalo. They were also dedicated to the Roman Catholic religion of their ancestors, and they did not wish to be outnumbered and absorbed by Protestants from Ontario.

Sir John Alexander Macdonald(1815-91), knighted for the great part he had played in bringing about confederation, became the first prime minister of the Dominion of Canada. Under his leadership the Intercolonial Railway connecting the Maritime Provinces with the St. Lawrence River was built, the Northwest Territories were acquired from the Hudson's Bay Company and, in return for his promise that a transcontinental railroad would be built within ten years, British Columbia agreed to join the Dominion. As a result of Macdonald's policies, by 1871 Canada stretched from the Atlantic to the Pacific.

RIEL'S WAY

Under the influence of their leader, Louis Riel (1844-85), an intelligent, resourceful but reckless and intemperate politician, they took their destiny into their own hands. Riel set up a local provisional government, and halted the new Canadian lieutenant governor, William McDougall, on the frontier of the colony. At the same time he occupied Fort Garry, the important Hudson's Bay post on the Red River. No attempt was made to break with Britain, however, and American attempts at informal intervention were repulsed. A form of democratic rule was established and law was enforced. But afterward Riel was rash enough to execute Thomas Scott, a rude and provocative English-speaking troublemaker who refused to accept his authority. With this act, Riel precipitated military intervention from Ottawa. Contingents of British and Canadian soldiers reached Fort Garry on August 24, only to find that Riel had fled. His rebellion, however, was successful, and it led to the creation of the province of Manitoba, of which Louis Riel is rightly considered the founding father. His people, the *métis,* were none too fairly dealt with by the new English-speaking settlers who soon had control of the province, and in 1885 Riel was to be summoned back from his American exile to lead another rebellion in the Northwest Territories.

BRITISH COLUMBIA

With the creation of the Province of Manitoba and the acquisition of the territories of the Hudson's Bay Company, Canada had been brought to the Rocky Mountains. To many colonists on the west coast it now seemed obvious that British Columbia should join Confederation. When the Dominion promised generous financial arrangements and to build a railroad to the coast, the final obstacle was removed. In 1871 British Columbia became the second of the new western provinces.

By then the permanence of the Union had been accepted by American leaders, and annexationist sentiment had died down in the U.S. Macdonald decided that the time had come to settle outstanding Canadian-American problems and put relations between the two nations on a new and firm footing. The Reciprocity Treaty had ended in 1866 and was not to be renewed. But the Treaty of Washington, which was signed in 1871, did formalize American acceptance of the permanence of the new Dominion and settled a number of outstanding differences between the United States and Britain. Canadian independence as yet only extended to do-

The Countess of Dufferin was the first railway locomotive to operate in western Canada. It was brought to Winnipeg, Manitoba, from the United States in 1877. The historic engine is now displayed near the Canadian Pacific Railway Station in Winnipeg.

mestic matters, and Britain signed treaties for Canada until after World War I.

THE PACIFIC SCANDAL

In 1873 Macdonald's government was brought down by the "Pacific Scandal," an affair that involved the subsidizing of Macdonald's party funds by financiers who were designated to build the railroad to the Pacific coast. The Liberal opposition made full use of the scandal to bring down the cabinet with charges of corruption. The public was infuriated. Macdonald had derived no personal financial advantage, but the charges of political corruption were clearly true, and he was compelled to resign.

One of Macdonald's last achievements before his resignation was to bring Prince Edward Island into the Confederation. He did this by appealing to the reasonable self-interest of the islanders, who were in economic trouble, and by giving them a boat service linking them commercially and socially with mainland Canada.

LIBERAL INTERLUDE

After Macdonald's fall, Alexander Mackenzie (1822-92), the head of the Liberal party, took office. In the election that followed, the Liberals won. The Liberal government lasted for five uneventful years, marked by the formation of a number of instruments of government, including the Supreme Court of Canada and the North-West Mounted Police, which later became the Royal Canadian Mounted Police, a corps of police officers legendary for their intelligence and heroism in keeping law and order in the vast, sparsely inhabited lands of western Canada.

The Mackenzie government proposed to build the Pacific railroad piecemeal and only insofar as the Dominion could afford to pay for it. Little building was done as a result.

In 1874 George Brown, on behalf of the government, had gone to Washington to try to effect a renewal of the Reciprocity Treaty with the United States. The agreement was successfully negotiated but failed to be ratified by the U.S. Senate. The U.S. was in fact steadily raising her tariffs. As the world depression that had begun in 1873 continued, and as business in Canada declined, Canadian manufacturers pressed for tariffs to foster and protect new industry.

THE NATIONAL POLICY

Macdonald immediately saw this pressure, along with the need to build the Pacific railroad, as a weapon he could use to get his party back into power. Using the name National Policy for his platform, he promised to lift the Dominion out of the economic doldrums and return to the task of nation building. Macdonald's campaign won him the general election of 1878, with a large majority.

Building the Canadian Pacific Railway

At this most opportune moment, an offer came to build the Pacific railroad from George Stephen, later Baron Mount Stephen (1829-1921), another of the Scots who helped to create the Canadian nation. Stephen was president of the Bank of Montreal. Gathering around him a powerful body of businessmen, he began to raise capital in the U.S. and in Europe. By the contract signed in Ottawa on Oct. 21, 1880, the newly formed Canadian Pacific Railway was committed to construct a line from the St. Lawrence Valley to the Pacific Ocean. In exchange the railroad was to receive from the government $25 million and a land grant of 25 million acres. The sections of line already laid were to be handed over to the company, free of charge.

TRACKS THROUGH THE MOUNTAINS

The construction task was awe-inspiring; it was material for legend. Finding and building a route above the north shore of Lake Superior and through the mountains of British Columbia was particularly difficult. Led by a great general manager, William Van Horne, the engineers, surveyors and workmen rose to the task. By 1886 trains were running from Montreal to Vancouver.

There had been many times when the project was near failure. It was carried through in spite of the harsh weather, the raw condition of the great land, deaths through accident, and, worst of all, political and financial troubles. At times both the London and New York money markets were hostile; the company was compelled to ask and receive government guarantees for its borrowings, and even so it was near bankruptcy before 1884. But Macdonald, ruthlessly determined, knew that the abandonment of the railroad would mean that the Canadian nation would be stillborn. He flung all his government's influence behind the company.

The Northwest Rebellion

The railroad brought a further problem to a crisis. The roots of the trouble were similar to those that had caused the Red River Rebellion. The *métis,* who were the rebels of the Red River, had migrated west to the banks of the Saskatchewan. The life of settled farm and town was alien to them. As the railroad crawled nearer to their lands, they saw their cherished way of life threatened for a second time. They pressed claims on the government for land with a "Bill of Rights." The government took no significant steps to conciliate them and ignored their petitions. In 1884 a *méti* deputation made the journey on foot to Montana to see Louis Riel, who had spent 15 years in exile after his headlong flight from Red River. By that time Riel had received treatment as a patient in a mental hospital. He was not, to say the least, the best possible leader for a people whose emotions were aroused by fear for their land and homesteads. Riel returned, and the *métis* brought out their rifles.

INDIAN ALLIES

This time they had allies in the plains Indians, who also feared that the advancing railroad would annihilate their way of life. They were hunters, and the once-great buffalo herds on which they had lived were dwindling. New settlers were beginning to take over the once-remote prairie lands.

In March 1885 the *métis* set up their own provisional government. Their style of warfare was skillful but outdated against strong forces

The Royal Canadian Mounted Police, originally the North-West Mounted Police, was established in 1873 to provide law and order in the sparsely settled lands of western Canada. In 1874 the first unit of 300 men journeyed to Oldman River in southern Alberta, where they built Fort Macleod and took up their police duty. Other Mounted Police posts were soon established. The Mounted Police cared for the settlers who followed, ended the whiskey trade with the Indians and brought criminals to justice. In 1904 "Royal" was added to the name in honor of their services, and in 1920 the organization was given its present name. The force today comprises about 4500 men and is Canada's federal police force.

This photograph, taken in 1884, shows Jean L'Hereux (standing on the left) and a North West Mountie (standing on the right), who conducted peaceful discussions with four chiefs of the Blackfoot Indians. The Blackfoot were the strongest military power on the northwestern plains. Until the 1830s they prevented trappers from hunting in the rich beaver country of the upper Missouri. The Blackfoot were buffalo hunters and made war upon neighboring tribes. Efforts to persuade them to turn to farming were of no avail, but by the 1880s the buffalo was almost exterminated and the Blackfoot tribes were greatly weakened by starvation. Thereafter they turned increasingly to farming and cattle raising.

with modern equipment. They struck quickly, however, with the aid of a number of Plains Indians, and attacked and seized a post at Duck Lake, between the two branches of the Saskatchewan. The Plains Indian chief, Big Bear, launched an attack on the mission at Frog Lake. The situation seemed extremely serious. In addition to the *métis*, Riel now had enlisted Indian war parties, and quick action was demanded. The railroad, the symbol of the trouble, was also the effective means of ending it.

RIEL EXECUTED

The government leaders took prompt action; using the railroad, they rushed well-armed troops to the scene of the trouble. More than 7000 men were raised in eastern Canada and hurried west. Before the rebels had time to gather strength, advance columns under the command of General Middleton were engaging them at Batoche. Riel was captured and the revolt crushed. Brought to trial at Regina, Riel was sentenced to death. His execution on November 16, together with that of eight Indians found guilty of murder during the uprising, created another problem for the government.

Many of the French Canadians in Quebec were sympathetic to the *métis'* cause and to the brave, brilliant and unbalanced man who was their champion. Riel's death on the scaffold aroused widespread resentment. It was seen by French Canadians as an act of political revenge upon one of their own people by the Protestant British of Ontario. The execution engendered a bitterness in English-French relations in Canada for many years.

DEATH OF MACDONALD

The general election of 1891 kept the Conservatives in power federally, but the rigors of the campaign were to lead to Macdonald's death in office. Throughout his long, often bitterly controversial career, the elder statesman had fought to preserve the transcontinental dominion he had created. At the age of 76, just after his last desperate electoral triumph, worn out by political struggles, he was struck down by paralysis and died on June 6, 1891.

The Liberals and Prosperity

With Macdonald's death the unity of the Conservative party was broken. Between 1891 and 1896, Canada had four Conservative prime ministers. The Liberals won the election of 1896, and their French-Canadian leader, Wilfred Laurier (1841-1919), became prime minister, a post he held until 1911.

By 1897 the depression that had begun in 1891 was ending. There was a flood of settlers to the west from Europe, the U.S. and eastern Canada. There was a general revival of trade and a prosperity such as the Dominion had never known before.

The flood of immigrants continued to arrive, right until 1914. Across the west there were more railroads and more towns springing up where there had been only trails and trading posts before. The great, rolling plains were now supplying wheat to the world markets, and the National Policy, continued by the Liberals, was helping to foster a number of prosperous industries in central Canada.

GOLD ON THE YUKON

The prospector and miner added another colorful page to the history of Canada, with the Klondike gold strike in 1896. The rush to the gold fields on the Yukon River that followed in the next two years helped to sweep away the remnants of the long depression in Canada and to bring a land boom and a new phase to railroad construction in western Canada.

The new prosperity and settlement of empty land helped to give a new unity to Canada and to strengthen the national sense of identity and self-confidence.

There was still, however, latent ill-feeling between English and French, which was exacerbated by events beyond Canada's shores.

The Defense Problem

In 1899 Canada found herself in a situation fraught with political difficulties. She had to make a decision on a subject that affected her whole position within the Brit-

This post in Saskatchewan was typical of North-West Mounted Police forts during the late 1800s. The Mounties policed 300,000 square miles of frontier country.

Oil derricks of the early 1900s. The depression of the 1880s and early 1890s in Canada gave way to a period of great economic expansion. For almost two decades Canada experienced unprecedented prosperity. The country's production grew, and settlers began to pour into the west. To accommodate the increasing activity, two more transcontinental railways were built.

ish Empire. With the outbreak of the South African war between the British and the Boers, Canada had to decide whether or not she was going to aid the mother country by sending troops to South Africa to support Britain. The English-speaking part of the population was in favor of sending troops to take part in the war. French-speaking Canadians, however, felt quite differently about the matter. Their opinion was that the war was no concern of theirs. If anything, bearing in mind the Conquest and the two Riel rebellions, their sympathies were more with the Boers. It was an opinion held strongly by some Liberals in England, too, where the war was not universally popular. The Canadian government, in response to the wishes of English-speaking Canadians, allowed a force composed of volunteers to set sail in October 1899. To avoid accusations from French-speaking Canadians that the country's money was being spent on a project to which they were opposed, the expenses of the Canadian force while in South Africa were paid by Britain. Before the war was over, more than 7000 Canadians had served in South Africa.

The question of how the government was to handle imperial relations in the case of war was to bedevil Canada again. This time, it was to play a part in Laurier's defeat in the 1911 elections.

In 1909 the problem of defense and foreign policy came to a head again. Germany and Britain were competing furiously in expanding their imperial navies. On both sides the burden of expenditure was crippling. In the case of the British government, it was felt that the colonies should share in part the expense of building the costly battleships. To many it seemed that Canada could no longer ignore her problems of defense. The question was, should she contribute to the building of Britain's fleet, or build her own? As a step toward sovereign nationhood, it was decided that Canada should build her own fleet, and in the following year, 1910, the Dominion parliament passed a bill creating a Canadian navy.

The passage of the Navy Bill aroused antagonism among many French-speaking Canadians. They had no wish to have a navy at all; they believed that it had come into being only because Britain was anxious to involve Canada in her wars. On the other hand Laurier, a good nationalist, believed Canada should be responsible for her own defense. Many French Canadians, however, led by Henri Bourassa, considered that Sir Wilfred Laurier, himself a French Canadian, had betrayed them to the English. Some English Canadians by contrast considered he had betrayed the Empire in not supporting an imperial navy. When the election came in 1911, enough French Canadians voted for the Quebec nationalists in Quebec to cut into the solid bloc of seats Laurier held in that province, and so contributed to Laurier's defeat.

RECIPROCITY

There was another factor that was to help defeat Laurier. During the few years preceding the election, the government had improved relations with the U.S. to such an extent that the question of reciprocity was again raised. In July 1911 the Congress of the United States passed an Act that mainly followed the outlines that Canada had previously tried to lay down without success. But free trade between Canada and the U.S. was denounced as a step toward eventual annexation by the U.S., at least by Canada's powerful business interests, which were now comfortably cushioned by the tariff. National pride, a wish to maintain the British connection and, above all, a desire not to be entangled with the U.S., brought many people to the polls determined to have nothing to do with reciprocity.

Sir Robert Borden (1854-1937), the leader of the Conservative party, came into power and, on taking office, immediately began to reexamine Canada's external policy. He was convinced that in her own interests Canada should play an active part in the defense of Britain. This meant a revision of the Liberals' original thinking on the question of defense. Firstly, the Liberal measure that Canada would have its own navy was to be abandoned. Instead, Canada would give Britain a sum of money to help boost the immediate strength of British naval power. Borden's Naval Bill for this contribution to Britain's navy, how-

Right: *The dramatic opening session of Parliament, at which the governor-general reads a message from the Queen of Canada.*

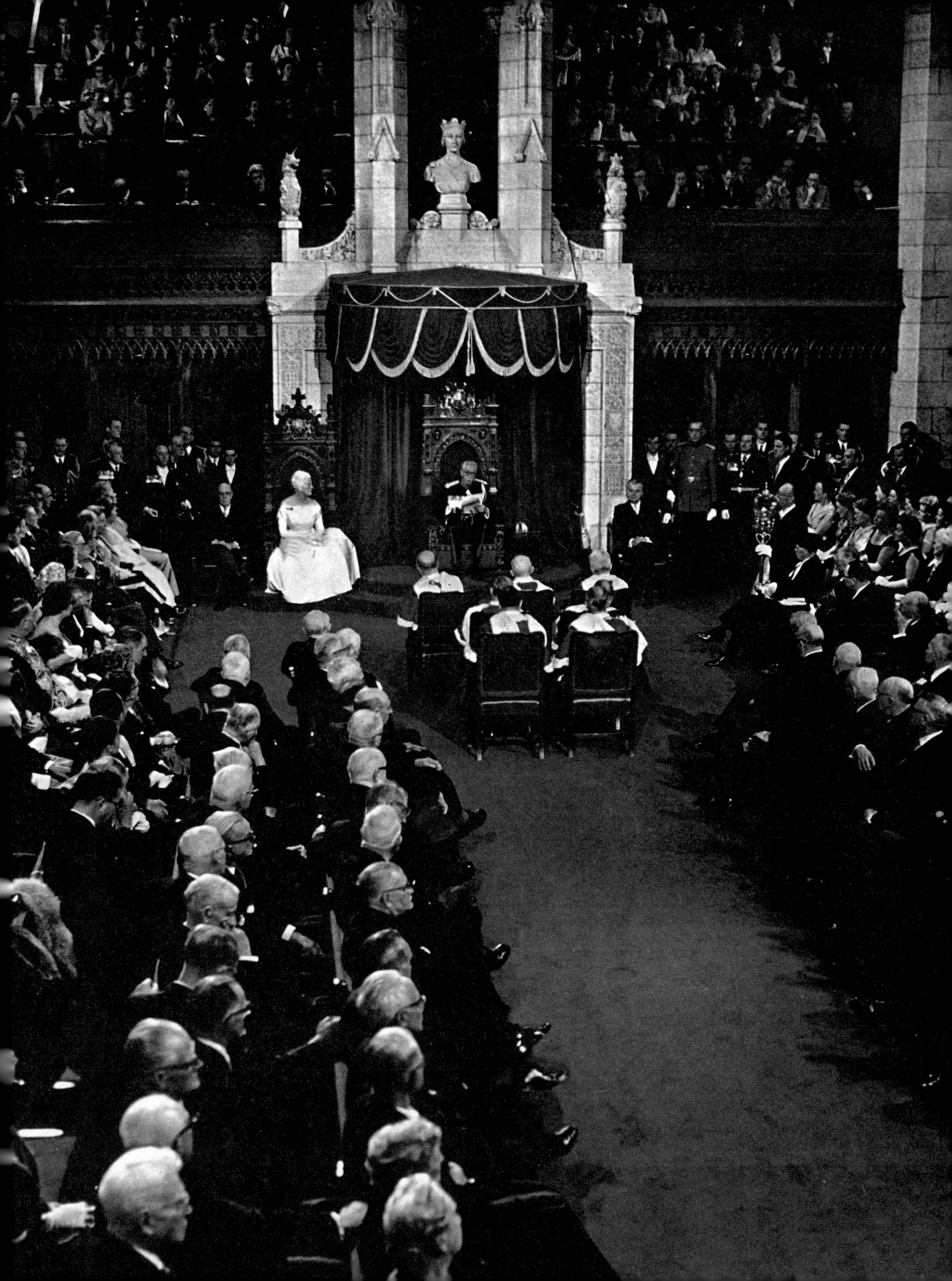

The Ministry of External Affairs seen from Parliament Buildings, Ottawa. Canada's role in World War I won for the nation recognition as an independent power. In the 1920s, Prime Minister William Lyon Mackenzie King (1874-1950) led Canada toward complete independence from Britain in shaping the country's foreign policy. He made it clear that Canada would no longer automatically follow Great Britain, and he insisted that Canada's representative alone sign the Halibut Treaty with the United States, whereas previous treaties of this nature had also been signed by the British minister. Canada's first legation was opened in 1927 in Washington, D.C.

ever, was rejected by a Liberal Senate, which still favored the original Laurier plan.

It had been Borden's intention to pursue the defense question by submitting plans to Britain based on the offer to take part in imperial defense and foreign policy, so long as it was based on a collective system in which both partners would exert their due and proper influence. However, he did not have a chance to put through his Navy Bill. In August 1914, World War I began.

A NATION IN WAR AND PEACE

FOR THE FIRST TIME IN HER HISTORY, Canada found herself fully involved in a war abroad. Despite the tensions that had been building up in Europe, and the arguments over the naval question, Canada had not given deep and serious consideration to the possibility of war. Europe had seemed a very long way off, and Canada had been preoccupied with her internal affairs. Nevertheless, when Germany struck at Belgium, Canadians entered into the war effort without reservation. At first most French Canadians were as concerned as English Canadians in their desire to support Britain and France against the invading Germans. Later, however, past and present ill treatment of French Canadians by the English-speaking majority led to a bitter struggle over the issue of conscription.

To deal with the emergency the government passed the War Measures Act in 1914. The first Canadian fighting men sailed for England in the autumn of 1914. Canadian troops were in action on the Western Front for four years.

On Land, Sea and in the Air

It was the first foreign war that Canada entered as a unified nation, and the Canadians made history. Their reputation for gallantry on the battlefields and in the air during World War I is remembered even to this day, when there has been another war to overshadow their exploits. They defended the front at Ypres, where they had massive casualties while holding their line against a heavy gas attack. In 1916 the Canadian Corps engaged in the great Somme advance, bearing the brunt of the attack, slogging through mud and blood. In 1917 they were at Passchendaele, and with inspired skill they captured Vimy Ridge. Their contribution to final victory can be measured by the fact that in this war Canada's losses were about equal to those of her giant neighbor, the U.S. On the sea the Canadians developed a cadre of Atlantic veterans who after the war used their experience to create the Royal Canadian Navy. During World War II this navy played a major role in the Atlantic convoy system.

In the air many Canadians became legendary "aces," duelists of supreme daring and skill in the two-man contests of those early days of aerial warfare. Captain William Avery ("Billy") Bishop, V.C. (1894-1956), later Air Marshal Bishop of the Royal Canadian Air Force, was officially recorded as shooting down 72 enemy aircraft. "Billy" Bishop embodied the legend of those early pioneers of war in the air and became a popular hero to boys throughout the Commonwealth.

After World War I

During the war, by the self-sacrificing generosity of its policies and the heroism of its soldiers, Canada defined its character more clearly as a nation. The Paris Peace Conference of 1919 brought Canada to the inner councils of the great powers. Borden made full use of the opportunity to demand unequivocally that Canada's status as an independent power be recognized, since her part in winning the war had been such a large one. Largely as a result of Borden's determination that his country's great role be appreciated in full, the Dominions were given separate representation at Versailles, and each, later, received a seat of its own in the League of Nations.

The Domestic Front

On the domestic front things were not quiet. A quick postwar boom had as quickly deflated into a slump, and there was much social unrest. Winnipeg was paralyzed by a general strike called by the Trades and Labor Council of the city to support the demands of the metal and building trades. Large public demonstrations were held. A force composed of special constables and militia was quickly gathered together and sent to quiet and disperse the demonstrators. This force found itself confronted with a shouting mob. Mounted Police drew their pistols and charged. The crowd was dispersed and the strike leaders were arrested. The brief postwar upsurge of the Canadian labor movement had been broken.

TROUBLE ON THE FARM

In agricultural regions, also, trouble was brewing. War-inflated farm produce prices had to be maintained if the industry was to be kept on its feet. As early as 1916, the Canadian Council of Agriculture, the national union of all the provincial farmers' organizations, had issued a call for a new agrarian policy of low tariffs and reciprocity with the United States.

Out of this unrest the United Farmers movement developed. In Ontario it won the 1919 election and took over the government in Toronto. The movement spread, and in a conference, in 1920, at Winnipeg the farmers founded the National Progressive party, which gained an astonishing success in the federal elections of 1921. However, its power declined steadily during the 1920s.

WILLIAM LYON MACKENZIE KING

The two old parties, the Conservatives and Liberals, each sought new leaders. After the retirement of Borden in 1920, a seasoned young statesman, Arthur Meighen (1874-1960), took his place as the leader of the Conservative government. His stay in office was short. In the general election of December 1921 he was beaten at the polls (outnumbered even by the Progressives) and replaced by William Lyon Mackenzie King, the new head of the Liberal party. Mackenzie King seemed to have all the qualifications that were needed at this particular time in Canada's history. He was a left-wing liberal who was already well known for the successful work he had done as a labor conciliator; and he had years of practical experience behind him under Sir Wilfred Laurier, first as deputy minister and then as minister of labor.

If the people had been expecting an immediate program of sweeping social reforms, however, they were to be disappointed. But King did lead Canada rapidly toward complete independence from Britain in the shaping of her foreign policy.

KING AND CHURCHILL

From the start King was determined that Canada should not be involved in any quarrel that was not her own. He also wanted her free to make her own decisions and no longer to be considered a colony. Canada was a nation, and King would not accept anything less than full recognition of her

As Canada's population grew and settlements spread, the stern-wheeler became a familiar sight on the many coastal and inland waterways. Where no railway existed it was the best means of reaching points from which mules and horses could be used to complete the journey to remote settlements. Here we see the stern-wheeler Thomas *on the Peace River in Alberta in 1929.*

status as such. His opportunity to make his stand clear came soon after he took office. In a violent quarrel that blew up between Turkey and Britain over the peace settlement in the Dardanelles, the then British colonial secretary, Winston Churchill, publicly warned Turkey that if the matter were not solved to Britain's satisfaction, there would be a war in which Turkey would have to fight all the Commonwealth nations. But Churchill, speaking for Britain, had taken this stand without consultation with the Commonwealth governments. This statement by Churchill, which seemed to commit Canada to war without prior consultation, aroused anger in Canada. When her military support was invited, King emphatically refused to commit Canada to any sort of cooperation, except after consultation with the Canadian parliament.

National Independence on the World Scene

The old idea that Canada and Britain should, as it were, automatically work side by side in diplomatic affairs was dead. If the idea's death was not made obvious by the Turkish incident, it was certainly made so in 1923, when Canada insisted that her representative alone should sign the Halibut Treaty with the United States. Previously it had been the custom to have the addition of the British minister's signature to a treaty of this nature. In the same year, the Imperial Conference stated that the Dominions now had the general right to conduct their own foreign policy. A definition of Dominion by the Imperial Conference of 1926 was written into the Statute of Westminster in 1931.

While loosening her imperial ties, Canada was also gradually becoming, after her close involvement in World War I, more and more preoccupied with her home problems. She was now much concerned with internal affairs, many of them of prewar origin, such as the issues of tariff and railroad policy. In this atmosphere the Conservatives made a strong recovery.

In the election of 1925 the Conservatives outnumbered the Liberals, but King continued to govern with the help of the Progressives, the party formed in 1920 by the farmers in the hope that it could introduce a program of lower tariffs and publicly owned utilities. On the issue of a constitutional dispute he had had with the governor-general, Lord Byng, in 1926, King beat the Conservatives in the general election that followed, and their leader, Arthur Meighen, retired.

The Great Depression

Mackenzie King's rule as prime minister was to last until 1930, undisturbed by any major crisis until the stock market boom collapsed in September 1929. This precipitated the general economic depression, which was made worse for the Canadian farmers by a severe and protracted drought.

If the Liberals had organized help for the farmers, they might have continued to hold the government. As it was, the government assumed a lethargic attitude, relying on what were considered the usual processes of a free economy to restore matters to order again.

RICHARD B. BENNETT

The new Conservative leader, Richard Bedford Bennett (1870-1947), had no drastically different approach to offer, but he did promise national aid to the provinces and increased protection to certain industries.

After nearly a decade of Liberal rule (interrupted only by a short-lived Conservative government during the King-Byng dispute of 1926), the country decided to give the Conservatives a chance. Bennett won the general election of 1930.

As soon as he was in office, Bennett set about trying to tackle the problems of the depression, problems that seemed to be worsening. He raised the tariff; he launched a small program of public works; and he set up a royal commission to study the mounting financial problems of the railroads. These measures proved quite inadequate.

By 1933 the depression was at its worst. Throughout the world millions of people were impoverished. As a primary producer Canada was very hard hit. The long drought was turning the prairies into arid wastes, and the price of wheat had sunk to its lowest level. The whole fabric of the Canadian society seemed to be disintegrating. Provincial and local governments faced a crippling burden of debt and an unprecedented need to supply their people with social services, but under the constitution they lacked the taxing powers needed to cope with these problems.

NEW PARTIES

There was a growing resentment among the unemployed, and new political movements sprang up. There was the Social Credit movement, under William Aberhart (1878-1943), a high school principal who had conceived the plan of a wider distribution of wealth among the people by means of monetary reforms—"social dividends," which would be paid by the government. He led his party to power in Alberta in 1935, where it has remained ever since. It has not really put social credit into practice, partly because monetary policy is a federal prerogative.

The Union Nationale in Quebec, a conservative party with slight resemblances to Mussolini's fascism, took power there in 1935 under Maurice Duplessis. He remained Quebec prime minister, except for a four-year period, until his death in 1959.

In addition there was the C.C.F., the Cooperative Commonwealth Federation, which grew out of the Progressive movement and was supported by western farm organizations. Closely associated with the labor movement, it advocated government planning and ownership of all the main industries. It was, in effect, a Socialist party, but of the English Fabian rather than the Marxist variety. There were no strong tendencies to fascism or communism in Canada.

In 1935, with a general election near, Bennett made a series of five broadcasts on the radio, outlining an extensive reform program inspired chiefly by Roosevelt's New Deal in the U.S. It was to meet the new economic and social demands of the time. Bold as the move was, it succeeded only in arousing the scepticism of a big section of the Conservative party; and the public did not believe in Bennett's political conversion to a principle of state intervention in the economy. He lost the general election, and the Liberals

Right: *The impressive Changing of the Guard ceremony at the Parliament Buildings.*

returned to power under Mackenzie King.

WORLD WAR II

SUCH PRECURSORS OF WORLD WAR as the Japanese invasion of Manchuria, the Italian attack on Abyssinia and international involvement in the Spanish Civil War were matters that the average Canadian did his best to ignore. They could be dismissed as being of no direct concern to Canadian interests. French Canadians in particular were violently opposed to being drawn into another "imperialist war." With his finger on the pulse of the people, Mackenzie King pursued a policy of isolation. Like England, France and the United States, Canada did her share to ensure that the League of Nations would take no action against fascist aggression, in spite of such warning voices as that of her greatest newspaper editor, John Dafoe of the Winnipeg *Free Press.*

When the time came for Canada to face the Munich crisis in September 1938, she was still holding to her isolationist position. After Munich, however, a change of feeling gradually became apparent, and during the winter of 1938-39 the true nature of Hitler's designs was brought home to the Canadian public to a degree not yet true in the United States. Canadian leaders, like those of Britain, reluctantly concluded that they must not allow Nazi aggression to proceed further.

This change of mood was reflected in a speech that Prime Minister King made at an official luncheon given to King George VI and Queen Elizabeth of Britain while they were on a visit to Canada in the spring of 1939. "Free institutions and democratic ideals," he said, "are dear to the hearts of your people in Canada as to the people in any other part of the empire. We regard their preservation as the common concern of all." When the German attack on Poland came, the Canadian people were ready to stand with Britain and France in attempting to stop it.

Parliament Buildings, Ottawa. During the 1930s the Canadian government directed its efforts toward overcoming the severe economic crisis of the depression. In foreign affairs the country kept itself free of involvement and followed a policy of isolation. Like most Western democratic nations, Canada ignored the implications of the Japanese attack on China and the difficulties building up in Europe. After the beginning of the dismemberment of Czechoslovakia at the Munich Conference in September 1938, the isolationist mood of the Canadian people began to change.

Lack of Preparation

Canada, however, like Britain and France, was unprepared for war. Canadians are not a military people. In battle they had proved their valor, but after 1918 the insanity of war became once more a remote possibility. Canada reduced the size of her army, air force and navy until they were little more than token forces. In 1939, on the brink of war, the total strength of the army, navy and air force was less than 10,000 men. The Royal Canadian Navy had only 13 ships, and the Air Force a handful of outdated aircraft.

It is therefore all the more remarkable that in World War II Canada was eventually able to raise a force of over 1,000,000 men and women, most of them volunteers.

Canada Declares War

After Hitler had defied the British ultimatum of Sept. 3, 1939, the Canadian parliament convened on September 7, and the government introduced a resolution to commit Canada to war against Germany. The debate was quiet, for the House had already resolved that it had no alternative but to go to war. When the vote was taken, only five members were in dissent. On September 10 Canada declared war.

French Canadians accepted this second war more readily than they had the first. Ernest Lapointe, Mackenzie King's chief French-Canadian lieutenant, appealed for national unity, and French Canadians responded by volunteering in large numbers for military service. But like Britain and France, the country was lulled into a false sense of security by the placid weeks of the "phony" war. As the government's policy had upset no one and the Conservative opposition was weak, it was not surprising that the Liberals easily won the general election called early in 1940. But the great awakening to the grim realities of the war were near at hand.

After Dunkirk

In April 1940 the Germans launched their successful invasions of Denmark and Norway. On May 10 they attacked the Netherlands and Belgium and swept everything before them. On June 17 France sued for peace. Hitler was now in effective control of the continent, and Canada was left as the second largest power in the war against Hitler's Europe.

Faced with disaster, Canada quickened her wartime production and began augmenting the armed services. The whole Canadian economy was placed under stringent governmental control. With the wholehearted and effective cooperation of business and labor leaders, and led by the minister of munitions and supply, the Rt. Hon. C. D. Howe, Canada turned out nearly $10 billion worth of war equipment, including 16,000 aircraft, 1000 naval and cargo ships, 8000 small craft, 50,000 tanks and gun carriers and 800,000 army trucks. The whole Canadian labor force was mobilized toward the most efficient prosecution of the war, but until 1944 the issue of conscription into the armed services had not come to a political crisis because of the large numbers of volunteers. Mackenzie King had tried to avoid conscription because French Canada was so strongly opposed to it, but in the autumn of 1944, when the war in Europe was reaching its peak and the Canadians on the battlefield were losing so many men, it became a question of keeping the army up to battle strength. The minister of defense. J. L. Ralston, demanded conscription and was supported by English-Canadian opinion in both major parties. It was a difficult situation for King; he had devoted his political life to the conciliation of the French and the English Canadians, and now he was faced with a situation that must antagonize one side or the other and increase the breach between them, whichever decision he made. He made a last desperate attempt to solve the problem by trying to secure volunteers among those men who had been called up under the National Resources Mobilization Act. The attempt to get sufficient volunteers was a failure. Mackenzie King was at last forced to authorize the sending of 16,000 men who had been conscripted for home service to the overseas battle area.

The anticipated storm of protest from French Canada did not break.

During World War II, though Canada's population was only 12,000,000, the nation's armed forces grew to 1,000,000 men and women. It was the grueling task of the Royal Canadian navy based in Halifax (shown here) to convoy the multitude of ships carrying men and supplies to Britain.

A number of Quebec Liberal votes went against the government in Parliament on this issue, but King's new chief lieutenant from Quebec, Louis St. Laurent, supported him completely. Mackenzie King's delaying policy over the issue had also convinced many that he had done everything he could to avoid a repetition of the antagonism of 1917-18.

Canadian Soldiers, Sailors and Airmen

In the Normandy invasion the burden of the first assault was borne equally by Canadian, British and American troops. After June 1944, the Canadians, with the British at Cannes and with the U.S. at Falaise, took part in key operations. They crashed through the German defenses into Belgium, liberating the great port of Antwerp and thus admitting vital supplies for the final struggle. They struck at many German strongholds and were victorious. Their contribution to the disintegration of the German army was of great importance in the final victory, and the Canadian First Army was among those who led the attack on the Rhineland.

They fought also in the grinding campaign that slowly and bloodily fought its way up the Italian peninsula, and it was a Canadian general to whom the Germans surrendered in Holland. Earlier in the war, Canadian troops had borne the burden of the ill-fated, heroic assault on Dieppe, which provided a preliminary testing for an invasion of the continent in 1942.

The role of the Royal Canadian Navy was less spectacular but no less grueling. During World War II the tiny peace-time navy was expanded until in 1945 it comprised nearly 100,000 men. Only a minor naval power in 1939, Canada acquired one of the world's largest fleets of convoy vessels. The Canadian navy after 1940 bore the chief burden of convoying ships across the grey, bleak vistas of the North Atlantic, carrying men and supplies to Britain. This was a service that involved much hardship from wind, rain, ice and the sudden engulfing storms characteristic of the ocean, as well as from the enemy. Quick battles were fought with hit-and-run German submarines, often operating in wolf-packs.

The expansion of the Royal Canadian Air Force between 1939 and 1945 was considerable. From a negligible strength in 1939, it had risen by 1945 to 250,000. Almost one-fourth of the bombers under British command that pummeled Germany during the last year of the war were supplied by the R.C.A.F. Canadian air crews also served in Africa, Asia and Italy and contributed to the convoy system by patrolling the British coasts.

Under the British Commonwealth Air Training Plan, Canada made another vitally valuable contribution to the war effort. Besieged Britain lacked free air space in which to train pilots: Canada provided it, and it was there that young airmen of all Commonwealth countries learned the craft of aerial military combat.

The population of Canada during the war years was about 12,000,000 men, women and children: of these more than 1,000,000 men and women joined the armed services. This was an awe-inspiring proportion when one takes into account that the overall figure of 12,000,000 included the aged and the ailing and also those active in farms and factories.

The Canadian coat of arms. The shield bears the royal arms of England, plus the lilies of France in the last quarter. At the bottom are three maple leaves, the emblem of Canada. The lion on the crest has a maple leaf in its dexter paw. Above the flanking lion and unicorn respectively are the Union Jack and the flag of old France. Above all is the crown of Great Britain. The motto refers to the fact that Canada extends from the Atlantic to the Pacific.

THE POSTWAR YEARS

WORLD WAR II ENDED IN AUGUST 1945 with the capitulation of Japan. Canada at peace was able to consider her position as a world power. This small nation was, until the recovery of western Europe and the rise of the great nations of Asia in the 1950s, the world's fourth greatest military and industrial power. She clearly could not return to a position of isolation and would have world-wide responsibilities in the postwar years.

Beginning in 1964 and lasting through 1967, Canada celebrated the 100th anniversary of the union of the colonies of British North America. To honor the conference held in 1864 in Charlottetown, at which the first steps were taken toward confederation, Queen Elizabeth II and her husband, Prince Philip, visited that city and the Queen dedicated the Fathers of Confederation Memorial Building, a striking new concert hall, theater and cultural center. The royal party was in Canada from October 5 to 13, traveling also to Quebec City, where the Queen addressed the Quebec legislature (shown here), and to Ottawa, the capital of the nation.

Postwar Responsibilities

The coming of the Cold War was brought forcibly home to the Canadian government and people in September 1945, when Igor Gouzenko, an official of the Russian embassy, sought the protection of the Royal Canadian Mounted Police. Gouzenko revealed that secret military information had been divulged to the U.S.S.R. Canada was clearly involved in the struggle between the two great powers, the U.S. and the U.S.S.R., and she played an important part in the creation of the North Atlantic Treaty Organization in 1949, as a defensive alliance against Russian power in Europe. Her chief security clearly lay in her close relationship with the United States. This had been put on a formal basis in 1940, with the establishment of the Permanent Joint Defense Board, and reinforced in 1957 with the creation of NORAD for the air defense of North America.

CANADA AND THE UNITED NATIONS

The details of the organization of the United Nations was a matter on which Canada voiced some definite views of her own, and she was to play a significant role in that body. It was obvious, of course, that the major powers would play the decisive roles in the postwar world, but there was also an important role for a middle power such as Canada to play. Through her external affairs minister, L. B. Pearson, Canada took the initiative during the 1950s in the creation of United Nations peace-keeping forces, and in the Gaza Strip, the Congo and Cyprus, Canadian troops formed the largest contribution to such forces.

THE COMMONWEALTH

In 1947 Canada took the initiative in persuading the original Commonwealth nations that their association might include republics, such as the newly independent India, as well as monarchies such as the older Dominions. A new pattern for the future was thus created. In 1960-61 Prime Minister Diefenbaker allied Canada with the Afro-Asian members of the Commonwealth against Britain and Australia, which were reluctant to antagonize South Africa.

DOMESTIC AFFAIRS

In the federal election of June 1945, Mackenzie King and his Liberal government were again returned, partly because they had presented a program of social reform to the people that borrowed heavily from the left-wing C.C.F. party. King was now nearing the end of his tenure of office. A personally unpopular man whose extreme caution and gift for dividing opponents and beclouding issues had infuriated many, he had nevertheless an uncanny ability to gauge public opinion. He governed the Dominion from 1921 to 1948, with only two breaks, briefly in 1926 and again between 1930 and 1935. He held the country together in the very strong divisions created by the conscription issue. He chose a powerful team of ministers and civil servants who performed magnificently through the war years and whose younger members even 20 years later were leading politicians, businessmen, and senior civil servants.

LOUIS S. ST. LAURENT

In 1948, Mackenzie King retired from political life, and Louis S. St. Laurent (1882-), a distinguished and scholarly French-Canadian lawyer whom King had persuaded to enter politics during the war, when he had become minister of justice, succeeded him. St. Laurent was completely bilingual in French and English and contributed much in his own person and by the strength of his government to the unity of Canada. It was significant, too, that a French-Canadian prime minister should commit Canadian troops to Europe in peace time and to a major role in the United Nations action in Korea. St. Laurent's first year in office, 1949, also saw the entry of Newfoundland into the Dominion as the tenth province.

The Road to Prosperity

The end of the Korean War marked a period of accelerating prosperity for Canada. The measures that had been taken to prevent a postwar slump had been effective; most Canadians were enjoying a new and unprecedented affluence. The production of new cars and kitchens and houses and a host of consumer goods kept the economy buoyant.

Discoveries of vast reserves of oil and natural gas in Alberta and of iron ore in Labrador and Quebec made Canada for the first time a significant exporter of these resources. Canada also became one of the world's leading uranium producers. Her steel industry expanded fivefold in the period 1945-65, and she continued to expand her two leading exports, wheat and pulp and paper products, during the 1960s. Great construction projects were undertaken, such as the St. Lawrence Seaway, the building of new towns like Kitimat and Schefferville, the construction of the Trans-Canada highway, transcontinental oil and gas pipelines, the world's longest television network, and an island in the St. Lawrence at Montreal, which was the site of the Expo 67 world's fair.

Aided by a high birth rate and an influx of nearly 3 million immigrants between 1946 and 1965, Canada's population reached 20 million in 1966.

Lester Bowles Pearson (1897-), Canadian statesman. Pearson joined the diplomatic service in 1928. He was the senior Canadian adviser at the Dumbarton Oaks (1944) and San Francisco (1945) conferences that led to the establishment of the United Nations. From 1948 to 1957 he served as foreign minister in the cabinet of Mackenzie King, and during much of that time he headed his country's delegation to the UN. For his services in behalf of the UN, which included mediating the Palestine crisis in 1947 and the Suez crisis in 1956, Pearson was awarded the 1957 Nobel Peace Prize. In 1958 he became the head of the Liberal Party, and when the Liberals won the 1963 elections Pearson became prime minister of Canada.

Political Change

During this long period of prosperity there was no serious political unrest. St. Laurent triumphed in the elections of 1949 and 1953. But by 1956 the Liberal government had been continuously in power for 21 years, and it was showing the effects of old age.

JOHN G. DIEFENBAKER

In 1957 the Liberals were defeated by the Conservative party, headed by John G. Diefenbaker (1895-). Since he had won only a plurality in 1957, Diefenbaker went to the polls again in 1958 and won 208 out of 265 seats.

By the end of 1957, Canada's economic climate was already beginning to change. There was an increase in unemployment and a pause in the postwar period of Canada's rapid growth. Diefenbaker was not a strong prime minister, and public confidence in his ability to govern gradually lessened. In the election of 1962 many voters turned to two smaller parties, the New Democrats and Social Credit, while others swung back to the Liberals, with the result that Diefenbaker lost nearly half his seats and was barely returned with a plurality.

LIBERALS IN OFFICE

The Liberals under Lester Pearson had begun to rebuild their party after the defeat of 1958 and to work out new policies. In the election held April 8, 1963, they won 129 seats, the largest number of any party, while the combined members of the other parties took 136. Pearson became prime minister as head of a minority government.

In the years that followed, the Liberals managed to weather several storms, including a dispute over the introduction of a new Canadian flag (showing a maple leaf on a white background, instead of the Red Ensign), and, later, one arising from charges of corruption and negligence against some cabinet ministers. The Liberal government faced another general election on Nov. 8, 1965, and was again returned without an overall majority.

In April 1968 Pearson retired and Pierre Elliott Trudeau succeeded him as Liberal party leader and as prime minister. Trudeau proceeded to dissolve parliament and to call for new general elections in the hope of securing a majority. The elections held on June 25, 1968, gave Trudeau and the Liberal party the firm majority they had sought.

FUNDAMENTAL DATES

c. 1000 Leif Ericsson discovers Canada.
1534-41 Jacques Cartier, French navigator, explores Canadian coasts and discovers the St. Lawrence River.
1608 Quebec is founded by Samuel de Champlain, Father of New France.
1627 Cardinal Richelieu, chief minister of France, forms the Company of One Hundred Associates to develop New France.
1665 Jean Talon arrives as intendant of New France.
1670 The Hudson's Bay Company is founded.
1758 First Assembly of Nova Scotia meets.
1759 Quebec falls to the British.
1774 The Quebec Act is passed.
1791 Act Creating Upper and Lower Canada is passed.
1837 Rebellions break out in the Canadas.
1848 Responsible government is granted in Canada and Nova Scotia.
1867 The Dominion of Canada is established by the British North America Act.
1870-71 Manitoba and British Columbia are created Canadian provinces.
1885 The Northwest rebellion is quelled and the Canadian Pacific Railway is completed.
1899 French and English Canadians are divided on participation in the South African (Boer) War.
1896-1913 Wheat boom and western settlement.
1905 Saskatchewan and Alberta are created Canadian provinces.
1914-18 Canada goes to war.
1919 Canada's part in Paris Peace Conference prepares the way for her becoming fully independent in foreign affairs with a seat in the League of Nations.
1931 The Statute of Westminster formalizes Canada's Dominion status.
1929-39 The world economic depression and drought bring hardship to the Canadian people.
1939-45 Canada declares war on Germany and builds up defense forces.
1945 Canada becomes a member of the U.N.
1949 Newfoundland joins Canada.
1956 Canada plays a major role in the U.N. over the Suez Crisis, for which Pearson is later awarded the Nobel Peace Prize.
1957 The Liberal government is defeated by Diefenbaker's Conservatives.
1967 The centenary of Confederation is celebrated with Expo 67.
1968 Pearson resigns and Trudeau becomes prime minister.

Prospect For Canada Today

Canada in the mid-60's, despite political and cultural divisions, was a country of almost limitless possibilities. Its natural wealth, developed and undeveloped, was immense, and it was already an advanced industrial state with the second-highest living standard in the world. The arts in Canada were at last coming fully of age in the mid-20th century. The Canadian people had matured slowly, and the national character was still being formed. Paradoxically, one of the nation's strengths derived from the very fact that created divisions: that Canada was a bilingual and bicultural state and had peoples, in addition to those of British and French extraction, from every part of the world, who for many years had been coming to make a new life in a new country. As a presence in world affairs Canada had the good fortune to be a strong middle power without an imperialist past, and therefore had an opportunity to work for peace in a way that could be accepted as fair and disinterested by nations of every race, size and ideological persuasion.

THE FINE ARTS

ESKIMO ART

THE FORM OF CANADIAN ESKIMO art has always been limited by the Eskimos' living conditions. Because the Eskimos migrated from the coast where they dwelt during the winter to the inland regions during the summer, their possessions had to be portable and utilitarian. As a result, Eskimo art is on a small scale. The availability of materials was also a determining factor; walrus tusks and bones as well as reindeer antlers and occasionally driftwood were the most commonly used materials during the prehistoric period (which actually lasted until the early 18th century).

The Dorset Culture

The Dorset culture of Canada began to take form during the 7th century B.C. and is believed to have disappeared in about 1300 A.D.

The Dorset culture was first recognized in 1925 from various objects in the National Museum of Canada at Ottawa, which had been excavated from sites at Cape Dorset on the Hudson Strait and Coats Island in the Hudson Bay. Since then, remains of the Dorset culture have been discovered throughout the entire region of northern Canada. According to radiocarbon dating and archaeological evidence, the oldest site, located on Southampton Island, existed in about 675 B.C.

DISTINGUISHING FEATURES

The art objects and decorated tools and weapons of the Dorset Eskimos have been distinguished from those of succeeding cultural periods and neighboring regions by virtue of their small size and delicacy, and the presence of deeply incised decorative lines. In addition, sculpted forms produced by the Dorset Eskimos are distinguishable by their extreme simplicity.

Incised geometric patterns appear on many utilitarian objects—knife handles, harpoons, spoons—produced by the Dorset Eskimos; as adornment was never allowed to interfere with the function of the tools or weapons, the designs are extremely simple.

Incised marks on sculpted animal and human forms, as well as on certain kinds of utilitarian objects, including spatulas, have a special significance that goes beyond decoration: They are supposed to represent, in an extremely abbreviated fashion, the skeleton and vital organs of a living being. The skeletal motif usually incorporates an "x" for the head, pairs of short slanting lines for the ribs and vertical lines for the legs.

The practice of portraying the internal structure as well as the external form, a type of "X-ray" art developed by many primitive cultures, reveals something of the way the Dorset Eskimos perceived the world around them; realistic art was, to them, not only a reproduction of what can be seen by the eye, but what is known to be there as well.

HUMAN FIGURES

Human figures carved by the Dorset Eskimos differ from those of other prehistoric Eskimo cultures: Not only were the faces carved with care, but great attention was also given to heads, arms and legs. This is exemplified by the walrus-tusk figurine of a male (c.1000 A.D., Eskimo Museum, Churchill, Manitoba), found on Igloolik Island, and by the small statue of a man with a boy on his shoulders (c.1000 A.D., Museum of Archaeology and Etnnology, Cambridge University, England), also excavated from a site on Igloolik Island.

ANIMAL CARVINGS

Carvings of animals are more numerous than those of human beings, and are usually naturalistic in form, although they, too, can be extremely stylized. Even the most

An example of a contemporary Eskimo print made from a soapstone plate. Since 1949 the Eskimos have begun to use their 2000-year-old art of engraving to produce such prints for sale in Canada, the United States and Europe.

naturalistic zoomorphic carvings are, however, very simple, showing the Dorset Eskimos' ability to bring out the characteristic features with a minimum of detail.

A large majority of these pieces of sculpture are representations of the creatures with which the Eskimos were most familiar—the walrus, whale, seal, polar bear, owl and reindeer.

Another category of this branch of their art is formed by carvings of animals which had disappeared from the Eskimos' hunting grounds, such as the musk ox (see page 86). Sculpture in this category was endowed with a magical power that was supposed to bring the animals back to Eskimo territory.

The Thule Culture

Soon after 1000 A.D., there was a mass migration of the Thule Eskimos of Alaska, who moved eastward along the Arctic coast of Canada to Greenland.

During a period of about 300 years, the Eskimos of the Thule culture who settled in Canada gradually took over the land as well as some of the traditions of the Dorset Eskimos; by about 1300, the latter were absorbed into the new population and their culture disappeared completely. The Thule Eskimos thrived in the Canadian Arctic until about 1700.

The most typical Thule carvings are representations of human beings, characterized by flat, featureless heads and the use of stumps to indicate arms and legs.

Among the most common examples of miniature carvings left by the Thule Eskimos are simply wrought birds, adorned with rows of dots. The function of these birds, which appear to be in a swimming position, was possibly magical, although recent evidence suggests that they might have been used as pieces in a game of chance.

The Historic Period

The degeneration of the Thule culture during the 18th century was due to two major factors: contact with the European settlers, and a marked decrease in the number of whales in the Arctic, related to a considerable climatic change in northern Canada. As a result, Thule art disappeared completely. With only a few minor exceptions, nothing was produced in the field of art by the Canadian Eskimos between the beginning of the 18th and the middle of the 19th century.

Eskimo art, which had been dying out as a result of environmental factors and the coming of the white man, is currently enjoying a rebirth stimulated by the interest of provincial governments and private art groups. The simplicity of form and the truncated arms and legs of this contemporary soapstone sculpture, Mother and Child, *is in the tradition of earlier Eskimo art.*

MODERN ESKIMO ART

Since about 1850, a new type of Eskimo art has emerged in Canada. Because sculpture made during the historic period has often been produced for trade or sale and has thus been governed by foreign standards, it has lost its traditional significance. The stylistic features of prehistoric sculpture have, however, been maintained in many cases, especially when the subjects are Eskimo in origin. This is exemplified by numerous animal carvings, including those of the walrus and the seal.

CONTEMPORARY SCULPTURE

During the last 20 years, there has been a revival in the production of Eskimo sculpture in the regions of Cape Dorset and other parts of Baffin Island. This has occurred largely as a result of the work of the Canadian J. A. Huston, who, with the support of the Canadian Handicraft Guild and the Department of Northern Affairs and Natural Resources, has encouraged the Eskimos to produce soapstone and ivory carvings for the commercial art market. The subjects include human figures, family groups (see this page), animals and even Eskimo spirits (see page 153).

PRINTS AND GRAPHIC ART

Since 1949 the Eskimos have also been encouraged to channel their 2000-year-old practice of engraving toward a new end—the production of prints, which are being sold in Canada, the U.S. and Europe. These prints are made from soapstone plates, which have been engraved either directly or from patterns (see page 151). The subjects, ranging from hunting scenes to representations of animals and birds (see page 154) are, however, generally unrelated to traditional Eskimo engraving, which was confined to abstract designs and symbolic forms.

This flat soapstone carving of an Eskimo spirit is typical of contemporary Eskimo art. The unsophisticated form, the embryonic limb and the simple features incised on the smooth surface lend a childlike quality to the figure.

INDIAN ART

THE INDIANS OF CANADA ARE NOT completely distinguishable from the other Indians of the North American continent, as most of their cultural regions extend into the U.S.

The Northwest Coast Indians

The territory that was occupied by the Northwest Coast Indians extended from the southern tip of Alaska through the Canadian coastal zone to central Oregon in the United States.

Artistically the most important cultural group in North America, the Northwest Coast Indians are famous for their wood carvings, which are paralleled in primitive art only by New Zealand Maori sculpture.

The tribes that form this culture—the Tlingit, Haida, Tsimshian, Bellacoola, Kwakiutl, Coast Salish and Nootka—shared the same basic way of life, which depended on the easy availability of food and an unending supply of wood.

The abundance of natural resources brought about two things: a culture that encouraged material wealth beyond personal needs and a great deal of leisure time. These in turn produced a large patron class with a demand for works of art, and a large number of professional artists to satisfy this need.

Artists were hired by wealthy members of society to produce carved poles, masks, costumes and other ceremonial paraphernalia, as well as household utensils, in order to establish or advance their social standing. Many of these objects were made to be given away under the *potlatch* system.

The heraldic nature of the society also played a role in the development of Northwest Coast Indian art. All objects, ranging from house posts to personal utensils, were adorned with heraldic emblems that served not only as personal signatures, but as symbols indicating family lineage and clan and tribal membership.

The art of the Northwest Coast Indians that has been handed down intact is almost exclusively in the form of wood sculpture and comes from the period that began in the early 18th century, just prior to the Indians' contact with Europeans, and ended in about 1910.

STYLES AND FORMS

Three-dimensional carvings are either naturalistic, as seen in some freestanding figures and masks, or abstract. The latter style, which is more common, is found on certain types of ceremonial pole. These incorporate a series of vertically arranged figures that merge into each other to form an overall pattern. In this case, only the trained eye can decipher the individual forms.

On the other hand, two-dimensional sculpture is always abstract. Humans, animals and mythological creatures also form the basis of carving found on flat surfaces, although in many cases, in order to create pleasing decorative motifs, they are distorted even further beyond recognition than they are in three-dimensional work. There are a number of conventional devices that the Northwest Coast Indians have developed to create these motifs. Most common is the splitting technique, in which a figure is cut down the middle and laid out flat so that all of its sides are visible at once. "X-ray" art—in which the internal as well as external parts of a creature are portrayed—was also used on occasion.

In general the carvings of the Northwest Coast Indians are extremely powerful. Surfaces are boldly wrought and brilliantly painted in strong hues, well exemplified by the poles in Stanley Park, Vancouver (see page 76). There are, however, some regional variations of style.

The Haida and Tsimshian Indians, situated in the northern and central coastal zones of Canada, were noted for the conventionalized design patterns that appeared in their two-dimensional low reliefs. During the late 19th century, however, their sculpture became more naturalistic, due to the influence of neighboring tribes. Haida art is further characterized by its technical precision, apparent in the carefully executed details, and by the fact that less emphasis than was usual in Northwest Coast art was placed on color (see page 77).

The Tlingit Indians, who lived in southern Alaska and the northern region of Canada's west coast, developed the most distinguished style; technically on a very high level, their carvings are outstanding for their powerful designs and strong colors.

CARVED POSTS AND POLES

As the Indians of the Northwest Coast did not practice totemism—a belief that certain animals are related by blood to families or groups—their sculpted posts are misnamed when referred to as "totem poles," even though this term is commonly applied to them.

The most important function of their sculpted posts was a heraldic one. The anthropomorphic and zoomorphic beings, as well as the mythological creatures, serve as symbols of family and tribal lineage and are sometimes used to depict the history or legends of individuals or groups. In addition, although the Indians of this region did not consider the figures they carved on their posts to be sacred or untouchable (another aspect of the totemic belief), they did feel that these creatures acted as guardian spirits, who could, for example, help a hunting expedition to be successful.

The posts are made from cedar columns, ranging from 10 to 70 feet in height and from one foot to three feet in diameter. Of the four major types, the most common is the memorial pole, placed along the beaches in front of the village dwellings. Erected on the death of chiefs, memorial poles are covered with heraldic symbols and forms that tell the tribe's history.

The second major category consists of mortuary posts, which are placed at each end of a chief's grave or, in some cases, are used to support the tomb itself. This type usually consists of a single human or animal motif (see page 155).

The third group consists of house posts. Some are placed a short distance from the house (see page 78), others on the house, forming part of the main façade and doorway; house interiors also have special kinds of posts that are placed along the walls or, in houses belonging to the wealthy, in the center

In an attempt to rehabilitate a culture threatened with extinction, as well as to revive a dying art form, government agencies and interested art groups are now encouraging the production of Eskimo art. The naïve character of Eskimo art is illustrated by the somewhat whimsical print on top. Below it is a sealskin painting called Dangers Facing the Seafarer, *done in a flat primitive style,*

This stylized, symbolic bird of the Haida Indians is characteristic of the ancient art of wood sculpture of the Northwest tribes. Such heraldic figures were used to represent family ancestors and tribal spirits. This example of the Haida Indian's craft is from the Queen Charlotte Islands.

of the room, marking the seat of honor. Usually shorter than posts found out-of-doors, interior house posts are adorned with family crests and carvings that tell family legends.

MASKS

The Northwest Coast Indians have produced some of the world's most outstanding masks made by primitive man. Beautifully designed and executed, there are static masks—some too large to be worn—and masks with movable parts, such as eyes, which are operated by a piece of string. In addition, there are mask-complexes, which have two and sometimes three faces that can be changed by the wearer. As with carvings on posts and poles, masks range from naturalistic representations to abstractions of both anthropomorphic and zoomorphic beings. Their meaning is also similar; they usually symbolize family lineage and position of rank within a clan or tribe. In addition, masks have an important function in secret societies and ceremonies (see page 156).

The Rocky Mountain Indians

The Rocky Mountain Indians lived a nomadic existence in the Rocky Mountain region of North America and in Canada were confined mainly to British Columbia.

The only distinguishing art product of the Rocky Mountain Indians is the decorated basket, created by the women of the various tribes. Either round or rectangular, the baskets are adorned with layers of applied geometric or zoomorphic forms, which are usually pale yellow, black or red. These motifs are purely decorative, lacking in symbolic significance.

The Woodland Hunters

The Woodland Hunters dwelt in the vast forest region of central Canada that extends from Alaska to Newfoundland.

The artistic expression of the nomadic Woodland Hunters was limited to the adornment of birch-bark canoes, containers, drums and grave-markers, as well as baskets, clothing and leather goods. In most cases, decoration on utilitarian objects is simple, but that on wearing apparel, usually in the form of embroidery or painting, can be quite elaborate.

The Woodland Farmers

The Woodland Farmers were situated in the regions of the Great Lakes and the upper St. Lawrence River. Living a less nomadic existence than the Woodland Hunters, the Woodland Farmers were able to develop more advanced forms of art.

By about 100 B.C., known as the Burial Mound I period, the Woodland Farmers were creating handmade pottery vessels, an art that reached its peak between the 14th and 18th centuries. At the same time, sculptured forms were made from antler, bone, shell and stone.

The Woodland Farmers of the Historic period are best known for the finely executed wood carvings that appear on many of their utilitarian objects. Carved pipes, in the shape of zoomorphic and anthropomorphic beings, represent their most distinguished products in this field.

Many of the masks used for festivals and by secret societies were also carved out of wood. For symbolic reasons, these were roughly hewn while still part of a living tree. After being cut down, they were refined, painted in red or black hues and decorated with, for example, strands of elm, used to represent hair.

The Plains Indians

Prior to the 18th century, the life of the Plains Indians was based on agriculture and hunting. This existence provided them with enough leisure to develop a variety of art forms, including sculpture, painting and embroidery, which were of an unusually high quality.

After the Plains Indians acquired the horse at the end of the 17th century, their traditional mode of life came to an abrupt end. As nomadic hunters, they wandered into the Great Plains region of Canada. The artistic expression of the Plains Indians was limited to glass-bead embroidery and skin-painting, which vary in form and meaning according to whether they were produced by women or men.

THE FRENCH COLONIAL PERIOD

ALTHOUGH CANADIAN ART IS IN THE mainstream of Western traditions, especially French, English and American, it has derived many of its characteristic features from the environment and history out of which it has evolved. The French colonial period may be defined as 1608-1759, from the first settlement at Quebec to the British conquest.

Very little of artistic importance was produced in Canada between 1608, when Quebec was founded, and 1660, the year a number of French settlers arrived in the new country. The introduction of art into New France during the last 40 years of the 17th century was largely due to the support of the Catholic Church, which served as a patron of the arts throughout the French colonial period. In 1668 the first great impetus was given to the arts when Laval, the first bishop of Quebec, established a school of arts and crafts at St. Joachim, near Quebec. This school trained not only sculptors and painters but carpenters and stone masons as well.

Architecture

The late 17th- and early 18th-century architecture of New France developed in the region of the St. Lawrence River. It consisted of rural structures—parish churches, village community buildings, cottages and manors—and urban architecture—churches, monasteries, government buildings and town houses. The latter appeared in Quebec, Montreal and Trois Rivières, the only towns then in existence.

Although the classical style of architecture, which prevailed in Paris during this era, appeared in only one building of New France—Château Saint-Louis (1691-1700) at Quebec, now replaced by Château Frontenac (see page 88)—some of its characteristic elements, including simplicity, clarity of form and symmetry, are evident in many of the major French colonial buildings.

There are also a few isolated examples in Canada of the influence of the Baroque style of the French provinces of the time.

MONASTERIES AND CONVENTS

The earliest religious buildings erected in New France were monasteries and convents, exemplified today by the Hôpital Général (1671-78) and the Ursuline Convent (c.1687), both at Quebec. The Hôpital Général, initially built as a Jesuit monastery of the Récollet Order, was turned into a hospital between 1695 and 1712. Although it has been added to several times, some of the original parts remain, including the basic monastic plan, which incorporates the refectory, chapel, cloister and kitchen.

The north and west sides of the Ursuline Convent are all that remain of the late 17th-century structure, the third erected on the same site. Extensive additions made between about 1850 and 1872, as well as during the early 20th century, gave the convent its present appearance.

URBAN CHURCHES

Old Notre Dame, the original parish church of Montreal (begun in 1672), was roughly modeled on the church of Saint Sulpice, at Paris. In 1722 the building was extensively redesigned to resemble more closely the Paris church. Its new plan, drawn up by Chaussegros de Léry (1682-1756), incorporated an elaborate Baroque façade, flanked by two tall towers. The façade and one of the towers were never executed, but the plan was used for a number of churches built near Montreal, as well as the church at Cap Santé (1754-73), near Quebec.

The church at Cap Santé still

A painting of the Thunderbird mask of the Kwakiutl Indians. The Thunderbird, a deity common to all the Northwest Coast Indians, was believed to have the form of a great eagle. The flight of the Thunderbird, always accompanied by a flock of smaller birds, was said to produce thunder and lightning. When soaring down from the mountains in search of whales, the Thunderbird would detach its snake belt and use it as a harpoon.

stands today, but Old Notre Dame was demolished in 1830, except for its façade, which was added to the Récollet church at Montreal (1706), destroyed in 1867.

TOWN HOUSES

The earliest forms of domestic dwelling in and around Montreal and Quebec were rows of attached houses, which shared common end gables set above the roof to prevent the spread of fire.

When this type of house, based on European town dwellings, developed in New France into a free-standing structure during the early 18th century, many of the original features, including the end gables, were preserved. This is exemplified by the Château de Ramezay (1704-23), at Montreal (see page 159).

RURAL CHURCHES

The rural churches of New France were based, in general, on medieval as well as 15th-, 16th- and 17th-century village churches of northern France. Characterized by their simplicity, the churches of New France usually have a steep-pitched roof, an arched doorway and a round window on the west façade, and a belfry on the roof above the main entrance. The belfry of the earliest churches incorporates a single or double lantern, topped by a needle-like spire.

Although the late 17th- and early 18th-century churches of New France were made of wood, they were usually rebuilt in stone some time after about 1710. This procedure is exemplified by the history of the parish church at Saint Pierre, on the Isle of Orleans, which was built in wood in 1676 and reconstructed in stone around 1716.

In 1722 New France was divided into 82 independent parishes, with the result that a great number of new churches were built. After this time, rural churches became slightly more elaborate and larger. Among the finest examples of the mid-18th-century churches is the parish church of Sainte-Famille (1743-46), also on the Isle of Orleans.

COUNTRY HOUSES

The earliest cottages built in New France, rectangular in shape, consist of low, white-washed walls made of stone rubble, high-pitched roofs and a chimney located either on the ridge of the roof or at one of its ends. Casement windows appear in the lower portion of the cottage; dormers are set in the roof.

After 1700 new features were added to this basic form. One of the first was the overhanging eave, which was sometimes curved at the base, as it was not supported from below. From this developed the veranda, created when posts were built to support the extending eaves. Although verandas appeared at about the same time in New York, it is possible that they evolved in both regions independently. As verandas are well suited to the Canadian climate, creating protection from sun and snow, they were not only incorporated into many cottages built between 1770 and 1800, but were added to a number of older dwellings as well.

The manor house, a larger and more elaborate version of the cottage, is represented by the Ferme St. Gabriel (1698), at Point St. Charles, near Montreal, and the presbytery (c.1686) at Batiscan, near Trois Rivières. They are among the oldest in the province of Quebec.

The art of portrait painting flourished in Canada during the late 18th and early 19th centuries. Many of the paintings were unsigned and, although similarities in styles are detected by experts, the names of the painters remain unknown. The traditional subjects of portraits were prominent citizens, such as the member of the Hurtubise family shown in this 18th-century painting titled Lady with a Dog. (The National Gallery of Canada, Ottawa)

Sculpture

Sculpture, mainly in the form of wood carving, was the most important art in New France. Its style was initially derived from religious works of the northern French provinces.

STYLISTIC DEVELOPMENTS

Some of the earliest extant carvings in Quebec, executed during the late 17th century, were made by Jacques Leblond de Latour (1670-

The principles of architecture brought to Canada by the early French settlers were based on the building methods of the north of France. The low rectangular shape of the building, the sharply pitched roof, the gables and the whitewashed rubble walls are characteristic features of the first dwellings. This house erected in Quebec in the early 1700s is an example of the type still found throughout the Quebec countryside.

1715), who was a master at the St. Joachim school of arts and crafts between 1690 and 1706.

Two French sculptors active in Quebec and Montreal at the turn of the century were Denis Mallet (c. 1670-1704), also an instructor at the school, and Charles Chaboillez (1654-1708), known for his work on an altar (1702) in the Récollet Church at Montreal.

Although the style of these early carvings reveals the artists' direct knowledge of European sculpture, the work was often crude. Human figures, for example, were often unnaturally proportioned, their expressions stereotyped, and their bodies bulkless and flat. This tendency was carried to its furthest extreme in folk art, produced by people untrained in the techniques of carving. At its best the effect is one of great power and moving simplicity.

SCULPTORS OF QUEBEC

While many carvers in the new country were breaking away from European styles, the Levasseur family of Quebec, which included the leading 18th-century sculptors of New France, helped to perpetuate French carving traditions. The most important members of the family were Noël (1680-1740), his sons François Noël (1703-94), and Jean Baptiste Antoine (1717-75), and his cousin Pierre Noël (1690-1770).

The most outstanding joint commission carried out by the family was the retable (altar wall) and altarpieces (1734-36) for the original chapel of the Ursuline Convent at Quebec, now preserved in the new chapel built in the early 20th century on the same site.

Of their later works, the best known is the altarpiece (1743-49) in the church at Sainte Famille, on the Isle of Orleans, which is Rococo in form.

The Levasseurs were succeeded by the Baillairgé family during the last quarter of the 18th century. Among its members were François (1759-1830), who worked in a French Classical style that he learned while studying in Paris, and Thomas (1791-1859), his son.

SCULPTORS OF MONTREAL

Leading 18th-century sculptors at Montreal were less influenced by European styles than their contemporaries at Quebec.

During the first half of the 18th century, the leading Montreal studio belonged to the Labrosse family, headed by Paul (1697-c.1760), known for his statuettes of apostles (1741) and an alterpiece (1742) in the parish church at Longueuil, near Montreal.

One of the most famous sculptors of the second half of the century was Philippe Liébert (1732-1804), from France. Although he usually worked in a style resembling that of the Levasseurs, his relief carvings on the sacristy doors (c.1772) at Sault au Récollet Church, which incorporate Biblical subjects and scenes based on the history of the parish, are quite original.

Painting

Although painting played a subordinate role to sculpture during the French Colonial period, it was in demand for the decoration of church interiors and for portraits.

FRENCH STYLES

The French style of painting was brought to New France during the 17th century. This was carried out by professional French painters who stayed in the new country for varying lengths of time. Among them was Jacques Leblond de Latour, better known as a sculptor, who painted religious pictures for the Quebec Seminary as well as a portrait of Bishop Laval.

The most important of these artists was Frère Luc (c.1614-85), a member of the Récollet Order. Active in Quebec between 1670 and 1672, he painted a number of religious scenes for the town's churches and monasteries in a style that reflects that of his master in Paris, Simon Vouet (1590-1649). Frère Luc also executed a number of portraits that are characteristically French in style.

DECLINE OF THE FRENCH STYLE

By the early 18th century the French style had become more primitive in the new country. This is exemplified by several votive pictures and portraits. Among the votive pictures are the *Votive Picture of Madam Riverin* (1701; Commemorative Chapel at Sainte Anne de Beaupré), which is almost completely devoid of a sense of space, and the tapestry-like *Votive of the Survivors of the Shipwreck at Lévis* (1754; Commemorative Chapel at Sainte Anne de Beaupré).

Toward the end of the 18th century, there was a return to the French style of painting, as a result of several painters from Quebec having studied in Europe. The most notable artist of the new trend was François Beaucourt (1740-94), whose *Portrait of a Negress* (1786; McCord Museum, Montreal) is reminiscent of contemporary French court paintings.

The Minor Arts

Various religious orders, especially that of the Ursuline nuns, were responsible for introducing the arts of needlework, embroidery, lacemaking and the gilding of church ornaments into the new country.

Silversmiths working in New France also maintained a high standard of craftsmanship. Among the most famous were Paul Lambert (1691-1749), François Ranvoyzé (1739-1819) and Laurent Amiot (1764-1839).

THE BRITISH COLONIAL PERIOD

THE FOUNDING OF AN ENGLISH colony at Nova Scotia (which also until 1784 included modern New Brunswick) marks the beginning of the British Colonial period in Canada (1749-1867). After the conquest of New France in 1759, English art styles were brought into the eastern townships of Quebec, as well as into parts of Upper Canada, now Ontario. This was done by English and Scottish settlers and the Loyalists who emigrated from the U.S. during the 1780s.

Architecture

As British Colonial architecture in Canada was based on 18th- and 19th-century English buildings as well as on Colonial architecture in America, derived from the same sources, it is essential to examine briefly English architectural styles during this period.

Early-18th-century English architecture was dominated by the works of Sir Christopher Wren (1632-1723), whose own major stylistic sources were Italian Renaissance and Baroque buildings. James Gibbs (1682-1754), Wren's most important successor, also derived inspiration from Italian buildings, as is evident in his most famous creation, St. Martin-in-the-Fields (1722-26). Gibbs was also among the followers of the Italian Renaissance architect, Andrea Palladio (1508-80); he helped to establish in England the Palladian style, which is often characterized by the presence of a portico embracing the two lower stories of the main façade, and by the use of heavy ornamentation.

Although based on Italian Renaissance architecture, the Georgian style of the later 18th century in England is less heavy than the Palladian style. Georgian architects worked in stone and red brick, using classical architectural motifs such as pilasters and pediments, and achieved their effect through a close regard for proportions and symmetry.

The Regency style, which prevailed in England from 1800 to 1830, differs from Georgian design mainly through the replacement of stucco and plaster, which lend themselves to finer details and refinements, with stone and brick.

English Neoclassical buildings, constructed during the 18th and 19th centuries, were based on, or were replicas of, ancient Greek and Roman structures.

THE GEORGIAN COLONIAL STYLE

In the British colonies of Canada, 18th- and early-19th-century buildings, both religious and secular, were based on Georgian structures of England and New England. In spite of the use of different materials (in many cases, wood replaced stone and brick), the essential features of the English Georgian style were maintained in the colonies; most notably, the symmetrical arrangement of windows and the use of classical ornamentation.

The earliest Georgian Colonial buildings of significance, which are based more on American than English structures, are located in Nova Scotia. These are represented by St. Paul's Church (1750) at Halifax (see page 162),St. Edward's Church (1788) at Clementsport, and the Perkins House (1767) at Liverpool.

THE REGENCY AND PALLADIAN STYLES

During the first decade of the 19th century, the English Regency style reached the Maritime Provinces. One of the best examples of the Regency style in Nova Scotia is Government House (1801) at Halifax, built by Isaac Hildreth (1741-1807). In Ontario, Regency architecture is exemplified by Poplar Hall (c.1800) at Maitland and by a number of town houses at Port Hope.

More popular, however, was the much older Palladian style, which also appeared in the British colonies of Canada around 1800. Province

One of the oldest town houses in Montreal is the Château de Ramezay, erected between 1704 and 1723 by the French governor of Montreal, Claude de Ramezay. The Château, a free-standing structure that took its characteristics from the "row houses," was purchased by the British as a governor's residence after the Treaty of Paris of 1763. Now a museum, the Château is a repository for memorabilia of the French Colonial period.

Wilhelm von Moll Berczy (1748-1813), an early portrait painter, came to Canada by way of America in 1792. Employed initially by the London Land Company as a colonizing agent, he ultimately settled in Montreal and turned to painting and architecture. This portrait of the colorful Mohawk chief, Joseph Brant, done in 1797, is believed to have been painted near the Indian's home at Burlington Bay on Lake Ontario. (The National Gallery of Canada, Ottawa)

House (1811) at Halifax, Nova Scotia, the original section of Osgoode Hall (1829) at Toronto, and the government building at St. John's in Newfoundland are among the best extant examples of the Palladian style in Canada.

THE NEOCLASSICAL STYLE

The Neoclassical style was the most widely used form of building in the British colonies of Canada between 1810 and 1850. Although many Neoclassical buildings were designed after English models, those constructed in the region of the southern border of Upper Canada were built according to the principles of the American Neoclassical architects, who based their structures more literally on ancient Greek and Roman buildings. The façade of St. Andrew's Church (1831) at Niagara-on-the-Lake, for example, was copied from engravings of an ancient Greek temple.

This Virgin and Child *wood sculpture of the School of Montreal was made by an anonymous woodcarver of the 18th century. Probably intended for the convent at Laprairie, it is believed to have been inspired by a statue given by Champlain to the Notre-Dame-des-Victoires in Quebec.* (The National Gallery of Canada, Ottawa)

Painting

Most of the paintings produced during the British Colonial period in Canada were executed by English or English-trained artists. The English painting tradition, especially that of the landscape, was important to the development of Canadian painting.

PORTRAITS

During the last two decades of the 18th century, as the British towns in Canada became more prosperous, there was a great demand for portrait paintings. This was met by a number of artists with varying degrees of training, who came from England and Europe.

Among them was Robert Field (c.1769-1819), who studied in London before he settled at Halifax in 1808. Considered to be the best portrait painter in the Maritime Provinces, Field painted some of Nova Scotia's most notable citizens.

Wilhelm von Moll Berczy (1748-1813), from Saxony, was active as a portrait painter in Quebec and Montreal. Among his most important works are two versions of *Joseph Brant, the Mohawk Chief* (1797, Quebec Seminary and the National Gallery of Canada; see above).

One of the leading 19th-century portrait painters, active in Upper Canada, was George Theodore Berthon (1806-92), who had studied under Jacques Louis David (1748-1825) while in Paris.

TOPOGRAPHICAL ARTISTS

English landscape painting first reached the British colonies of Canada by way of the topographical artists—amateur artists trained to record their surroundings in drawings and watercolor paintings. Most of the topographical artists active in the British colonies of Canada were officers in the Royal Engineers and Royal Artillery.

In the Maritime Provinces an especially large number of scenes and events were recorded by topographical artists. Among the earlier examples is *Wolfe's Expedition at Miramichi* (c.1759, the National Gallery of Canada) by Hervey Smyth (active 1759-70).

William Eager (c.1796-1839), from Ireland, produced records of scenes and historical events in the Maritime Provinces, using a style resembling that of leading English watercolorists of the time.

The most interesting topographical artist of the Maritime Provinces was, however, Thomas Davies (c. 1737-c.1812), who produced minutely detailed and richly colored landscapes (see page 164).

Topographical artists who worked in the province of Quebec included the Scotsman George Heriot (1766-1844), whose watercolors are close in style to English classical landscapes.

Richard Short (active 1759-64), who also worked in Quebec as well as in the Maritime Provinces, produced carefully wrought pictorial records of buildings, which are invaluable today to the student of architectural history.

Best known of the professional topographical artists was William Henry Bartlett (1809-54), who published books of landscapes executed in many parts of the world, including one entitled *Canadian Scenery* (1842).

KRIEGHOFF, KANE AND WHALE

During the middle decades of the 19th century, a group of painters flourished who devoted their attention to frontier and pioneer life and to landscapes. The three most significant were Cornelius Krieghoff (c. 1815-72), Paul Kane (1810-71) and Robert Whale (1805-87).

Krieghoff studied in both Holland and Germany, then went to the U.S. and, in about 1840, to Canada, where he spent most of the rest of his life.

His brightly colored landscapes and genre paintings show the influence of the Düsseldorf Academy, where he studied, as well as of 17th-century Dutch paintings. Among his tremendous output—over 700 works—are interior scenes, such as *The Studio* (c.1845, the National Gallery of Canada); portraits; pure landscapes, including *The Falls on the River Saint Anne* (1854, Breakey Collection, Quebec); and paintings based on Indian life. He is best known for his pictures of everyday habitant life in Quebec (see page 165).

Paul Kane emigrated from Ireland as a young boy. After extensive travels through the U.S. and Europe, where he studied paintings by the great masters, Kane returned, in 1844, to Toronto with plans to paint scenes of the prairies and Pacific coastal regions of Canada. Between 1846 and 1849, with the aid of the Hudson's Bay Company, Kane journeyed to Fort Vancouver and back, making small sketches of the country and its inhabitants. Many of

The first Canadian painting of a "conversation picture," that is, an animated group of figures, was Wilhelm von Moll Berczy's painting of The Woolsey Family *(1809), a prosperous merchant family of Quebec. An amusing notation on the back of the painting, written by J. W. Woolsey, the principal figure in the painting, reads: "The family group represented in this picture was painted in 1809, by Mr. Berczy, an amateur, assisted by his own son William. The eight portraits cost ten pounds each, the dog Brador was added without cost."* (The National Gallery of Canada, Ottawa)

these were enlarged into paintings, and some were reproduced in his book, *The Wanderings of an Artist Among the Indians of North America* (1859).

Some of Kane's well-known paintings, such as *Portrait of an Indian* (Royal Ontario Museum, Toronto; see page 119) and *Indian Camp* (Toronto Art Gallery; see page 114), show what great care he took to record all details of costume, decoration, and modes of Indian life. However, owing to the influence of European painting, Kane's works often possess qualities of the "grand manner;" this is especially evident in the aristocratic poses and expressions he has superimposed on his subjects.

The third artist in this group was the lesser known Robert Whale. Born in Cornwall, England, he studied in London before moving to Brantford, in Upper Canada, around 1850. Whale's early Canadian paintings—portraits and scenes of the Grand River region—were executed in a style that idealizes and elevates his subjects. His later works, exemplified by *Niagara Falls* (c. 1870, the National Gallery of Canada), combine a professional academic approach with a primitive type of style.

PLAMONDON

Among French-Canadian painters of the 19th century, Antoine Plamondon (1804-95), who had had some formal training in Paris, successfully combined the Canadian folk-art tradition with the French classical style. This is best seen in his portrait of the nun *Sœur Saint-Alphonse* (1841, the National Gallery of Canada).

THE LATER NINETEENTH CENTURY

DURING THE PERIOD FOLLOWING Confederation (1867), when the colonies of Canada were united into a self-governing dominion, there was an upsurge of nationalistic feeling, which was reflected in the arts.

However, the traditional borrowings of art styles from England, France and the U.S. did not cease, especially in the field of architecture.

Architecture

A large majority of the buildings constructed in Canada during the second half of the 19th century were based on the English neo-Gothic style. Features of Gothic Revival buildings, basically derived from medieval European architecture, include the use of the pointed arch in windows, doors and constructional supports, an emphasis on vertical elevation, and elaborate ornamentation.

The neo-Gothic style first appeared in Canada during the 1820s in the form of added ornamentation. This is exemplified by the neo-Gothic tower that was added to the otherwise Georgian church of St. John (1824) at Belfast, on Prince Edward Island.

Typical of the earliest Gothic Revival buildings in Canada are the church of Notre Dame (1829) at Montreal (see page 163), designed by the Irish-American James O'Donnell (1774-1830), and the basilica of Notre Dame (1841-46) at Ottawa.

The neo-Gothic style of the mid-1840s is well represented by the Anglican cathedral at St. John's (1846) in Newfoundland (see page 166). designed by the English architect Sir George Gilbert Scott (1811-78); and by Fredericton Cathedral (1845) at New Brunswick, modeled on a 13th-century parish church in Norfolk, England, by Frank Wills (1827-c.1857), who also designed Christ Cathedral at Montreal (1856).

The two most important commissions of the 1850s, carried out in an elaborate and sumptuous Victorian manner, were University College (1856), Toronto, and the central unit of buildings on Parliament Hill (1859-67), Ottawa (see page 147).

University College was designed in a Norman style by Frederick William Cumberland (1821-81), who had studied under Sir Charles Barry (1795-1860), architect of the Houses of Parliament at Westminster in London. Thomas Fuller (1822-98) was responsible for the Parliament Buildings in Ottawa (which were destroyed by fire in 1916 and replaced in 1919), and for its Library (1876), which has a magnificent dome (see page 167).

During the 1870s and 1880s, the late neo-Gothic style was used for all types of structure, from office buildings to grand country mansions; it still dominates the appearance of many major Canadian cities, especially those on the east coast.

THE ROMANESQUE REVIVAL

Reaction during the 1870s against the over-elaborate neo-Gothic style brought about a revival of the Romanesque style. This, characterized by its monumentality, heavy masonry and rounded arches, was first achieved on the American continent

St. Paul's, built at Halifax, Nova Scotia, in 1750, is the oldest Anglican church in Canada. The wooden building, designed in the Georgian style of New England, was built of timbers brought from Boston. The vaults beneath the church, which is popularly called the "Westminster Abbey of the New World," contain the remains of many prominent figures of Canadian history.

The Church of Notre Dame de Montreal is one of the finest examples of the neo-Gothic revival of the early 19th century. Built in the 1820s, it is one of the largest churches in North America. The elaborate structure and the complex tracery of ornamental detail are characteristic of neo-Gothic ecclesiastical architecture.

by Henry Hobson Richardson (1838-86) of Massachusetts.

Richardson's style is reflected in such Canadian buildings as Victoria College (1891), Toronto, designed by William Storm (1826-92), and Windsor Station (c. 1890), Montreal.

Painting

After Confederation, a number of local and national institutions were founded to encourage Canadian-born artists. Among these were the Royal Canadian Academy and the National Gallery of Canada, both established in 1880.

Among the leaders of late-19th-century Canadian painting was John Fraser (1838-98) who worked in the leading photographic studio, Notman's, in Montreal and Toronto. He gathered many artists to work for his company and was himself a fine Canadian landscape painter.

Robert Harris (1849-1919), though born in Wales, spent most of his childhood on Prince Edward Island. After studying in London and Paris, he settled in Montreal, where he began his career as an art teacher and painter. Harris' portraits and group studies show his ability to combine photographic realism with well-balanced composition.

THE TURN OF THE CENTURY

CANADIAN ART BEGAN TO TAKE ON a different form during the last years of the 19th century. This was largely due to the influx of new European styles, which tended toward richness and elegance.

Architecture

The École des Beaux-Arts at Paris, as well as schools in London and New York, where almost all architects of the period, whatever their nationality, wished to study, set the pace for the architectural styles in Canada at the turn of the century. At these institutions, students were required to study the history of architectural styles and how they could be applied to contemporary design. As a result, at these schools a specific style was allocated for every type of building—the Classical mode for banks and railway stations; the Gothic for churches, universities and government houses; the Georgian or Tudor for domestic dwellings; and the Italian Renaissance for office buildings.

Canadian architects were governed, to a large extent, by these academic principles. Henry Sproatt (1866-1934), for example, designed Great Hall, Hart House (1914), at the University of Toronto, in the English Gothic Perpendicular style (see page 191). In this instance, the English variant of the Gothic style was chosen in an attempt to recapture the atmosphere of the colleges at Oxford and Cambridge. The new central block of the Parliament Buildings at Ottawa (1919-27) was also Gothic in style (see pages 145 and 146).

Canadian architects also turned to Scottish castles and French châteaux in an effort to find a distinctively Canadian style that would blend with the Canadian landscape. The rugged Scottish castle served as a model for what is now the National Museum of Canada (1808) at Ottawa. The château style appears in such buildings as the Château Laurier (1910) at Ottawa, designed by D. H. MacFarlane (1874-1949), and the Canadian Pacific Hotel (1913) at Banff (see page 121). In some instances, elements from both castles and châteaux were combined to form what is known as the château-baronial style. This is best exemplified by Château Frontenac at Quebec (see pages 7 and 129).

Painting

At the turn of the century a variety of painting styles were being simultaneously employed in Canada. These ranged from the realistic style of the 1880s to Post-Impressionism.

As in architecture, the academic

Artists the world over have been inspired by the beauty and grandeur of Niagara Falls, first painted in 1698 by Père Hennepin. William Green (1760-1823), a visiting London artist, captured the falls' misty splendor in this painting dated 1804. (The National Gallery of Canada, Ottawa)

Captain Thomas Davies (c. 1737-1813), one of the finest of topographical artists, was trained in the authentic recording of landscapes at the Royal Military Academy at Woolwich, England. Davies' A North View of Fort Frederick *is a fine example of his perceptive and minutely detailed work.* (The National Gallery of Canada, Ottawa)

Cornelius Krieghoff (c. 1815-72), an itinerant musician and artist in Europe, emigrated to the New World and from 1840 to 1872 portrayed the lives of the French-Canadian settlers in many of his more than 700 paintings. Habitant Farm *(1849) captures the isolation of a small farm against the vast snowscape, yet conveys a feeling of the warmth of family life through the use of bright colors and the intimate grouping of the figures.* (The National Gallery of Canada, Ottawa)

approach to art that developed in Paris had an effect on Canadian painting at the turn of the century.

LANDSCAPE PAINTING

Horatio Walker (1858-1938) was inspired by members of the French Barbizon School, as reflected in his paintings of scenes executed on the Isle of Orleans.

Homer Watson (1855-1936) produced a number of landscapes of his native Grand River region. Executed in a semi-realistic style, his early paintings are reminiscent of the Hudson River School of the U.S., while his later creations show a strong similarity to the work of the English painter John Constable (1776-1837). Ozias Leduc (1864-1955) spent most of his life at St. Hilaire, near Montreal, where he produced small canvases filled with a mysterious atmosphere all their own.

IMPRESSIONISM

Impressionism, which developed in France during the 1860s, did not reach Canada until about 1900. It first appeared in the work of a few of those Canadian painters who

A passionate admirer of Indian life, the documentary painter Paul Kane (1810-71) devoted all his creative energies to the representation of North American Indians. White Mud Portage, *inspired by a three-year journey that he took through the western Canadian wilderness, is painted in a realistic style that is characterized by an infinite care for details.* (The National Gallery of Canada, Ottawa)

Above: *Construction of St. John's Anglican Cathedral, which was designed by Sir George Gilbert Scott (1811-78), was begun in 1847. The cathedral is considered a fine example of neo-Gothic architecture of the mid-19th century.*

Below: *The ornate interior of the Parliamentary Library was painstakingly rebuilt over a four-year period after the disastrous fire of 1952. More than half a million volumes are available here to Members of Parliament.*

had trained in Paris. Among them were Aurèle de Foy Suzor-Côté (1869-1937) and Maurice Cullen (1866-1934). Suzor-Côté used the impressionist style in his paintings of Quebec country and village scenes, exemplified by *Winter Landscape* (1909, the National Gallery of Canada). Cullen concentrated on winter landscapes of the Montreal area, using blues, violets, purples and pinks in a typically impressionistic fashion.

POST-IMPRESSIONISM

The Post-Impressionist movement in France, initiated by Cézanne (1839-1906), Gauguin (1848-1903), and van Gogh (1853-90), had an effect on at least two Canadian artists: James Wilson Morrice (1865-1924) and Ernest Lawson (1873-1939).

Morrice spent most of his life in Paris, where he became the first Canadian painter to gain international fame. His first artistic inspiration came from the paintings of the American James McNeill Whistler (1834-1903), who also spent most of his career in Paris. While he was associated with the *Fauve* movement (1905-08) and during the last phase of his life, Morrice turned to the use of brilliant colors and lively compositions, derived largely from the art of Henri Matisse (1869-1954).

Lawson's style was based on paintings by a group of New York artists who had been influenced by the *Fauves*. The most distinguishing quality of Lawson's paintings, such as *Misty Day* (c.1915, the National Gallery of Canada), is their richness of color and form.

Sculpture

Sculpture produced in Canada around 1900 was also governed by the principles of French Academicism.

The first Canadian sculptor of importance was Louis Philippe Hébert (1850-1917), who was trained in Paris. He is well known for his numerous bronze statues and memorials, which adorn the public buildings and squares of many Canadian cities. Among them is the *Queen Victoria Monument* (1901), on Parliament Hill at Ottawa.

THE NATIONAL MOVEMENT

THE NATIONAL MOVEMENT IN CANADIAN art, most evident in painting, occurred between 1913 and 1933.

Architecture

While the variety of architectural styles that appeared in Canada at the turn of the century continued to prevail up to about 1930, there was a minor movement toward a more functional, uniquely Canadian mode of building. The most significant work in this field was produced by engineers, whose designs were governed by the function of the structure, whether it was a factory, a bridge or a grain elevator. Ornamentation was discarded, and buildings gained any aesthetic appeal they might have from the arrangement of windows and of the simple geometric blocks of which the buildings were made.

Much of the inspiration for this type of construction came from the Chicago School, which developed under Louis Sullivan (1856-1924) and Frank Lloyd Wright (1869-1959). Ottawa's Daly Building (c. 1900), for example, was governed by the principles of the Chicago School.

Painting

Between 1910 and 1913, a group of eight young artists, most of them from an engraving firm, gathered at Toronto. Their common interest was landscape painting, which they pursued while on weekend holidays and sketching trips in the Georgian Bay region and in northern Ontario.

Members of the group were J. E. H. MacDonald (1873-1932) and Tom Thomson (1877-1917); Arthur Lismer (1885-) and F. H. Varley (1881-), who came from England in 1912; and Lawren Harris (1885-). They were joined by Franklin Carmichael (1890-1945), Frank Johnston (1888-1949) and A. Y. Jackson (1882-).

The group's leading spirit was Tom Thomson. Self-taught, he began sketching out-of-doors in about 1911. Although his earlier works are dark and somber, by 1913, through the influence of Jackson, he was painting in brighter colors and using a more spontaneous style.

During his brief career, Thomson completed only about 30 large paintings (see page 168). However, a number of his sketches, which represent his best work, have also been preserved.

GROUP OF SEVEN

Some members of this group along with other Canadian painters became official war artists during World

Above: *The Parliamentary Library in Ottawa, one of the greatest examples of neo-Gothic architecture in North America, was designed by Thomas Fuller (1822-98) and completed in 1876. Part of a complex of three buildings, the library combines 12th- and 13th-century Gothic features taken from English, French, German, Flemish and Italian buildings.*

Below: *The Center Block, Parliament's main building, was one of two destroyed by fire in 1916 and rebuilt in 1919. The interior, with its intricate lace work of stone, attempts to maintain the Gothic spirit of Thomas Fuller's brilliant original design, which was constructed 1859-67.*

War I. They reassembled in 1919-20, when they became known as the Group of Seven, and painted the rugged landscape of the Canadian Shield in bright, strong colors and stark, simple forms. They also tended toward creating a flat, decorative surface pattern, which Thomson had developed in his paintings of 1916 and 1917.

After 1922 the membership of the Group was somewhat altered. After Johnston left, he was replaced by Alfred Casson (1898-), in 1926; Edwin H. Holgate (1892-) and Lemoine Fitzgerald (1890-1956) joined in 1931 and 1932, respectively. In 1933, the Group of Seven was succeeded by a larger organization, the Canadian Group of Painters.

INDEPENDENT ARTISTS

There were several artists who, although contemporary with the Group of Seven, developed almost completely independently of them and at the same time stood apart from the National Movement.

The three most important were Emily Carr (1871-1945), John Lyman (1886-), and David Milne (1882-1953).

Emily Carr's earliest paintings were mostly based on British Columbian Indian life and landscapes. Her first important outside stimulus came from the *Fauves*, whom she studied in Paris in 1910 and 1911. After her return to Canada, she painted in brilliant colors and bold patterns,

Left: *Emily Carr (1871-1945), a student of the* Fauves *in France, found her work rejected by her countrymen on her return to Victoria in 1911. Discouraged, she gave up painting for 15 years until, through the interest of the Group of Seven and a growing public recognition, she regained confidence in her work. Her love of the West Coast Indian culture and of the great forests is reflected in the brooding solemnity of the heraldic figures in* Heina. (The National Gallery of Canada, Ottawa)

Below: *The Group of Seven, dissatisfied with the conventional renderings of the Canadian landscape by traditionalist painters, attempted through a bold and evocative use of form and color to convey the rugged majesty and power of the land. In* Approaching Snow Storm, *Tom Thomson (1877-1917), a leading spirit of the Group, reflects their impressionistic and often decorative style.* (The National Gallery of Canada, Ottawa)

The paintings of Alex Colville (1920-) convey, through the meticulous building up of detail as well as the clarity of each object, a quality called "magic realism." The subtle balance and the attention to detail of Hound in Field *typify his realistic style.* (The National Gallery of Canada, Ottawa)

and her work was rejected in her old province; as a result she stopped painting for over 15 years.

Encouraged by some eastern Canadian painters, including members of the Group of Seven, she began painting again about 1928. Her later works, often based on totem poles or the deep British Columbian forests, have a violent rhythm or a mysterious brooding quality about them (see page 168).

John Lyman opposed the nationalistic style of the Group of Seven in favor of the French decorative style that he learned from Matisse. Even in his landscapes of Canadian scenes, he maintained the qualities of French design and color, avoiding anything that would endow his work with a regional or national character.

David Milne's first artistic training was acquired in New York, where he was profoundly influenced by modern American and European paintings exhibited at the Armory Show of 1913, to which he himself contributed.

In 1928 Milne returned to Canada, and during the last years of his life he lived in extreme poverty in rural Ontario.

Sculpture

A number of sculptors were also involved in the National Movement, several of them directly influenced by the Group of Seven. This had varying effects on sculptural forms. For example, while Elizabeth Wyn Wood (1903-1966) attempted to reproduce landscapes in relief carvings, Frances Loring (1887-) executed portrait busts which show the same strength as the Group's paintings.

CONTEMPORARY ART

Contemporary art in Canada may be dated from 1933, the year the Group of Seven was dissolved. At that time, national art styles were beginning to be submerged in modern, international modes of art.

Architecture

THE INTERNATIONAL STYLE

The styles of Mies van der Rohe (1886-), Le Corbusier (1887-1965) and Walter Gropius (1883-), as they developed in Europe and the U.S., first appeared in Canada during the 1930s. One of the earliest buildings to contain elements of these styles is the T. H. and B. Railway Station (1933), Hamilton, which consists of a grouping of simple cubic shapes, adorned with windows wrapped around its curved corners.

International–style architecture, which can be seen in almost all major cities of the world, has become, since about 1950, the most commonly used building form in Canada. Characteristic features include the use of reinforced concrete or steel-frame constructions, which are usually penetrated by numerous symmetrically arranged windows.

There have been some architects, notably in Vancouver, who have attempted to break away from internationalism in an effort to create a modern Canadian style. This is best seen in certain houses on the west coast, which break away from austerity to blend with the natural

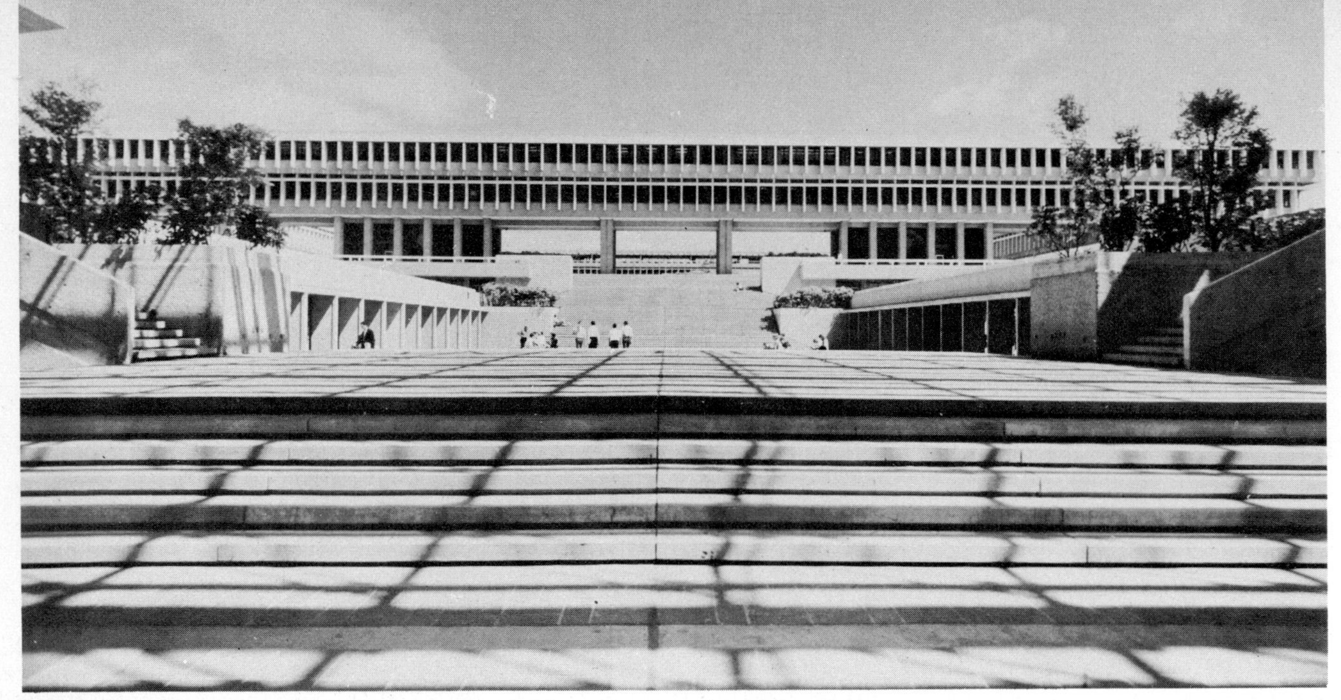

Above: *Designed by Arthur Erickson and Geoffrey Massey, the Simon Fraser University, near Vancouver, is a brilliant example of the style of architecture developing in the 1960s, which reflects a break with the bleak functionalism of the prior decade. The university, which opened Sept. 9, 1965, combines bold horizontal structures and broad flights of stairs around immense courtyards.*

Below: *One of the Group of Seven, J. E. H. MacDonald (1873-1932), a retiring and contemplative man, interpreted the beauty of the Algoma wilderness through a style characterized by the use of brilliant colors thickly applied. He had a passionate love of the land and in later years spent a great deal of time in the mountain solitude of the Rockies.* Leaves in the Stream *reveals in its swirling flow MacDonald's intense feeling for the country.*

surroundings. The new Shakespearean Festival Theater (1956-57) at Stratford, Ontario (see page 196), designed by Robert Fairfield, is another type of modern construction. Three unique masterpieces of the 1960s are Arthur Erickson's Simon Fraser University (see page 170), John Andrews' Scarborough College and the Finnish architect Viljo Revell's Toronto City Hall (see this page).

Above: *The growth of a new style of architecture in Canada is exemplified by this masterpiece of the 1960s, the unique City Hall in Toronto, designed by the Finnish architect Viljo Revell.*

Painting

REPRESENTATIONAL PAINTING

One group of contemporary Canadian painters has perpetuated the national landscape tradition by portraying scenes of Canada in a representational style. Although many of the artists in this category were inspired by the Group of Seven, they worked in a more subjective fashion than the Group, moving toward a greater simplicity of form.

In the paintings of Charles Comfort (1900-), for example, natural shapes have been abstracted into geometric masses, thus creating a surrealistic quality sometimes referred to as "magic realism."

Closely related to Comfort's paintings are those by Carl Schaefer (1903-), who has often reproduced abstract designs found in nature, as has Will Ogilvie (1901-). The New Brunswicker Alex Colville (1920-) is one of Canada's finest painters and the most influential "magic realist" painter (see page 169).

There are also several representational painters who execute portraits, most notably Edwin Holgate, who was a member of the Group, and Jack Humphrey (1901-). One of the few great portrait painters Canada has produced is an original member of the Group of Seven, Frederick Varley.

THE MONTREAL SCHOOL

Between 1939 and 1955, several artists working in Montreal formed a loosely organized group out of which developed an art movement or school of painting.

The basic unifying factors that held these painters together were their violent reaction against regionalism and the influence of the School of Paris—Matisse, Picasso and the Surrealists.

Contrary to the Canadian tradition, the human figure was their most important subject. As seen in the paintings of Goodridge Roberts

Below: *In* October on the North Shore, *Arthur Lismer (1885-), one of the Group of Seven, reveals through the use of bold colors and giant forms the strong impression made on him by the northern Lake Superior wilderness. Dedicated to the improvement of art education, he founded the Children's Art Center in Toronto and subsequently was invited by the Republic of South Africa to set up a similar institution there. Since 1940 he has been educational supervisor of Montreal's Museum of Fine Arts.*

(1904-), the human form was, however, used as a means of creating decorative patterns and pleasing shapes.

Alfred Pellan (1906-) was largely responsible for introducing the Surrealist and Abstract styles of France to the Montreal painters.

Léon Bellefleur (1910-), a Surrealist, was especially inspired by Pellan's art. Other Montreal painters who turned to Surrealist and Abstract styles as a result of Pellan's work include Jacques de Tonnancour (1917-), a pupil of Goodridge Roberts.

Perhaps the greatest Canadian painter of all was Paul Émile Borduas (1905-60), who helped to initiate Automatism (a variant of the Surrealist style, which attempts to portray the subconscious as a vital and active force). Borduas had a large following in Montreal during the 1940s and 1950s, which included the action painter Jean Paul Riopelle 1923-), now a resident of Paris. Riopelle's works, represented by *Wandering* (see below), are characterized by his use of iridescent colors applied with a spatula in small segments over the entire surface of the canvas.

VANCOUVER AND THE WEST COAST

Two artists lead the school of painting in Vancouver that began to develop in 1940. They are Jack Shadbolt (1909-), whose abstract paintings are based on organic forms such as roots, seeds and blades of grass, and B. C. Binning (1909-), known for his semi-abstract, decorative style, akin to that of Ben Nicholson.

Joseph Plaskett (1918-) and Donald Jarvis (1923-) of Vancouver execute paintings that show their concern for man's position in modern city life. Plaskett's paintings usually portray an isolated human being in a figurative style. Jarvis, on the other hand, has created an expressive cubistic style, which he uses to portray groups of human figures.

TORONTO

At present, Toronto is again developing a regional school of painting. Abstract Expressionism, the style being used by most contemporary Toronto artists, was first introduced into the city during the 1950s by a group known as the Painters Eleven, which has since been disbanded. Among its members were William Ronald (1926-), Harold Town (1924-) and Kazuo Nakamura (1926-).

Among the younger generation of Toronto painters experimenting with various contemporary styles are Graham Coughtry (1931-), Tony Urquhart (1934-) and Michael Snow (1930-).

Sculpture

One important contemporary sculptor, Louis Archambault (1915-), began his career as a ceramist. Influenced by the Abstract styles of painting in Montreal, where he has spent much of his life, Archambault turned to creating abstract forms in sculpture, represented by such bird forms as *L'Oiseau de Fer* (1950, the National Gallery of Canada). Younger sculptors include Gerald Gladstone, Armand Vaillancourt, Josef Drenters, Richard Turner and Robert Murray.

Jean Paul Riopelle (1923-), one of the young modernists and an acknowledged leader in the school of abstract expressionism. Together with Paul Emile Borduas, he established the mode of Automatism, a form of Surrealism that attempts to exalt the subconscious into an active, creative force. This intuitive art form was proclaimed by them in the manifesto Refus Global. *The style is shown here in Riopelle's* Wandering.

THE LITERATURE

FORGING A NATIONAL LITERATURE

Two Cultures

THE ENGLISH-CANADIAN AND THE French-Canadian literatures have developed in isolation from each other.

Until recently it has not been common for either French- or English-Canadian works to be translated into the other language. In fact, Canadian culture is not strictly bilingual. In Canada, two peoples who have originated from separate nations are living side by side; for a long period, in literature at least, they have almost totally ignored each other. The circumstances that caused their literatures to prosper independently were fostered by the first Canadian historians, who documented either the French or the English colonial history as though the other nation did not exist; and by schools, which propagated exclusively either the French or the English culture.

There is developing, however, among both French and English Canadians, a feeling of greater respect for the customs and heritage of the other.

Origins of French-Canadian Literature

The English victory, referred to by French Canadians as *la conquête* (the conquest), eventually precipitated among the French Canadians a feeling of unity and nationalism. However, for about 80 years the lack of any important French-Canadian literature reflected their lack of self-confidence and a real doubt about the possibility of their survival as a people. *Histoire du Canada* (The History of Canada) by François X. Garneau (1809-66), the heroic story of New France and of French Canada through early settlement, conquest and rebellion, published between 1845 and 1848, was the symbol and the instrument of a new French-Canadian awareness, and in fact marks the real beginning of French-Canadian literature. Young writers of the time, such as Antoine Gérin-Lajoie (1824-82), Joseph Octave Crémazie (1822-79) and Henri Raymond Casgrain (1831-1904), were inspired by the work of Garneau.

Encouragement and Publicity

Although dependent on different cultures, and flowering and declining at different periods, the French- and English-Canadian literatures have certain factors in common.

With educated people concentrated in the towns and communications poor, the emergence of a writer tended to depend on the efforts of a critic or publisher, who could discover and promote the local literary talent within his town.

PUBLISHER AND BOOKSELLER

It was generally true that the early Canadian writers gathered round one man, who encouraged their writing and was the motivating force behind the crop of literary journals each movement produced.

Joseph Howe (1804-73), publisher, politician and himself a poet, played such a role in Halifax, where he published the literary journal the *Nova Scotian* (1828-41), in which the jurist Thomas Chandler Haliburton (1796-1865) made his name as a writer. Haliburton was the first Canadian writer of major importance, and his accounts of Samuel Slick, the Yankee Clockmaker in Nova Scotia, contributed directly to a tradition of North American humor of which Mark Twain and Stephen Leacock are two leading examples. Joseph Octave Crémazie, bookseller and poet, was the center of the School of Quebec, and Henri Raymond Casgrain (1831-1904), a Roman Catholic priest, was its mentor and critic. Casgrain initiated three important literary reviews in the 1860s.

LITERARY PERIODICALS

These literary periodicals propounded the theories of the movements that inspired them. Until re-

Abbé Henri Raymond Casgrain (1831-1904), a Roman Catholic priest and critic, was a major figure in the School of Quebec, a group of writers who represented the first true flowering of French-Canadian literature. The Quebec School found a ready outlet for their work in the three literary reviews founded by the Abbé.

Oliver Goldsmith (1794-1861) is considered the first native-born, English-speaking Canadian poet. Named after his famous granduncle, Goldsmith wrote The Rising Village *(1825) in imitation of his granduncle's poem,* The Deserted Village. *Imbued with the simple values of a small, colonial society, the poem extolls the happy life of Loyalist settlers in the Acadian wilderness.*

cently, when their role was, to some extent, taken over by the anthologists, they were the primary means by which emergent poets could publicize their works before gaining enough confidence and support to publish a full collection of poems.

The Week (1883-96) published the poetry of Charles George Douglas Roberts (1860-1943), William Bliss Carman (1861-1929), Archibald Lampman (1861-99) and Duncan Campbell Scott (1862-1947), the leading poets of a regional and descriptive school of poetry. The organ of the School of Montreal, the periodical *Soirées du Château de Ramezay* (Evenings in the Château de Ramezay) publicized the rejection of the Romantic and patriotic tradition espoused by a young group of writers headed by the poet and critic Jean Charbonneau (1875-1960).

ENGLISH-CANADIAN LITERATURE

The Nova Scotian School

IN THE LATE 18TH CENTURY NOVA Scotia was the most advanced of the English provinces in Canada. The educated United Empire Loyalists from the newly independent U.S. flooded into the predominantly French populated territory after 1783 and established a centralized government. The port of Halifax, rich from trade that had accrued during the English blockade of European ports at the time of the Napoleonic Wars, became the cultural center of the colony and the birthplace of the first English-Canadian literary movement.

HYMNS AND SATIRES

Little had been written up to that time. The Puritan New Englander Henry Alline (1748-84), an immigrant to Nova Scotia, had published *Hymns and Spiritual Songs* in 1802 and a *Life and Journal* in 1806 of his experiences as a wandering preacher.

The Rev. Jonathan Odell (1737-1818), a Loyalist immigrant, wrote satires in the 18th-century style, mocking the North American rebels. Thomas McCulloch (1776-1843), a Presbyterian minister and educator, also found time to write a series of coarse and humorous fictional letters in a local newspaper, based on the local scene. The first literary movement began with Joseph Howe, at whose literary club the authors he had promoted in the *Nova Scotian* journal met for discussion and criticism. An American publisher's son and an immigrant, Howe, at the age of 24, edited his own newspaper. His wide culture was self-taught, but it inspired him to wish for an indigenous Canadian literature. His political interest prompted him to print a satirical and soon widely popular column by Thomas Chandler Haliburton.

A spirited and lucid writer himself, Howe published his *Western Rambles* (1828) and *Eastern Rambles* (1830) as a result of his travels through Nova Scotia to observe at first hand how it was being governed.

PIONEER EPIC

Howe was the patron and publisher of Canada's first poet, Oliver Goldsmith (1794-1861), a grandnephew of the Anglo-Irish writer of the same name.

Anxious to prove himself worthy of his kinsman, the author of *The Deserted Village* and *The Vicar of Wakefield,* the Canadian Oliver Goldsmith produced a poem, modeled in form on his granduncle's poem, called *The Rising Village* (1825).

In well-marshalled heroic couplets, he described in this work the struggles against the Indians, the difficulties of the first settlers, the villages and life of his day and his hope for Canada's future.

SAM SLICK

Haliburton was, by contrast, an original. His satiric anecdotes about the double-dealings of Sam Slick among the easily duped Nova Scotians appeared in the *Nova Scotian* in 1835. Sam Slick of Slickville became a famous figure throughout the English-speaking world. His adventures were combined in *The Clockmaker; or, the Sayings and Doings of Samuel Slick, of Slickville* (1837-40), *The Attaché, or Sam Slick in England* (1843-44), *Sam Slick's Wise Saws and Modern Instances* (1853) and *Nature and Human Nature* (1855).

Haliburton used Sam Slick to show up the minor but insidious corruption in politics and money and daily life that had become a part of the life of the colony and was making the Nova Scotians the prey of Slicks in real life.

Never cruel but invariably revealing beneath his boisterous humor, Haliburton wrote a racy, informal chronicle of the life of his times.

Haliburton emigrated to England in 1856 and became a Member of the British Parliament, which he remained until his death.

PIONEER AUTOBIOGRAPHY

The *Literary Garland* published poems by two sisters, Mrs. Catherine Parr Traill (1802-99) and Mrs. Susanna Moodie (1803-85), better known for their autobiographies *Roughing It in the Bush* (1852) by Mrs. Moodie and *The Backwoods of Canada* (1836) by Mrs. Traill.

These sisters, married to army officers, were educated women and had emigrated from England. Prolific and articulate authors, they are remembered for their humorous and lightly snobbish but truthful accounts of their experiences in the new country.

JOHN RICHARDSON

One of the first Canadian novelists was John Richardson (1796-1852). Richardson was born in Canada and had an Indian grandmother. He first went to England as an army officer. As correspondent of *The Times* of London, he returned to Canada, where he was stranded. Discharged by *The Times* because of his unacceptable views on the need for reform in the administration of the colony, he turned to free-lance writing to make a living.

Richardson had both a journalist's and a soldier's grasp of a dramatic situation and created tense scenes of battles and duels in his three-volume novel *Wacousta, or The Prophecy: A Tale of the Canadas* (1832); this book dealt with Pontiac's 1763 campaign in Michilimackinac and the siege of Detroit. As a sequel to *Wacousta,* he wrote one of his best books, *The Canadian Brothers* (1840), which is remarkable for its description of war with the Indians.

CHARLES HEAVYSEGE

Charles Heavysege (1816-76) was a working-class immigrant who was an avid reader of Shakespeare, Milton and the Bible.

In his narrative poems, mostly on Biblical subjects (*Saul,* 1857; *Jezebel,* 1867), he attempted a rousing and dramatic style.

The exaggeration evident in Heavysege's vivid but frequently gruesome imagery is equally pronounced in his rhetoric. Sensitive to the rhythm of language and intoxicated by its richness, he sometimes allowed his enthusiasm to lead him into ludicrous effect where he had meant to be dramatic. In *Count Filippo* (1860), Paphiana is told: "Dead, dead is Hylas; shot, young Hylas, shot. Banished into the air, Paph; blown point-blank into the world-wide welkin, shattered, shivered. All shattered, shivered, shot; oh shotting shame!"

Longfellow acclaimed Heavysege as "the greatest dramatist since Shakespeare."

Nationalism

Growing Canadian nationalism was crowned in 1867 by the Federation of British North America.

The author and jurist Thomas Chandler Haliburton (1796-1865), known for his satirical Sam Slick stories, was the first Canadian writer to win an international reputation. Strongly conservative in his political views, he became alienated from his contemporaries; in 1856 he emigrated to England and became a Member of Parliament, a position he held until his death.

The writing of Hugh MacLennan (1907-) is noteworthy for its treatment of Canadian society. Barometer Rising *(1941) focuses on the disastrous explosion of 1917 in Halifax and shows the main character growing into a new awareness of himself as a Canadian. In* Two Solitudes *(1945), MacLennan deals with the conflicts between English and French Canadians.* The Watch That Ends the Night *(1959) tells of the world of depression, the growing resistance to fascism, and World War II.*

The role of the writers was recognized as crucial, for they could, by expressing the patriotic feelings of their nation, unify the newly federated Canadians into one people.

McLACHLAN AND SANGSTER

A working-class Scots immigrant who was typical of his new country was Alexander McLachlan (1818-96), who compared the poverty he had escaped to the opportunities he found in Canada in his poem *Young Canada, or Jack's as Good as His Master.*

Charles Sangster (1822-93) anticipated the wave of nationalism that was to inspire, toward the end of the century, what has been named Canada's Golden Age of poetry. Sangster was a widely admired poet who took his self-imposed role as Canada's national poet seriously, although his sentimental pastorals are no longer very highly regarded.

MAIR, KIRBY AND OTHERS

The works of Charles Mair (1838-1927) were published in the years following Federation. In 1868 he produced his first collection, *Dreamland and Other Poems,* followed by *Collected Poems* in 1901.

Believing that to draw on one's national history is to "create an original and distinctive literature," he gave expression to the patriotism that was to become a feature of English-Canadian poetry in his poem *The Last Bison* (1890). His rhetorical verse drama *Tecumseh* (1886) treats the fate of the oppressed and dwindling Canadian Indians.

In 1887 *The Golden Dog,* a historical novel by William Kirby (1817-1906), was published.

Kirby, a journalist who edited the Niagara *Mail* from 1850 to 1863, spent about 11 years researching the way of life in Quebec while the town was under French rule. He used his material as a backdrop to *The Golden Dog.* Sympathetic to the old-world loyalties and the religious traditions of the French Canadians, he recreated them so that they genuinely came alive in his book.

Horatio Gilbert Parker (1862-1932, famous for his flamboyant romance *Seats of the Mighty* (1896), also wrote tales of the western pioneers. Parker's stories, such as *Pierre and His People* (1892), sentimentalized his characters by making them more passionate, strong and silent than life.

Literature of the New Dominion

A crop of periodicals heralded the emergence of a new generation of writers after Confederation. The *Canadian Monthly* (1872-82), *Nation* (1874-76) and *The Week* (1883-96) published the poetry of the leaders of the Romantic-nationalist movement—Charles Roberts, Bliss Carman, Archibald Lampman and Duncan Campbell Scott. The work of Carman and Roberts, who were brought up in the university town and provincial capital of Fredericton, New Brunswick, marks the beginning of a Canadian national literature in English.

Although not the best poet of the Confederation group of writers, Roberts was their leader. His *Orion and Other Poems* (1880) marked a new departure in Canadian literature.

After his brief but significant editorship of *The Week,* Roberts wrote a *History of Canada,* pub-

Mazo de la Roche (1885-1961), in her novel Jalna *(1927) and its sequels, wrote a tempestuous family saga that spanned a period from before the American Civil War to the 1950s. Her romantic idyl of the Whiteoaks family won her an enormous popular following.*

lished in 1902, and worked in journalism in New York. His nationalism suffused his patriotic poems, *An Ode for the Canadian Confederacy* and *Collect for Dominion Day.* Didactic and rhetorical in his more ambitious poetry, he was best when he confined his observations to country scenes. The titles of some of his poems indicate their domestic nature: *The Farmer's Winter Morning; The Oat-Threshing; The Pea Fields; In the Old Barn.* The lyrics are simple, and though Roberts had an eye for a salient detail, he created his effects by evoking a hazy mood picture. *The Kindred of the Wild* (1902) and his prose animal stories were very popular.

BLISS CARMAN

Bliss Carman, who published about 20 collections of poetry between 1893 and 1905, was a poet of landscapes, whose technique was to suggest a scene rather than to describe it exactly, sketching its details indistinctly.

His world resembled the scene he describes in one poem, a "vast dreamland," splashed with dramatic colors like the "smouldering west," or the "running gold" of a stream at sunset. Bliss Carman was a master of verbal melody and the careless or broken rhythmic patterns that convey his varied moods.

Journalist, politician, part-time poet and publisher of the Nova Scotian, *Joseph Howe (1804-73) was instrumental in bringing the first English-Canadian writers of major importance to the attention of the public. As a political reformer, Howe helped to enlarge the freedom of the press by winning his famous trial of 1835-36, in which he was charged with libeling the magistrates of Halifax when he accused them of maladministration.*

ARCHIBALD LAMPMAN

Archibald Lampman was a pastoral poet, whose best descriptions are of heat and drowsiness. The languor hanging over his harvest scenes and lazy country afternoons echoes in the intentionally sluggish pace of his words; he created a trance-like atmosphere. Yet, by sharpening rhythms and choosing his words for their associations of energy and sharpness, Lampman captured the crispness of cold weather in such sonnets as *Winter Evening* and *A January Morning.*

Toward the end of his short life, he wrote the longer poem *The City of the End of Things,* an indictment of urbanization, a nightmarish vision of an accursed town, where the only light comes from the furnaces where robot slaves labor, and the only sounds are the "inhuman music" of industrial work.

At the Long Sault: May, 1660 (written in 1898), describing the defense of Montreal, concludes with a similar outcry against wolfish and hostile social forces that destroy all that is good in men and women.

DUNCAN CAMPBELL SCOTT

The strength evident in Lampman's last poems is a feature of the poems of Duncan Campbell Scott, and it places these works apart from the main stream of the Romantic movement.

Duncan Campbell Scott wrote poems of conflict and pain, set in wild landscapes far removed from the pastoral peace that reigns in the poems of his contemporaries. He has a dramatic vision that imparts a feeling of action, even of violence. Many of his poems have violent subjects: an eagle swooping on its prey; an old squaw abandoned by her tribe to die in the winter cold (*The Forsaken*); or sudden death.

In *The Piper of Arll,* one of his most famous poems, the tragedy of the drowned ship is muted by the dream-like atmosphere founded on the undisturbable renewal and peace of nature.

OTHER ROMANTIC POETS

Isabella Valancy Crawford (1850-87) wrote dramatic poems, many of which, set in the same untamed backgroud as Duncan Campbell Scott's, achieve an intense imagery and excitement.

Frederick George Scott (1861-1944) and William Wilfred Campbell (1861-1918) might also be classified as Romantic poets, akin to Roberts and Carman.

Regionalism

Toward the end of the 1890s the enthusiasm that accompanied Confederation began to lose momentum. This slackening of purpose led to emigration to the United States by some Canadians, and a literary slump among the writers.

The generation of writers that followed the economic slump lacked the unifying patriotic aim of their predecessors, which had raised their Romantic poetry to technical and poetic excellence.

Best Sellers

The new writers all followed their own bent. The more successful brought something new to the Canadian literary scene, best sellers.

The subjects of the best sellers were mainly regional. One type was the patriotic frontier romance, and its most successful practitioners were Ralph Connor (1860-1937), Robert W. Service (1874-1958), Tom MacInnes (1867-1951) and Norman Duncan (1871-1916).

Tom MacInnes himself lived the frontier life described in his ballads, and his undisciplined poetry evokes the wild life and free women of gold-rush days. Robert W. Service was more sentimental and more popular. Deliberately exploiting the public taste for Yukon ballads, he wrote in a colloquial style. His treatment of his subjects was frequently coarse or crudely sentimental; he himself called his approach "synthetic," but the excitement generated by such ballads as "The Shooting of Dan McGrew," "The Cremation of Sam McGee," and by his *Rhymes of a Red Cross Man* (1916), based on his experiences in World War I, made him one of the best-selling ballad-writers of his time.

The novelist Ralph Connor (pseudonym of the Rev. Charles William Gordon), blended the roughness of life in lumber- and mining-camp settings with naïve but fervent Christianity. His characters are tough but always redeemed by conversion to better motives. His first novel, *Black Rock* (1898), was published in a religious magazine.

LUCY M. MONTGOMERY

Another type of regionalism that attracted a widely responsive audience was the regional idyll. This was carried to its height by Lucy Maud Montgomery, creator of *Anne of Green Gables* (1908) and *Anne of Avonlea* (1909).

Robert Service (1874-1958), called Poet of the Yukon and sometimes the Canadian Kipling, lived and wrote for many years in a rustic cottage, the remains of which are seen in this photograph. Despite his English upper-middle-class background—his father was a banker—at the age of 20 he emigrated to Canada, arriving with only $5 in his pocket. His ballads of the Klondike with its gold seekers and desperados brought him international fame.

Lucy Montgomery escaped the triviality and the false pathos of many other exponents of the regional idyll. But one of the best was William Henry Drummond (1854-1907), who evoked the life of the French-Canadian peasant in a patois he invented to characterize his subjects. The poetry of Marjorie Pickthall has a scope restricted to a description of the effects of light and shadow, to capturing a flash of color or the note of a bird; but she composed with a craftsman's ear for sound and rhythm. She was a lyrical and graceful poet in the English pre-Raphaelite style.

STEPHEN LEACOCK

One man who was capable of standing apart from his age and region to comment on and laugh at it was the English-born satirist Stephen Butler Leacock (1869-1944). *Sunshine Sketches of a Little Town* (1912), one of his best-known works, is an indulgent parody of the sleepy, provincial town of Mariposa. Mariposa thinks itself bustling and up-to-date, but makes itself ridiculous whenever it bestirs itself to copy a fashion from the metropolis.

Leacock's satire is unobtrusive beneath his affection for his characters, though it sharpens in *Arcadian Adventures with the Idle Rich* (1914), an indictment of upper-class hypocrisy and materialism.

Leacock was not a reforming satirist; he was a humorist who had the sharp eye of a journalist, and his anger was never so pronounced as to lead him to bitterness. His works also include *Literary Lapses* (1910), *Nonsense Novels* (1911), *Moonbeams from the Larger Lunacy* (1915) and the autobiographical sketch *The Boy I Left Behind Me* (1946).

Poetry Since 1920

World War I has little place in Canadian literature, but its end marked the end of escapism. New poets and novelists were ready to take on the challenge of realism in subject matter and innovation in style.

The ferment of the 1920s was expressed in a variety of politico-literary magazines, led by *The Canadian Forum* (founded in 1920). The new theories did not bear fruit until the 1930s, when in 1936 the leading experimental poets combined to produce the anthology *New Provinces*.

Two of the early modernists were W. W. Eustace Ross (1894-), whose collection *Laconics* was published in 1930; and Raymond Knister (1900-32), a keen and objective observer of rural life. The former poet achieved a rare economy of style in his best poems, which present a vivid succession of images in the fewest possible words.

Canada's most celebrated humorist is Stephen Butler Leacock (1869-1944). As a lecturer and author his satire was always mellow, and the deep affection he had for people is clearly seen in his work. For many years a professor of economics and political science at McGill University, Leacock was a beloved campus character, and often wore a battered old hat and an overcoat with missing buttons. (Photo: Karsh-Ottawa)

EDWIN JOHN PRATT

The major poet of the 1920s, and an outstanding figure in the whole history of Canadian literature, was Edwin John Pratt (1883-1964). Pratt's work stands outside the modernist movement, the poet's originality lying not in his technique, which is traditional, but in his choice and treatment of subject matter.

Pratt's first collection, *Newfoundland Verse* (1923), already showed the poet's considerable gifts for observation and narrative, and it is these qualities that give his later, narrative poems their grandeur. After the humorously fantastic tale of *The Witches' Brew* (1925) and the descriptions of conflicts in nature in *The Titans* (1926), Pratt turned to human tragedies in *The Roosevelt and the Antinoe* (1930), a tale of shipwreck and rescue, *The Titanic* (1935), a powerful and accurately documented narrative of the famous shipwreck disaster, and *Brébeuf and His Brethren* (1940), which deals with the martyrdom of a Jesuit priest. *Towards the Last Spike* (1952) deals with the building of the Canadian Pacific Railway.

'NEW PROVINCES'

The five poets who, with Pratt, were represented in the anthology *New Provinces* (1936) show, in their work, the various individual strains that made the modernist movement a vital force in Canadian literature.

Arthur J. M. Smith (1902-) and Leo Kennedy (1907-), who both make much use of symbols and allusions, were influenced by the Anglo-American poet T. S. Eliot (1888-1965). Frank R. Scott (1899-) is representative of a trend, at that period, toward social criticism and satire. His work is distinguished by a skilled use of colloquial language and natural speech rhythms.

One of the most gifted new poets of the 1930s was Abraham Moses Klein (1909-). In style his work also shows the influence of Eliot; his originality comes from his deep understanding of the religion and history of the Jewish people. The last of this group of poets, Robert Finch (1900-), is most remarkable for the intensity and intricacy of his language and rhythms.

POETS OF THE 1940s

Two poets whose work was first recognized in the 1940s are Dorothy Livesay (1901-) and Earle Birney (1904-). Dorothy Livesay is a poet who strives to express reality as she sees it through experimental forms of verse. The collection *Day and Night* (1944) is filled with unhappiness and anger at the state of the world at that time. Earle Birney, in his work, has tried to reflect the attitudes of the Canadian. The collection *Now Is Time* (1945) includes a number of war poems expressing the Canadian's reaction to World War II. Recent collections of Birney's work are entitled *Ice Cod Bell or Stone* (1962) and *Near False Creek Mouth* (1964).

A number of younger poets began to make their names in the early post-World War II period. They include Patricia Kathleen Page (1916-), a highly introspective poet; Raymond Souster (1921-), much of whose inspiration is found in the life of Toronto; and Irving Layton (1912-), a bitter enemy of puritanism and intellectualism in Canadian society.

RECENT POETRY

In the most recent period one of the main problems tackled by new poets has been that of forming new kinds of poetic unities by the subtle linking of separate poems. This idea lies behind some of the work of James Reaney (1927-), whose collection *A Suit of Nettles* (1958) is a set of 12 eclogues on the pattern of the *Shepheardes Calendar* of the 16th-century English poet Edmund Spenser. A later collection, entitled *The Dance of Death at London, Ontario,* was published in 1963.

In the collection *The Boatman* (1957), Jay Macpherson (1931-) links individual poems by means of recurring symbols, by references and counter-references and by the development, throughout the collection, of particular themes.

Other significant poets of this period are Phyllis Webb (1927-), Eli Mandel (1922-), whose poetry shows a keen vision in which the realistic and the mythic are skillfully combined, and Margaret Avison (1918-), who, although she has been writing since 1939, published her first book of poetry in 1960.

Two of the best younger poets to emerge in recent years are Daryl Hine (1936-) and Leonard Cohen (1934-).

Prose Fiction Since 1920

A good deal of prose fiction in the English language has been written in Canada since 1920, but of this mass the greater part has consisted of light novels of no literary value. Only a few modern Canadian novelists—notably Morley Callaghan (1903-), Mazo de la Roche (1885-1961), Hugh MacLennan (1907-) and Mordecai Richler (1931-)—are widely known outside their own country.

HISTORICAL NOVELS

Many Canadian writers have tried their hands at historical fiction. Very highly regarded by her contemporaries was Lily Adams Beck (d.1931), who wrote historical romances under the pseudonym E. Barrington, but her works are now regarded as over-written.

A much better writer of historical novels was Frederick John Niven (1878-1944), whose trilogy *The Flying Years* (1935), *Mine Inheritance* (1940) and *The Transplanted* (1944) traces the development of the Canadian Prairies with documentary accuracy and fine descriptive power. *The Viking Heart* (1923) by Laura Goodman Salverson (1890-) was another notable contribution to Canadian historical fiction.

Since 1940 novelists have continued to draw themes from Canadian history. Two such writers are the Nova Scotians Thomas H. Raddall (1903-) and Will R. Bird (1891-).

IDYLL AND REALISM

In the 1920s and 1930s the contemporary Canadian scene was treated by two widely differing schools of writers. Writers of the so-called regional idyll, the best known of whom is Mazo de la Roche, wrote of particular areas of Canada in a loving, idealistic way. Mazo de la Roche made her reputation with *Jalna* (1927), the first of a series that was eventually to comprise 16 novels treating the history of the Whiteoaks family. Set in rural Ontario, the *Jalna* books, although somewhat sentimental, stand out from other novels of the same genre by the skillful evocation of the environment and the almost Dickensian vividness of the characters.

Other writers of this same period, notably a group who are sometimes described as the "Prairie school," attempted a realistic portrayal of life in its harsher aspects. The best of these realistic novelists was Frederick Philip Grove (1871-1948), who wrote five novels set in the Canadian Prairies, among which are *Our Daily Bread* (1928), *The Yoke*

Stephen Butler Leacock (1869-1944), historian, political scientist and world-famous humorist, spent his summers in this cottage, which, together with his library, has been made into a museum. This intensely human writer, a gentle satirist of human foibles, has been translated and read in countries as divergent as Norway and Japan.

of Life (1930) and *Fruits of the Earth* (1933).

MORLEY CALLAGHAN

A writer whose work reflects the mood of urban rather than rural Canada, and of Toronto in particular, is Morley Edward Callaghan. His first novel, *Strange Fugitives* (1928), which shows the influence of the American writer Ernest Hemingway, is the story of a bootlegger and portrays man as a helpless creature whose destiny is determined by the forces of heredity and environment and by the irrational urges of his subconscious.

In later works Callaghan evolved the controversial philosophy of "human personalism," by which he saw the fullest development of the Christian personality in a self-sacrificing love which must inevitably clash with human institutions and society. This was first expressed in *Such is My Beloved* (1934) and developed in his later works, notably *The Loved and the Lost* (1951) and *A Passion In Rome* (1961).

The fame of E. J. Pratt (1883-1964), one of Canada's greatest poets, rests principally on his epics. His narratives, breaking away from the old romantic tradition of Canadian poetry, are noted for their cosmic scope. In The Titanic *(1935) Pratt describes with power the famous ship disaster;* Brébeuf and his Brethren *(1940) deals with the martyrdom of a Jesuit priest, and* Toward the Last Spike *(1940) tells of the building of the Canadian Pacific Railway.*

NOVELISTS OF CANADIAN SOCIETY

The work of Hugh MacLennan (1907-) is principally noteworthy for its treatment of Canadian society and of a Canadian consciousness. In *Barometer Rising* (1941), which deals with the disastrous 1917 explosion in Halifax, Nova Scotia, centers on the emergence of its hero from the old and narrow colonialism into a new human and national awareness. His *Two Solitudes* (1945), less successful as a novel and more explicitly dominated by its theme, is about French and English Canada. *The Watch That Ends the Night* (1959) is set in the world of the depression, the resistance to fascism and World War II.

Robertson Davies (1914-) is a satirist, whose main butt is the provincial society of southern Ontario. His works include an important group of one-act and full-length plays, the fictional journals *The Diary of Samuel Marchbanks* (1947) and *The Table Talk of Samuel Marchbanks* (1949), and three novels about Salterton (which resembles Kingston), Ontario, culminating in *A Mixture of Frailties* (1958).

IMMIGRANT NOVELISTS

A number of the finest modern Canadian novelists were born in Britain. Malcolm Lowry (1909-57) lived for several years in poverty near Vancouver. Recognized as a great writer after his death, he is best remembered for his powerful poetic novel *Under the Volcano* (1947). Brian Moore (1921-) is an Irishman whose novels deal with the struggle of the individual to come to terms with life. One of his best-known works, about an Irish immigrant in Montreal, *The Luck of Ginger Coffey* (1960), was made into a successful film.

David Walker (1911-), a Scottish-born writer, has concentrated on popular appeal in *Geordie* (1950) and *Where the High Winds Blow* (1960).

MORDECAI RICHLER

The most interesting of the younger generation of Canadian novelists is Mordecai Richler. In *The Acrobats* (1954) and *Son of A Smaller Hero* (1955) the main characters are self-absorbed and somewhat passive, but in later works, for instance *The Apprenticeship of Duddy Kravitz* (1959), the protagonists are more self-assertive. Richler's *The Incomparable Atuk,* published in 1963, is a broad satire. He is a writer of intellectual power, an ironist with a considerable reputation extending beyond Canada.

FRENCH-CANADIAN LITERATURE

Creation of a Tradition

ALTHOUGH FOR SOME GENERATIONS it seemed that the conquest and the arrival of English-speaking immigrants might lead to the submergence of French Canada, in the end the struggle to retain the French language, faith and customs gave French Canadians a strong sense of cohesion and nationalism that found expression in their literature.

It is customary to date the beginnings of the French-Canadian literary tradition from the *Histoire du Canada* (History of Canada) of François Xavier Garneau, which began to appear in 1845.

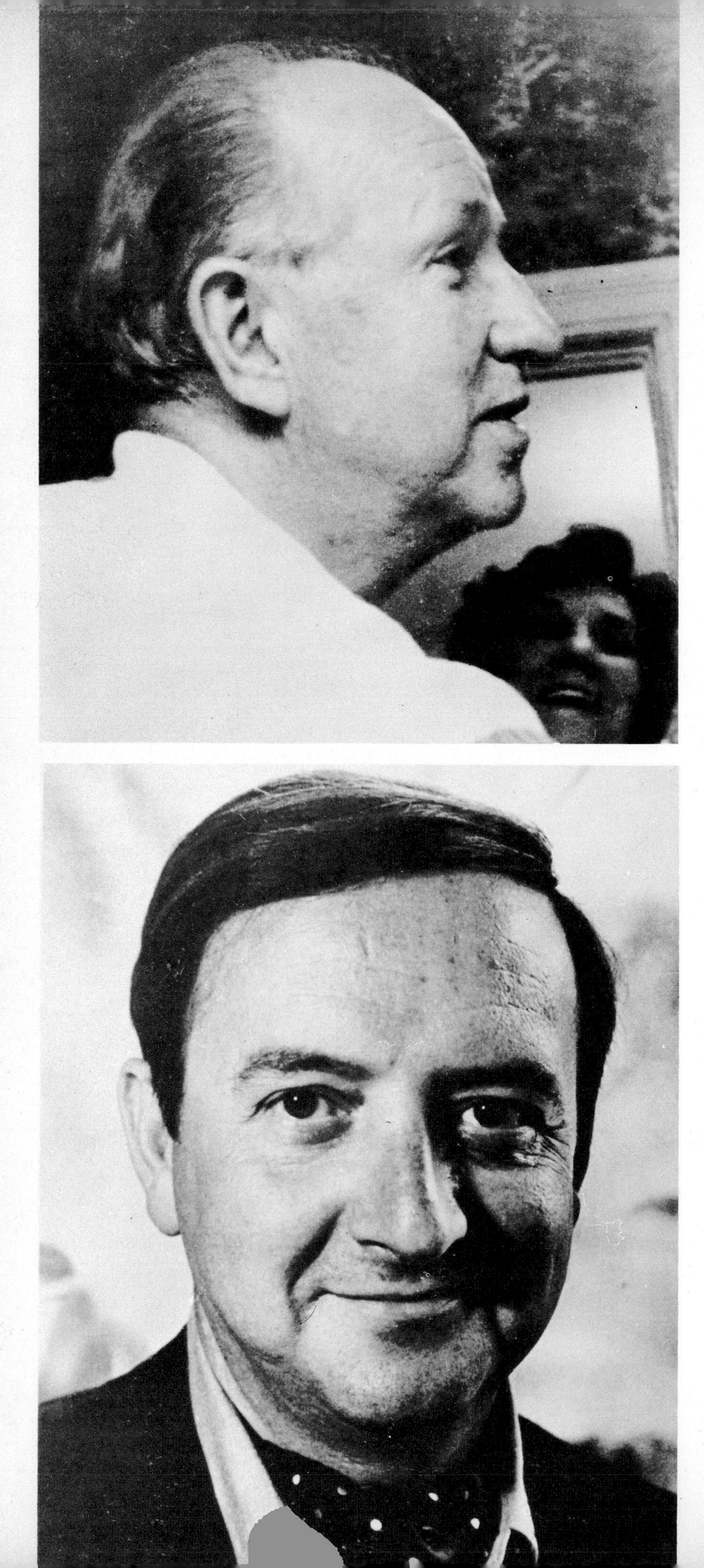

Morley Callaghan (1903-), Toronto-born novelist, is concerned in his work with the plight of the individual in a hostile environment. His novels abound in acute psychological insights and exhibit a great mastery of suspense.

IMPORTS FROM FRANCE

Garneau's work, although it inaugurated a new era of national self-awareness and of literary production, was itself the culmination of a smaller nationalist movement that was heralded, in 1817, by the foundation in Montreal of the periodical *l'Aurore* (Dawn), by Michel Bibaud (1782-1857).

From Bordeaux, Bibaud also imported the cultural periodical *La Ruche d'Aquitaine*, which printed selections from contemporary French work that enabled the Montrealese to keep in touch with currents of thought in France.

POPULAR LEGENDS

While Bibaud was the forerunner of the French-Canadian writers who were to look to France for their models, Philippe Aubert de Gaspé (the younger) inspired authors who preferred to find their own country, Canada, enough for their purposes. His novel *Le Chercheur de trésor* (The Treasure Seeker), which appeared in 1837, drew its setting and plot from rural Canada.

Gaspé's novel was followed by two other important works of fiction: *Les Fiancés de 1812* by Joseph Doutre, published in 1844, about the reactions of French-Canadian society to British rule; and *Charles Guérin* (1852) by the prolific novelist and poet Pierre Joseph Olivier Chauveau (1820-90).

PATRIOTIC NOSTALGIA

The heroic role of the French in the history of Canada was first exploited by Pierre Chauveau and Louis Joseph Cyprien Fiset (1827-98), poets who illustrated the pathos of the Indian defeats as a means of exalting French military honor.

Georges Étienne Cartier (1814-73) and Antoine Gérin-Lajoie (1824-

Brian Moore (1921-), the prize-winning novelist, is best known for his novel The Luck of Ginger Coffey, *about the difficulties of an immigrant Irishman in adjusting to a new environment. Himself an immigrant Irishman, Moore was brought to the attention of a wide audience when his book was made into a successful motion picture in 1960.*

82) expressed the hold that the beauty of Canada had begun to exert on their countrymen; they spoke no longer as expatriate Frenchmen, but as Canadians in whom separation from Canada evoked a cruel nostalgia. Cartier's *O Canada, Mon Pays, Mes Amours* (O Canada, My Country and My Love; 1835) and Lajoie's *Un Canadien Errant* (The Wandering Canadian; 1838) became national songs.

Poetic Patriots

OCTAVE CRÉMAZIE

Patriotism and religion were to be dominant themes in French-Canadian literature until the end of the century. They were exemplified in the works of the first important French Canadian poet, Joseph Octave Crémazie.

Crémazie composed in his head and wrote down his poems in a hasty dash just before publication, which lent an occasional clumsiness to his alexandrines. He was the French-Canadian national poet, echoing their bitter feelings of betrayal and defeat and their hopes of liberation in his narrative poems.

Octave Crémazie and his friend, the priest and critic Henri Raymond Casgrain, were the leaders of a school of writers who met in the back room of Crémazie's bookshop in the 1850s. Together they founded the periodical *Journal de Quebec,* in which many of Crémazie's poems appeared. This was followed by *Les Soirées Canadiennes* (Canadian Evenings, 1861-65), whose object was to record French-Canadian customs that were in danger of dying out.

Financially bankrupt, Crémazie, in 1862, went into exile in France, where he lived in depression and penury until his death.

DIDACTIC CRITIC

The Abbé Casgrain's influence as a critic extended to the end of the 19th century. He presented literature as a quasi-sacred and patriotic manifestation. "If... a literature is a mirror of the manners, character, tendencies and genius of a nation... ours should be serious, thoughtful, religious.... Above all, our literature must be essentially pious and religious. This is the only cause that can give rise to a literature and its only reason for existence."

Casgrain's didacticism did not prove restrictive; rather, it afforded writers a purpose and a discipline. His review *Le Foyer Canadien* (The Canadian Hearth; 1863-66) serialized some of the first Canadian novels, and his *Revue Canadienne,* founded in 1864, survived into the 20th century. But when put into practice, the Abbé Casgrain's literary influence was less laudable; when the elder Philippe Aubert de Gaspé, for example, gave him the manuscript of his historical novel *Les Anciens Canadiens* (1863) to revise, the Abbé destroyed some of its spontaneity by tampering with the writer's style.

REMINISCENCES

Philippe Aubert de Gaspé, father of Philippe Aubert the younger, who already has been mentioned as important as a pioneer of the nationalist movement and the author of *Le Chercheur de trésors,* published his novel when he was 77 and wrote his *Mémoirs* when he was 80. The *Mémoirs,* free from the superimposed plot Gaspé tacked onto his novel, are a disorderly, spontaneous and humorous account of life during Gaspé's youth, before the influence of the English in Canada had made itself felt. Gaspé recalls the way of life of his youth with extraordinary detail and spices his reminiscences with anecdotes.

PIONEER NOVEL

Gaspé's carefree spirit did not influence other writers. More typical of French Canada was Antoine Gérin-Lajoie, who, as well as composing the nostalgic song *Un Canadien Errant,* wrote two patriotic novels advocating, as he saw it, the duty of Canadians to return to the pioneer work in the fields and thus preserve the integrity of their traditions, instead of deserting their country to work in the U.S. The novels *Jean Rivard, le Défricheur* (Jean Rivard, the Pioneer; 1862) and *Jean Rivard, Economiste* (1864) are gauchely written, but their message was widely echoed.

Authentic accounts of the trials of the pioneers appeared in the short stories of Joseph Charles Taché (1820-94) *Forestiers et Voyageurs* (Foresters and Travelers; 1863); Taché had himself led the life he described.

HISTORICAL FICTION

Novelists found a lighter outlet for patriotism in romantic historical fiction. Among many writers of this period are Joseph Marmette (1844-95), Napoléon Bourassa (1827-1916) and Georges de Boucherville (1814-94).

The first generation of French-Canadian authors discovered a range of subjects that were taken up with greater literary ease and a less trammeled poetic inspiration by their followers, among whom the lyric poet Louis Honoré Fréchette was a leader.

Leonard Cohen (1934-), shown here in a scene from the National Film Board's documentary Ladies and Gentlemen, Mr. Cohen, *is one of the best of the younger poets to emerge in Canada in recent years. Since World War II a number of poets have achieved recognition, including the highly introspective Patricia Kathleen Page (1916-); Raymond Souster (1921-), who found his inspiration in the everyday life of Toronto; and Irving Layton (1912-), whose values are opposed to the puritanism in Canadian society.*

The Romantic Writers

Fréchette, like his contemporaries Pamphile Lemay (1837-1918), Nérée Beauchemin (1850-1931), Alfred Garneau (1836-1904), William Chapman (1850-1917) and Adolphe Poisson (1849-1922), drew heavily on French Romanticism for his forms and his masters. In addition, the subjects favored by the French Romantics were among those the Canadian poets had already been struggling to express.

But there was between the original French Romantics and their Canadian followers considerable difference of emphasis. The European poetic revolt against the classical dominance of reason and form at the expense of subjectivity and emotion was unnecessary to the Canadian poets, whose past had not been cramped by an outworn literary tradition.

While echoing the lyricism and appreciation of nature typical of the French Romantics, the French Canadian poets missed some of the passion.

LOUIS FRÉCHETTE

Fréchette, while Canada's great French Romantic poet, was also a journalist and a politician who sat in the Federal House of Commons from 1874 to 1878. His political experience and his contacts with a wide range of people gave him a certain detachment, which comes out in his humorous prose stories *Originaux et Détraqués* (Odd characters, 1892).

Fréchette's career in current affairs ran parallel to his work as a lyric poet of strikingly beautiful imagery, gifted with a natural facility and ease in composition. This gift won him an award from the French Academy for his collection *Fleurs boréales* (Northern flowers, 1881) and made him the first French-Canadian poet to be recognized outside his country.

NATIONAL EPIC

Fréchette's most ambitious work is his epic, *La Légende d'un peuple* (The History of a people; 1887). It borrows its form and inspiration from Victor Hugo's *La Légende des siècles*, but the content is original. About 3000 lines long, it is a series of loosely connected odes to the glory of Canada: the land, the explorers and the soldiers being used to project an idealized and heroic picture of Canada's history.

PAMPHILE LEMAY

Pamphile Lemay is more modest in his aims. His love for his country is a deep-seated, almost religious feeling, which he expresses through his more restricted descriptions of rural laborers in country scenes. In 1899 he recorded with loving observation the daily experiences of the country people and the tales that had sprung up round the heroes of the French struggles against the British, in his *Contes Vrais* (True tales).

His collections *Essais poétiques* (1865) and *Les Gouttelettes* (Droplets, 1904) are written with a graceful and delicate treatment of the rural life he found so attractive. Pamphile Lemay is more intimate than his predecessors, but his attitude toward his meditations, though melancholy, is serene.

NÉRÉE BEAUCHEMIN

The melancholy that familiar country sights inspired in Lemay has no place in the work of Nérée Beauchemin, a Romantic poet similarly attracted by the peace and close-knit life of rural communities. To the end of his life he practiced as a doctor among the people he described in *Floraisons matutinales* (Early efflorescence; 1897), *Patrie intime* (Familiar country; 1928) and the posthumously published *Choix de poésies* (Selection of poems; 1950).

ROMANTIC NOVELISTS

Jules-Paul Tardivel (1851-1905) wrote his novel *Pour la patrie* (For one's country; 1895) to propagate his extremist nationalist views on the superiority of the French-Canadian people and their faith.

Laure Conan (1845-1924) preached similar views with greater finesse in her sentimental novels, *Un Amour vrai* (A true love story; 1878), *L'Oublié* (The Man they forgot; 1900), and *La Sève Immortelle* (The Undying sap; 1924). Her beliefs in patriotic honor and religious purity form the core of her plots, and the public was attracted by the novel element of character analysis in her books.

The effect of the geography of Canada on its emergent literature has been incalculable. From Goldsmith's The Rising Village *(1825) through the long tradition of the pastoral poets to the Whiteoaks of* Jalna *(1927) of de la Roche, a romantic and often idealized attachment to the land has persisted. The tone of Canadian literature has been likened to that of Russian writing because of its intimate association with a beautiful, vast, and often inhospitable land.*

The School of Montreal

The School of Montreal was first founded in 1895 by a group of young poets. Disenchanted with the values that had hitherto prevailed in poetry, they wished to avoid, as they saw it, the rigidly conservative rural Canadianism of their predecessors and to break away from the now-outdated French models of Romanticism. They were anxious to draw their language closer to the purity of the French spoken in France rather than to give a Canadian color to their works by using provincial dialect.

The rhetoric and optimism of a large-scale semi-narrative work like Fréchette's *La Légende d'un peuple* was replaced by carefully worked lyrics. The work of the Montreal poets was informed by self-doubt, religious doubt and, in the rare cases when they wrote about their own society, a questioning of the moral values on which it was based.

With Jean Charbonneau (1875-1960) as leader, Émile Nelligan (1879-1941), Albert Lozeau (1878-

1924), Charles Gill (1871-1918), Gonzalve Désaulniers (1863-1934), Alfred Des Rochers (1901-), Lucien Rainier (1877-1956) and Joseph-Arthur Lapointe followed in the tradition of the French Parnassian and Symbolist schools and the art for art's sake movement.

One of their meeting places was Ramezay Castle, which gave its name to their literary periodical. The periodical brought the movement wider publicity than similar magazines had brought their predecessors, because in the last decade of the 19th century, literacy and education had expanded.

CRITICS

The rise of the new school coincided with the emergence of two critics of decisive importance.

Camille Roy (1870-1943) was a literary scholar versed in the literatures of Greece, Rome and France and an advocate of close ties with France. Louis Dantin (the pseudonym of Eugène Sears; 1866-1945), a critic of strong individual preferences, encouraged young writers and, in 1904, wrote an important introduction to Émile Nelligan's poems.

JEAN CHARBONNEAU

Jean Charbonneau, the head of the Montreal School, remained faithful to its ideals long after others had left the School; he wrote a collection in 1952, *Sur la borne pensive* (On the pensive boundary), in the same style as his first poems, *Les Blessures* (The Wounds; 1912). Romantic in attitude and prosaic in style, Charbonneau was more influential as the critic of the School than as a poet. In 1935 he published an important history of its development, *L'école littéraire de Montréal*.

ÉMILE NELLIGAN

The School's first poet was Émile Nelligan, who joined the group after the triumphant reception of his "*La Romance du vin*" (Ballad of the wine harvest). Nelligan's reign lasted only two years, before he became insane at the age of 19, but the example of his achievement, that so exactly translated the hitherto academic theories of the School toward a new style, left its mark on his contemporaries.

The richness of his vocabulary and exotic nature of his images are best seen in the sonnets "Le Vaisseau d'or" (The Ship of Gold), "*Le Cloître noir*" (The Black cloisters) and "*L'Idiote aux cloches*" (The Idiot and the church bells).

The career of George E. Cartier (1814-73) was of greater importance to the political history of Canada than to the tradition of literature, but his O Canada, Mon Pays, Mes Amours *(1835) achieved immense popularity and became a national song. After the Rebellion of 1837, he took refuge for several months in the United States, returning to Canada to work for the Confederation. For his service in the interest of unification, Cartier was made a Baronet of the United Kingdom in 1868.*

CHARLES GILL

Charles Gill was the most ambitious and the most original of the group. It is for his aims rather than for his achievements that he is famous. The work he actually put to paper is small, and as he published nothing during his lifetime, after his death his sister had to gather together the fragments of his epic, his translations of Horace and his few finished poems. In 1919 they appeared as *Le Cap d'éternité* (The Peak of eternity) and *Étoiles filantes* (Shooting stars).

The 12 songs of *Le Cap d'éternité*, which Charles Gill had reworked more than once, were intended as part of a scheme of 10 books and 35 songs, which was to be a lyrical hymn in praise of Canada. The author would have linked each book by a description of one of Canada's great rivers and embroidered each song with evocations of the sights and histories along each waterway.

ALBERT LOZEAU

Charles Gill intended to be a poet of immense sights and an all-embracing philosophy. Albert Lozeau, by contrast, was a poet of detail. Confined to his chair by paralysis that immobilized him when he was 25, and restricted to one view of the changing seasons through his window, he minutely described what he saw, such as leaves of frost on the windowpane; these his imagination transformed into fruits and flowers of silver. He imagined what lay beyond his window or conjured up chaste visions of a quiet, companionable love that would enrich his solitude.

Lozeau wrote of how depression, boredom and pain had schooled him to a patient humility that freed his soul to dream. Writing with careful precision, in spite of his melancholy, he conveyed best the joys of intimacy and the delight the imagination may find in detail. His works are included in *l'Âme solitaire* (The Lonely spirit; 1907), *Le Miroir des jours* (A Mirror of the days; 1912) and *Lauriers et feuilles d'érable* (Laurels and maple leaves; 1916).

GONZALVE DÉSAULNIERS

Gonzalve Désaulniers turned to the Canadian woods for inspiration and called his first collection *Les Bois qui chantent* (The Singing forests; 1930). Sensitive to the interior life he imagined in trees, he fused his personality with the spirit he felt emanating from the forests, describing their beauty and history.

Nature, to Désaulniers, was the medium through whose goodness he could understand men. His sympathy for the dying race of Indians led him to paint slightly incongruous pictures of them acting in a chivalric manner, expressed in efficient alexandrines in his long poem *Pour la France* (1918). He was an idealist and an optimist, distinguished by his intuitive sensibility toward all natural objects.

PAUL MORIN

The second generation of the French Canadian Parnassians includes Paul Morin (1889-) and René Chopin (1885-1953).

Paul Morin set his best poems in the East. He has a chameleon-like gift of absorbing foreign atmospheres, which he translates into his poems by appealing to all the senses. He evokes the smells of oil, oranges and spices, the inertia and heat; but he is equally at home embroidering fantastic pictures around a medieval illumination *Le Paon d'émail* (The Enameled peacock; 1911) or painting a scene in provincial France.

A stylist whose fluency sometimes has led him into artifice, Paul Morin composes generally in a free and supple meter. With his pictures of Eastern gardens and market scenes, he has brought new vistas into French-Canadian poetry. His collection *Poèmes de cendres et d' or* (Poems of ashes and gold) appeared in 1922.

RENÉ CHOPIN

René Chopin's imagination transformed the Canadian landscapes of his poetry into scenes of magic and fantasy. The title of his collection *Le Cœur en exil* (The Heart in exile) of 1913 sums up his feeling of being divorced from the material world and at one with nature, whose ways he interpreted. Reality, for him, did not reside in the world, but in the past and the future, in man's emotions and desires.

To supplement his meager earnings as a lawyer, the lyric poet and politician Louis Frechette (1839-1908) turned to journalism. His liberalism, boldly expressed in editorial attacks on politicians, soon brought about his dismissal from the newspaper. Moving to Chicago, he continued writing articles violently attacking home politicians until he was able to return to the Canadian political scene. He ultimately won a seat in the Canadian House of Commons. Considered a great romantic poet, Frechette wrote lyric poems filled with strikingly beautiful imagery. His most ambitious work was the historical epic La Legende d'un peuple *(1887).*

The first close examination of life in post-World War II Montreal was undertaken by Gabrielle Roy (1909-) in her prize-winning novel Bonheur d'occasion *(1945). Her study of the failures and castoffs of a modern, industrialized city, written with detailed realism, marked the opening of a new era in French-Canadian literature.*

Regionalism

ESCAPISM

Roughly contemporary with the Montreal movement was the trend toward regionalism in poetry and fiction. Although the regionalists could claim to be true to life, in that their idylls of pioneer virtues were based on the truth whereas the followers of Émile Nelligan followed the fantasies of their imaginations, they were equally escapist.

SETTLER NOVELS

Louis Hémon's novel *Maria Chapdelaine* (1916) released a flood of imitations. Although French by birth, Hémon recorded an authentic picture of the life of the settler in Quebec.

Georges Bugnet (1879-) was a settler, and his best novel, *La Forêt* (The Forest; 1935), draws on his experience of the isolation and feeling of defenselessness of the pioneer in the immense Canadian forests. In *Nipsya* (1924) he attempted, less successfully, a solution to the problem of the Indian's equivocal place in Canadian society.

PASTORALS

Englebert Gallèze (1875-1955), whose real name was Lionel Leveille, and Blanche La Montagne-Beauregard (1889-1960) were unpretentious in their love of the regions they inhabited and described in their poetry.

Englebert Gallèze described the appearance, the work and the habits of the people, their folklore and their good humor. Although nostalgically attracted by the life of pristine virtue he saw in his straw-hatted, pipe-smoking peasants, he was capable of a certain satirical detachment. He wrote in a light, singing tone in his collections *La Claire fontaine* (The Pure spring; 1913) and *Chante, rossignol, chante* (Sing, nightingale, sing; 1925).

Blanche Lamontagne devoted almost all her poetry to sentimental but sincere evocations of the countryside; her works include *Visions Gaspésiennes* (1913) and *Ma Gaspésie* (1928).

Alfred DesRochers forms a link between the Montreal and pastoral attitudes, and the acceptance of realism. Controlled and precise in form, he does not sentimentalize his mainly regional subjects. The dirt and smells of the farmyard figure as prominently as more conventionally poetic details in his collection *A l'Ombre de l'Orford* (In the Shadow of Orford; 1929).

Realism

Bonheur d'occasion (1945; Eng. trans.: *The Tin Flute,* 1947) by Gabrielle Roy (1909-) marked the opening of a new era in the history of the French-Canadian novel.

The action of the book takes place in industrial Montreal during World War II. The setting is realistic, and the characters are chosen from the hitherto unexplored class of drunks and failures. The novelist's vision of love is similarly revolutionary, for she treats it without romantic illusions. She describes a poverty-stricken household where ill-temper and bad health master love and place barriers between the people.

Bonheur d'occasion won the French Prix Fémina and was followed by *La Petite Poule d'eau* (1951; Eng. trans.: *Where Nests the Water Hen,* 1951). *La Montagne secrète* (Eng. trans.: *The Secret Mountain,* 1962) was published in 1961.

PROMINENT REALIST NOVELISTS

Among the exponents of the new-found realism are: Roger Lemelin (1919-), with his trilogy *Au pied de la pente douce* (1944), *Les Plouffe* (1948) and *Pierre le Magnifique* (1952); Yves Thériault (1915-), a novelist in revolt against restrictive and brutal social conditions, who published *Les Vendeurs du temple* (1951), about social bigotry, and *Cul-de-sac* (1961), about alcoholism; Jean-Charles Harvey (1891-), who wrote *Demi-civilisés* (1934) aimed at the upper classes of a corrupt society; Jean Jules Richard, whose novel *Neuf jours de haine* (Nine days of hate; 1948) is set during World War II; Jean Simard (1916-), critic of the cruelty and ugliness in contemporary society in *Les Sentiers de la nuit* (Night Paths; 1959); Gerrard Bessette (1920-), critic of French-Canadian society, whose *Le Libraire* (1960) is an ironic account of a love affair; and André Langevin (1927-) who wrote *Evadé de la nuit* (Night escape; 1951) and *Le Temps des hommes* (The Era of Men; 1956). The most powerful of these novelists, however, was Philippe Panneton, who wrote under the pen-name Ringuet and is best known for his early work *Trente arpents* (Thirty acres, 1942). Among the leading poets of the past 25 years have been Saint Denys Garneau, Alain Grandbois and Anne Hébert.

A number of French-Canadian authors have taken as their subject the life of the pioneers, of which this wheelwright's shop is reminiscent. Turning from the ugliness of a spreading urban and industrial society, such writers as Louis Hémon (1880-1913), Englebert Gallèze (1875-1955), Blanche La Montagne-Beauregard (1899-1960) and Alfred Des Rochers (1901-) generally wrote of pastoral themes and often viewed with affection and nostalgia the simple, virtuous ways of bygone times.

THE THEATER

Progress in the development of the theater in Canada has always been hampered not only by the difficulties of a scattered population and lack of financial support, but also by the preoccupations of a pioneer people who have undertaken the great task of carving a nation out of a vast territory. For novelists and poets social attitudes are less important, since their work can at least appeal to a scattered minority, but the theater, by its very nature, must rely on concentrated support.

In recent years, however, building on the foundation laid down by the persistent efforts of amateur movements, a new era has begun. Regional centers have been set up, not only encouraging the appreciation of foreign playwrights but also beginning to stimulate interest in Canadian dramatists.

As an awareness of national identity has evolved, so has a pride in the nation's artistic achievements. The change in cultural climate is reflected in the growing success of annual festivals, in the foundation of more and more permanent theaters and in the increased status of drama criticism.

THE ENGLISH-LANGUAGE THEATER

Literary Drama

ALTHOUGH HE WAS ACCLAIMED BY many of his contemporaries as a worthy follower in the path of Shakespeare and Milton, English Canada's first literary playwright, Charles Heavysege (1816-76), wrote no plays that can actually be performed. An Englishman who worked in Canada as a cabinetmaker and journalist, Heavysege wrote many sonnets and long narrative poems as well as verse dramas, including *Saul* (1857), *Count Philippo, or The Unequal Marriage* (1860) and *Jephthah's Daughter* (1865). Though these works were widely read in their day, modern attempts to revive them have failed, mostly because of the pompous, grandiose nature of the verse.

A more strongly nationalist spirit was expressed in the English-language historical verse drama *Tecumseh* (1886) by Charles Mair (1838-1927). The theme of Mair's work is patriotic, but its stirring effects are marred by the unconvincing biblical style in which the Indians are made to speak. Its most remarkable feature is non-dramatic, being the minute observation contained in the passages descriptive of nature.

Such verse dramas as these, which also include the works of Wilfred Campbell (1861-1918)) and Marjorie Pickthall (1883-1922), were widely appreciated in Canada, but they were clearly not intended to be performed and they had little

Sarah Bernhardt, shown here during her 1880 visit to Montreal, was one of the many foreign performers who visited Canada as guest artists before native Canadian theater had developed. Bernhardt starred in several plays, including Hernani. *She revisited the country in 1891 and 1905.*

Vincent Massey (1887-1967), the first native-born governor-general of Canada (1952-59), was one of the most influential figures of the little theater movement. As a member of the University of Toronto's board of directors, he was instrumental in the creation of the Hart House theater (1919).

or no influence on the development of Canadian theater.

Live Theater

Virtually the only Canadian theatrical representations during the 19th century consisted of adaptations of popular melodramas to local settings. Apart from these, Canadians had little opportunity to experience live theater except through the sporadic appearances of English or American touring companies.

As early as February 1786 an English company playing in Albany had moved to Montreal. Its members had been associated with Lewis Hallam, who had played Shakespeare for the first time in North America in 1752. In 1826 the great English actor Edmund Kean made his Montreal debut as Richard III, following this with Shylock, Othello and King Lear. In later years Canada saw the work of other celebrated English actors and actresses, including Charles Kean, Charles and Fanny Kemble, William Charles Macready, Sir Henry Irving, Ellen Terry, Mrs. Patrick Campbell, Sir Johnston Forbes-Robertson, Sir John Martin-Harvey and George Arliss; America was represented by such actors as Edwin Forrest, John Wilkes Booth, E. H. Sothern, Walter Hampden and John Barrymore. From Europe's theater came Tomaso Salvini, Adelaide Ristori, Sarah Bernhardt and Louis Jouvet among many others.

These tours, which at one time were quite regular, were significant in that they made the theater an integral part of Canadian social life; they created the need for permanent buildings to accommodate them and, more important, they sowed the seeds of love for the theater. These were to take root and blossom, after World War I, into what became known as the "Little Theater Movement."

The Little Theaters

Touring had to stop eventually in Canada because of rising transportation costs and also because of increased competition from the motion picture industry, which took over most of the theaters—the Royal Alexandra in Toronto is, in fact, the sole survivor of that epoch.

It was between 1930 and 1940 that amateur theatrical activity came into its own, but there were pioneers of importance in the field before and immediately after World War I.

THE PLAYERS' CLUB

One of the most flourishing theatrical societies was founded in 1913 at the University of Toronto. Its first performance under the direction of the United States-trained Roy Mitchell, was given in the hall of Victoria College; this was the beginning of a repertory series, mostly of one-act plays by such established writers as Ibsen and Shaw, but also including some by Canadian dramatists.

Vincent Massey, who was to be an influential force in the development of the Canadian theater, was on the board of directors and, like his younger brother Raymond, later a well-known actor in the United States, he also took an active part in the society's productions.

HART HOUSE THEATER

Another significant event in Toronto's early theater life came in 1919 with the opening of Hart House Theater, also linked with the city's university. Built by the Massey Foundation (Vincent Massey was chairman of the Board of Syndics until his appointment as Canadian High Commissioner in London in 1935) as part of the Central Students' Building, it seats 300 and has a very well equipped stage. In 1966 it became part of the University of Toronto's Drama Center, after 20 seasons of student productions under the direction of Robert Gill (from 1946 to 1966), which produced such leading Canadian actors as William Hutt, Kate Reid, Eric House and Donald Davis.

Hart House maintained a consistently high level in its presentations, and the directors were adventurous in their choice of plays—in 1927 they performed the first all-Canadian program, consisting of one-act plays by Isobel Ecclestone Mackay (1875-1928), Duncan Campbell-Scott (1862-1944) and Mazo de la Roche (1879-1961), whose

Whiteoaks (1936) enjoyed immense success in London and on Broadway. This phase of Hart House activity terminated with World War II, during which it was shut down. Then in 1946 Gill was brought from Carnegie Tech to re-open it. The Drama Center, which succeeded the Gill regime, was launched in October 1966 under the chairmanship of Clifford Leach.

REGIONAL ACTIVITY

In Saskatchewan the Regina Amateur Dramatic Society was formed by English actors as early as 1912. In 1926 the group re-formed as the Regina Little Theater Society, and it still flourishes under this name. Under the patronage of the then governor-general, Lord Bessborough, the Saskatchewan Drama League was founded in 1932.

In the same year Lord Bessborough gave further proof of his enthusiasm for the theater by founding the Masquers' Club in Winnipeg, which, in 1933, won first prize for its entry in the first Dominion Drama Festival.

Vancouver had its Little Theater in 1922, and London, Ontario, acquired one in 1934 by the process of assembling all its existing amateur groups. By 1945 the London group was able to move into the Grand Theater, and in 1966 it opened its second theater, for experimental productions.

Between the Wars

The Little Theater movement created a great feeling of optimism and vigor and, of course, enlarged the scope for indigenous playwrights. But the Canadian theater still lagged behind the Canadian novel and poetry; when a contest for dramatists was held in the late 1920s it was specified that the entrants should deal in effect with themes connected with "the great outdoors"—this at a time when the other arts were turning to more sophisticated themes.

MERRILL DENISON

Although he left for America quite early in his career, Merrill Denison (1893-) wrote several one-act comedies and a full-length play in Canada. All his work contrasts with that of his contemporaries because it is essentially theatrical. It has the qualities of realism

Above: *The Royal Alexandra Theater in Toronto, with some of the audience outside during intermission. Of the city's theaters at which Victorian and Edwardian touring artists appeared, the Alexandra is the only one still carrying on its legitimate-theater tradition. Most of the others have been converted into motion picture houses.*

Below: *The Hart House Theater, since 1966 part of Toronto University's Drama Center, was opened in 1919. Built by the Massey Foundation as part of the Central Students' Building (seen here), it was intended to be an experimental art theater for the community as well as for the students. The theater has presented a broad spectrum of the world's dramatic literature, ranging from an all-Canadian program in 1927 to* Lysistrata *in 1966, the first play presented under the auspices of the Drama Center.*

Lord Bessborough, governor-general of Canada, (1931-35) lent his influence and patronage to the little-theater movement. In 1932, under his aegis, the Saskatchewan Drama League and the Masquers' Club in Winnipeg were founded. A devoted benefactor of the theater, he was one of those inspired leaders who helped keep it alive during the 1920s and '30s.

and conciseness; it is well constructed; and the dialogue is convincing and often witty.

Although Denison's short plays are comedies, the mood is generally one of satire, and the audience is often made aware of the dark, cruel aspects that lie beneath what is superficially comic. Hence it is not surprising that in his only full-length Canadian play Denison should have made a clean break with the comic genre.

Marsh Hay, which can be regarded as the best Canadian play of the 1920s, bears comparison with the work of the United States dramatist Eugene O'Neill. It takes as its theme the stultifying effect a backwoods environment can have on the moral, intellectual and emotional life of the inhabitants, but finally the author makes no judgment—he simply presents the situation for his audience's assessment.

DIGNITY AND INTELLECT

Other dramatists of the 1920s did not achieve the high reputation of Denison, but their work has many estimable qualities. *Pierre* (1926), for example, by Duncan Campbell-Scott, is a domestic tragedy that conveys a certain dignity in its portrayal of the return of a ne'er-do-well son to his home in rural Quebec. *The Translation of John Snaith* (1926), by Britton Cook, which is set in northern Ontario during World War I, is particularly impressive for its intellectual strength, although, as is often the case, the complexity of ideas outweighs the actual dramatic presentation, which tends to be melodramatic.

GWEN PHARIS RINGWOOD

The next step forward in the development of Canadian drama is marked by the work of Gwen Pharis Ringwood (1910-), who wrote some of the best plays of the 1930s. This writer's work rises above the undistinguished, grim sociological dramas produced by many of her contemporaries. Some were written in conjunction with the Alberta Folk Lore project, and most are devoted in some way to the problems of living on the land. *Still Stands the House* recreates with uncompromising realism the atmosphere of despair that reigned in Alberta during the time of depression and drought; *Dark Harvest* is similar in tone, but *The Courting of Marie Jenvrin* is a more lighthearted comedy about a French-Canadian girl and her suitors in Northwest Territories.

JOHN COULTER

The earlier plays of Irish-born John Coulter (1888-) appeared in the 1930s. *Oblomoff,* Coulter's dramatization of the 19th-century Russian Ivan Alexandrovich Goncharov's novel, and *The Drums Are Out,* which deals with the Irish Civil War, both show the dramatist's understanding of dialogue and construction. Coulter's more recent work, such as *Riel* (1962), a powerful historical piece in two parts, describing the Northwest rebellion and the insurgent leader's trial and execution, makes use of the same qualities to good effect. It was performed by the New Play Society and later by the Canadian Broadcasting Corporation. His *Deirdre of the Sorrows* was set to music by Dr. Healey Willan for the Canadian Broadcasting Corporation, revived by the Royal Conservatory Opera School in 1966 and included in the 1966-67 season of the Canadian Opera Company.

SIGNS OF RENEWAL

In 1932 promise of a new phase in Canadian theater came when the Dominion Drama Festival was initiated. This great national contest, which, except during wartime, has been an annual event in Canada, begins with a series of regional preliminary competitions; the finals take place in various host cities. Over the years the festival has done much to create a sense of coordination and of a common theatrical tradition.

The Professional Theater

During the 1930s depression, with its grim economic difficulties, Canadian drama had been provided principally through the medium of radio. Among the playwrights who began to make their names in this field were Joseph Schull (1910-), who showed a liking for lyrical symbolism in scripts such as *The Bridge* and *The Legend of the Ghost Lagoon,* and Lister Sinclair (1921-), who later developed a mordant satirical style in *We All Hate Toronto, Socrates,* performed in Toronto Museum Theater in 1952, and *Encounter By Moonlight.*

Although it might be said that working for the radio diverted the energies of potential theatrical playwrights, it often happened that writers, like actors, were able to earn a reasonably good living through radio, and later television, while at the same time working, less remuneratively, for the theater. It also meant that dramatists had opportunity to experiment and discover forms and styles that suited their particular talents.

POTENTIAL OF RADIO AND TELEVISION

The arrival of television drama furthered opportunities for the Canadian writer. It is certain that the development of both media, radio and television, gave new impetus to the growth of professional theater. Like the Little Theater movement, this came after a world war at a time when there was a new spirit of determination to build for the future. The added challenge of competition brought another spur—new groups began to appear and old ones were revived.

But in many cases, after the first flush of enthusiasm had died down, audiences resumed their old apathy and theaters had to close. One exception was The New Play Society, formed in 1947 in Toronto by Dora Mavor Moore and her son Mavor; this group was extremely active during the 1950s and it still continues, although it now restricts itself to running a drama school.

NEW WRITERS FOR THE THEATER

One of the most prolific and successful of contemporary Canadian playwrights is the versatile critic and essayist Robertson Davies (1914-), whose work is mainly satirical and especially distinguished for its inventiveness. From the one-act farce *Eros at Breakfast* (1949), Davies moved on to a full-length play, *Fortune My Foe* (1949), about a Canadian professor lured south by American money. Among his other best plays are *At My Heart's Core* (1950),

The Canadian Opera production of Deirdre of the Sorrows, *with libretto by the Canadian dramatist John Coulter and music by Dr. Healey Willan. Coulter (1888-) is one of Canada's outstanding playwrights. His plays, which also include* Oblomoff, *a dramatization of Goncharov's novel,* The Drums Are Out, *about the Irish civil war, and* Riel, *which describes the Northwest rebellion and Riel's trial and execution, exhibit a keen ear for dialogue and a masterful understanding of theatrical construction.*

A Masque of Aesop (1952), written for a cast of boys, and *A Jig for the Gypsy* (1954).

Other successful plays were written by Ted Allen (1916-), who wrote *The Moneymakers,* about a scriptwriter in Hollywood, before he moved to London, England, and wrote for television, the West End and, later, Broadway. Norman Williams published a volume of short plays under the title *Worlds Apart* (1956), which was followed by a three-act play, *To Ride a Tiger* (1957). George W. Blackburn had success in Ottawa with the comedy *A Button Missing,* which broke a 30-year record at the Ottawa Little Theater and was acquired for London's West End, though it was never produced. A London production did follow Mary Jukes's 1956 comedy *Every Bed Is Narrow,* first presented at the Crest under the direction of Herbert Whittaker, then taken to London in 1957 by Anna Deare Wiman and produced at the Winter Garden Theater.

The poet and dramatist James Reaney (1926-) is one of the most interesting dramatists of the day. He has a preference for pastoral comedy that gives an outlet for lyricism, but his themes and characters often have a complexity that may not always be apparent through the surface comedy. Among his works is numbered *The Killdeer,* first produced by the Coach House Theater in Toronto in 1960, then presented by the Glasgow Citizens Theater in Scotland in 1966.

The Stratford Festival

The opening of the Stratford Festival Theater in July 1953 started a new era in the development of Canadian theater. The idea of holding a festival in Stratford, Ontario, to celebrate the greatness of Shakespeare was first proposed by a Stratford-born journalist, Tom Patterson. In 1952 the English director Tyrone Guthrie was called in to advise on the project; whereas the intention had been to stage plays in the open air, he suggested instead that a tent-theater should be erected, with an open stage instead of the conventional proscenium arch.

The theater's first season opened with a performance of Shakespeare's *Richard III,* in which the English actor Alec Guinness played the title role. On the following night *All's Well That Ends Well* starring Guinness and Irene Worth was staged, and the success of the venture was confirmed. Both plays were produced by Guthrie and designed by the celebrated English designer Tanya Moiseiwitsch, who also designed the Stratford stage.

Since 1953 the festival has continued in its declared policy, not only to stimulate interest in Shakespeare but also to advance the development of the arts in Canada. Its success has increased steadily; in 1956 the tent was taken down and, while the company was appearing at Scotland's Edinburgh Festival in *Henry V* and *Oedipus Rex,* a permanent building was erected.

The Stratford theater is revolutionary in concept; it is based on a modern adaptation of the Elizabethan structure and has a platform stage with a balcony and trapdoors, seven acting levels and nine major entrances. The amphitheater has a steep slope and surrounds the stage on three sides; there is also a balcony which, although it brings the theater's seating capacity up to 2258, involves little loss of the intimate relationship between actors and audience, since no seat is farther than 65 feet from the stage.

In 1955 Michael Langham took over artistic direction from Guthrie. In 1964 the festival company took three productions to Chichester, England, a theater inspired by Canada's Stratford, with great success. It has initiated a series of school matinees, which, since 1958, have taken place in the fall of each year. Students come from all over the country to attend performances of Shakespeare's plays and informal talks given afterward by leading members of the company.

A further stimulus to the growth of Canada's theater talent is the Tyrone Guthrie Award, which is made annually and covers all aspects of the theatrical arts. Promising young writers, actors, directors and designers receive scholarships to enable them to travel or study.

The Shaw Festival, reflecting Canada's burgeoning interest in the theater, opened its first season at the old Court House Theater at Niagara-on-the-Lake, Ontario, in 1963. Shown here is a scene from the 1966 production of Shaw's Misalliance, *directed by Barry Morse, the London-born actor.*

The Shaw Festival

It has been said that if the Stratford Festival had not been founded when it was, a similar festival would have emerged elsewhere in Ontario, for the time was ripe. Some indication that this theory is true was given by the appearance and rapid development of a second festival, one devoted to the work of George Bernard Shaw and established in the old Court House at Niagara-on-the-Lake, Ontario.

Launched in 1962 by Brian Doherty, a lawyer with one hit play, *Father MaLachy's Miracle,* to his credit and some experience as an impresario, it started in 1964 under the direction of Andrew Allan, who had won a great reputation as director of the "Stage" series on the Canadian Broadcasting Corporation's national radio network. Allan had introduced a series of leading players, including John Drainie, Lorne Green, Robert Christie, Ruth Springford, Budd Knapp, Jane Mallett and Tommy Tweed, all of whom became well-known names prior to the emergence of television; he had also done much to develop a number of radio playwrights. Allan guided the Shaw Festival through its first three professional seasons. In 1963 he presented *Androcles and the Lion, You Never Can Tell, How He Lied to Her Husband* and *The Man of Destiny;* in 1964, *Heartbreak House, The Dark Lady of the Sonnets, Village Wooing* and *John Bull's Other Island;* and in 1965, *Pygmalion, The Millionairess* and the festival's first non-Shavian play, Sean O'Casey's *Shadow of a Gunman.* Barry Morse, a London-born actor who had become part of the Canadian scene before making an international name in the television series "The Fugitive," replaced Andrew Allan as artistic director in 1966, when the Court House Theater was improved under the direction of the Festival designer, Lawrence Schaffer. That season *Man and Superman, Misalliance* and *The Apple Cart* were staged, with Morse and Edward Gilbert directing.

The Stratford Festival, an idea first proposed by Tom Patterson, a Stratford-born journalist, began in 1953 when it opened with Richard III *under the direction of Tyrone Guthrie. The second-night performance of* All's Well That Ends Well, *with Alec Guinness and Irene Worth (shown here), established the Festival as a resounding success and inaugurated a new era in the development of Canadian theater.*

TOURING THEATER

Especially important in Canada, with its widely scattered population, is the growth of such companies as the Canadian Players, which toured the country, visiting both large and small communities and bringing theater to many people who have no other opportunity to see it.

The group was originally formed in 1954 by Tom Patterson and Douglas Campbell for Stratford Festival actors who wanted to continue working together in the winter season. In 1964 they performed a contemporary work, *All About Us,* a survey of Canadian history composed by Len Peterson from a series of actual documents and original sketches. The work met with a mixed reception. The company was reminded of the high standards of its early days, when Douglas Campbell took a bare-bones production of Shaw's *Saint Joan* out with his wife, Ann Casson, daughter of Dame Sibyl Thorndyke, who created the role of Saint Joan, in the title role; the company included William Hutt, William Needles and Bruno Gerussi. Other touring productions of note followed, including *Hamlet,* with Hutt, *Peer Gynt,* with Gerussi, and many other non-Shakespearean productions.

In 1966 the Canadian Players inaugurated its first season in Toronto, at the Central Library Theater, while maintaining its touring on a reduced scale. Under the management of Marigold Charlesworth and Jean Roberts, formerly with the Red Barn Theater, it staged well-received productions.

The season was well received, winning most of the honors in the Theater Awards presented by the Toronto *Telegram,* but financially it was not a success because of the limited capacity of the Central Library Theater. As the Crest Theater had encountered similar difficulties and had lost its artistic director, Murray Davis, the boards of the two organizations decided upon amalgamation, with Miss Charlesworth and Miss Roberts as artistic directors.

THE VANCOUVER FESTIVAL

The festival idea had emerged in Vancouver in 1958, when the town set up a large-scale Vancouver International Festival under the direction of Nicholas Goldschmidt, the conductor. Its first original work, in a program mingling attractions from the Far East with those of Europe and North America, was the Canadian play, *The World of the Won-*

The permanent theater of the Stratford Festival, erected in 1956, is based on the open Elizabethan stage, a concept suggested by Tyrone Guthrie and designed by Tanya Moiseiwitsch. Although the theater has a fairly large capacity (2258 seats), the amphitheater, which surrounds the stage on three sides, affords the audience the intimacy of smaller houses, since no seat is more than 65 feet from the stage.

derful Dark, based on West Coast Indian themes by Lister Sinclair.

The Manitoba Theater Center

Over the last decade or so the professional theater has become more firmly established in widely scattered, heavy-population centers.

A major force in the movement has been the foundation of the Manitoba Theater Center in Winnipeg. A unique enterprise, growing out of the Winnipeg Little Theater in 1958, it was particularly ambitious because there had been virtually no professional theater in Winnipeg since 1936, when the John Holden Players decided to move east.

By 1966 the Manitoba Theater Center had proved itself. Its main-stage productions attracted increasingly larger audiences, and the small studio theater provided valuable scope for experiments; tours on a Manitoba circuit have expanded yearly, and visits to schools, a student drama festival, special children's theater productions and seasonal drama classes for children are conducted.

The Manitoba Theater Center also has attempted an exchange of regional productions; it brought the Red Barn Company's production of *Mrs. Warren's Profession* by George Bernard Shaw from the Central Library, Toronto. Among the original plays the Manitoba Theater Center has produced are Len Peterson's *Look Ahead,* Patricia Joudry's *Teach Me How to Cry* (a Dominion Drama Festival winner) and Bernard Slade's *A Very Close Family,* as well as a number of children's plays.

Toronto Theater

Toronto, long an active theatrical center, had not the advantages of isolation that enabled Winnipeg's and Quebec's cultural workers to develop. It has always had the competition of theater from abroad. In recent years, the 3200-seat O'Keefe Center and the 1400-seat Royal Alexandra Theater in Toronto have seen the latest New York shows on tour and, occasionally, London productions on their way to Broadway.

Of the indigenous theaters, the Crest most deserves top consideration as successor to the two semi-professional theater companies, the New Play Society and Jupiter Theater, the latter an organization started by John Drainie, Lorne Green and other performers. Both have made many important contributions to the development of an indigenous Toronto Theater in the matters of audiences, playwrights and players.

The Crest ran for 13 years under the management of members of the Davis family, who launched it in 1954. It had begun as a summer theater operation called The Straw Hat Players, in the Muskoka area of Ontario. There Murray and Donald Davis gathered together fellow actors from Hart House Theater, under the direction of Robert Gill, for summer seasons.

The winter operation of the Davis brothers and their sister, Barbara Chilcott, was launched under the direction of Murray Davis, who stayed with the company until he retired in 1966. Its productions ranged from modern stock comedies and Agatha Christie mysteries to Shaw, Chekhov and Shakespeare, but it recognized its responsibility to Canadian playwrights and produced such works as Robertson Davies' *Royal Stewart* and *Jig For a Gypsy,* Stanley Mann's *Gift of the Serpent,* John Gray's *Bright Sun at Midnight, To Ride a Pink Horse* and *Emmanuel Xoc.*

Then, before the opening of its 1964 season, the Crest experienced severe financial difficulties. It rallied when a fund-raising campaign brought in over $80,000, and the new season included *The Severed Head, The Deputy,* and *The Provoked Wife.*

But at the end of the 1965-66 season, it was decided to amalgamate with the Canadian Players, the touring organization that had run into financial difficulties after its first season at the Central Library, Toronto. The result of the merger, under the artistic directorship of Marigold Charlesworth and Jean Roberts, was to be known as The Crest Canadian Foundation and continue to operate as both a local Toronto theater and a touring operation.

A third theater of note in Toronto is Workshop Productions, an improvisational group headed by George Luscombe with Jack Winter as dramaturgist, which has staged some interesting experimental work at its studio, notably *Hey, Rube, Before Compeigne* and *The Mechanic.* In 1965 it also began summer seasons in the park at Stratford, Ontario, across the river from the Stratford Festival.

The Neptune Theater, Halifax

The Neptune Theater, the Maritimes' principal regional theater, was founded in 1963, based on a brief presented to the Canada Council by Leon Major and Jack Gray. Leon Major became artistic director for the first season in Halifax' old Garrick Theater, which had been taken over as a movie house. The first production was Shaw's *Major Barbara,* with a company of Toronto actors. The first program also listed *Mary, Mary; The Four Poster* and *Antigone* (by Anouilh). Although financing proved difficult, the theater survived to offer a Centennial season including *Henry IV (Part One); The Crucible, The Physicists, A Shot in the Dark* and a new work, *The Sleeping Bag,* by the Halifax playwright Arthur L. Murphey. Previously it had staged one other new play, *Chevalier Johnson* by Jack Gray.

Other Maritime operations have included a professional theater in the Playhouse, Fredericton, under the management first of Alexander Gray and later Brian Swarbrick. It has confined itself to professional operations in summer.

The Charlottetown Festival, located in the Confederation Center opened for 1964, has been operated by Mavor Moore on a policy of all-Canadian programming. Its attractions have included a musical version of *Anne of Green Gables,* from the L. M. Montgomery novel; a Stephen Leacock program, given by John Drainie and others; *The Adventures of Private Turvey,* a musical version of the Earle Birney book made by Donald Harron and Norman Campbell; and a revival of *The Ottawa Man,* Mavor Moore's adaptation of Gogol's *The Inspector General* using a Canadian setting. Performers have included Barbara Hamilton, Peter Mews, Jack Duffy, Kate Reid and other leading players from the Toronto stage.

Vancouver Theater

As well as its International Festival, Vancouver has had many theater groups, leading up to the Playhouse Company, which gained a new lease of life after a doubtful first season in 1963-64. It occupies a small theater built as an adjunct to the big Queen Elizabeth Theater as a home for local companies. A professional operation was sought for the Playhouse, and Malcolm Black was selected as artistic director. It had its first popular success with Eric Nichol's comedy, *Like Father, Like Fun,* which went on to the Royal Alexandra in the summer of 1966. The position of the Playhouse Company was strengthened by a merger between it and the long-established Holiday Theater, which had proved successful under the direction of Joy Coghill, specializing in touring children's theater.

The Neptune Theater in Halifax, founded in 1963 through the efforts of Leon Major and Jack Gray, is the Maritimes' principal regional theater. A full-time repertory company, the Neptune Theater, besides its regular season of plays, presents children's plays and gives seminars and high school matinees as well as touring the area. The Neptune has endeavored to encourage the work of Canadian playwrights by presenting new plays such as Chevalier Johnson *by Jack Gray and* The Sleeping Bag *(shown here in the 1966 production) by Arthur L. Murphey of Halifax.*

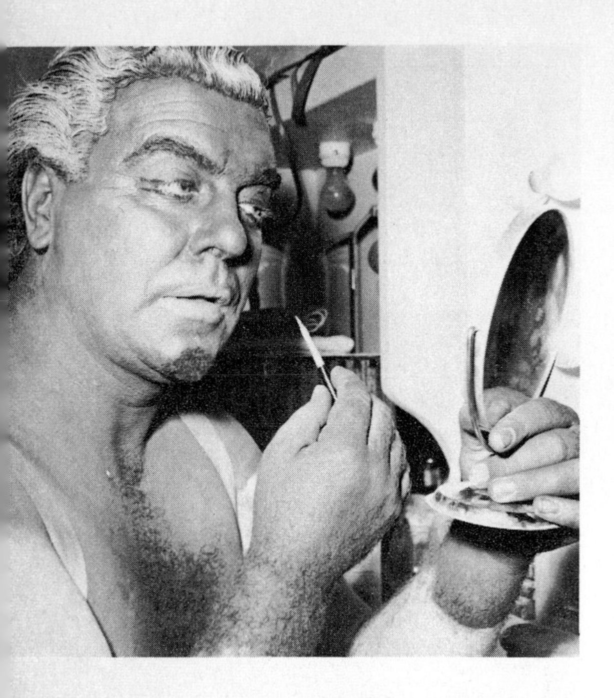

Douglas Campbell, a man of prodigious energy, started his career with London's Old Vic Theater. In 1953 he became associated with the Stratford Festival and for nine years was a leading member of the company, also directing a number of productions. During these years he worked with devotion in support of regional theater. When Tyrone Guthrie went to Minnesota to establish the Tyrone Guthrie Theater in Minneapolis, Campbell soon followed.

Also in Vancouver is the Frederick Wood Theater at the University of British Columbia, opened by Dorothy Somerset, and the Arts Theater, a more popular operation.

VICTORIA THEATER

When the old McPherson Playhouse was deeded to the City of Victoria in 1964, it became a major part of the new Centennial Square, acquiring a handsome new lobby and adjoining restaurant. It also acquired a company called the Bastion Theater, headed by Peter Mannering, which offered a full season of plays. The McPherson reopened with an Elsa Lanchester one-woman show, followed by a season of special attractions, many staged by community groups. But it also included a visit from the Vancouver Playhouse with Anouilh's *Ring Round the Moon*. The auditorium, carefully restored, also saw *Dark of the Moon* presented by the Bastion Theater Studio. This was the group that was groomed to occupy the McPherson Playhouse. In 1965-66, the Bastion Theater staged a season of eight regular plays, plus six for children.

EDMONTON THEATER

The Citadel Theater in Edmonton is a late addition to the growing circuit of Canada's regional theaters. It was launched in 1965 by Joseph Shocter, a wealthy lawyer of Edmonton who had invested in Broadway shows. He purchased the home of the Salvation Army (hence the theater's name) and engaged John Hurlbut to head his first company. On Hurlbut's death, he invited Robert Glenn and Robert Kalfin, both from New York, to complete the season. Plays offered that first year were *Who's Afraid of Virginia Woolf?*, *Death of a Salesman*, *Never Too Late*, *Come Blow Your Horn* and *The Glass Menagerie*. The Citadel, which seats 277, includes a luxury restaurant on the premises.

Also in Edmonton is Gordon Peacock's Studio Theater at the University of Alberta, and the Torches Theater, a summer operation also maintained by the university.

In Calgary, the Betty Mitchell Theater (named after Dr. Betty Mitchell, whose Workshop 14 dominated Calgary theater for many years) was included in the Calgary Allied Arts Center.

The National Theater School

One of the most influential features of recent theatrical activity in Canada is the growth of the National Theater School, which graduated its first class in 1963. This unique institution, which provides three-year training for both French- and English-speaking students in their own theatrical traditions, was planned by Michel St. Denis, at the invitation of members of the Dominion Drama Festival; it was set up with the help of the Canadian Theater Center. It depends heavily on the Canada Council and the Arts Councils of Quebec, Ontario and Saskatchewan. With courses in acting and in all aspects of theater production and design, the school supplies talent to regional theaters across the country as well as to the Stratford Festival and the Canadian Broadcasting Corporation.

To preserve the bicultural aspect of the institution, insisted upon by St. Denis from the beginning, the National Theater School is located in Montreal but holds its summer session at Stratford, with close connections to the festival. Its directors have included Powys Thomas and David Peacock, of the Seattle University drama department.

Celebrating Confederation

In addition to an elaborate program of international attractions for Expo 67, the world exposition coinciding with the celebration of Canada's 100th anniversary of Confederation, a program of tours will take leading musical, operatic and dramatic groups around the country under the banner of Festival-Canada, sponsored by the Centennial Commission. The Centennial was also celebrated by the planned erection of new cultural centers across the country. The principal one is the complex centered in the heart of the capital city, Ottawa, planned to include an opera and ballet house, a large-scale theater and a small experimental theater. The elaborate operation was announced for completion in 1969. Montreal's addition to its *Grande Salle de la*

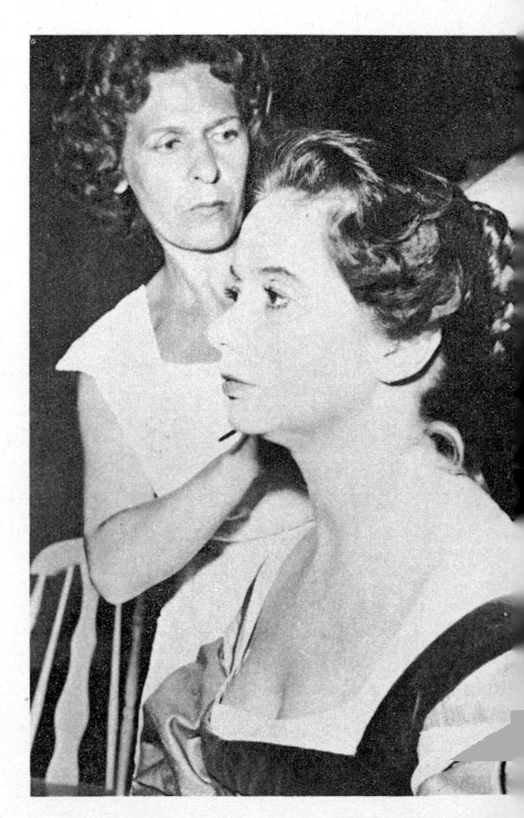

Kate Reid, one of Canada's foremost actresses, began her career in the Hart House Theater in Toronto and has since performed in the leading theaters of Canada as well as having a number of successes on Broadway. Here she is seen preparing for the role of Emilia in Shakespeare's Othello, *her debut performance at the Stratford Festival Theater in 1959.*

Place des Arts, a handsome concert hall, was to be two smaller auditoriums, a theater and a concert hall.

CANADA'S FRENCH THEATER

IN FRENCH CANADA, THE DEVELOPMENT of the theater, like that of other cultural activities, has been largely influenced by the people's determination to retain their own distinctive characteristics. Before the British conquest of 1759, companies in Quebec had drawn exclusively on French classics for their repertories, but after the fall of Quebec, French Canada was for many years cut off from the mother country.

French Canadians were forced to conserve and be isolationist; this was their only protection against assimilation by the British. In one sense this had inhibiting effects on the growth of a fully developed culture, but in another sense the common danger acted as a stimulant, and the desire to preserve a clear national identity became the French Canadians' passionate concern. Nationalist themes became the chief inspiration of French-Canadian artists and writers.

In modern times French-Canadian culture has fully asserted itself, and there is a greater sense of freedom in cultural cooperation. Between French and English companies there are, for instance, some exchanges of theatrical productions as well as tours and collaboration.

French Canada's most active center is Montreal, but a good theatrical foundation is also being established in Quebec City.

Colonial Theater

The earliest recorded theatrical performance took place in French Canada in 1606. The piece, a *gaillardise en rime*, or comedy in verse, was called *Le Théâtre de Neptune*, and it was presented, under the direction of its author, Marc Lescarbot, in the newly settled Port Royal, now Annapolis Royal, Nova Scotia. It set a precedent for performances of a similar nature that were to flourish, especially between 1636 and 1640, in Quebec.

In 1646, some ten years after its performance in Paris, *Le Cid* by Pierre Corneille reached the stage in New France, and this was followed by other productions of successes already established in the mother country. But toward the end of the century the Puritan movement began to exert its powerful influence, and the theater was suppressed. It was kept alive through the efforts of Jesuit priests, who had a tradition of cultivating good drama; these priests staged performances of classics and plays of a religious nature within their colleges.

English invasion in 1759 brought obstacles to the development of French native drama, but nevertheless, by 1790 the first permanent French theater had been opened in Quebec and the same year saw the first performance, in Montreal, of a play written in French on Canadian soil; the author was the French-born playwright Joseph Ques-

A new awareness in French Canada of the importance of the theater is giving rise to contests and festivals to encourage French-Canadian writers, and is leading to the establishment of little theaters. An example is La Poudrière, the Montreal International Theater, which was opened in 1958 in a converted powder magazine in the 140-year-old fortress Ile Sainte Hélène, Montreal, Quebec.

nel, and the play was called *Colas et Colinette.*

The Nineteenth Century

During the 19th century the masterpieces of the French classical playwrights began to exert their influence on the writing of French Canadians: Pierre Petitclair (d. 1860), taking Molière as his model, produced *Grifon, ou la vengeance d'un valet* (Grifon, or a Servant's Revenge; 1837) and *La Donation* (The Donation; 1842), while A. Gerin Lajoie, whose chief work was *Le jeune Latour* (Young Latour; 1844), preferred the tragic genre as exemplified by the plays of Corneille.

As in British Canada, love of the theater was nourished by the visits of celebrated actors and actresses from the mother country. A particular success was scored by the great French actress Sarah Bernhardt (1844-1923), who first played in Montreal in 1880 in *La dame aux camélias* by Alexandre Dumas *fils* and in *Hernani* by Victor Hugo. This great artist revisited Canada in 1891 and 1905.

Prewar Success

During the early years of this century, before the beginning of World War I, the theater seemed to have reached a peak of success. New theaters were springing up, and more and more touring companies were arriving from Paris. French-Canadian actors and actresses were even becoming known in France, and such was the atmosphere of nationalist zeal and enthusiasm that competition from the movie industry held no fears for the theater manager.

But the war, with its attendant financial difficulties, brought a slump in theatrical activity and some years were to pass before the next period of renewal.

The Pioneer Movement

The years immediately before World War II were more fruitful for theater in French Canada. In 1938 a theater troupe known as *Les Compagnons de Saint Laurent* was formed by Père Émile Legault (1906-). Starting with the performance of religious plays, the company gradually added secular drama—usually French classics such as the plays of Molière or Racine—to its repertory until it had built up a selection of good productions with particular appeal to young audiences.

COSMOPOLITAN REPERTORY

In 1942 the group acquired a semi-professional status with its move into *L'Ermitage* theater. On these premises it extended its repertory to embrace such French writers as Jean Anouilh, André Obey, Jean Giraudoux, Edmund Rostand and the Spanish Federico García Lorca. British and American theater was represented by T. S. Eliot's *Murder in the Cathedral,* Thornton Wilder's *Our Town* and Tennessee Williams' *The Glass Menagerie.*

RIVAL GROUPS

From 1943 to 1948 Pierre Dagenais ran a rival group to *Les Compagnons;* it was known as *L'Équipe* (The Team) and was composed of radio actors. Before succumbing to lack of financing, this group presented a wide variety of productions, including *Tessa (The Constant Nymph)* by Margaret Kennedy, *Marius, Fanny* and *César,* the trilogy by Marcel Pagnol, and plays by Jean Cocteau. In an early bicultural exchange, Dagenais directed *King Lear* for the Shakespeare Society of Montreal while Herbert Whittaker directed Shaw's *L'Homme et Les Soldats (Arms and the Man)* for *L'Équipe.*

'LE RIDEAU VERT'

The place of *L'Équipe* was taken in 1948 by a company known as *Le Rideau Vert* (The Green Curtain), founded by Yvette Brind'Amour. Until *Les Compagnons* disbanded in 1952 this company remained their sole competitor.

In their first home, the pocket theater *L'Anjou,* which had seats for 90 people, *Le Rideau Vert* company performed an adventurous series of plays on a monthly repertory basis, with an annual revue. They presented unusual experimental plays by foreign writers and also gave opportunities to Canadians such as Roger Sinclair, with *La Boutique aux Anges* (Angel Store), and Marcel

Gratien Gélinas (1909-), shown here with his puppet likeness, created the fresh and witty character of Fridolin in 1938 in his first stage appearance and became an overnight success. Besides being a respected actor—his performance in Tit-Coq *left no room for imitators—Gélinas in 1958 opened* La Comédie Canadienne, *a 1200-seat theater planned as a showcase for the plays of Canadians.*

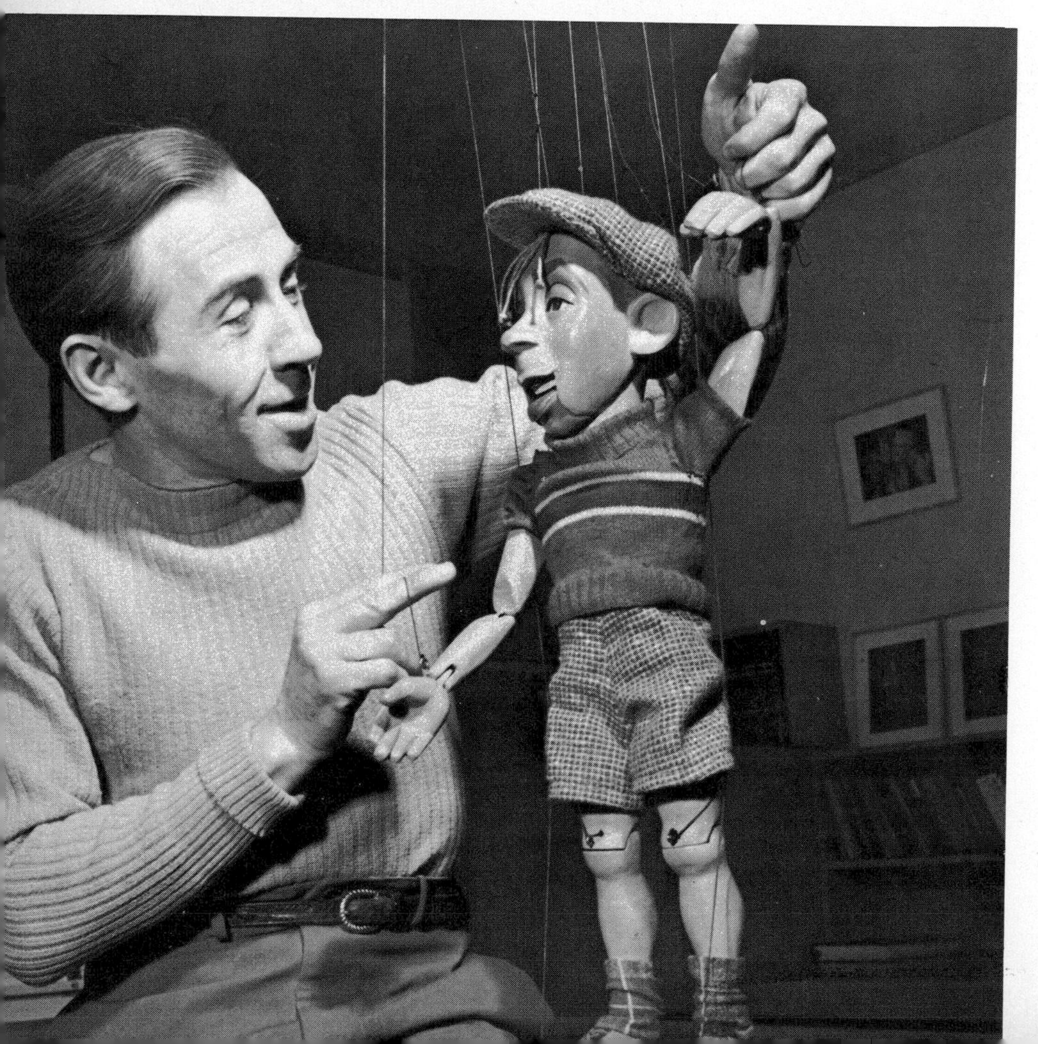

Established in 1952 under the direction of Celia Franca, a former member of the Sadler's Wells Ballet, the National Ballet of Canada is one of three major professional dance companies in the country. Along with the Royal Winnipeg Ballet, formed in 1939, and Les Grands Ballets Canadiens, *founded in 1952, it has benefited from the phenomenal rise in the popularity of ballet in Canada. To further the training of young Canadians, the National Ballet School, modeled on the schools in Russia and Great Britain, was established in 1959. Lois Smith and Earl Kraul, leading dancers of the National Ballet of Canada, appear here in a performance of* La Sylphide.

Gagnon, the novelist, who wrote *Edwige*.

In 1960 the company moved into the more spacious surroundings of *Le Théâtre Stella*, which holds 400 seats. It continues to maintain high standards without relinquishing its varied and ambitious program. In 1964 it was invited by the French minister of culture, André Malraux, to visit Paris with a production of *L'Heureux Stratagème* (Clever Tactics) by Marivaux.

Gratien Gélinas

The year 1938, during which *Les Compagnons de Saint Laurent* gave their first performances, also witnessed the first stage appearance of Gratien Gélinas (1909-). Gélinas' previous acting experience had been in a popular radio soap-opera, "Le Curé du Village" (The Village Priest), but the success of his characterization of Fridolin, a fresh and wittily presented personality that made immediate and nation-wide impact on the Canadian public, made him abandon radio and devote himself to revue.

'TIT-COQ'

The character Gélinas had evolved gave rise to a series of *Fridolinons* whose popularity remained unequaled until 1950 when Fridolin's creator produced another outstanding stage personality in *Tit-Coq;* this was to dominate the theatrical scene for many years, with 200 shows in Montreal alone. *Tit-Coq* told the story, in witty and realistic terms, of an illegitimate son, who, because of the conventions of society, suffered all kinds of indignities until love brought him self-respect. The play had great popular appeal, and because of the originality of its characterization and, perhaps, the overwhelming personality of its creator, it left no room for imitators.

Literary Trends

The writers of the period seemed more concerned with the literary than the dramatic qualities of their plays. Some examples are *Un Fils à tuer* (A Son to be Killed; 1949) a historical tragedy on the theme of the deserter by Eloi de Grandmont; a peasant drama, *Le Marcheur* (The Walker; 1950) by the novelist Yves Thériault (1916-); *Polichinelle* (1950), a verse fantasy by Lomer

A scene from Klondike, *a historical musical by Jacques Languirand, resident playwright of* Le Théâtre du Nouveau-Monde, *and presented in a spectacular production in 1966. The action of the play takes place during the gold rush and centers on two main characters, who sit isolated and bored in their room with the feeling that a day wasted is an accomplishment. This vital French-Canadian theater in Montreal, established in 1951, reflects the growing interest of the French Community in theater.*

Gonin; and *Rose Latulippe* (1951), a romantic comedy based on a French-Canadian legend by the actor Jean-Louis Roux.

The plays of Paul Toupin are particularly restrained, unaffected by contemporary trends and with *Choix* (The Choice; 1951) is set in France during the Nazi occupation, *Brutus* (1952) is a pure and classical tragedy and *Le Mensonge* (The Lie; 1952) takes place in 15th-century Brittany.

The work of the prolific writer Marcel Dubé (1930-) is, on the other hand, much more theatrical in character. Between 1952 and 1960 he had six of his plays produced; three of them appeared first on television: *Zone* (1952), *Le Barrage* (The Dam; 1956), *Chambre à Louer* (Room to Let; 1955), *Le Temps des Lilas* (Lilac Time; 1958), *Un Simple Soldat* (A Simple Soldier; 1959) and *Florence* (1960).

Theater for the New World

On Oct. 9, 1951, Molière's *L'Avare* (The Miser) was performed by the newly formed company *Le Théâtre du Nouveau Monde,* (or Theater of the New World; the T.N.M., as it is known), for which the plays of Molière provided a constant source of success. After its first season the company experienced various setbacks through fire and financial problems, but it survived and was able to mount a successful production of *Tartuffe,* also by Molière, in 1953. Its first presentation in the English language was *Come Back, Little Sheba,* by William Inge, in 1954, and in the same year came the T.N.M.'s first production of an original French-Canadian play, *La Fontaine de Paris,* by Eloi de Grandmont.

In 1955 the T.N.M. was invited to the Paris International Arts Festival, where its production of three one-act plays by Molière was received with great enthusiasm. The same kind of reception was accorded by English-speaking audiences at Stratford, Ontario, the following year. A more recent success abroad was the company's 1965 appearance in England at the Commonwealth Arts Festival, where it performed *L'École des Femmes* (School for Wives) by Molière.

But the T.N.M. is by no means restricted to Molière in its choice of plays. Its productions have ranged from *L'Échange* (The Exchange) by Paul Claudel in 1956 and *Le Pain Dur* (Stale Bread) by the same author in 1963, to *Irma la Douce* by Alexandre Breffort, also in 1963.

THE MANAGEMENT

The artistic director of the T.N.M. is the versatile Jean Gascon; Gascon works on all the company's important productions, in which he often takes a leading part. Gascon is also an associate director of the Stratford Festival Theater, where he has produced *Othello* and *The Comedy of Errors* as well as the operas *Cosi fan Tutte, Mahagonny* and, in 1966, *Don Giovanni.* The company now has a resident playwright in Jacques Languirand, a writer previously much influenced by new-wave theater but who has turned now to local themes; one of these was his collaboration with Gabriel Charpentier on the musical production *Klondike,* also performed at the 1965 Commonwealth Arts Festival in England.

Languirand's appointment as official dramaturgist is a significant part of the T.N.M.'s search for a more secure basis for cultural development.

In April 1964 it was announced that the company would reorganize as a non-profit-making venture, so as to qualify for a government subsidy. As yet they have no permanent home: they spend the summer season in a playhouse at Repentigny, which looks from the outside like an Indian stockade; when winter comes they move back to the city, where they stage productions in the Orpheum, formerly a cinema, holding 1000 seats.

INTIMATE THEATER

In 1953 two former members of *Les Compagnons de Saint Laurent,* Jacques Letourneau and Monique Lepage, formed a small company under the name of *Le Théâtre-Club,* using a high school as their theater. Among their most noted successes have been *Le Barrage* (The Dam) by Marcel Dubé, *Quand la Moisson sera Courbée* (When the Harvest Is Over) by Roger Sinclair, and *Les Violons de l'Automne* (Autumn Violins) by Jacques Languirand, but the group is particularly well known for its imaginative productions for young people.

'LA COMÉDIE CANADIENNE'

In 1961 *Le Théâtre-Club* was invited to use the facilities of *La Comédie Canadienne.* This 1200-seat theater, the best equipped in Canada, had been planned by the energetic

Gratien Gélinas as a show-place for Canadian dramatic work, but the venture met with great financial difficulties, and not long after its opening in 1958 Gélinas had to compromise and allow the building to be used for movies and as a music hall. In 1966 he was able to return to his original objectives and take over the theater.

THE AVANT-GARDE

The activity, however short-lived, of small avant-garde French-Canadian theaters has had an extremely invigorating effect on larger, more orthodox enterprises. Montreal has several amateur groups of the former kind, including *Les Apprentis-Sorciers* and *Les Saltimbanques*, but it also has supported a professional experimental theater in *Le Théâtre de L'Egrégore,* which, during the 1961-62 season, acquired its own premises with an Elizabethan-style stage and room for an audience of 130. This dynamic company was run by Françoise Berd and Jacques Languirand who decided on an Ionesco play, *Le roi se meurt* (Exit the King), for the opening production in their new theater. One of their most popular successes was *Naïves Hirondelles* (Naïve Swallows) by Roland Dubillard, but their choice of plays before and since ranged from Anton Chekhov to Alfred Jarry, Jean Genet and Samuel Beckett.

FOUNDATION FOR THE FUTURE

The new awareness of the importance of the theater has given rise to, or encouraged the development of, festivals, contests for French-Canadian writers and such activities as the tours of *Les Jeunes Comédiens* (The Young Players), a group of French-speaking graduates of the National Theater School who are now sponsored by the Canadian Players. All these combine to assure the healthy growth of the French-Canadian theater of the future.

THE BALLET

ALTHOUGH IT WAS THE LAST OF THE performing art forms to be established in Canada, ballet has developed with almost phenomenal speed. Within the space of ten years, from 1939 to 1949, the number of amateur companies in Canada had leapt from three to twenty, and at present the country has three fully professional ballet companies.

The Royal Winnipeg Ballet

This group, founded in 1939 by Gweneth Lloyd as the Winnipeg Ballet Club, gained professional status in 1951, when it became known as the Winnipeg Ballet. Its year of triumph was 1953, when it became the first British Commonwealth ballet company to receive the honor of a British Royal Charter. In 1965 it was invited to participate in the Commonwealth Festival, held in London, and had an excellent critical reception.

The Royal Winnipeg Ballet is the first Canadian company to have evolved an individual tradition and characteristic style; this is largely due to the efforts of its artistic director, Arnold Spohr, who joined the company in 1945 as a dancer and became director in 1950. Spohr has encouraged foreign talent—for example, as guest artists or teachers—but he has built up a company largely of Canadian-born dancers, with such exceptions as the ballerina Sonia Taverner, who trained with the Royal Ballet in England, and the male principals Frederic Strobel and Richard Rutherford, from the U.S.

During the course of its history, the company has staged many original ballets, and it now provides a worthy vehicle for the work of Canada's leading native-born choreographer, Brian Macdonald, who became an official member of the company in 1965. Macdonald's ballets include *The Darkling* (1959), *Les Whoops-de-doo, A Court Occasion, Prothalmion,* which has been performed in Russia, and more recently, *Pas d'Action* and *Aimez-vous Bach?*, which received a Gold Star for the best abstract ballet in the Paris International Festival in 1964. In 1964 Macdonald won great critical acclaim for his choreography in the company's contribution to the annual dance festival that takes place at Jacob's Pillow, Massachusetts. Although in 1965 he was appointed *chef de ballet* for the Opera House in Stockholm, Sweden, he continued to create for the Royal Winnipeg Ballet.

In 1963 the company made its first tour abroad with a highly successful visit to Jamaica at the

Margery Lambert is shown dancing the Oriental number from the Nutcracker *in a production by* Les Grands Ballets Canadiens. *The youngest of the professional ballet companies,* Les Grands Ballets Canadiens *is based in Montreal. Founded by the Latvian choreographer Ludmilla Chiriaeff, the company has grown in scope and status, and in 1964 Anton Dolin, the renowned English dancer, became artistic adviser.*

Nutcracker, Act I. *A lavish production of the National Ballet Company in which the complete Tchaikovsky score is used. Scenes from other ballets in the repertoire of the National Ballet of Canada appear on these pages.*

time of that country's independence celebrations.

During the 1963-64 season *Mayerling*, a ballet by the English choreographer Peter Darrell, was given its premiere in Winnipeg, and at the 1966 Stratford Festival the company presented, at the Avon Theater, a new ballet, *Rose Latulippe* by Brian Macdonald. This, the first full-length ballet with a Canadian theme, is based on an old French-Canadian legend.

The National Ballet of Canada

The National Ballet of Canada, founded in 1952, has its base in Toronto. There 40 dancers and a 24-piece orchestra work under the direction of Celia Franca, who was brought from England on the recommendation of Dame Ninette de Valois, director of the Royal Ballet.

Highlights of the company's repertory have included a return visit by the Canadian-born Melissa Hayden, now prima ballerina in George Balanchine's New York City Ballet, who danced with her former colleagues in 1963 in *Swan Lake* and *Coppelia* and in Balanchine's *Serenade*. In 1966 Rudolf Nureyev took over the leading role in *La Sylphide* when Erik Bruhn of the Royal Danish Ballet, who was the National Ballet's guest star, injured his knee in performance.

In 1964 the company acquired John Cranko's *Romeo and Juliet*, which they first performed at *La Place des Arts* in Montreal. The ballet was designed by Jurgen Rose as it had been at Stuttgart.

Also in 1964 Grant Strate, assistant to the artistic director, saw his ballet *The House of Atreus* brought to life in Ottawa, with music by Harry Somers and sets and costumes by Harold Town.

The company's 13th season opened at the O'Keefe Center in Toronto with a new Christmas production of *The Nutcracker*. For the 1966-67 season it engaged Erik Bruhn to produce a new production of *Swan Lake*, Eugene Valukin of the Bolshoi Ballet to stage *Bayaderka* and Herno Heiden to create a new work, *La Prima Ballerina*.

Les Grands Ballets Canadiens

The youngest of Canada's professional ballet companies, *Les Grands Ballets Canadiens*, is based in Montreal. In 1963 it staged the first full-length ballet to be choreographed in Canada, *Cendrillon* (Cinderella), by Ludmilla Chiriaeff. In the same year Anton Dolin staged his *Pas de Quatre* for it, and in 1964 he joined the company as artistic director.

In the fall of 1963 the company was the first to perform in the newly completed *Grande Salle de la Place des Arts* in Montreal.

The main event of the 1964 season was the performance of a new ballet, *Medea*, with choreography by Brydon Paige and electronic music by Georges Savaria.

The National Ballet School

The most important advance of any Canadian ballet company was that of the National Ballet when it established, in September 1959, the National Ballet School, an institution combining academic and balletic instruction on a full-time basis, as do schools in Russia and Great Britain. The only one of its kind on the North American continent, the National Ballet School was established by Celia Franca, artistic director of the National Ballet, and Betty Oliphant, ballet mistress of the National Ballet. Its academic excellence won the approval of the Ontario Department of Education, to which it is responsible, through the high marks obtained by the students, while its balletic instruction was approved by the great Soviet ballerina Galina Ulanova, when she paid an official visit to the school during the Bolshoi's 1962 visit and took a class with its pupils. This led to an exchange by which Eugene Valukin was lent to the National Ballet School by the Bolshoi to teach, and Betty Oliphant visited Moscow and Leningrad. The pupils graduating with top honors are assured a place in the National Ballet company, but Miss Oliphant, herself a pupil of Tamara Karsavina, regards the duty of the establishment to be a national school to train Canadian dancers for other Canadian companies, as well as for companies abroad. Veronica Tennant, who danced Juliet with the National Ballet in 1966, was one of the first of the school's graduates to acquire soloist status, followed by Martine von Hamel and Karen Bowes.

Nutcracker, Act II.

Triptych. *A modern dance ballet based on Mozart's Clarinet Concerto in A. There is no story. The entire ballet is treated in pure dance terms.*

THE MUSIC

The Indian Tradition

PRIOR TO THE ARRIVAL OF THE Europeans, the Canadian Indians had a well developed tradition of ceremonial music.

The songs of the Northwestern interior Indians were sung to express religious feelings, to help heal the sick, to celebrate battle victories, to mourn death, and even to seal peace between tribes, and they are often very beautiful. The songs were marked with clear, musical drum beats and were sung in intricate, guttural languages. The scales employed were usually pentatonic.

Differing from the songs of the Northwestern interior Indians, those of the Indians on the sea coast were usually not so musically appealing. Whereas the Northwestern interior Indians' music was an integral part of daily life, the coastal tribes' songs were usually sung only at rites and ceremonies. The songs were somewhat brooding and melancholy in nature; the coastal Indians' voices were harsh and throaty; and the drums used were muffled and hollow-sounding.

La Sylphide, *Act I. This classical ballet by Herman Lovensjöld was first produced in Copenhagen in 1836. It is based on the tragic story of a mortal's love for a sylph.*

The Early Colonists

With the first explorers and settlers, two new musical traditions were introduced to Canada—secular folk music and church music.

The production of Romeo and Juliet *(an international prize-winning dance replica of Shakespeare's play), as it was presented on CBC television.*

FOLK MUSIC

French-Canadian folk songs derive from the stock of traditional French songs brought over to Canada by the original French explorers. French-Canadian songs are rhythmical, and they usually contain solo parts that alternate with a chorus or refrain. The refrains reflect the activities and feelings of the early French immigrants. Some of the best known songs are *À la Claire Fontaine* and *Auprès de Ma Blonde.*

English-Canadian folk songs are made up of both songs from the Old World and songs of local origin. The local songs are usually either tragic ballads, dealing with death and disaster, or shorter, more humorous tunes of recent origin, based on local happenings. Many show distinct Irish influences. Newfoundland has remained the richest area for these songs.

Early Church Music

Because among the first settlers there were many priests, the first organized European music in Canada was church music. Founded in 1608, Quebec became the center of musical as well as missionary and commercial activity. As early as 1635, elements of Gregorian chant and musical notation were taught to French and Indian boys by the priests, and some years later the Ursuline Sisters began to instruct girls in music. Over the succeeding years, the church formed choirs and organized concerts of both sacred and secular music.

CONFLICT WITH FOLK MUSIC

As church and folk music became more widespread in Canada, they also became more divergent. Throughout the 18th century and most of the 19th century, there was conflict between the two. Folk music had become a part of everyday life, but it drew forth some opposition from the church, which associated it with social evils, such as drunkenness and loose living. This attitude of the church was especially marked in the early Protestant settlements.

The Eighteenth Century

The war between France and England brought to Canada a new form of music, the music of the regimental bands, which became the backbone of instrumental music for a whole century. The bands performed regularly—at social gatherings, theater performances, and public concerts. At the end of the war in 1763, many members of these army bands chose to remain in Canada, and in most cases they contributed to music as teachers or performers.

SERIOUS SECULAR MUSIC

The activities of the regimental bands fostered an appreciation of serious secular music in Canada during the 18th and early 19th centuries. Bands were formed in many towns, and as a result the number of concerts and performances increased, especially during the last decade of the century.

Although significant advances

Solitaire. *The dance tells the story of a young girl's search for companionship, her rejection and loneliness.*

were made in the musical life of Canada in the 18th century, religious hostility was still apparent, and even the use of musical instruments in church was sometimes opposed. As a result of these attitudes, the growth of serious music was somewhat hindered. Even wealthy people rarely patronized the musical arts, and a career in music was looked down upon.

Musicians and music lovers had to work very hard to raise the quantity and quality of their art. It was only as the result of their pioneer efforts that musical societies were formed.

The Nineteenth Century

During the 19th century, as towns grew and a strong middle class emerged, urban musical life developed rapidly. Music societies became plentiful, as did music teachers. There was an increasing demand for instruments; music appeared on the curriculum in educational institutions; and a number of native compositions were written.

MUSIC SOCIETIES

In the first half of the century, music societies were often the only source of musical activity and appreciation. Among these societies were: the Amateur Glee Club (founded in 1837), in Halifax, the Montreal Philharmonic Society (1848), the Société de Musique (1837), also in Montreal, the Choral Society (1845), in Toronto, and the Harmonic Society for the Cultivation of Sacred Music, formed in Quebec in 1820, and in Nova Scotia in 1828.

CONCERTS AND OPERA

During the mid-19th century, concerts became more frequent and more oriented toward a classical repertoire. In 1858 the Philharmonic Society of Hamilton performed *The Creation* by Haydn, with an orchestra of 25 and a chorus of 90. The Montreal Philharmonic Society (1877-99), with Guillaume Couture as its conductor, gave almost 90 concerts, and performed such works as Mozart's *Requiem* and Beethoven's *Ninth Symphony*.

The Canadian Opera Company production of Salomé *by Richard Strauss, with Margaret Tynes as Salomé, Phil Stark as Herod and Arlene Meadows as Herodias. In 1946 about 500 people attended a concert of operatic selections at Hart House on the University of Toronto campus; the performers were students of the Royal Conservatory Opera School, which had just started its activities. The public response was so encouraging that within a few years it became necessary to move the performances to the larger Royal Alexandra Theater. These successes provided the stimulus for the formation in 1954 of the professional Opera Festival Company. In 1959 the company adopted its present name, and two years later it moved to the modern, 3200-seat O'Keefe Center for the Performing Arts.*

Around 1853, in Toronto, Bellini's *Norma* was the first opera performed in Canada. During the 1889-90 season, 26 different operas were performed in Toronto. In 1846, the Société des Amateurs Canadiens of Quebec performed Jacques Rousseau's opera, *Le Devin du Village*, and in the 1890s opera classes in Halifax gave successful public performances of two operas.

MUSICAL COMPOSITION

No significant headway in musical composition in Canada was made until the 19th century. Prior to this, practically all music was composed for the church, and there was no distinctive style or school of Canadian composers. One notable 18th-century exception to the exclusive concern with religious music was the French-Canadian Joseph Quesnel (1749-1809), who wrote music for operas and plays. One of his works, *Colin and Colinette*, was performed in 1790 in Montreal and in 1808 in Quebec.

Throughout the 19th century, although most composers still continued to write for the church, other types of music were written. Calixa Lavallée (1842-91), a French-Canadian, was Canada's first composer to create an impressive body of work. His compositions include *O Canada*, later to become the national anthem. Other French-Canadian composers of note were Romain-Octave Pelletier, Joseph Vézina, Guillaume Couture and Alexis Contant.

Sir Ernest MacMillan (1893-), composer, conductor, pianist, lecturer and author, has composed many fine works, generally featuring the voice. As the conductor of the Toronto Symphony Orchestra from 1931 to 1956, he was instrumental in building the group into an excellent musical ensemble. MacMillan's ability and influence have put him in the forefront of Canada's musical life. (Photo: Karsh-Ottawa)

Composition among the English-Canadians began a little later in the century. Their music also was written chiefly for church and choral purposes, and rarely for the stage. Charles Harriss (1822-1932), Albert Ham (1858-1940) and Edward Broome (1868-1932) were among the composers of note. The most important Anglo-Canadian composers of Ontario were Wesley Forsyth (1863-1937), who wrote songs and compositions for piano, and Clarence Lucas (1866-1947), who wrote operas and orchestral works.

Most 19th-century compositions by both French- and English-Canadians were not published until the early 20th century, as in 19th-century Canada there was still little interest and support for native compositions. Performers were considered far more important than composers, and, because of this, many of Canada's finest composers were forced to go elsewhere if they wished to earn a living by writing music. Notable 19th-century works not published until the early 20th century include Harriss' opera *Torquil*, performed in 1900; Contant's oratorio *Cain*, performed in 1905 in Montreal; and Couture's oratorio *Jean Le Précurseur*, performed in Montreal in 1923.

MUSIC PUBLICATION

In the 19th century music became a business. Before the 1850s the bulk of musical publications had been imported, but by the middle of the century, sheet music was being printed in Canada, and in 1860 the first native musical periodical in French, *L'Artiste*, was published. The first Canadian music magazine to be published in English was the *Music Journal*, published in Toronto in 1887. Within the next 20 years, at least ten magazines on music appeared.

INSTRUMENT-BUILDING

Before the 19th century, musical instruments, like printed music, had been imported; however, importing was costly and hazardous, and the European instruments did not stand up well to Canada's climate. Many Canadian immigrants proved capable of making very fine instruments, and so this home industry developed rapidly. Organs were first made in Canada around 1820, and piano-making began a little later.

MUSICAL EDUCATION

Musical education in Canada in the early 1800s was inadequate, and those who sought a serious musical training had to go abroad.

In the 1840s, music was finally

Healey Willan (1880-), the dean of English-speaking Canadian composers, has an impressive and varied list of works to his credit. He holds the distinction of having written the first Canadian grand opera, Deirdre of the Sorrows.

accepted as a part of middle-class education, and it appeared in the curricula of several colleges. The first music doctorate was conferred on James P. Clark by the University of Toronto. By World War I, 50 doctoral degrees had been conferred.

Several music conservatories were opened in the second half of the 19th century, among them the Quebec Académie de Musique (1868), the Toronto Conservatory (1886), the Halifax Conservatory (1887), and the McGill Conservatorium (1904) in Montreal.

The Twentieth Century

During the 20th century, music has become a very important part of cultural life in Canada. The country has experienced a tremendous growth in population and prosperity, and the people have had more leisure time for the study and rehearsal of music. Regimental bands and church groups have lost their once supreme importance, and the new leaders of music in Canada are the composers, conductors, senior conservatory staffs and the Canadian Music Center.

MUSIC FESTIVALS

Music festivals became increasingly popular during the early 20th century and have provided a valuable stimulus to the musical life of Canada. The first Canadian music festival was held in May 1908, at Edmonton. There were a large number of entries, and their performances were of a high caliber. Other provinces, and cities, were quick to follow suit: Saskatchewan (1909), Manitoba (1919), and Vancouver (1923). In addition to these, many smaller district festivals were held in the western provinces.

In the eastern provinces music festivals did not begin until several years later. In Ontario, they began in 1923, and today there are at least 25 festivals held in that province.

The response to festivals was lively, and often whole towns would take part in the festival spirit. Over 95 music festivals are held annually in Canada today, and they attract more than 30,000 entries, ranging from soloists to full orchestras. In addition, there are two organizations that concern themselves solely with music festivals: the Federation of Canadian Music Festivals, and Les Festivals de Musique du Quebec.

YOUNG MUSICAL ARTISTS

An important outgrowth of Canada's music festivals has been the growing interest in native Canadian musical artists. Due to the vastness of the country and the expense of travel, many of the finest young artists were formerly unable to give concert recitals on a tour. Then, around 1940, in western Canada, the Young Artists Series was formed for the purpose of sending young performers on tours. Now Ontario's educational authorities organize and subsidize musical tours of their province. Les Jeunesses Musicales du Canada, founded in 1949 by Gilles Lefebvre, operates chiefly in the province of Quebec. This organization arranges recitals by Canadian and also foreign artists, and holds annual music competitions at its summer camp at Mount Orford.

The National Youth Orchestra, founded in 1960, has been a tremendous success since its inception. Led by Walter Susskind, the former conductor of the Toronto Symphony Orchestra, the N.Y.O. has offered intensive summer training in Toronto and Stratford by top Canadian and U.S. instructors. The N.Y.O. also gives concerts in these two cities and makes a western tour of such cities as Vancouver, Winnipeg, and Edmonton.

In 1963, the Canadian Music Center (which is jointly financed by the Canada Council and the Composers, Authors and Publishers Association of Canada) initiated a project whereby 15 established composers would come to Toronto to work with music teachers and school orchestras on a creative music course for young people. The aim of this project was to introduce new compositions to teachers and students for future inclusion in school music programs; to familiarize students with contemporary music; and, also, to encourage the composers to write for young people.

Among the many Canadian musical artists who have achieved international recognition are the great contralto, Maureen Forrester; Lois Marshall, soprano, who won the Naumberg Award in New York in 1952; and Betty Jean Hagen, violinist, also a Naumberg winner in 1950 and a winner of the Pathé-Marconi Prize in Paris. Perhaps the outstanding pianist of his generation, and a musicologist of note as well, is the Canadian Glenn Gould. Among Canadian-born opera singers who have achieved world standing at the top of their profession are Raoul Jobin, Jon Vickers, Léopold Simoneau and George London. There are dozens of Canadian-trained opera singers who now take leading roles in the opera houses of Europe and the United States.

COMPOSERS

The most outstanding English-Canadian composer of the early 1900s is Healey Willan (1880-), the dean of English-speaking composers in Canada. He has an impressive and varied list of works to his credit, including two symphonies, a piano concerto, chamber music, choral works and a radio opera, *Transit through Fire*. Willan is also noted for writing the first Canadian opera, *Deirdre of the Sorrows*.

Another musician whose ability and influence have put him at the forefront of Canada's musical life is Sir Ernest MacMillan (1893-), conductor, composer, organist, pianist, lecturer and author. He has composed many fine works, including a series designed for musical education. MacMillan has been conductor of the Toronto Symphony and of the Mendelssohn Choir.

The leading French-Canadian composer of the early 1900s is Claude Champagne (1891-), whose distinguished works include *Suite Canadienne*, for choir and orchestra, *Symphonie Gaspésienne*, and *Paysanne*, for small orchestra. Many of Champagne's works have been influenced in style and theme by French-Canadian folk songs.

Another composer of note, of later date, is John Weinzweig (1913-), who has written many orchestral works, including five *Divertimenti*, a violin concerto, works for piano, vocal compositions, many radio and motion-picture scores and a ballet, *The Red Ear of Corn*. Weinzweig has a very individual style, and he has widely employed the themes and idioms of Indian and French-Canadian folk songs. He is a noted music teacher and was the first president of the

A regimental band leads a parade through the historic Saint Louis Gate, Quebec. During the early years of settlement in Canada two forms of music became widespread: church music and folk music. However, after the British conquest (1759) a new kind of music became common—the music of the regimental band. At the close of the war in 1763 many members of these bands chose to remain in Canada, and their activities helped to foster an appreciation of serious secular music. For a century the music of the regimental band was the backbone of instrumental music in Canada.

In 1908 a few musicians in Toronto organized under the leadership of Frank Welsman. In 1923 the group was joined by other musicians, and under the direction of Dr. Luigi von Kunits they practiced and performed the works of major composers in their spare time. In the 1930s, with the noted Sir Ernest MacMillan as conductor, the orchestra was able to arrange full-length programs. The group's activity has since increased rapidly, and today the Toronto Symphony Orchestra is an example of Canada's growing musical maturity. In 1965 the 29-year-old Seiji Ozawa, a graduate of Tokyo's Toho School of Music and winner of several international music awards, was named Music Director.

Canadian League of Composers, founded in 1951.

English-speaking Canada has produced a number of very fine composers. Barbara Pentland has worked in a variety of forms and media, and has written orchestral works, scores for ballet, radio and film, and vocal works, one of which is a chamber opera, *The Lake.*

Udo Kasemets has written pieces inspired by John Cage and a number of other contemporary American composers. Harry Somers has composed a great variety of orchestral work and chamber music; recognized as Canada's leading contemporary composer, he is one of the most versatile and intellectually demanding.

Godfrey Ridout has written vocal works and symphonies and two études for strings. Among the outstanding younger composers are Harry Freedman and Norma Beecroft, both of Toronto.

There have been a great many impressive modern French-Canadian composers. Jean Papineau-Couture, grandson of the great Canadian composer Guillaume Couture, is a composer, professor of music and pianist. His representative works include *Concerto Grosso, First Symphony,* and a violin and piano sonata.

Clermont Pepin has written a number of symphonies, two concertos for piano and orchestra, solo and chamber music, vocal music, and music for the ballet and theater. Among his works are *Guernica,* a symphonic poem inspired by Picasso's painting, and *Hyperbolas,* for string quartet.

Pierre Mercure, in addition to being a progressive and individualistic modern composer, is a conductor and music producer for television. Among his works are *Cantate une Joie*; *Kaleidoscope,* a symphonic fantasy for full orchestra; and *Pantomine,* for wind, brass and percussion instruments. Mercure has been a leader in the search for new forms and styles of music in Canada and has written some impressive works of electronic music.

Louis Applebaum is Canada's most famous composer for motion pictures and television and has composed for the Stratford Shakespeare Festival, where he has been musical director. Maurice Blackburn has also written for radio, films and television.

ORCHESTRAS AND OPERAS

Canada's first symphony orchestra, L'Orchestre Symphonique de Quebec, was founded in 1902. Today there are at least 30 orchestras in operation. Almost all the provinces have at least one functioning orchestral group, with Ontario and Quebec having the largest concentration.

The Canadian Opera Company puts on about five new opera productions a year and can count on a highly successful short season in Toronto and on the road. Since government subsidies are not yet large enough to make it a year-round operation, many of its leading performers and graduates of the brilliantly successful Royal Conservatory Opera School in Toronto leave to accept permanent positions abroad. The quality of its recent productions has been extremely high, and near, capacity houses suggest that there is a rapidly growing audience. The composer Harry Somers has been commissioned by the C.B.C. and by a private foundation to write two operas in the centennial year 1967.

THE FILM

Canadian film-makers are respected throughout the world for the quality of their achievements in the field of documentary cinema. But, for financial reasons, they have seldom ventured into full-length feature film production. It is only recently that backers have shown willingness to invest; and as a result the industry is only just beginning to gain ground. However, even now it shows great promise.

THE EARLY DAYS

IN THE 1890s, IN MONTREAL, TWO Frenchmen exhibited a motion picture camera that their countrymen, the Lumière brothers, had invented in 1895. This prepared public interest for the appearance of the Kinetoscope, an invention of the American Thomas Edison (1847-1931).

The Kinetoscope

The Kinetoscope was in effect a coin-operated peep-show. Only one person at a time could view the pictures. At first it created a great sensation and became popular at fairs and in amusement arcades, but most people, at least initially, saw it as a passing fad. At first Edison's own company took no interest in enlarging the picture for presentation to audiences instead of individuals, but others were more far-sighted and were quick to recognize the idea's great potential. Edison did not abandon the peep-show technique until 1896, when he adopted the projector developed by C. F. Jenkins and Thomas Armat the previous year.

When various engineering problems had been overcome, Canadian firms lost no time in preparing projections for the public. Leader in the field was the Ottawa Street Railway Company, which began to make a series of short films in 1895. They were followed by the Massey-Harris company, which made films for publicity purposes; and in 1900, the Canadian Pacific Railway produced a series of short films aimed at attracting immigrants.

Encouraged by this kind of activity, a businessman, John Griffin, opened the country's first regular movie theater, the Theatorium, in Toronto in 1905. Building up his business into the Griffin Amusement Company, Griffin went on to acquire theaters all over Canada. But it was not until 1916 that the first luxury-class cinema, the Regent Theater, was built by a group of Toronto businessmen.

The National Film Board of Canada, destined to have world-wide influence on the development of the documentary film, came into being in 1939. John Grierson (1898-) was appointed as the Board's first commissioner, and during the six years of his tenure he raised Canadian film-making to a lively and respected industry. He was the first to use the term "documentary," and his definition of the genre as "the creative treatment of actuality" led to the filming of current happenings without the use of actors or artificial backgrounds.

Early Feature Films

The first authentic Canadian production of a serious feature-length film came in 1914 with the appearance of *Evangeline,* the work of the Canadian Bioscope Company in Halifax, Nova Scotia. The same year saw the production in Montreal of *The Battle of the Long Sault,* and by 1917 *The Foreigner* had been completed in Winnipeg.

In those early days of film-making the name of the director was not given, and it was not until after World War I that the name of a Canadian director appeared on the screen for the first time. The name was that of L. E. Ouimet, who was the owner of several movie theaters. Ouimet made his first venture into the world of film production with *Madeleine de Vèrcheres* (1925), a historical film with Estelle Belanger in the title role; it proved such a success that Ouimet was encouraged to make *Why Get Married?* (1926), with Paul Cazeneuve and Andrée Lafayette, *Blue Waters* (1927) and *Destiny* (1927).

By 1928 the industry had gained enough ground for the Canadian International Film Company to launch the production of a series of short films known as the Douglas Bright Comedies.

THE FILM SOCIETY MOVEMENT

Within a few years enough Canadian public interest had been aroused in the art of the film for a flourishing film society movement to have begun; but, despite cultural successes, the Canadian film industry found itself in financial difficulties and in 1939 the Canadian government decided to intervene and develop a national cinema.

THE NATIONAL FILM BOARD

THE NATIONAL FILM BOARD OF Canada, which was to exert such an all-pervading influence on documentary cinema, came into being in 1939 and set up its headquarters in Ottawa. Intended as an official government agency for the production and distribution of films, it gained recognition as the best organization of its kind in the world.

John Grierson

A famous British documentary director, John Grierson (1898-), who had been working in the United States, was appointed as the board's first film commissioner. During Grierson's six years in office he managed, against great odds, to raise Canadian film-making from a small, backward, almost unknown local activity into a lively, cultural and commercial industry with clearly stated aims and aspirations. By 1941 the N.F.B. had moved its headquarters to Montreal and was already producing films under its own name.

The Art of the Documentary

Grierson was the first to apply the term documentary to the cinematic genre that became his particular preoccupation. His definition of the documentary as "the creative treatment of actuality" led him to believe in the validity of filming what is actually happening, without the use of actors or artificial backgrounds.

During the years of World War II, Grierson, who had already worked with British directors such as Paul Rotha (1907-), Basil Wright (1907-), Henry Watt (1906-) and with the American Robert Flaherty (1884-1951), famed for his *Nanook of the North* (1922), gathered around him in Canada a group of capable young directors, artists, writers and technicians. Men like Stuart Legg, Raymond Spottiswoode, Norman McLaren and George Dunning combined their talents to make documentary films that gave substance to Grierson's faith in the genre as a vital new art form, philosophically more significant than fiction.

The pressing need to convey information to the population of Canada scattered throughout the enormous country was partly fulfilled during the war by such films as *Canada Carries On* and *The World in Action* series. Both illustrate the kind of technique that has become a hallmark of the Canadian documentary.

In such cases, where it is vital to pack as much information as possible into the 20-minute, or less, time allowance, the method used is extremely concentrated; brief shots follow closely upon one another and sound is skillfully counterpointed in a way that produces a strong, lucid impact on the mind of the spectator.

The N.F.B. has produced hundreds of short films on a vast range of subjects including agriculture, geography, the creative arts, health and hygiene, social welfare, natural resources and industry, science, sports, recreation and travel, transport and communications and world affairs.

A few examples of the films made during World War II give some indication of the wide variety of subjects dealt with: *Trans-Canada Express* (1944) was made by Sydney Newman to reveal some of the unappreciated beauties of the Canadian countryside; *Accidents Don't Happen* (1944) pointed up the dangers of carelessness while working at machines and in plants; *Neuro-Psychiatry* provided an elementary course on the importance of basic psychiatric knowledge; *White Safari* (1943) was a geographical lesson in the form of a big-game hunt; and *Vegetable Insects* (1944) was a zoological entertainment.

An impressive series made just after the war by Robert Anderson incorporated the use of animation and live photography in its telling treatment of psychiatric problems in everyday life; these included *The Feeling of Rejection* (1947), *The Feeling of Hostility* (1948) and *Dependency* (1949).

OUTSIDE INFLUENCES

The Restrictions of Sponsorship

THE DOMINATING INFLUENCE OF THE Canadian government film agency and the fact that, because of the sponsorship system, films were always obliged to have an extra-cinematic function inevitably had an inhibiting effect on Canada's film-makers. The lack of opportunity for free expression and the persistence of the documentary as the predominant form led in some cases to stilted, unadventurous styles. Directors lost their freshness of approach; they tended to fall into stale, mannered presentation. In addition there was a dearth of the kind of informed criticism that is so necessary a stimulant to the creative arts.

Film Festivals

Much-needed encouragement was provided after World War II by the development of the Canadian film festival movement. This had important effects on the industry by stimulating the competitive spirit and instilling the need to entertain rather than merely to instruct. Vancouver, Montreal and Stratford for a time held annual festivals. Increasingly important, Montreal has a competitive week now of Canadian features together with a display devoted to the films of one foreign nation. In 1965 the special short film program was given over entirely to animated cartoon films.

The Coming of Television

The inauguration of Canadian television in 1953 brought another source of sponsorship and distribution. Films made for television require different techniques, and the challenge jolted Canadian directors into new and original methods of approach. The medium also gave scope for the development of dialogue and dramatic narrative forms.

One of the earlier ventures was a serial history for children called *The Adventures of Pierre Radisson;* this film was produced by Omega Productions for the Canadian Broadcasting Corporation. In 1956 a short film on alcoholics, *Skid Row,* set a high standard with its penetrating observation of an acute and painful social problem. In the 1960s with major documentaries such as *The Mills of the Gods,* a film about the war in Vietnam made for CBC television, the Canadian documentary maintained and expanded its position of international leadership. The Wilderness Awards, for films made for Canadian television, provided a further stimulus.

ANIMATION

TELEVISION PROVIDED AN EXCELLENT outlet for the work of artists such as

Wayne and Shuster as they appeared in their comic version of The Last of the Mohicans, *presented on CBC television in May 1966. Born in Toronto, John Wayne and Frank Shuster have since their teens formed an inseparable team. Shortly after graduating from the University of Toronto they turned to comedy work, and in 1942, when they enlisted in the Army, they were assigned to the Canadian Army Show, which toured camps in Canada and overseas. After the war Wayne and Shuster performed regularly on radio, and in 1954 they made their first appearance on television when they started a monthly show for the CBC. Their humor and skits have since been seen and enjoyed by millions.*

Norman McLaren, George Dunning, Jim Mackay, Grant Munro, Jean-Paul Ladouceur and Gerald Potterton who all worked on animated films for the N.F.B.

Animation is the term applied to films which are shot frame by frame (such as films based on art work, cartoons, drawings or puppets) instead of "live."

Norman McLaren

Norman McLaren (1914-), an immigrant from Scotland, joined the N.F.B. in 1941 and has proved one of its most adventurous and successful artists. He has experimented with an enormous range of animation techniques and has opened up many new fields for other artists to explore.

Working like a medieval miniaturist, McLaren often paints with special pens and brushes onto the film itself. Sometimes he synthesizes music by a complex series of blobs and lines; the sounds produced are unlike those of any instrument but have an odd percussive quality about them; volume and pitch can be controlled by altering the shape of the marks or the density of the paint.

The first full-length feature film commissioned by the N.F.B. was Pour la suite du monde *(For the continuation of the world; 1962), a scene of which is shown here. Directed by Pierre Perrault and Michel Brault, the film deals with the difficult existence of the whale-fishing community on Île aux Coudres in the St. Lawrence River. At times using purely documentary sequences, the film depicts whaling methods and provides an incisive glimpse into the lives of these hard-working people, who have preserved their dialect and traditional customs.*

The fact that there is no need for the direct intervention of the camera means that the artist can be much more free and spontaneous in his work. As he draws the gradation of movement onto successive 35-mm. frames, he can see immediately whether he is achieving the desired effect. McLaren used this method in, for example, his witty shorts on economics, *Five for Four* and *Dollar Dance,* both made in 1943.

A different technique devised and explored by McLaren is that of drawing with a brush lengthwise down a strip of film undivided by frames. *Fiddle-de-Dee* (1947) and *Begone Dull Care* (1949) illustrate the metamorphosis of painting that takes place when the film is run through; a completely abstract pattern of moving lines and forms is seen dancing about in time to carefully coordinated music. The effect may be full of humor. The technique is completely straightforward, with no need for camera work or processing.

In *Chalk River Ballet* (1949), which evoked the dance of spheres, McLaren achieved a remarkably convincing impression of three-dimensional objects moving toward and away from the camera; to do so he used only flat cut-out disks of different sizes, which could be moved about on a flat surface.

The same kind of technique was used in *C'est l'aviron* (1945), the sixth in a series of shorts by different artists on French-Canadian folksongs, which was acclaimed by Pablo Picasso as a new advance in the art of the film. By using flat paper cut-outs on a painted background and by zooming and panning the camera, McLaren gives the spectator the impression that he is moving through a landscape of woods and streams. The folksong is one the pioneers sang as they made their way by canoe along Canada's great rivers.

McLaren's many other films, including *La Poulette Grise* (1947), *A Phantasy* (1951), *Neighbours* (1952), *Blinkety Blank* (1955), *Rhythmetic* (1956), *Chairy Tale* (1957), *Le Merle* (The Blackbird; 1959) and *Festival* (1961), reveal his extraordinarily inventive imagination and technical versatility. McLaren's movies have won awards at film festivals throughout the world.

George Dunning

George Dunning, born in Toronto in 1920 and now working in England, made for the N.F.B. an interesting series of experiments with animation techniques. In 1944 with *Cadet Rousselle* (Young Rousselle) he brought an old French folksong to life on the screen through the use of jointed metal figures, which were animated by a hand held under the camera. A year later in *Grim Pastures,* he drew simple figures on paper and lit them from below. This particular method was to be developed in 1949-50 when Dunning achieved remarkable effects by painting on glass plates shot with light from below and above.

WOLF KOENIG

Another N.F.B. artist, Wolf Koenig (1927-), who later moved into the documentary field, was responsible for evolving a special animation technique; this involves perforating the film frame by frame with holes of different shapes and sizes so as to produce patterns whose movements can be aligned with a suitable sound-track.

The Artistic Documentary

Colin Low (1926-), who now controls the animation unit of the N.F.B., joined the board as a designer in 1952 and two years later made his highly praised *Corral.* This film depicts, in lyrical terms without any spoken commentary, the struggle between a man and a horse on a ranch in Alberta.

Low's subsequent films share a common theme in that they all mingle the past and the present with a more or less nostalgic feeling for the days of the early pioneers or the traditional way of life of the indigenous Indian. *City of Gold,* which won an award at the 1957 Cannes festival, makes use of animation to recreate the era of the Klondike gold rush; *Circle of the Sun* (1960)